In this book Herman Bierens provides a mathematically rigorous treatment of a number of timely topics in advanced econometrics. His subjects include nonlinear estimation, maximum likelihood theory, ARMA and ARMAX models, unit roots and cointegration, and nonparametric regression, together with an extensive and thorough treatment of the necessary probability theory. The book is uniquely self-contained, providing the reader with a selection of the latest developments in econometric theory, plus the required introductory material on each topic. It will be used by graduate students of econometrics and statistics, and is particularly suitable for self-tuition.

Topics in advanced econometrics

Topics in advanced econometrics

Estimation, testing, and specification of cross-section and time series models

HERMAN J. BIERENS

Robert H. and Nancy Dedman Trustee Professor of Economics
Southern Methodist University, Dallas, USA

CAMBRIDGE
UNIVERSITY PRESS

Published by the Press Syndicate of the University of Cambridge
The Pitt Building, Trumpington Street, Cambridge CB2 1RP
40 West 20th Street, New York, NY 10011-4211, USA
10 Stamford Road, Oakleigh, Melbourne 3166, Australia

First published 1994
First paperback edition published 1996

Printed in Great Britain at the University Press, Cambridge

A catalogue record for this book is available from the British Library

Library of Congress cataloguing in publication data

Bierens, Herman J., 1943–
Topics in advanced econometrics / Herman J. Bierens.
p. cm.
Includes bibliographical references.
ISBN 0 521 41900 X (hard)
1. Econometrics. I. Title.
HB139.B533 1993
330'.01'5195–dc20 92-47068 CIP

ISBN 0 521 41900 X hardback
ISBN 0 521 56511 1 paperback

CE

Contents

Preface

This book covers topics in advanced econometrics that I have taught in graduate econometrics programs of the University of California at San Diego, Southern Methodist University, Dallas, the Netherlands Network of Quantitative Economics, Tinbergen Institute, and the Free University, Amsterdam. The selection of the topics is based on my personal interest in the subjects, as well as lack of availability of suitable textbooks in these areas.

Rather than providing an encyclopedic survey of the literature, I have chosen a presentation which fills the gap between intermediate statistics and econometrics (including linear time series analysis) and the level necessary to gain access to the recent econometric literature; in particular, the literature on nonlinear and nonparametric regression, and advanced time series analysis. The ultimate goal is to provide the student with tools for independent research in these areas. This book is particularly suitable for self-tuition, and may prove useful in a graduate course in mathematical statistics and advanced econometrics.

The first four chapters contain enough material to fill a half-semester graduate course in asymptotic theory and nonlinear inference if one skips some of the material involved, and a full semester course if not. In teaching such a half-semester course I usually skip the details of the proofs in chapter 2, and focus on the relations between the various modes of convergence only. Also, I usually skip the sections of chapter 2 and chapter 4 dealing with non-identically distributed samples, and only sketch the proof of the uniform law of large numbers for the i.i.d. case (theorem 2.5.7). Section 3.3 is related to chapter 5, so if you skip chapter 5 then you may skip section 3.3 as well.

Chapter 5 requires knowledge of the material in section 3.3 and chapter 4. I have used this chapter in a short (12 hours) graduate course on model misspecification testing.

Chapters 6, 7 and 8 form a unity, and I have used them in a half-semester course on (non)linear time series modeling, without the sections on heterogeneous time series. Chapters 1–3 are prerequisite for this course.

I have used the parts of chapter 9 on unit roots for a short (12 hours) topics course. Chapter 1 is prerequisite for this course, together with an understanding of the α-mixing concept explained in chapter 6.

Finally, chapter 10 stands on its own, except section 10.7 which requires knowledge of the α-mixing and υ-stability concepts and related convergence results in chapter 6. I have used this chapter, without section 10.7, in a short (12 hours) graduate course on nonparametric estimation.

The first five chapters of this book have been disseminated in draft form as working papers. I am grateful to Anil Bera, Alexander Georgiev, and Jan Magnus for suggesting additional references, and to Lourens Broersma, Shengyi Guo, Helmut Lütkepohl, Johan Smits, Ton Steerneman and Baoyuan Wang, for suggesting various improvements.

Most of the work on this book was done while affiliated with the Free University, Amsterdam, and the sections on maximum likelihood and cointegration were written while enjoying the hospitality of the Center for Economic Research, Tilburg University.

1

Basic probability theory

The asymptotic theory of nonlinear regression models, in particular consistency results, heavily depends on uniform laws of large numbers. Understanding these laws requires knowledge of abstract probability theory. In this chapter we shall review the basic elements of this theory as needed in what follows, to make this book almost self-contained. For a more detailed treatment, see for example Billingsley (1979) and Parthasarathy (1977). However, we do assume the reader has a good knowledge of probability and statistics at an intermediate level, for example on the level of Hogg and Craig (1978). The material in this chapter is a revision and extension of section 2.1 in Bierens (1981).

1.1 Measure-theoretical foundation of probability theory

The basic concept of probability theory is the *probability space*. This is a triple $\{\Omega,\mathfrak{F},P\}$ consisting of:

— An abstract non-empty set Ω, called the *sample space*. We do not impose any conditions on this set.

— A non-empty collection $\mathfrak{F}$ of subsets of Ω, having the following two properties:

$$\text{If } E \in \mathfrak{F} \text{ then } E^c \in \mathfrak{F}, \tag{1.1.1}$$

where E^c denotes the complement of the subset E with respect to Ω: $E^c = \Omega\backslash E$.

$$\text{If } E_j \in \mathfrak{F} \text{ for } j=1,2,..., \text{ then } \cup_j E_j \in \mathfrak{F}. \tag{1.1.2}$$

These two properties make $\mathfrak{F}$, by definition, a *Borel field* of subsets of Ω. (Following Chung [1974], the term "Borel field" has the same meaning as the term "σ-Algebra" used by other authors.)

— A *probability measure* P on $\{\Omega,\mathfrak{F}\}$. This is a real-valued set function on $\mathfrak{F}$ such that:

$$P(\Omega)=1, \tag{1.1.3}$$

$$P(E) \geq 0 \text{ for all } E \in \mathfrak{F}, \tag{1.1.4}$$

$E_j \in \mathfrak{F}$ for $j = 1,2,\ldots$ and
$E_{j_1} \cap E_{j_2} = \emptyset$ if $j_1 \neq j_2$ imply $P(\cup_j E_j) = \sum_j P(E_j)$. (1.1.5)

Example: Toss a fair coin. The possible outcomes are head (H) or tail (T). Thus $\Omega = \{H,T\}$. The collection $\mathfrak{F}$ of all subsets of Ω, i.e.,

$$\mathfrak{F} = \{\Omega, \emptyset, \{H\}, \{T\}\}$$

is a Borel field. Finally, the appropriate probability measure in this case is

$$P(\{H\}) = P(\{T\}) = \tfrac{1}{2}, P(\Omega) = 1, P(\emptyset) = 0.$$

Let X be a *random variable* (r.v.) and let F be its distribution function. In the measure-theoretical approach of probability theory a random variable is considered as a real-valued *function* on the set Ω denoted by:

$$X = x(.)$$

with value $x(\omega)$ at $\omega \in \Omega$, such that for every real number t:

$$\{\omega \in \Omega : x(\omega) \leq t\} \in \mathfrak{F}.$$

The *distribution function* F with value F(t) at $t \in R$ is then defined by:

$$F(t) = P(\{\omega \in \Omega : x(\omega) \leq t\}),$$

which will often be denoted by the shorthand notation:
$F(t) = P(X \leq t)$.

Example: In the coin tossing case the function

$$x(H) = 1, x(T) = 0$$

determines a random variable X. The corresponding distribution function is:

$$F(t) = 1 \text{ if } t \geq 1,$$
$$F(t) = \tfrac{1}{2} \text{ if } 0 \leq t < 1,$$
$$F(t) = 0 \text{ if } t < 0.$$

It is not hard to see that the axioms (1.1.1) and (1.1.2) imply:

$$E_n \in \mathfrak{F}, n = 1,2,\ldots \Rightarrow \cap_n E_n \in \mathfrak{F}$$

and that from (1.1.3), (1.1.4) and (1.1.5):

$$P(\emptyset) = 0, P(E^c) = 1 - P(E), P(E \cup D) + P(E \cap D) = P(E) + P(D),$$
$$E \subset D \Rightarrow P(E) \leq P(D \backslash E) + P(E) = P(D),$$

$E_n \subset E_{n+1}$, $E = \cup_n E_n \Rightarrow P(E_n) \to P(E)$ as $n \to \infty$,
$E_n \supset E_{n+1}$, $E = \cap_n E_n \Rightarrow P(E_n) \to P(E)$ as $n \to \infty$,
$P(\cup_n E_n) \leq \sum_n P(E_n)$,

where all sets involved are members of $\mathfrak{F}$. The distribution function F(t) is *right continuous*:

$$F(t) = \lim_{\varepsilon\downarrow 0} F(t+\varepsilon),$$

as is easily verified, and it satisfies

$$F(\infty) = \lim_{t\to\infty} F(t) = 1\ ,\ F(-\infty) = \lim_{t\to-\infty} F(t) = 0.$$

Furthermore, by F(t−) we denote:

$$F(t-) = \lim_{\varepsilon\downarrow 0} F(t-\varepsilon),$$

which clearly satisfies $F(t-) \leq F(t)$.

A finite dimensional *random vector* can now be defined as a vector with random variables as components, where these random components are assumed to be defined on a *common* probability space. Moreover, a *complex random variable* Z can be defined by $Z = X + i\cdot Y$ with real valued random variables X and Y defined on a common probability space as real and imaginary parts, respectively.

Next we shall construct a Borel field $\mathfrak{B}^k$ of subsets of R^k such that for every set $B \in \mathfrak{B}^k$ and any k-dimensional random vector X on a probability space $\{\Omega,\mathfrak{F},P\}$ we have

$$\{\omega \in \Omega : x(\omega) \in B\} \in \mathfrak{F}, \tag{1.1.6}$$

because only for such subsets B of R^k can we define the probability

$$P(X \in B) = P(\{\omega \in \Omega : x(\omega) \in B\}), \tag{1.1.7}$$

Let $\mathfrak{C}$ be the collection of subsets of R^k of the type

$$\times_{m=1}^{k}(-\infty,t_m],\ t_m \in R,$$

and let $\mathfrak{G}$ be the Borel field of all subsets of R^k. Clearly we have $\mathfrak{C} \subset \mathfrak{G}$ (meaning $E \in \mathfrak{C} \Rightarrow E \in \mathfrak{G}$). But next to $\mathfrak{G}$ there may be other Borel fields of subsets of R^k with this property, say $\mathfrak{G}_a$, $a \in A$, where A is an index set. Assuming that all Borel fields containing $\mathfrak{C}$ are represented this way, we then have a non-empty collection of Borel fields $\mathfrak{G}_a$, $a \in A$, of subsets of R^k such that $\mathfrak{C} \subset \mathfrak{G}_a$ for each $a \in A$. Now consider the collection

$$\mathfrak{B}^k = \cap_{a\in A}\mathfrak{G}_a.$$

Since each $\mathfrak{G}_a$ is a Borel field, it follows that this collection $\mathfrak{B}^k$ is a Borel field of subsets of R^k and since $\mathfrak{C}$ is contained in each $\mathfrak{G}_a$ it follows that $\mathfrak{C}$

$\subset B^k$. We shall say that the Borel field $\mathfrak{B}^k$ is the *minimal Borel field* containing the collection $\mathfrak{C}$, and for this particular collection $\mathfrak{C}$ it is called the *Euclidean Borel field.* Summarizing:

> *Definition 1.1.1.* Let $\mathfrak{C}$ be any collection of subsets of a set Γ and let the Borel fields of subsets of Γ containing $\mathfrak{C}$ be $\mathfrak{G}_a$, $a \in A$. Then $\mathfrak{G} = \cap_{a \in A}\mathfrak{G}_a$ is called the *minimal Borel field* containing $\mathfrak{C}$.

> *Definition 1.1.2.* Let $\mathfrak{C}$ be the collection of subsets of R^k of the type
>
> $\times_{m=1}^{k}(-\infty,t_m]$, $t_m \in R$.
>
> The minimal Borel field $\mathfrak{B}^k$ containing this collection is called the *Euclidean Borel field* (also called the Borel σ-Algebra) and the members of $\mathfrak{B}^k$ are called *Borel sets.*

The concept of Borel sets is very general. Roughly speaking, any subset of R^k you can imagine is a Borel set. For example, each singleton in R^k is a Borel set, the area in a circle is a Borel set in R^2, the circle itself and the straight line are Borel sets in R^2, the (hyper)cube is a Borel set, etc. Thus, "almost" every subset of R^k is a Borel set. However, there are exceptions, but the shape of a set in R^k that is not a Borel set is complicated beyond our imagination. See Royden (1968, pp. 63-64) for an example.

We show now that for any Borel set B and any r.v. X on $\{\Omega,\mathfrak{F},P\}$, (1.1.6) is satisfied. Let $\mathfrak{D}$ be the collection of all Borel sets B such that (1.1.6) is satisfied. Then $\mathfrak{D} \subset \mathfrak{B}^k$. If $\mathfrak{D}$ is also a Borel field then $\mathfrak{B}^k \subset \mathfrak{D}$ (and hence $\mathfrak{B}^k = \mathfrak{D}$) because $\mathfrak{B}^k$ is the minimal Borel field containing the collection $\mathfrak{C}$ in definition 1.1.2, whereas obviously the collection $\mathfrak{D}$ contains $\mathfrak{C}$. So it suffices to prove that $\mathfrak{D}$ is a Borel field. However, this is not too hard and therefore left to the reader. This proves the first part of theorem 1.1.1. below. The proof of the second part is left as an easy exercise.

> *Theorem 1.1.1.* For any random vector X in R^k defined on $\{\Omega,\mathfrak{F},P\}$ and any Borel set B in R^k we have $\{\omega \in \Omega : x(\omega) \in B\} \in \mathfrak{F}$. The collection $\mathfrak{F}\{X\}$ of sets $\{\omega \in \Omega : x(\omega) \in B\}$ with B an arbitrary Borel set in R^k is a Borel field itself, contained in $\mathfrak{F}$.

Consequently the definition (1.1.2) is meaningful for Borel sets. In fact, by defining a measure μ on the Euclidean Borel field $\mathfrak{B}^k$ as

$$\mu(B) = P(X \in B) = P(\{\omega \in \Omega : x(\omega) \in B\})$$

for any Borel set B in R^k we have created a probability measure on $\{R^k,\mathfrak{B}^k\}$. This probability measure μ is often referred to as the probability measure *induced* by X. Moreover, the Borel field $\mathfrak{F}\{X\}$ is called the *Borel field generated by* X. This concept plays an important role in defining conditional expectations.

We are now able to define a (joint) distribution function on R^k. Let X be a random vector in R^k defined on a probability space $\{\Omega,\mathfrak{F},P\}$. The product sets

$$\times_{j=1}^{k}(-\infty,t_j]$$

are Borel sets in R^k, where the t_j's are the components of a vector $t \in R^k$. Thus:

$$\{\omega \in \Omega : x(\omega) \in \times_{j=1}^{k}(-\infty,t_j]\} \in \mathfrak{F}.$$

The (joint) *distribution function* F, say, of X is now defined for all $t \in R^k$ by:

$$F(t) = P(\{\omega \in \Omega : x(\omega) \in \times_{j=1}^{k}(-\infty,t_j]\}) = \mu(\times_{j=1}^{k}(-\infty,t_j]),$$

where μ is the probability measure induced by X. However, F(t) will often also be denoted by the shorthand notation:

$$F(t) = P(X \leq t).$$

Clearly, F is uniquely determined by μ. The reverse is also true, i.e.

> *Theorem 1.1.2.* Given a distribution function F on R^k there exists a *unique* probability measure μ on $\{R^k, \mathfrak{B}^k\}$ defining F.

Proof: Similarly to Royden (1968, proposition 12, p. 262).

Theorem 1.1.2 implies that there is a one-to-one correspondence between a distribution function F and its defining probability measure μ. We shall employ this result later in defining mathematical expectations.

Exercises

1. Show that (1.1.1) and (1.1.2) imply $\cap_j E_j \in \mathfrak{F}$.
2. Consider the collection $\mathfrak{F}$ of subintervals of [0,1] with rational-valued endpoints, together with their complements and *finite* unions and intersections. Show that $\mathfrak{F}$ is not a Borel field. (Hint: Use the fact that irrational numbers can be written as limits of rational numbers.)
3. Let $\mathfrak{F}$ be a Borel field of subsets of Ω. Let $A \in \mathfrak{F}$ and let $\mathfrak{G}_A$ be the collection of all subsets of the type $A \cap B$, where $B \in \mathfrak{F}$. Prove that $\mathfrak{G}_A$ is a Borel field of subsets of A.
4. Let $\Omega = \{1,2,3,4,5\}$ and let $\mathfrak{C}$ be the collection consisting of the two subsets {2}, {4}. Prove that the minimal Borel field containing $\mathfrak{C}$ consists of the following sets: Ω, $\emptyset$, {2}, {4}, {2}∪{1,3,5}, {4}∪{1,3,5}, {2,4}, {1,3,5}.

5. Prove that the following subsets of R^2 are Borel sets:
   a rectangle
   the area in a circle
   a straight line
6. Is the set Q of rational numbers a Borel set in R?
7. Let $\mathfrak{C}$ be the collection of all intervals of the type [a,b], where a and b are finite and $a < b$. Prove that the minimal Borel field containing $\mathfrak{C}$ is just the Euclidean Borel field.
8. Complete the proof of theorem 1.1.1.
9. Prove that a distribution function is always right continuous.
10. Let $S = \{1,2,3,4\}$, let Ω be the set of all pairs (x_1,x_2) with $x_1 \in S$, $x_2 \in S$, $x_1 < x_2$, let $\mathfrak{F}$ be the Borel field of all subsets of Ω and let P be a probability measure on $\{\Omega, \mathfrak{F}\}$. Define the random variable Y as follows:

    $y(\omega) = 1$ if $\omega = (x_1,x_2)$ with $x_1 + x_2$ odd.
    $y(\omega) = 0$ if $\omega = (x_1,x_2)$ with $x_1 + x_2$ even.

    — Determine the Borel field $\mathfrak{F}\{Y\}$ generated by Y.
    — All points in Ω have equal probability. Derive the distribution function F(y) of Y.
11. A bowl contains 9 white balls and 1 red ball of equal size. Draw randomly one ball and assign to it the value $X_1 = 1$ if the ball is red and the value $X_1 = 0$ if the ball is white. Draw randomly a second ball without replacing the first ball, and assign the value $X_2 = 1$ to it if it is red and the value $X_2 = 0$ if it is white. Consider the vector $Y = (X_1,X_2)'$. Define a sample space Ω and a Borel field $\mathfrak{F}$ of subsets of Ω such that together:
    — Y is a random vector
    — $\mathfrak{F}$ is equal to the Borel field generated by Y.
    Also, define an appropriate probability measure P.

1.2 Independence

Let $X_1,X_2,...$ be a sequence of random variables with corresponding probability spaces $\{\Omega_1,\mathfrak{F}_1,P_1\},\{\Omega_2,\mathfrak{F}_2,P_2\},...$ respectively. It is possible to construct a new probability space, $\{\Omega,\mathfrak{F},P\}$, say, such that the X_j's can be regarded as *independent* random variables on $\{\Omega,\mathfrak{F},P\}$ (see Chung [1974, section 3.3]). Independence means:

> *Definition 1.2.1* Let $X_1,X_2,...$ be random vectors defined on a common probability space. This sequence of random vectors is called *(totally) independent* if for any conformable sequence (B_j) of Borel sets,

$$P(\cap_j \{\omega \in \Omega: x_j(\omega) \in B_j\}) = \Pi_j P(\{\omega \in \Omega: x_j(\omega) \in B_j)\}$$

and it is called *mutually (or pairwise) independent* if for $j_1 \neq j_2$, X_{j_1} and X_{j_2} are independent.

As an example, consider the tossing of a fair coin. Assign to X_j the value 1 if the outcome of the j-th tossing is head (H) and assign the value 0 if the outcome is tail (T). Then X_j is a random variable defined on the probability space $\{\Omega_j, \mathfrak{F}_j, P_j\}$, where

$$\Omega_j = \{H,T\},\ \mathfrak{F}_j = \{\emptyset, \{H\}, \{T\}, \{H,T\}\}$$
$$P_j(\emptyset) = 0,\ P_j(\{H,T\}) = 1,\ P_j(\{H\}) = P_j(\{T\}) = \tfrac{1}{2}.$$

Now let Ω be the set of all one-sided infinite sequences of H and T, for example, let $\omega = (H,H,T,T,H,T,T,T,H,H,H,T,\ldots)$ be such an element of Ω. We could take as $\mathfrak{F}$ the collection of all subsets of Ω, including the empty set. Now x_j can also be defined on $\{\Omega, \mathfrak{F}\}$, as follows. Let

$$x_j(\omega) = 1 \text{ if the j-th element of } \omega \text{ is H},$$
$$x_j(\omega) = 0 \text{ if the j-th element of } \omega \text{ is T}.$$

Each set $E \in \mathfrak{F}$ can be written as $E = E_{j,1} \cup E_{j,2}$, where $E_{j,1}$ and $E_{j,2}$ are disjoint sets defined by:

$$E_{j,1} = \{\omega \in E : \text{j-th element of } \omega \text{ is H}\},$$
$$E_{j,2} = \{\omega \in E : \text{j-th element of } \omega \text{ is T}\}.$$

Of course, $E_{j,1}$ or $E_{j,2}$ may be empty. Now define

$$\delta(E_{j,i}) = ½ \text{ if } E_{j,i} \neq \emptyset,\ \delta(E_{j,i}) = 0 \text{ if } E_{j,i} = \emptyset,\ i = 1,2,$$
$$P(E) = \Pi_j[\delta(E_{j,1}) + \delta(E_{j,2})].$$

Then (X_j) is a sequence of independent random variables defined on the common probability space $(\Omega, \mathfrak{F}, P)$.

1.3 Borel measurable functions

If X is a r.v. and f(x) is a real function on R, is then f(X) a r.v.? The answer is: not always. There are functions (see for example Royden [1968, problem 3.28]) for which this is not the case. The condition for f(X) being an r.v. is that for all $t \in R$ we have

$$\{\omega \in \Omega : f(x(\omega)) \leq t\} \in \mathfrak{F},$$

where $\{\Omega, \mathfrak{F}, P\}$ is the probability space involved, and referring to theorem 1.1.1 we see that this will be the case if for every $t \in R$,

$$\{x \in R : f(x) \leq t\} \text{ is a Borel set in R.}$$

Functions satisfying the latter condition are called *Borel measurable.*

Now consider a real function $f(x_1,...,x_k)$ on R^k and r.v.'s $X_1,...,X_k$ on $\{\Omega,\mathfrak{F},P\}$. If for every $t \in R$ the set

$$B_t = \{(x_1,...,x_k) \in R^k : f(x_1,...,x_k) \leq t\}$$

is a Borel set in R^k then

$$\{\omega \in \Omega : f(x_1(\omega),...,x_k(\omega)) \leq t\} \in \mathfrak{F}$$

for every $t \in R$ and hence $f(X_1,...,X_k)$ is an r.v. Also such functions are called Borel measurable.

> *Definition 1.3.1* A real function $f(x)$ on R^k is called *Borel measurable* if for every $t \in R$ the set $\{x \in R^k : f(x) \leq t\}$ is a Borel set in R^k.

A first example of a Borel measurable function is the so-called *simple function*:

> *Definition 1.3.2.* A real function $f(x)$ on R^k is called a simple function if there are finite real numbers $b_1,...,b_n$ and Borel sets B_j, $j = 1,2,...,n$ with $B_{j_1} \cap B_{j_2} = \oslash$ if $j_1 \neq j_2$, such that
>
> $$f(x) = \sum_{j=1}^{n} b_j I(x \in B_j),$$
>
> where $I(.)$ is the indicator function, i.e.,
>
> $$I(x \in B_j) = 1 \text{ if } x \in B_j;\ I(x \in B_j) = 0 \text{ if } x \notin B_j.$$

Simple functions differ from the well-known step functions in that for step functions the disjoint sets B_j are restricted to intervals. Since intervals are Borel sets, step functions are simple functions.

Realizing that for a simple function f the set $\{x \in R^k : f(x) \leq t\}$ is always a finite union of Borel sets, we have:

> *Theorem 1.3.1* Simple functions are Borel measurable.

From this result we can derive other Borel measurable functions using the following theorem.

> *Theorem 1.3.2* Let $f_1,f_2,...$ be a sequence of Borel measurable functions on R^k. Then the functions $\max\{f_1,...,f_n\}$, $\min\{f_1,...,f_n\}$, $\sup_n f_n$, $\inf_n f_n$, $\limsup_{n\to\infty} f_n$ and $\liminf_{n\to\infty} f_n$ are also Borel measurable.

Proof: We only consider the case $k = 1$. Moreover, it is not hard to see that if f is Borel measurable then so is $-f$, hence it suffices to prove the theorem for the "max" and "sup" cases. Let

$$h_n(x) = \max\{f_1(x),...,f_n(x)\}.$$

Then

$$\{x \in R : h_n(x) \leq t\} = \cap_j\{x \in R : f_j(x) \leq t\},$$

which is a Borel set since the f_j's are Borel measurable. Moreover, replacing n by ∞ we see that $\sup_n f_n(x)$ is Borel measurable. Since

$$\limsup_{n\to\infty} f_n(x) = \inf_n \sup_{k\geq n} f_k(x)$$

and since $\inf_n g_n(x)$ is Borel measurable if the g_n are Borel measurable, it follows directly that $\limsup_{n\to\infty} f_n(x)$ is Borel measurable. Q.E.D.

Along the same lines it can be shown:

> *Corollary 1.3.1* If $X_1, X_2, X_3, ..$ are random variables defined on a common probability space, then so are $\max\{X_1,...,X_n\}$, $\min\{X_1,...,X_n\}$, $\sup_n X_n$, $\inf_n X_n$, $\limsup_{n\to\infty} X_n$ and $\liminf_{n\to\infty} X_n$.

From theorems 1.3.1 and 1.3.2 it follows now:

Theorem 1.3.3 Continuous real functions on R^k are Borel measurable.

Proof: We prove the theorem for the univariate case $k = 1$ only. Let

$$f_n(x) = f(x) \text{ if } -n < x \leq n;\ f_n(x) = 0 \text{ elsewhere},$$
$$f_{nm}(x) = \sum_{j=0}^{m-1} \sup_{x\in B_{jnm}}(x) \cdot I(x \in B_{jnm}),$$

where

$$B_{jnm} = (-n + 2n \cdot j/m, -n + 2n(j+1)/m].$$

Then the $f_{nm}(x)$'s are simple functions. Since by the continuity of f, $f_n(x) = \lim_{m\to\infty} f_{nm}(x)$, it follows from theorem 1.3.2 that the $f_n(x)$'s are Borel measurable. The theorem follows now from theorem 1.3.2 and the fact that

$$f(x) = \lim_{n\to\infty} f_n(x) = \limsup_{n\to\infty} f_n(x) = \liminf_{n\to\infty} f_n(x). \quad \text{Q.E.D.}$$

Let f be any Borel measurable function on R^k. Since the functions $\max\{0,x\}$ and $\max\{0,-x\}$, $x \in R$, are continuous and hence Borel measurable, it follows that

$$f^+(.) = \max\{0, f(.)\},\ f^-(.) = \max\{0, -f(.)\}$$

are non-negative Borel measurable functions. Moreover, we obviously have

$$f = f^+ - f^-. \tag{1.3.1}$$

This representation is important because it means that without loss of generality we can limit our attention to non-negative Borel measurable functions. Thus the following theorem gives a full characterization of Borel measurable functions:

> *Theorem 1.3.4* A non-negative real function f on R^k is Borel measurable if and only if there is a non-decreasing sequence of simple functions φ_n on R^k such that for each $x \in R^k$,
>
> $0 \le \varphi_n(x) \le f(x), \lim_{n\to\infty}\varphi_n(x) = f(x)$

Proof: Take for given non-negative Borel measurable f and integers m with $1 \le m \le n2^n$,

$\varphi_n(x) = (m-1)/2^n$ if $(m-1)/2^n \le f(x) < m/2^n$; $\varphi_n(x) = n$, otherwise.

Then the φ_n's have all the required properties. Since by theorem 1.3.1 the simple functions φ_n are Borel measurable, the limit is Borel measurable - by theorem 1.3.2. Q.E.D.

Combining (1.3.1) and theorem 1.3.4 now yields:

> *Theorem 1.3.5* A real function on R^k is Borel measurable if and only if it is a (pointwise) limit of a sequence of simple functions on R^k.

Exercises

1. Let f be a Borel measurable real function on R^k and let B be an arbitrary Borel set in R. Prove that the set $\{x \in R^k: f(x) \in B\}$ is a Borel set in R^k. (Hint: Use a similar argument to that in the proof of theorem 1.1.1.)
2. Let f and g be Borel measurable real functions on R. Prove that $f+g$ and $f-g$ are Borel measurable. (Hint: Use theorem 1.3.5.)
3. Prove that the product of two simple functions on R^k is a simple function itself.
4. Let f and g be simple functions on R, where $g(x) \neq 0$ for $x \in R$. Prove that f/g is a simple function.
5. Consider the real function

   $f(x) = x$ if x is rational, $f(x) = -x$ if x is irrational.

   Prove that f is Borel measurable.

1.4 Mathematical expectation

The theorems 1.3.4 and 1.3.5 can be used for defining the mathematical expectation of f(X), where f is a Borel measurable function on R^k and X is a random vector in R^k defined on a probability space $\{\Omega,\mathfrak{F},P\}$, as a limit of mathematical expectations of simple functions. The latter expectations are defined as follows:

Definition 1.4.1 Let f(x) be the simple function on R^k as defined in definition 1.3.2. and let X be a random vector in R^k defined on a probability space $\{\Omega,\mathfrak{F},P\}$. Then the mathematical expectation of f(X) is defined by:

$$E\,f(X) = \sum_{j=1}^{n} b_j P(\{\omega \in \Omega : x(\omega) \in B_j\}) = \sum_{j=1}^{n} b_j \mu(B_j),$$

where μ is the probability measure on $\{R^k,\mathfrak{B}^k\}$ induced by X.

For any non-negative Borel measurable function we define:

Definition 1.4.2 Let f(x) be a non-negative Borel measurable function on R^k and let X be a random vector in R^k. Then

$$E\,[f(X)] = \sup E\,[\varphi(X)],$$

where the supremum is taken over all the simple functions satisfying $0 \leq \varphi(x) \leq f(x)$.

Using the representation (1.3.1) we now have:

Definition 1.4.3 Let f(x) be a Borel measurable function on R^k and let X be a random vector in R^k. If

$$E\,[f^+(X)] < \infty \text{ and/or } E\,[f^-(X)] < \infty,$$

then $E\,[f(X)] = E\,[f^+(X)] - E\,[f^-(X)]$.

This is also denoted by the general integral with respect to the measure P of the probability space on which X is defined:

$$E\,[f(X)] = \int f[x(\omega)]P(d\omega) = \int f(x)dP$$

(the latter integral is simply a shorthand notation for the former) or by the integral with respect to the measure μ induced by X:

$$E\,[f(X)] = \int f(x)\mu(dx).$$

If both $E\,[f^+(X)] = \infty$ and $E\,[f^-(X)] = \infty$, the mathematical expectation and the corresponding integral are undefined. Moreover, for any set $\Lambda \in \mathfrak{F}$ we define:

$$\int_\Lambda f[x(\omega)]P(d\omega) = \int y(\omega)P(d\omega),$$

where

$$y(\omega) = f[x(\omega)] \text{ if } \omega \in \Lambda,\; y(\omega) = 0 \text{ if } \omega \in \Omega\backslash\Lambda,$$

provided that the latter integral is defined. Similarly, we define for arbitrary Borel sets B in R^k:

$$\int_B f(x)\mu(dx) = \int g(x)\mu(dx),$$

where:

$$g(x) = f(x) \text{ if } x \in B,\ g(x) = 0 \text{ if } x \notin B$$

The mathematical expectation is often denoted by the classical Riemann–Stieltjes integral (see Rudin [1976]):

$$E[f(X)] = \int f(x)dF(x), \tag{1.4.1}$$

where F is the joint distribution function of the random vector X. Strictly speaking this definition requires that the function f can be written as a pointwise limit of step functions (compare Rudin [1976, ch. 6]). If so, then (1.4.1) is also a mathematical expectation according to the general definition, for step functions are obviously simple functions. For notational convenience we shall often use the notation (1.4.1) even if f is not a pointwise limit of step functions. Thus:

> *Definition 1.4.4* $\int f(x)dF(x) = \int f(x)\mu(dx)$, where μ is the probability measure defining F. Moreover, $\int_B f(x)dF(x) = \int_B f(x)\mu(dx)$ for Borel sets B in R^k.

Most of the properties of the general integral with respect to a probability measure go through for the classical Riemann–Stieltjes integral with respect to the distribution function F, and in the following we shall assume that the reader is familiar with them. (Otherwise, see for example Chung [1974] and Royden [1968].) Some of these properties are listed below since they are frequently used in this book. Assuming that the integrals and mathematical expectations involved are well defined, these properties are:

— Let X and Y be random variables defined on the probability space $\{\Omega, \mathfrak{F}, P\}$. Let Λ and Λ_n be sets in $\mathfrak{F}$. Let α and β be real numbers. We have:

$\int_\Lambda(\alpha x + \beta y)dP = \alpha\int_\Lambda xdP + \beta\int_\Lambda ydP$.
If the Λ_n's are disjoint, then $\int_{\cup\Lambda_n} xdP = \sum_n \int_{\Lambda_n} xdP$.
If $x(\omega) \geq 0$ for every $\omega \in \Lambda$, then $\int_\Lambda xdP \geq 0$.
If $x(\omega) \leq y(\omega)$ for every $\omega \in \Lambda$, then $\int_\Lambda xdP \leq \int_\Lambda ydP$.
$|\int_\Lambda xdP| \leq \int_\Lambda |x|dP$.

These properties are not hard to verify from definitions 1.4.2 and 1.4.3. See also Kolmogorov and Fomin (1961, ch. 7), for related properties of the Lebesgue integral.

— If $X_1, X_2, \ldots, X_n, \ldots$ are independent random variables or vectors and if $f_1(x), f_2(x), \ldots, f_n(x), \ldots$ are conformable Borel measurable functions, then:

$$E[\Pi_j f_j(X_j)] = \Pi_j\{E[f_j(X_j)]\}.$$

— *Chebishev's inequality*. If φ is a Borel measurable function on R such that $\varphi(x)$ is positive and monotonically increasing on $(0,\infty)$ and $\varphi(x) = \varphi(-x)$, then for every r.v. X and every $\delta > 0$ we have $P(|X| > \delta) \leq E[\varphi(X)/\varphi(\delta)]$.

— *Holder's inequality*. Let X and Y be random variables. Then for $p > 1$ and $1/p + 1/q = 1$,

$$|E(X \cdot Y)| \leq E|X \cdot Y| \leq \{E[|X|^p]\}^{1/p}\{E[|Y|^q]\}^{1/q}.$$

(For $p = 2$ we have the well-known *Cauchy-Schwarz inequality*.)

— *Minkowski's inequality*. Let X and Y be random variables. If for some $p \in [1,\infty]$, $E[|X|^p] < \infty$ and $E[|Y|^p] < \infty$, then

$$\{E[|X + Y|^p]\}^{1/p} \leq \{E[|X|^p]\}^{1/p} + \{E[|Y|^p]\}^{1/p}.$$

— *Liapounov's inequality*. Let X be a r.v. Then for $1 \leq p \leq q \leq \infty$,

$$\{E[|X|^p]\}^{1/p} \leq \{E[|X|^q]\}^{1/q}.$$

(This follows straightforwardly from Holder's inequality by putting $Y = 1$ and replacing X by $|X|^p$ and p by q/p.)

— *Jensen's inequality*. Let φ be a convex real function on R and let X be a random variable such that $E[|X|] < \infty$, $E[|\varphi(X)|] < \infty$. Then

$$\varphi(E(X)) \leq E[\varphi(X)].$$

(N.B. Convex real functions are Borel measurable.)

Since the mean of a finite number of non-random variables in R may be considered as a mathematical expectation, it follows from Holder's inequality that for real numbers x_j, y_j, $p > 1$, $1/p + 1/q = 1$:

$$|(1/n)\textstyle\sum_{j=1}^n x_j y_j| \leq \{(1/n)\textstyle\sum_{j=1}^n |x_j|^p\}^{1/p}\{(1/n)\textstyle\sum_{j=1}^n |y_j|^q\}^{1/q}, \qquad (1.4.2)$$

and consequently, taking $y_j = 1$,

$$|\textstyle\sum_{j=1}^n x_j|^p \leq n^{p-1}\textstyle\sum_{j=1}^n |x_j|^p,\ p \geq 1. \qquad (1.4.3)$$

The latter inequality is a sharpening of the following trivial but useful inequality:

$$|\textstyle\sum_{j=1}^n x_j|^p \leq n^p(\max|x_j|)^p \leq n^p\textstyle\sum_{j=1}^n |x_j|^p,\ p > 0. \qquad (1.4.4)$$

Moreover, by Minkowski's inequality we have for $1 \leq p < \infty$,

$$\{(1/n)\sum_{j=1}^{n}|x_j+y_j|^p\}^{1/p} \leq \{(1/n)\sum_{j=1}^{n}|x_j|^p\}^{1/p} + \{(1/n)\sum_{j=1}^{n}|y_j|^p\}^{1/p}. \quad (1.4.5)$$

Finally we shall also use (in chapter 2) the following result.

Theorem 1.4.1 Let X be a r.v. on $\{\Omega,\mathfrak{F},P\}$ such that $E[|X|] < \infty$. Let (Λ_n) be a sequence of sets in $\mathfrak{F}$ such that $\lim_{n\to\infty}P(\Lambda_n) = 0$. Then:

$$\lim_{n\to\infty}\int_{\Lambda_n}|x(\omega)|P(d\omega) = 0.$$

Proof: Let for n = 1,2,...,

$$\Delta_n = \{\omega \in \Omega : |x(\omega)| \geq n\};\ \Gamma_n = \{\omega \in \Omega : n \leq |x(\omega)| < n+1\}.$$

From the fact that

$$\int|x(\omega)|P(d\omega) = \int_{\cup_{n=0}^{\infty}\Gamma_n}|x(\omega)|P(d\omega) = \sum_{n=0}^{\infty}\int_{\Gamma_n}|x(\omega)|P(d\omega) < \infty$$

we conclude that

$$\int_{\Delta_n}|x(\omega)|P(d\omega) = \sum_{k=n}^{\infty}\int_{\Gamma_k}|x(\omega)|P(d\omega) \to 0 \text{ as } n \to \infty.$$

The theorem now follows from:

$$\int_{\Lambda_n}|x(\omega)|P(d\omega) = \int_{\Lambda_n\cap\Delta_k}|x(\omega)|P(d\omega) + \int_{\Lambda_n\cap\Delta_k^c}|x(\omega)|P(d\omega)$$
$$\leq \int_{\Delta_k}|x(\omega)|P(d\omega) + \int_{\Lambda_n\cap\Delta_k^c} kP(d\omega) \leq \int_{\Delta_k}|x(\omega)|P(d\omega) + kP(\Lambda_n)$$

by letting first $n \to \infty$ and then $k \to \infty$. Q.E.D.

Exercises

1. Prove the first set of properties of the integral with respect to a probability measure for finite-valued random variables.
2. Prove the second property for simple functions of independent random variables.
3. Prove Chebishev's inequality. (Hint: Write $E[\varphi(X)] = E[\varphi(|X|)] = E[\varphi(|X|)]I[\varphi(|X|) > \varphi(\varepsilon)] + E[\varphi(|X|)]I[\varphi(|X|) \leq \varphi(\varepsilon)]$.)
4. Prove Holder's inequality. (Hint: Denote $a = |X|^p/\{E[|X|^p]\}$, $b = |Y|^q/\{E[|Y|^q]\}$, $Z = a^{1/p}b^{1/q}$, and use the concavity of ln(.) to show that $\ln(Z) \leq \ln[(1/p)a + (1/q)b]$.
5. Prove Jensen's inequality for the case that X is discretely distributed, i.e.,

   $$P(X = x_j) = p_j > 0\,;\, j=1,...,n\,;\, \sum_{j=1}^{n}p_j = 1.$$

1.5 Characteristic functions

A special and very useful mathematical expectation is the so-called characteristic function:

Definition 1.5.1 Let X be a random vector in R^k with distribution function F. The *characteristic function* of this distribution is the following complex-valued function $\varphi(t)$ on R^k:

$$\varphi(t) = E[\exp(i \cdot t'X)] = E[\cos(t'X)] + i \cdot E[\sin(t'X)],$$

where $t \in R^k$ is a non-random vector.

Distributions are fully determined by their characteristic functions: *distributions are equal if and only if their characteristic functions are equal.* For absolutely continuous distributions this one-to-one correspondence can even be stated explicitly in an inversion formula. We recall that a distribution function F on R^k is absolutely continuous if there exists a non-negative function f on R^k, called the density of F, satisfying:

$$F(t) = \int_{\{u \leq t\}} f(u)du$$

(where u and t are vectors in R^k). For such distributions we have the following results.

Theorem 1.5.1 (Inversion formula for characteristic functions) Let F be a distribution function on R^k and let φ be its characteristic function. If φ is absolutely integrable then F is absolutely continuous and its density F satisfies:

$$f(x) = (1/2\pi)^k \int \exp(-i \cdot t'x)\varphi(t)dt$$
$$= (1/2\pi)^k \int \cos(t'x)\mathrm{Re}[\varphi(t)]dt + (1/2\pi)^k \int \sin(t'x)\mathrm{Im}[\varphi(t)]dt.$$

Proof: Cf. Wilks (1963).

Moreover, we have:

Theorem 1.5.2 A distribution function F is continuously differentiable up to the m-th order if its characteristic function $\varphi(t)$ satisfies $\int |t|^m |\varphi(t)|dt < \infty$.

This can be proved by generalizing theorem 1.5.1 to derivatives, realizing that by the condition of the theorem we may differentiate m times under the integral.

Exercises

1. The distribution F on R has characteristic function $\exp(i \cdot t)$. Determine F.
2. The distribution F on R has characteristic function $\exp(-|t|)$. Determine the density of F.
3. Let X be a r.v. with characteristic function $\varphi(t)$. Show that for $m = 1,2,\ldots$,

   $$E[X^m] = [(d/dt)^m \varphi(t)|_{t=0}]/i^m,$$

   provided $E[|X|^m] < \infty$.

1.6 Random functions

A random function is a function which is a r.v. for each value of its argument. Usually random functions occur as functions of both random variables and parameters, for example the sum of squares of a regression model. Their definition is similar to that of random variables:

> *Definition 1.6.1* Let $\{\Omega,\mathfrak{F},P\}$ be a probability space and let Θ be a subset of R^k. The real function $f(.) = f(.,\omega)$ on $\Theta\times\Omega$ is called a (real) random function on Θ if for every $t \in R$ and every $\theta_0 \in \Theta$, $\{\omega \in \Omega : f(\theta_0,\omega) \leq t\} \in \mathfrak{F}$.

However, dealing with random functions one must be aware of some pitfalls. First, if f(.) is a random function on an uncountable subset Θ of a Euclidean space, then $\sup_{\theta\in\Theta}f(\theta)$ and $\inf_{\theta\in\Theta}f(\theta)$ are not automatically random variables, because

$$\{\omega \in \Omega : \inf_{\theta\in\Theta}f(\theta,\omega) \leq t\} = \cup_{\theta\in\Theta}\{\omega \in \Omega : f(\theta,\omega) \leq t\}$$

and

$$\{\omega \in \Omega : \sup_{\theta\in\Theta}f(\theta,\omega) \leq t\} = \cap_{\theta\in\Theta}\{\omega \in \Omega : f(\theta,\omega) \leq t\}$$

are then *uncountable* unions and intersections, respectively, of members of the Borel field $\mathfrak{F}$ and therefore not necessarily members of $\mathfrak{F}$ themselves. Another pitfall is that if θ is a random vector in an uncountable subset Θ of a Euclidean space and if f(.) is a random function on Θ , then $f(\theta)$ is not necessarily a random variable, because

$$\{\omega \in \Omega\text{: } f(\theta(\omega),\omega) \leq t\}$$
$$= \cup_{\theta_1\in\Theta}[\{\omega \in \Omega\text{: } f(\theta_1,\omega) \leq t\}\cap\{\omega \in \Omega\text{: } \theta(\omega) = \theta_1\}]$$

is an uncountable union of members of $\mathfrak{F}$. These problems can be overcome if we assume that the random function f(.) is *separable* (see Gihman and Skorohod [1974], ch. 3, sec. 2]). However, in this study we shall only deal with random functions of the type $f(.) = \varphi(.,X)$, where φ is a Borel measurable real function on $\Theta\times R^m$ with Θ a compact Borel set in R^k, and X is a random vector in R^m. If in addition $\varphi(.,x)$ is for each $x \in R^m$ a continuous function on Θ we do not need the separability concept, because of the following theorem:

> *Theorem 1.6.1* Let Θ be a compact set in R^k and let $\varphi(\theta,x)$ be a Borel measurable real function on $\Theta\times R^m$ which is continuous in θ for each $x \in R^m$. There exists a mapping $\theta(x)$ from R^k into Θ with Borel measurable components such that
>
> $$\varphi(\theta(x),x) = \sup_{\theta\in\Theta}\varphi(\theta,x).$$

Consequently the supremum involved is a Borel measurable real function on R^m. Moreover, if $\varphi(\theta,x)$ is continuous on $\Theta \times R^m$ then $\sup_{\theta\in\Theta}\varphi(\theta,x)$ is a continuous function on R^m.

Proof: Jennrich (1969).

(N.B. Compact sets in R^k are Borel sets.)

Of course, a similar result holds for the 'inf' case. The condition in theorem 1.6.1 that the set Θ is compact (hence bounded) is not strictly necessary for the Borel measurability of $\sup_{\theta\in\Theta}\varphi(\theta,x)$ and $\inf_{\theta\in\Theta}\varphi(\theta,x)$, provided that

$$\Theta_n = \Theta \cap \{\theta \in R^k : |\theta| \leq n\}$$

is compact for each n. Then we have:

$$\sup_{\theta\in\Theta}\varphi(\theta,x) = \lim_{n\to\infty}\sup_{\theta\in\Theta_n}\varphi(\theta,x),$$
$$\inf_{\theta\in\Theta}\varphi(\theta,x) = \lim_{n\to\infty}\inf_{\theta\in\Theta_n}\varphi(\theta,x),$$

which by theorems 1.3.2 and 1.6.1 are Borel measurable functions.

Let us return to more general random functions. The properties of a random function f(.) may differ for different ω in Ω. For two points ω_1 and ω_2 in Ω it is for example possible that $f(\tau,\omega_1)$ is continuous and $f(\tau,\omega_2)$ is discontinuous at the same τ.

In this study we shall always consider properties of random functions holding almost surely, which means that a property of $f(.) = f(.,\omega)$ holds for all ω in a set $E \in \mathfrak{F}$ with $P(E) = 1$. Thus, for example, the statement: "f(.) is a.s. continuous on Θ" means that there is a null set N such that $f(.,\omega)$ is continuous on Θ for all $\omega \in \Omega\backslash N$.

Exercises:

1. Let X be uniformly distributed on [0,1] and let for $\Theta \in [0,1]$,

   $$f(\theta) = 1 \text{ if } X \geq \theta,\ f(\theta) = 0 \text{ if } X < \theta.$$

   Is $f(\theta)$ a random function on [0,1]?
2. Let X be N(0,1) distributed and let for $\theta \in R$,
   $f(\theta) = \theta$ if θ is rational, $f(\theta) = -\theta$ if θ is irrational.

   Prove that f(X) is a continuously distributed random variable.
3. Let for $x \in R$ and $\theta \in R$,

   $$\varphi(x,\theta) = 1-(\theta-2)^2 \text{ if } 1 \leq \theta \leq 3 \text{ and } x > 0,$$
   $$\varphi(x,\theta) = [1-(\theta-2)^2]/[1+x^2] \text{ if } 1 \leq \theta \leq 3 \text{ and } x \leq 0,$$
   $$\varphi(x,\theta) = 1-(\theta+2)^2 \text{ for } -3 \leq \theta \leq -1 \text{ and } x \leq 0,$$
   $$\varphi(x,\theta) = [1-(\theta+2)^2]/[1+x^2] \text{ if } -3 \leq \theta \leq -1 \text{ and } x > 0,$$
   $$\varphi(x,\theta) = 0 \text{ elsewhere,}$$

and let $\hat{\theta}$ be such that

$$\varphi(\hat{\theta}(x),x) = \sup_{\theta \in [-3,3]} \varphi(\theta,x).$$

— Is φ continuous?
— Determine $\hat{\theta}(x)$.
— What is your conclusion regarding the second part of theorem 1.6.1?

2

Convergence

In this chapter we consider various modes of convergence, i.e., weak and strong convergence of random variables, weak and strong laws of large numbers, convergence in distribution and central limit theorems, weak and strong uniform convergence of random functions, and uniform weak and strong laws. The material in this chapter is a revision and extension of sections 2.2–2.4 in Bierens (1981).

2.1 Weak and strong convergence of random variables

In this section we shall deal with the concepts of convergence in probability and almost sure convergence, and various laws of large numbers. Throughout we assume that the random variables involved are defined on a common probability space $\{\Omega,\mathfrak{F},P\}$. The first concept is well known:

> *Definition 2.1.1* Let (X_n) be a sequence of r.v.'s. We say that X_n converges in probability to a r.v. X if for every $\varepsilon > 0$, $\lim_{n\to\infty}P(|X_n - X| \leq \varepsilon) = 1$, and we write: $X_n \to X$ in pr. or $\mathrm{plim}_{n\to\infty}X_n = X$.

However, almost sure convergence is a much stronger convergence concept:

> *Definition 2.1.2* Let (X_n) be a sequence of r.v.'s. We say that X_n converges almost surely (a.s.) to a r.v. X if there is a *null set* $N \in \mathfrak{F}$ (that is a set in $\mathfrak{F}$ satisfying $P(N) = 0$) such that for every $\omega \in \Omega\backslash N$, $\lim_{n\to\infty}x_n(\omega) = x(\omega)$, and we write: $X_n \to X$ a.s. or $\lim_{n\to\infty}X_n = X$ a.s.

Note that this definition is equivalent to:

$X_n \to X$ a.s. if $P(\{\omega\in\Omega: \lim_{n\to\infty}x_n(\omega) = x(\omega)\}) = 1$.

A useful criterion for almost sure convergence of random variables is given by the following theorem.

> *Theorem 2.1.1* Let X and $X_1,X_2,...$ be random variables. Then $X_n \to X$ a.s. if and only if

$$\lim_{n\to\infty} P(\cap_{m=n}^{\infty}\{|X_m - X| \le \varepsilon\}) = 1 \text{ for every } \varepsilon > 0. \qquad (2.1.1)$$

Proof: First we prove that $x(\omega) = \lim_{n\to\infty} x_n(\omega)$ pointwise on $\Omega\backslash N$ implies (2.1.1). Let $\omega_0 \in \Omega\backslash N$. Then for every $\varepsilon > 0$ there is a number $n_0(\omega_0,\varepsilon)$ such that

$$|x_n(\omega_0)\ x(\omega_0)| \le \varepsilon \text{ for all } n \ge n_0(\omega_0,\varepsilon).$$

Now consider the following set in $\mathfrak{F}$.

$$A_n(\varepsilon) = \cap_{m=n}^{\infty}\{\omega \in \Omega : |x_m(\omega) - x(\omega)| \le \varepsilon\}.$$

Then $\omega_0 \in A_{n_0(\omega_0,\varepsilon)}(\varepsilon)$ and hence $\omega_0 \in \cup_n A_n(\varepsilon)$. Thus we have:

$$\Omega\backslash N \subset \cup_n A_n(\varepsilon)$$

and consequently

$$P(\Omega\backslash N) \le P(\cup_n A_n(\varepsilon)).$$

But $P(\Omega\backslash N) = P(\Omega) - P(N) = 1$ since N is a null set, hence

$$P(\cup_n A_n(\varepsilon)) = 1.$$

Since $A_n(\varepsilon) \subset A_{n+1}(\varepsilon)$, we have $A_k(\varepsilon) = \cup_n^k = 1 A_n(\varepsilon)$ and thus

$$\lim_{n\to\infty} P(A_k(\varepsilon)) = \lim_{n\to\infty} P(\cup_{n=1}^{k} A_n(\varepsilon)) = P(\cup_n A_n(\varepsilon)) = 1,$$

which proves the first part of the theorem.

Next we prove that if $\lim_{n\to\infty} P(A_n(\varepsilon)) = 1$ for every $\varepsilon > 0$ then there exists a null set N such that

$$x(\omega) = \lim_{n\to\infty} x_n(\omega) \text{ pointwise on } \Omega\backslash N\ .$$

For $\delta > 0$ put $N_\delta = \Omega\backslash\cup_n A_n(\delta)$. Then $N_\delta \in \mathfrak{F}$ and

$$P(N_\delta) = P(\Omega) - P(\cup_n A_n(\delta)),$$

hence N_δ is a null set. Define

$$N = \cup_k N_{1/k}.$$

Then N is a countable union of null sets in $\mathfrak{F}$ and therefore a null set itself. Let $\omega_0 \in \Omega\backslash N$, then $\omega_0 \in \cap_k(\cup_n A_n(1/k))$. Suppose that k is arbitrarily chosen but fixed. Then $\omega_0 \in A_n(1/k)$. Therefore, there exists an $n_0 = n_0(1/k)$ such that

$$|x_n(\omega_0) - x(\omega_0)| \le 1/k \text{ for } n \ge n_0(1/k).$$

It is obvious now that $x_n(\omega_0)$ converges to $x(\omega_0)$ pointwise on $\Omega\backslash N$. This proves the "only if" part of the theorem. Q.E.D.

From this theorem we see that

Corollary 2.1.1 $X_n \to X$ a.s. implies $X_n \to X$ in pr.

Proof: Note that

$$\cap_{m=n}^{\infty}\{|X_m - X| \leq \varepsilon\} \subset \{|X_n - X| \leq \varepsilon\}$$

and consequently

$$P(\cap_{m=n}^{\infty}\{|X_m - X| \leq \varepsilon\}) \leq P(|X_n - X| \leq \varepsilon). \qquad \text{Q.E.D.}$$

The following simple but important theorem provides another useful criterion for almost sure convergence.

Theorem 2.1.2 (Borel–Cantelli lemma) If for every $\varepsilon > 0$,

$$\textstyle\sum_n P(|X_n - X| > \varepsilon) < \infty,$$

then $X_n \to X$ a.s.

Proof: Consider the set

$$A_n(\varepsilon) = \cap_{m=n}^{\infty}\{\omega \in \Omega\colon |x_n(\omega) - x(\omega)| \leq \varepsilon\} = \cap_{m=n}^{\infty}\{|X_n - X| \leq \varepsilon\}.$$

From theorem 2.1.1 it follows that it suffices to show

$P(A_n(\varepsilon)) \to 1$ or, equivalently, $P(A_n(\varepsilon)^c) \to 0$.

But

$$A_n(\varepsilon)^c = \cup_{m=n}^{\infty}\{|X_m - X| > \varepsilon\},$$

and hence

$$P(A_n(\varepsilon)^c) \leq \textstyle\sum_{m=n}^{\infty} P(|X_m - X| > \varepsilon).$$

Since the latter sum is a tail sum of the convergent series

$$\textstyle\sum_n P(|X_n - X| > \varepsilon)$$

we must have

$$\textstyle\sum_{m=n}^{\infty} P(|X_n - X| > \varepsilon) \to 0 \text{ as } n \to \infty,$$

which proves the theorem. Q.E.D.

The a.s. convergence concept arises in a natural way from the strong laws of large numbers. Here we give three versions of these laws.

Theorem 2.1.3 Let (X_j) be a sequence of *uncorrelated* random variables satisfying $E[X_j - EX_j)]^2 = O(j^\mu)$ for some $\mu < 1$. Then

$$(1/n)\textstyle\sum_{j=1}^{n}[X_j - E(X_j)] \to 0 \text{ a.s.}$$

Proof: This theorem is a further elaboration of the strong law of large numbers of Rademacher–Menchov (see Révész [1968, theorem 3.2.1] or Stout [1974], theorem 2.3.2), which states:

Let (Y_j), $j > 0$, be a sequence of orthogonal random variables (orthogonality means that $E(Y_{j_1}Y_{j_2}) = 0$ if $j_1 \neq j_2$). If

$$\sum_j(\log j)E(Y_j^2) < \infty$$

then $\sum_j Y_j$ converges a.s. (which means that $Z = \sum_j Y_j$ is a.s. a finite valued random variable). Now let $Y_j = [X_j - E(X_j)]/j$. Then

$$\sum_j(\log j)E(Y_j^2) = \sum_j(\log j)O(j^{\mu-2}) < \infty \text{ for } \mu < 1,$$

hence $\sum_j[X_j - E(X_j)]/j$ converges a.s. From the Kronecker lemma (see Révész [1968, theorem 1.2.2] or Chung [1974, p.123]) it follows that this result implies the theorem under review. Q.E.D.

Theorem 2.1.4 Let (X_j) be a sequence of *uncorrelated* random variables satisfying:

$$\sup_n(1/n)\sum_{j=1}^n E[|X_j - E(X_j)|^{2+\delta}] < \infty \text{ for some } \delta > 0.$$

Then $(1/n)\sum_{j=1}^n [X_j - E(X_j)] \to 0$ a.s.

Proof: The moment condition in this theorem implies

$$E[|X_j - E(X_j)|^{2+\delta}] = O(j),$$

so that by Liapounov's inequality

$$E\{[X_j - E(X_j)]\}^2 \leq \{E[|X_j - E(X_j)]|^{2+\delta}\}^{2/(2+\delta)} = O(j^{2/(2+\delta)}).$$

The theorem now follows from theorem 2.1.3. Q.E.D.

If the X_j's are independent identically distributed (i.i.d.) the condition on the second moment is not needed:

Theorem 2.1.5 (Strong law of large numbers of Kolmogorov) Let (X_j) be a sequence of i.i.d. random variables satisfying $E(|X_1|) < \infty$. Then

$$(1/n)\sum_{j=1}^n X_j \to E(X_1) \text{ a.s.}$$

Proof: Chung (1974, theorem 5.4.2).

We already have mentioned that almost sure convergence implies convergence in probability. There is also a converse connection, given by the following theorem.

Theorem 2.1.6 Let X and $X_1, X_2, \ldots$ be r.v.'s. Then $X_n \to X$ in pr. if and only if every subsequence (n_k) of the sequence (n) contains a further subsequence (n_{k_j}) such that

$$X_{n_{k_j}} \to X \text{ a.s. as } j \to \infty \qquad (2.1.2)$$

Proof: Suppose that every subsequence (n_k) contains a further subsequence (n_{k_j}) such that (2.1.2) holds, but not that $X_n \to X$ in pr. Then there exist numbers $\varepsilon > 0$, $\delta > 0$, and a subsequence (n_k) such that

$$P(|X_{n_k} - X| \le \varepsilon) \le 1\text{-}\delta,$$

hence for every further subsequence we have the same, which contradicts our assumption. Thus the "if" part is now proved. Next, suppose that $X_n \to X$ in pr. Then for every positive integer k,

$$\lim_{n\to\infty} P(|X_n - X| > 1/2^k) = 0 .$$

For each k we can find an n_k such that

$$P(|X_{n_k} - X| > 1/2^k) \le 1/2^k,$$

hence

$$\sum_k P(|X_{n_k} - X| > 1/2^k) \le \sum_k 1/2^k < \infty$$

and consequently:

$$\sum_k P(|X_{n_k} - X| > \varepsilon) < \infty \text{ for every } \varepsilon > 0.$$

By the Borel–Cantelli lemma it follows now that $X_{n_k} \to X$ a.s., which proves the "only if" part. Q.E.D.

Theorem 2.1.7 Let X and $X_1, X_2, \ldots$ be r.v.'s such that (a) $X_n \to X$ a.s. or (b) $X_n \to X$ in pr.,respectively. Let f(x) be a Borel measurable real function on R. If f is continuous on a Borel set B such that $P(X \in B) = 1$, then (a) $f(X_n) \to f(X)$ a.s. or (b) $f(X_n) \to f(X)$ in pr., respectively.

Proof
(a) There is a null set N_1 such that for every $\varepsilon > 0$ and every $\omega \in \Omega\backslash N_1$,

$$|x_n(\omega) - x(\omega)| \le \varepsilon \text{ if } n \ge n_0(\omega,\varepsilon).$$

Let $N_2 = \Omega\backslash\{\omega \in \Omega: x(\omega) \in B\}$. Then N_2 is a null set in $\mathfrak{F}$ and $x(\omega)$ is for every $\omega \in \Omega\backslash N_2$ a continuity point of f. Thus for every $\varepsilon > 0$ and every $\omega \in \Omega\backslash N_2$ there is a number $\delta(\varepsilon,\omega) > 0$ such that:

$$|f(x_n(\omega)) - f(x(\omega))| \le \varepsilon \text{ if } |x_n(\omega) - x(\omega)| \le \delta(\varepsilon,\omega),$$

hence for every $\varepsilon > 0$ and every $\omega \in \Omega\backslash(N_1 \cup N_2)$ we have:

$$|f(x_n(\omega)) - f(x(\omega))| \le \varepsilon \text{ if } n \ge n_0(\omega,\delta(\varepsilon,\omega)).$$

Since $N_1 \cup N_2$ is a null set in $\mathfrak{F}$, this proves part (a) of the theorem.
(b) For an arbitrary subsequence (n_k) we have a further subsequence

(n_{k_j}) such that (2.1.2) holds and consequently by part (a) of the theorem:

$$f(X_{n_{k_j}}) \to f(X) \text{ a.s.}$$

By theorem 2.1.6 this implies $f(X_n) \to f(X)$ in pr. Q.E.D.

Remark: Thus far in this section we have dealt only with random variables in R. However, generalization of the definitions and the theorems in this section to finite dimensional random vectors is straightforward, simply by changing random *variable* to random *vector*. The only notable extension is:

> *Theorem 2.1.8* Let $X_n = (X_{1n},...,X_{kn})'$ and $X = (X_1,...,X_k)'$ be random vectors. Then $X_n \to X$ a.s. (in pr.) if and only if for each j, $X_{jn} \to X_j$ a.s. (in pr.).

Exercises

1. Let (X_j) be a sequence of random variables such that for each j

   $E(X_j) = \mu$, $E[(X_j - \mu)^2] = \sigma^2$, $\sup_j E[|X_j - \mu|^3] < \infty$,
   $\text{cov}(X_j, X_{j-m}) = 0$ if $m > 1$, $\text{cov}(X_j, X_{j-m}) \neq 0$ if $m = 1$.

   Prove that $(1/n)\sum_{j=1}^n X_j \to \mu$ a.s. (Hint: Let $Y_{1j} = X_{2j}$, $Y_{2j} = X_{2j+1}$. Prove first that for $i = 1,2$, $(1/n)\sum_{j=1}^n Y_{ij} \to \mu$ a.s.)
2. Let (Y_j), $j > 0$, be a sequence of random variables satisfying $E(Y_j) = 0$, $E(Y_j^2) = 1/j^2$ and let $X_n = (Y_n)^n$, $n = 1,2,...$ Prove that $X_n \to 0$ a.s. (Hint: Combine Chebishev's inequality and the Borel–Cantelli lemma.)
3. Let $X_{n,m}$ and X_m be random variables, where $n = 1,2,...$ and $m = 1,2,...$ such that for $m = 1,2,...,k < \infty$, $X_{n,m} \to X_m$ a.s. as $n \to \infty$. Prove that

   $$\max_{m=1,2,...,k} |X_{n,m} - X_m| \to 0 \text{ a.s.}$$
4. Let (X_j) be a sequence of i.i.d. random variables satisfying $E(X_j) = 0$, $0 < E(X_j^2) < \infty$. Prove that

   $$[(1/n)\sum_{j=1}^n X_j]/[(1/n)\sum_{j=1}^n X_j^2] \to 0 \text{ a.s.}$$
5. Let X be a random variable satisfying

   $$P(X = 1) = P(X = -1) = ½.$$

   Let $Y_n = X^n$, $n = 1,2,...$ Does Y_n converge a.s. or in pr.?
6. Prove theorem 2.1.8.

2.2 Convergence of mathematical expectations

If X and $X_1, X_2, \ldots$ are random variables or vectors such that for some $p > 0$, $E(|X_n - X|^p) \to 0$ as $n \to \infty$, then it follows from Chebishev's inequality that $X_n \to X$ in pr. The converse is not always true. A partial converse is given by the following theorem.

Theorem 2.2.1 If $X_n \to X$ in pr. and if there is a r.v. Y satisfying $|X_n| \le Y$ a.s. for $n = 1,2,\ldots$ and $E(Y^p) < \infty$ for some $p > 0$, then $E(|X_n - X|^p) \to 0$.

Proof: If $P(|X| > Y) > 0$ then $X_n \to X$ in pr. is not possible, hence $|X| \le Y$ a.s. Since now $|X_n - X| \le 2Y$ there is no loss of generality in assuming $X = 0$ a.s. We then have:

$$\int |x_n(\omega)|^p P(d\omega) = \int_{\{|x_n(\omega)| > \varepsilon\}} |x_n(\omega)|^p P(d\omega) + \int_{\{|x_n(\omega)| \le \varepsilon\}} |x_n(\omega)|^p P(d\omega)$$
$$\le \varepsilon^p + \int_{\{|x_n(\omega)| > \varepsilon\}} y(\omega)^p P(d\omega).$$

The theorem follows now from theorem 1.4.1. Q.E.D.

Putting $p = 1$ in theorem 2.2.1 we have:

Theorem 2.2.2 (Dominated convergence theorem) If $X_n \to X$ in pr. and if $|X_n| \le Y$ a.s., where $E(Y) < \infty$, then $E(X_n) \to E(X)$.

We shall use this theorem to prove first Fatou's lemma which in turn will be used to prove the monotone convergence theorem.

Theorem 2.2.3 (Fatou's lemma) If $X_n \ge 0$ a.s., then $E(\liminf_{n\to\infty} X_n) \le \liminf_{n\to\infty} E(X_n)$.

Proof: Put $X = \liminf_{n\to\infty} X_n$ and let $\varphi(x)$ be any simple function satisfying $0 \le \varphi(x) \le x$. Put $Y_n = \min[\varphi(X), X_n]$. Then $Y_n \to \varphi(X)$ in pr. because

$$P(|\min[\varphi(X),X_n] - \varphi(X)| \ge \varepsilon) = P(X_n \le \varphi(X) - \varepsilon) \le P(X_n \le X - \varepsilon) \to 0.$$

Moreover, since $\varphi(x)$ is a simple function we must have $E[\varphi(X)] < \infty$. From the dominated convergence theorem and from $Y_n \le X_n$ a.s. it follows now:

$$E[\varphi(X)] = \lim_{n\to\infty} E(Y_n) = \liminf_{n\to\infty} E(Y_n) \le \liminf_{n\to\infty} E(X_n).$$

Taking the supremum over all such simple functions φ it follows now from definition 1.4.2 that the theorem holds. Q.E.D.

Theorem 2.2.4 (Monotone convergence theorem) Let (X_n) be a nondecreasing sequence of r.v.'s. Then

$$E(\lim_{n\to\infty} X_n) = \lim_{n\to\infty} E(X_n) \le \infty.$$

Proof: Since our sequence (X_n) is nondecreasing, we have:

$\lim_{n\to\infty} X_n = \liminf_{n\to\infty} X_n$, $\lim_{n\to\infty} E(X_n) = \liminf_{n\to\infty} E(X_n)$,

so that by Fatou's lemma, $E(\lim_{n\to\infty} X_n) \leq \lim_{n\to\infty} E(X_n)$. However, for any n we have $X_n \leq \lim_{n\to\infty} X_n$ a.s. because X_n is nondecreasing, hence $E(X_n) \leq E(\lim_{n\to\infty} X_n)$ and consequently

$\lim_{n\to\infty} E(X_n) \leq E(\lim_{n\to\infty} X_n)$.

This proves the theorem. Q.E.D.

Exercises

1. Let Y_n be defined as in exercise 5 of section 2.1. Does $E(Y_n)$ converge?
2. Let (f_n) be a sequence of Borel measurable real functions on R^k and let μ be a probability measure on $\{R^k, \mathfrak{B}^k\}$. Suppose there exists a non-negative Borel measurable real function g on R^k such that

   $\sup_n |f_n(x)| \leq g(x)$, with $\int g(x)\mu(dx) < \infty$.

   Moreover, assume that $f(x) = \lim_{n\to\infty} f_n(x)$ exists for each x in a set $S \subset R^k$ with $\mu(S) = 1$. Prove that

   $\lim_{n\to\infty} \int f_n(x)\mu(dx) = \int f(x)\mu(dx)$.

   (This is another version of the dominated convergence theorem.)

2.3 Convergence of distributions

If X and $X_1, X_2, \ldots$ are r.v.'s with distribution functions F, F_1, $F_2, \ldots$, respectively, then one would like to say that X_n converges in distribution to X if for every $t \in R$, $F_n(t) \to F(t)$. However, if X and F are given and if we define $X_n = X + 1/n$, then:

$F_n(t) = P(X_n \leq t) = P(X \leq t - 1/n) = F(t - 1/n)$,

so that for every discontinuity point t_0 of F we have:

$\lim_{n\to\infty} F_n(t_0) = \lim_{n\to\infty} F(t_0 - 1/n) = F(t_0-) < F(t_0)$,

while intuitively we would expect that in this case we also have convergence in distribution. Furthermore, if $X_n = X + n$ we have:

$F_n(t) = P(X_n \leq t) = F(t-n) \to F(-\infty) = 0$ for every t.

Thus not every sequence of distribution functions converges to another distribution function. In the latter case we say that the convergence is improper.

> *Definition 2.3.1* A sequence $(F_n(t))$ of distribution functions converges properly pointwise if $F_n(t) \to F(t)$ pointwise for all

continuity points of F, where F is a distribution function. We then write: $F_n \to F$ properly pointwise.

The exclusion of discontinuity points avoids the complication that otherwise the function $F(t) = \lim_{n\to\infty}F_n(t)$ may not be right continuous. In view of the above example we now define:

Definition 2.3.2 A sequence (X_n) of random variables (or random vectors) converges in distribution to X, if their underlying distribution functions (F_n), F, respectively, satisfy $F_n \to F$ properly pointwise. We then write: $X_n \to X$ in distr.

Remark: If this "limit" distribution F is the distribution function of (for example) the normal distribution $N(\mu,\sigma^2)$, we shall also write: $X_n \to N(\mu,\sigma^2)$ in distr.

There is a close connection between proper pointwise convergence of distribution functions and convergence of mathematical expectations, as is shown by the following theorem. This theorem is fundamental as it allows for a variety of applications.

Theorem 2.3.1 Let F and F_n, n = 1,2,... be distribution functions on R^k. Then $F_n \to F$ properly pointwise if and only if for every bounded continuous real function φ on R^k,

$$\int\varphi(t)dF_n(t) \to \int\varphi(t)dF(t).$$

Proof: Since the proof for the general case $k > 1$ is a straightforward extension of that for $k = 1$, we assume $k = 1$. Suppose $F_n \to F$ properly pointwise. For given $\varepsilon > 0$ we can always find continuity points a and b of F such that $F(b)-F(a) > 1-\varepsilon$. Let φ be any bounded continuous real function on R with uniform bound 1 (which is no restriction). By the uniform continuity of φ on [a,b] we can find continuity points $t_2,t_3,\ldots,t_{m-1}$ of F satisfying $a = t_1 < t_2 < \ldots < t_{m-1} < t_m = b$ and

$$\sup_{t\in(t_i,t_{i+1}]}\varphi(t) - \inf_{t\in(t_i,t_{i+1}]}\varphi(t) \leq \varepsilon$$

for i = 1,2,...,m-1. Now define:

$$\psi(t) = \inf_{t\in(t_i,t_{i+1}]}\varphi(t) \text{ for } t \in (t_i,t_{i+1}],\ i=1,2,\ldots,m\text{-}1,$$
$$\psi(t) = 0 \text{ elsewhere.}$$

Then

$$0 \leq \varphi(t) - \psi(t) \leq \varepsilon \text{ for } t \in (a,b],\ 0 \leq \varphi(t) - \psi(t) \leq 1 \text{ for } t \notin (a,b],$$

hence

$$|\int\psi(t)dF_n(t) - \int\varphi(t)dF_n(t)| \leq \int_{\{t\in(a,b]\}}\varepsilon dF_n(t) + \int_{\{t\notin(a,b]\}}dF_n(t)$$

$$= \varepsilon(F_n(b) - F_n(a)) + 1 - F_n(b) + F_n(a)$$
$$\to \varepsilon(F(b) - F(a)) + 1 - F(b) + F(a) \le 2\varepsilon.$$

Moreover,

$$\int\psi(t)dF_n(t) = \textstyle\sum_{i=1}^{m-1}\{\inf_{t\in(t_i,t_{i+1}]}\varphi(t)\}(F_n(t_{i+1}) - F_n(t_i))$$
$$\to \textstyle\sum_{i=1}^{m-1}\{\inf_{t\in(t_i,t_{i+1}]}\varphi(t)\}(F(t_{i+1}) - F(t_i)) = \int\psi(t)dF(t)$$

and

$$|\int\varphi(t)dF(t) - \int\psi(t)dF(t)| \le 2\varepsilon.$$

So we have:

$$|\int\varphi(t)dF_n(t) - \int\varphi(t)dF(t)| \le 4\varepsilon + |\int\psi(t)dF_n(t) - \int\psi(t)dF(t)| \le 5\varepsilon$$

for sufficiently large n, which proves the "only if" part of the theorem.

Now let u be a continuity point of F and define

$$\varphi(t) = 1 \text{ if } t \le u,\ \varphi(t) = 0 \text{ if } t > u,$$

$$\varphi_{1,m}(t) = 1 \text{ if } t \le u - 1/m,$$
$$\varphi_{1,m}(t) = m.u - m.t \text{ if } t \in (u - 1/m, u],$$
$$\varphi_{1,m}(t) = 0 \text{ if } t > u,$$

$$\varphi_{2,m}(t) = 1 \text{ if } t \le u,$$
$$\varphi_{2,m}(t) = m.u + 1 - m.t \text{ if } t \in (u, u + 1/m],$$
$$\varphi_{2,m}(t) = 0 \text{ if } t > u + 1/m.$$

Then $\varphi_{1,m}$ and $\varphi_{2,m}$ are bounded continuous functions on R satisfying $\varphi_{1,m}(t) \le \varphi(t) \le \varphi_{2,m}(t)$, hence for m = 1,2,... and $n\to\infty$:

$$\int\varphi_{1,m}(t)dF_n(t) \le F_n(u) = \int\varphi(t)dF_n(t) \le \int\varphi_{2,m}(t)dF_n(t),$$
$$\int\varphi_{1,m}(t)dF(t) \le F(u) = \int\varphi(t)dF(t) \le \int\varphi_{2,m}(t)dF(t).$$

Moreover:

$$0 \le \int(\varphi_{2,m}(t) - \varphi_{1,m}(t))dF(t) \le \int_{\{t\in(u-1/m,u+1/m]\}}dF(t)$$
$$= F(u+1/m) - F(u-1/m).$$

Since u is a continuity point of F, $F(u + 1/m) - F(u - 1/m)$ can be made arbitrarily small by increasing m, hence $F_n(u) \to F(u)$, which proves the "if" part. Q.E.D.

A direct consequence of this theorem is that:

Theorem 2.3.2 $X_n \to X$ in pr. implies $X_n \to X$ in distr.

Proof: By theorem 2.1.7 it follows that for any continuous function φ we have $X_n \to X$ in pr. implies $\varphi(X_n) \to \varphi(X)$ in pr., whereas by theorem

2.2.2, $\varphi(X_n) \to \varphi(X)$ in pr. implies $E[\varphi(X_n)] \to E[\varphi(X)]$ if φ is a bounded continuous function. Q.E.D.

The converse of this theorem is not generally true, but it is if X is constant a.s., that is: $P(X = c) = 1$ for some constant c. In that case the proper limit F involved is:

$F(t) = 1$ if $t \geq c$, $F(t) = 0$ if $t < c$.

The proof of this proposition is very simple:

$$P(|X_n - c| \leq \varepsilon) = P(c-\varepsilon \leq X_n \leq c+\varepsilon) = F_n(c+\varepsilon) - F_n((c-\varepsilon)-)$$
$$\to F(c+\varepsilon) - F(c-\varepsilon) = 1$$

for every $\varepsilon > 0$, since $c+\varepsilon$ and $c-\varepsilon$ are continuity points of F. Thus:

Theorem 2.3.3 Convergence in distribution to a constant implies convergence in probability to that constant.

Let X_n and X be random vectors in R^k such that $X_n \to X$ in distr. and let f be any continuous real function on R^k. For any bounded continuous real function φ on R it follows that $\varphi(f)$ is a bounded continuous real function on R^k, so that by theorem 2.3.1,

$E[\varphi(f(X_n))] \to E[\varphi(f(X))]$

and consequently $f(X_n) \to f(X)$ in distr. Thus we have:

Theorem 2.3.4 Let X_n and X be random vectors in R^k and let f be a continuous real function on R^k. Then $X_n \to X$ in distr. implies $f(X_n) \to f(X)$ in distr.

Remark: The continuity of f in theorem 2.3.4 is an essential condition. For example, let X be a *continuously* distributed random variable, let X_n the value of X rounded off to n decimal digits and let

$f(x) = 1$ if x is rational, $f(x) = 0$ if x is irrational.

Then $X_n \to X$ in distr. and f is Borel measurable. However, $f(X_n) = 1$ a.s. and $f(X) = 0$ a.s., which renders $f(X_n) \to f(X)$ in distr. impossible.

A more general result is given by the following theorem.

Theorem 2.3.5 Let X_n and X be random vectors in R^k, Y_n a random vector in R^m and c a non-random vector in R^m. If $X_n \to X$ in distr. and $Y_n \to c$ in distr., then $f(X_n,Y_n) \to f(X,c)$ in distr. for any continuous real function f on $R^k \times C$, where C is some subset of R^m with interior point c.

Proof: Again we prove the theorem for the case $k = m = 1$ since the proof of the general case is similar. It suffices to prove that for any bounded continuous real function φ on R^2 we have $E[\varphi(X_n,Y_n)] \rightarrow E[\varphi(X,c)]$, because then $E[\psi(f(X_n,Y_n))] \rightarrow E[\psi(f(X,c)]$ for any bounded continuous real function ψ on R, which by theorem 2.3.1 implies $f(X_n,Y_n) \rightarrow f(X,c)$ in distr.

Let M be the uniform bound of φ and let F_n and F be the distribution functions of X_n and X, respectively. For every ε we can choose continuity points a and b of F such that:

$$P(X \in (a,b]) = F(b) - F(a) > 1 - \varepsilon/(2M).$$

Moreover, for any $\delta > 0$ we have:

$$\begin{aligned}|E[\varphi(X_n,Y_n)] - E[\varphi(X_n,c)]| &\leq \int_{\{x_n\in(a,b]\}}|\varphi(x_n,y_n) - \varphi(x_n,c)|dP \\ &\quad + \int_{\{x_n\notin(a,b]\}}|\varphi(x_n,y_n) - \varphi(x_n,c)|dP \\ &\leq \int_{\{x_n\in(a,b]\}\cap\{|y_n-c|\leq\delta\}}|\varphi(x_n,y_n) - \varphi(x_n,c)|dP \\ &\quad + 2M{\cdot}P(\{X_n\in(a,b]\}\cap\{|Y_n-c|>\delta\}) + 2M{\cdot}P(X_n\notin(a,b]) \\ &\leq \int_{\{x_n\in(a,b]\}\cap\{|y_n-c|\leq\delta\}}|\varphi(x_n,y_n) - \varphi(x_n,c)|dP \\ &\quad + 2M{\cdot}P\{|Y_n-c|>\delta\} + 2M(1-F_n(b)+F_n(a)).\end{aligned}$$

Since by theorem 2.3.3, $Y_n \rightarrow c$ in pr., we have

$$P(|Y_n - c| > \delta) \rightarrow 0 \text{ for any } \delta > 0,$$

whereas

$$\lim_{n\rightarrow\infty} 2M(1-F_n(b)+F_n(a)) = 2M(1-F(b)+F(a)) < \varepsilon.$$

Furthermore, since $\varphi(t_1,t_2)$ is uniformly continuous on the bounded set

$$\{(t_1,t_2) \in R^2\text{: } a < t_1 \leq b, |t_2 - c| \leq \delta\},$$

provided that δ is so small that this set is contained in $R^k \times C$, we can choose δ such that the last integral is smaller than ε. So we conclude:

$$E[\varphi(X_n,Y_n)] - E[\varphi(X_n,c)] \rightarrow 0.$$

Since obviously $E[\varphi(X_n,c)] \rightarrow E[\varphi(X,c)]$ because $X_n \rightarrow X$ in distr., the theorem follows. Q.E.D.

Remark: It should be stressed that the constancy of c is crucial in theorem 2.3.5. Thus, for example, $X_n \rightarrow X$ in distr. and $Y_n \rightarrow Y$ in distr., where X and Y are nonconstant random variables, does *not* generally imply $X_n + Y_n \rightarrow X + Y$ in distr. or $X_nY_n \rightarrow X{\cdot}Y$ in distr. For example, let

$$\begin{pmatrix} X_n \\ Y_n \end{pmatrix} \sim N_2\left(\begin{pmatrix} 0 \\ 0 \end{pmatrix}, \begin{pmatrix} 1 & \rho \\ \rho & 1 \end{pmatrix}\right); \begin{pmatrix} X \\ Y \end{pmatrix} \sim N_2\left(\begin{pmatrix} 0 \\ 0 \end{pmatrix}, \begin{pmatrix} 1 & 0 \\ 0 & 1 \end{pmatrix}\right).$$

Consequently, theorem 2.1.8 does *not* carry over to convergence in distribution.

Finally we note that convergence in distribution is closely related to convergence of characteristic functions:

Theorem 2.3.6 Let (F_n) be a sequence of distribution functions on R^k and let (φ_n) be the sequence of corresponding characteristic functions. If $F_n \rightarrow F$ properly pointwise, then $\varphi_n(t) \rightarrow \int \exp(i \cdot t'x)dF(x)$ pointwise on R^k. If $\varphi_n(t) \rightarrow \varphi(t)$ pointwise on R^k and $\varphi(t)$ is continuous at $t = 0$ then there exists a unique distribution function F such that $\varphi(t) = \int \exp(i \cdot t'x)dF(x)$ and $F_n \rightarrow F$ properly pointwise.

Proof: Cf. Feller (1966).

This theorem is basic for proving central limit theorems. Moreover, the following corollary of theorem 2.3.6 is very useful in proving *multivariate* asymptotic normality results.

Theorem 2.3.7 Let (X_n) be a sequence of random vectors in R^k. If for all vectors $\xi \in R^k$, $\xi'X_n$ converges in distribution to a normal distribution $N(\mu'\xi, \xi'\Lambda\xi)$, where Λ is a positive (semi) definite matrix, then X_n converges in distribution to the k-variate normal distribution $N_k(\mu, \Lambda)$.

Proof: We recall that the characteristic function of the k-variate normal distribution $N_k(\mu, \Lambda)$ is given by

$$\exp(i.\mu't - \tfrac{1}{2}t'\Lambda t)$$

(see, for example, Anderson [1958]). Now consider a random vector $X = (X_1, \ldots, X_k)'$ in R^k with mean vector

$$E(X) = (E(X_1), \ldots, E(X_k))' = (\mu_1, \ldots, \mu_k)' = \mu$$

and variance matrix

$$E[(X-\mu)(X-\mu)'] = \big(E[(X_i-\mu_i)(X_j-\mu_j)]\big) = \Lambda.$$

(Recall that if Λ is a singular matrix then the normal distribution involved is said to be singular). Suppose that for every vector ξ in R^k, $\xi'X$ is normally distributed. Then $\xi'X \sim N(\xi'\mu, \xi'\Lambda\xi)$, hence for every $t \in R$ and every $\xi \in R^k$,

$$E[\exp(i \cdot t\xi'X)] = \exp[i \cdot t\mu'\xi - \tfrac{1}{2}t^2\xi'\Lambda\xi].$$

Substituting $t=1$ now yields

$$E[\exp(i\cdot\xi'X)] = \exp[i.\mu'\xi - \tfrac{1}{2}\xi'\Lambda\xi] \text{ for all } \xi \in R^k,$$

which is just the characteristic function of the k-variate normal distribution $N_k[\mu,\Lambda]$. Q.E.D.

Exercises

1. Let Y_n be defined as in exercise 5 of section 2.1. Does Y_n converge in distribution?
2. Let (X_n) be a sequence of independent $N_k(\mu,\Lambda)$ – distributed random vectors in R^k, where Λ is nonsingular. Let

   $$\hat{\Lambda} = (1/n)\textstyle\sum_{j=1}^n (X_j - \mu)(X_j - \mu)'.$$

   Prove that

   $$(X_n - \mu)'\hat{\Lambda}_n^{-1}(X_n - \mu) \rightarrow \chi_k^2 \text{ in distr.}$$

   (Hint: Use the fact that the elements of an inverse matrix are continuous functions of the elements of the inverted matrix, provided the latter is nonsingular.)
3. The χ_n^2 distribution has characteristic function

   $$\varphi_n(t) = (1 - 2it)^{-n/2}.$$

   Let $X_n = Y_n/n$, where Y_n is distributed $\chi_n{}^2$. Prove $X_n \rightarrow 1$ in pr., using theorem 2.3.6 and the fact that $(1 + z/n)^n \rightarrow e^z$ for real or complex-valued z.

2.4 Central limit theorems

In this section we consider a few well-known central limit theorems (CLT), which are stated here for convenience. The first one is the standard textbook CLT (see, for example, Feller [1966]):

> *Theorem 2.4.1* Let $X_1, X_2, X_3,\ldots$ be i.i.d. random variables with $E(X_j) = \mu$, $\text{var}(X_j) = \sigma^2 < \infty$. Then
>
> $$(1/\sqrt{n})\textstyle\sum_{j=1}^n (X_j - \mu) \rightarrow N(0,\sigma^2) \text{ in distr.}$$

Proof: Let $\varphi(t)$ be the characteristic function of $X_j - \mu$, and let $\psi_n(t)$ be the characteristic function of $(1/\sqrt{n})\sum_{j=1}^n (X_j - \mu)$. Then

$$\psi_n(t) = \varphi(t/\sqrt{n})^n.$$

Moreover, it follows from exercise 3 in section 1.5 that for the first and second derivatives φ' and φ'' of φ,

$$\varphi'(0) = 0; \varphi''(0) = -\sigma^2,$$

hence by Taylor's theorem,

$$\varphi(t/\sqrt{n}) = 1 + \tfrac{1}{2}(t^2/n)\varphi''(\lambda_{nt}t/\sqrt{n}),$$

where $\lambda_{nt} \in [0,1]$. Denoting

$$a_n = \tfrac{1}{2}t^2\varphi''(\lambda_{nt}t/\sqrt{n}),$$

it now follows easily from the continuity of φ'' and the well-known result

$$\lim_{n\to\infty}a_n = a \text{ implies } \lim_{n\to\infty}(1+a_n/n)^n = \exp(a),$$

that

$$\lim_{n\to\infty}\psi_n(t) = \exp(-\tfrac{1}{2}t^2\sigma^2),$$

which is the characteristic function of the $N(0,\sigma^2)$ distribution. The theorem follows now from theorem 2.3.6. Q.E.D.

The next central limit theorem is due to Liapounov. This theorem is less general than the Lindeberg-Feller central limit theorem (see Feller [1966] or Chung [1974]), but its conditions are easier to verify.

Theorem 2.4.2 Let

$$S_n = \textstyle\sum_{j=1}^{k_n}X_{n,j},$$

where for each n the r.v.'s $X_{n,1},\dots,X_{n,k_n}$ are independent and $k_n\to\infty$. Put

$$E(X_{n,j}) = \alpha_{n,j},\ \alpha_n = \textstyle\sum_{j=1}^{k_n}\alpha_{n,j},$$
$$\sigma^2(X_{n,j}) = E[(X_{n,j}-\alpha_{n,j})^2] = \sigma^2_{n,j},\ \sigma^2_n = \textstyle\sum_{j=1}^{k_n}\sigma^2_{n,j},$$

assuming $\sigma^2_n < \infty$ (but *not* necessarily $\limsup_{n\to\infty}\sigma^2_n < \infty$). If for some $\delta > 0$,

$$\lim_{n\to\infty}\textstyle\sum_{j=1}^{k_n}E[|(X_{n,j}-\alpha_{n,j})/\sigma_n|^{2+\delta}] = 0$$

then $(S_n-\alpha_n)/\sigma_n \to N(0,1)$ in distr.

Proof: Chung (1974, p.209).

A special case of theorem 2.4.2 is:

Theorem 2.4.3 For each $n \geq 1$ let $X_{n,j}$, $j=1,\dots,n$, be independent random variables with $E(X_{n,j}) = 0$. If

$$\lim_{n\to\infty}(1/n)\textstyle\sum_{j=1}^{n}E(X^2_{n,j}) \to \sigma^2$$

and

$$\lim_{n\to\infty}\textstyle\sum_{j=1}^{n}E(|X_{n,j}/\sqrt{n}|^{2+\delta})=0 \text{ for some } \delta > 0 \tag{2.4.1}$$

then $(1/\sqrt{n})\sum_{j=1}^{n}X_{n,j} \to N(0,\sigma^2)$ in distr.

Remark: Note that condition (2.4.1) holds if

$\sup_n(1/n)\sum_{j=1}^{n}|X_{n,j}|^{2+\delta} < \infty$

Exercises

1. Let (X_j) be a sequence of i.i.d. random vectors in R^k with

   $E(X_j) = \mu$, $E[(X_j-\mu)(X_j-\mu)'] = \Lambda$,

   where Λ is nonsingular. Let

   $\bar{X} = (1/n)\sum_{j=1}^{n}X_j$,
   $\hat{\Lambda} = (1/n)\sum_{j=1}^{n}(X_j-\bar{X})(X_j-\bar{X})'$,
   $Y_n = n(\bar{X}-\mu)'\hat{\Lambda}^{-1}(\bar{X}-\mu)$.

   Prove that $Y_n \to \chi_k^2$ in distr. (Cf. exercise 2 of section 2.3).
2. Let (U_j) be a sequence of i.i.d. random variables satisfying $E(U_j) = 0$, $E(U_j^2) = 1$. Let $X_j = U_j + U_{j-1}$. Prove that

   $(1/\sqrt{n})\sum_{j=1}^{n}X_j \to N(0,4)$ in distr.

2.5 Further convergence results, stochastic boundedness, and the O_p and o_p notation

2.5.1 Further results on convergence of distributions and mathematical expectations, and laws of large numbers

The condition in theorem 2.3.1 that the function φ is bounded is only necessary for the "if" part. If we assume proper pointwise convergence then convergence of expectations will occur under more general conditions, as is shown in the following extension of the "only if" part of theorem 2.3.1.

> *Theorem 2.5.1* Let (F_n) be a sequence of distribution functions on R^k satisfying $F_n \to F$ properly pointwise. Let $\varphi(x)$ be a continuous real function on R^k such that
>
> $\sup_n\int|\varphi(x)|^{1+\delta}dF_n(x) < \infty$ for some $\delta > 0$.
>
> Then $\int\varphi(x)dF_n(x) \to \int\varphi(x)dF(x)$.

Proof: Define for $a > 0$

$$\varphi_a(x) = \varphi(x) \text{ if } |\varphi(x)| \le a,\ \varphi_a(x) = a \text{ if } \varphi(x) > a,$$
$$\varphi_a(x) = -a \text{ if } \varphi(x) < -a. \qquad (2.5.1)$$

Obviously $\varphi_a(x)$ is a bounded continuous real function on R^k, hence by theorem 2.3.1:

$$\int\varphi_a(x)dF_n(x) \to \int\varphi_a(x)dF(x) \tag{2.5.2}$$

Moreover,

$$|\int\varphi(x)dF_n(x) - \int\varphi_a(x)dF_n(x)| \le 2\int_{|\varphi(x)|>a}|\varphi(x)|dF_n(x)$$
$$\le 2.a^{-\delta}\int|\varphi(x)|^{1+\delta}dF_n(x) = O(a^{-\delta}) \tag{2.5.3}$$

uniformly in n, and similarly we have:

$$|\int\varphi(x)dF(x) - \int\varphi_a(x)dF(x)| \le 2a^{-\delta}\int|\varphi(x)|^{1+\delta}dF(x) = O(a^{-\delta}) \tag{2.5.4}$$

provided

$$\int|\varphi(x)|^{1+\delta}dF(x) < \infty \tag{2.5.5}$$

The theorem follows easily from (2.5.2) through (2.5.4) by letting first n $\to \infty$ and then a $\to \infty$. Thus it suffices to show that (2.5.5) is true. Now observe that $|\varphi_a(x)|^{1+\delta}$ is monotonic nondecreasing in a and that $|\varphi_a(x)|^{1+\delta} \to |\varphi(x)|^{1+\delta}$ as $a \to \infty$. It follows therefore from the monotone convergence theorem (theorem 2.2.4) and theorem 2.3.1 that:

$$\int|\varphi(x)|^{1+\delta}dF(x) = \lim_{a\to\infty}\int|\varphi_a(x)|^{1+\delta}dF(x)$$
$$= \lim_{a\to\infty}\lim_{n\to\infty}\int|\varphi_a(x)|^{1+\delta}dF_n(x)$$
$$\le \lim_{n\to\infty}\int|\varphi(x)|^{1+\delta}dF_n(x) \le \sup_n\int|\varphi(x)|^{1+\delta}dF_n(x) < \infty \tag{2.5.6}$$

This result completes the proof of theorem 2.5.1. Q.E.D.

Along similar lines we can prove the following version of the weak law of large numbers.

Theorem 2.5.2 Let $X_1,X_2,...$ be a sequence of independent random vectors in R^k, and let $(F_j(x))$ be the sequence of corresponding distribution functions. Let $\varphi(x)$ be a continuous function on R^k. If

$(1/n)\sum_{j=1}^n F_j \to G$ properly, pointwise

and

$\sup_n(1/n)\sum_{j=1}^n E(|\varphi(X_j)|^{1+\delta}) < \infty$ for some $\delta > 0$

then $\text{plim}_{n\to\infty}(1/n)\sum_{j=1}^n\varphi(X_j) = \int\varphi(x)dG(x)$.

Proof: Consider the function $\varphi_a(x)$ defined in (2.5.1). Then obviously by the independence of the X_j's, the boundedness of $\varphi_a(x)$ and Chebishev's inequality

$$\text{plim}_{n\to\infty}(1/n)\sum_{j=1}^n\{\varphi_a(X_j) - E[\varphi_a(X_j)]\} = 0, \tag{2.5.7}$$

while from theorem 2.3.1 it follows

$$\lim_{n\to\infty}E[(1/n)\sum_{j=1}^{n}\varphi_a(X_j)] = \int\varphi_a(x)dG(x).$$

Hence

$$\text{plim}_{n\to\infty}(1/n)\sum_{j=1}^{n}\varphi_a(X_j) = \int\varphi_a(x)dG(x). \tag{2.5.9}$$

Moreover, since $\varphi_a(x)$ is bounded, it follows from (2.5.9) and theorem 2.2.1 that

$$E[|(1/n)\sum_{j=1}^{n}\varphi_a(X_j) - \int\varphi_a(x)dG(x)|] \to 0 \text{ as } n \to \infty. \tag{2.5.10}$$

Furthermore, similarly to (2.5.3) it follows that

$$\text{limsup}_{n\to\infty}E[|(1/n)\sum_{j=1}^{n}\varphi(X_j) - (1/n)\sum_{j=1}^{n}\varphi_a(X_j)|] \to 0 \text{ as } a \to \infty \tag{2.5.11}$$

and, similarly to (2.5.4), that

$$|\int\varphi(x)dG(x) - \int\varphi_a(x)dG(x)| \to 0 \text{ as } a \to \infty. \tag{2.5.12}$$

Combining (2.5.10), (2.5.11), and (2.5.12) we see that

$$\lim_{n\to\infty}E[|(1/n)\sum_{j=1}^{n}\varphi(X_j) - \int\varphi(x)dG(x)|] \to 0. \tag{2.5.13}$$

The theorem follows now from (2.5.13) and Chebishev's inequality. Q.E.D.

Remark: The difference of this theorem from the classical weak law of large numbers is that the finiteness of second moments is *not* necessary.

If we combine theorems 2.1.4 and 2.5.1 we easily obtain the following strong version of theorem 2.5.2.

> *Theorem 2.5.3* Let the conditions of theorem 2.5.2 be satisfied, and assume in addition that
>
> $$\sup_n(1/n)\sum_{j=1}^{n}E[|\varphi(X_j)|^{2+\delta}] < \infty \text{ for some } \delta > 0. \tag{2.5.14}$$
>
> Then $(1/n)\sum_{j=1}^{n}\varphi(X_j) \to \int\varphi(x)dG(x)$ a.s.

The continuity condition on the function φ in theorems 2.5.2 and 2.5.3 is mainly due to theorem 2.5.1, i.e., without this condition theorem 2.5.1 is not generally true. Suppose for example

$$\varphi(x) = x^2 \text{ if x is rational, } \varphi(x) = -x^2 \text{ if x is irrational.}$$

Then $\varphi(x)$ is a Borel measurable real function on R. The proof of this proposition is left as an exercise. Now let X be a random drawing from an absolutely continuous distribution, say the standard normal distribution, and let X_n be the value of X rounded off to n decimal digits. Then $X_n \to X$ in distr., hence the distribution function F_n of X_n converges properly to the distribution function F of X. However, since X is a.s. irrational we have:

$$E[\varphi(X)] = \int -x^2 dF(x) = -1$$

whereas X_n is a.s. rational and thus

$$E[\varphi(X_n)] = \int x^2 dF_n(x) \rightarrow \int x^2 dF(x) = 1.$$

This counter-example shows that theorem 2.5.1 does not carry over for general Borel measurable functions φ. In order that a similar result to that in theorem 2.5.1 does hold for Borel measurable functions we need a stronger convergence in distribution concept, namely setwise proper convergence:

> *Definition 2.5.1.* Let (F_n) be a sequence of distribution functions on R^k with corresponding sequence (μ_n) of probability measures on $\{R^k,\mathfrak{B}^k\}$ (cf. section 1.1). This sequence (F_n) converges properly *setwise* if for each Borel set B in $\mathfrak{B}^k$, $\lim_{n\rightarrow\infty}\mu_n(B) = \mu(B)$, where μ is a probability measure on $\{R^k,\mathfrak{B}^k\}$. We then write $F_n \rightarrow F$ properly setwise, where F is the distribution function induced by μ.

Using this concept and definition 1.4.4 we can now state:

> *Theorem 2.5.4* Let F_n and F be distribution functions on R^k. Then $F_n \rightarrow F$ properly setwise if and only if for every *bounded Borel measurable* real function φ on R^k,
>
> $$\lim_{n\rightarrow\infty}\int\varphi(x)dF_n(x) = \int\varphi(x)dF(x).$$

Proof: The "if" part is easy and therefore left to the reader. Moreover, the "only if" part follows easily from definition 1.3.2 if φ is a simple function. Thus, assume that φ is not simple. From the proof of theorem 1.3.4 it easily follows that for arbitrary $\varepsilon > 0$ and each bounded Borel set B we can construct a simple function ψ such that

$$|\psi(x)-\varphi(x)| < \varepsilon \text{ if } x \in B, \ \psi(x) = 0 \text{ for } x \notin B.$$

Moreover, we may choose B such that

$$\mu(B) = \int_B dF(x) > 1-\varepsilon.$$

Furthermore, since

$$\mu_n(B) = \int_B dF_n(x) \rightarrow \mu(B)$$

there exists an n_ε such that

$$\mu_n(B) > 1-2\varepsilon \text{ if } n \geq n_\varepsilon.$$

Thus we have for $n \geq n_\varepsilon$

$$
\begin{aligned}
|\int\varphi(x)dF_n(x) - \int\varphi(x)dF(x)| &\leq |\int_B\varphi(x)dF_n(x) - \int_B\varphi(x)dF(x)| \\
&\quad + |\int_{R^k\backslash B}\varphi(x)dF_n(x) - \int_{R^k\backslash B}\varphi(x)dF(x)| \\
&\leq |\int_B(\varphi(x) - \psi(x))dF_n(x)| + |\int_B(\varphi(x) - \psi(x))dF(x)| \\
&\quad + |\int_B\psi(x)dF_n(x) - \int_B\psi(x)dF(x)| + M\mu_n(R^k\backslash B) + M\mu(R^k\backslash B) \\
&\leq \varepsilon\cdot\mu_n(B) + \varepsilon\cdot\mu(B) + 3\varepsilon M + |\int_B\psi(x)dF_n(x) - \int_B\psi(x)dF(x)| \\
&\leq (2+3M)\varepsilon + |\int\psi(x)dF_n(x) - \int\psi(x)dF(x)|,
\end{aligned}
$$

where M is the bound of $\varphi(x)$. Since the second term converges to zero (for ψ is simple) and the first term can be made arbitrarily small, the theorem follows. Q.E.D.

Now observe from the proof of theorem 2.5.1 that the continuity of φ and φ_a is only necessary for (2.5.2). However, if $F_n \to F$ properly setwise then (2.5.2) carries over for Borel measurable φ_a, as we have just shown in theorem 2.5.4. Consequently we have:

Theorem 2.5.5 Let (F_n) be a sequence of distribution functions on R^k satisfying $F_n \to F$ properly setwise. Let $\varphi(x)$ be a Borel measurable real function such that

$\sup_n\int|\varphi(x)|^{1+\delta}dF_n(x) < \infty$ for some $\delta > 0$.

Then $\int\varphi(x)dF_n(x) \to \int\varphi(x)dF(x)$.

Replacing theorem 2.5.1 by theorem 2.5.5 the laws of large numbers (theorems 2.5.2 and 2.5.3) can now be generalized to:

Theorem 2.5.6 Let (X_j) be a sequence of independent random vectors in R^k, and let $(F_j(x))$ be the sequence of corresponding distribution functions. Let $\varphi(x)$ be a Borel measurable real function on R^k. If

$(1/n)\sum_{j=1}^n F_j \to G$ properly setwise

and

$\sup_n(1/n)\sum_{j=1}^n E[|\varphi(X_j)|^{1+\delta}] < \infty$ for some $\delta < 0$

then $\text{plim}_{n\to\infty}(1/n)\sum_{j=1}^n\varphi(X_j) = \int\varphi(x)dG(x)$.

Theorem 2.5.7 Let the conditions of theorem 2.5.6 be satisfied. If

$\sup_n(1/n)\sum_{j=1}^n E[|\varphi(X_j)|^{2+\delta}] < \infty$ for some $\delta > 0$,

then $(1/n)\sum_{j=1}^n\varphi(X_j) \to \int\varphi(x)dG(x)$ a.s.

Finally we consider convergence of random variables of the type

$(1/n)\sum_{j=1}^{n}\varphi_j(X_j)$,

where the φ_j's are Borel measurable (respectively, continuous) functions.

Theorem 2.5.8 Let X_j be a sequence of independent random vectors in R^k and let (φ_j) be a sequence of Borel measurable (continuous) real functions on R^k. Denote $Y_j = \varphi_j(X_j)$ and let F_j be the distribution function of Y_j. If

$(1/n)\sum_{j=1}^{n}F_j \rightarrow G$ properly setwise (pointwise)

and

$\sup_n(1/n)\sum_{j=1}^{n}E[|\varphi_j(X_j)|^{1+\delta}] < \infty$ for some $\delta > 1$ $(\delta > 0)$

then $(1/n)\sum_{j=1}^{n}\varphi_j(X_j) \rightarrow \int ydG(y)$ a.s. (in pr.).

We shall not use this theorem in the sequel, but it is stated because its proof is a useful exercise.

2.5.2 Stochastic boundedness, and the O_p and o_p notation

Definition 2.5.2 A sequence X_n of random variables or vectors is called stochastically bounded if for every $\varepsilon \in (0,1)$ there exists a constant M such that $\inf_n P(|X_n| \leq M) \geq 1-\varepsilon$.

Analogously to the well-known notation O(.) for a nonrandom sequence x_n: $x_n = O(a_n)$ if $|x_n| \leq Ma_n$ for some $M < \infty$ and a positive sequence a_n, stochastic boundedness is often denoted by: $X_n = O_p(1)$. More generally, the notation $Y_n = O_p(a_n)$ means that Y_n/a_n is stochastically bounded. Furthermore, analogously to the notation o(.) we denote $Y_n = o_p(a_n)$ if $\text{plim}_{n\rightarrow\infty}Y_n/a_n = 0$, hence $o_p(1)$ stands for a random variable that converges in probability to zero. Note that $Y_n = O_p(a_n)$ with $a_n = o(1)$ implies $Y_n = o_p(1)$, and that $X_n = O_p(1)$ and $Y_n = o_p(1)$ imply $X_nY_n = o_p(1)$.

The following two theorems give easy sufficient conditions for stochastic boundedness.

Theorem 2.5.9 Convergence in distribution implies stochastic boundedness, and so does convergence in probability.

Proof: Exercise 3.

Theorem 2.5.10 If $\sup_n E(|X_n|^{\delta}) < \infty$ for some $\delta > 0$, then $X_n = O_p(1)$.

Proof: Exercise 4.

For example, if $X_1,...,X_n$ is a random sample from a distribution with $E(|X_j|^2) < \infty$, then by theorems 2.4.1 and 2.5.9,

$$(1/n)\sum_{j=1}^{n}[X_j - E(X_j)] = O_p(1/\sqrt{n}).$$

Exercises

1. Prove theorem 2.5.8.
2. Restate theorems 2.5.2 and 2.5.6 for double arrays $(X_{n,j})$, $j=1,...,n$, $n=1,2,...$ of random vectors in R^k and prove the modified theorems involved.
3. Prove theorem 2.5.9.
4. Prove theorem 2.5.10.

2.6 Convergence of random functions

In dealing with convergence of random functions, one should be aware of some pitfalls. The first one concerns pointwise a.s. convergence. Let $f(\theta)$ and $f_n(\theta)$ be random functions on a subset Θ on R^k such that for each $\theta \in \Theta$, $f_n(\theta) \to f(\theta)$ a.s. as $n \to \infty$. At first sight we would expect from definition 2.1.2 that there is a null set N and an integer function $n_0(\omega,\theta,\varepsilon)$ such that for every $\varepsilon > 0$ and every $\omega \in \Omega \backslash N$,

$$|f_n(\theta,\omega) - f(\theta,\omega)| \leq \varepsilon \text{ if } n \geq n_0(\omega,\theta,\varepsilon).$$

However, reading definiton 2.1.2 carefully we see that this is not correct, because *the null set N may depend on* θ: $N = N_\theta$. Then, again at first sight, we might reply that this does not matter because we could choose $N = \cup_{\theta\in\Theta}N_\theta$ as a null set. But the problem now is that we are not sure whether $N \in \mathfrak{F}$, for only countable unions of members of $\mathfrak{F}$ are surely members of $\mathfrak{F}$ themselves. Thus although $N_\theta \in \mathfrak{F}$ for each $\theta \in \Theta$, this is not necessarily the case for $\cup_{\theta\in\Theta}N_\theta$ if Θ is uncountable. Moreover, even if $\cup_{\theta\in\Theta}N_\theta \in \mathfrak{F}$, it may fail to be a null set itself if Θ is uncountable. For example, let $\Theta = \Omega = [0,1]$, let P be the Lebesgue measure on [0,1] and let $N_\theta = \{\theta\}$ for $\theta \in [0,1]$. Then $P(\cup_{\theta\in\Theta}N_\theta) = P(\Omega) = 1$, while obviously the N_θ's are null sets.

The second pitfall concerns uniform convergence of random functions. As is well known, uniform convergence of (real) *non-random* functions, for example $\varphi_n(\theta) \to \varphi(\theta)$ uniformly on Θ as $n \to \infty$, can be defined by

$$\sup_{\theta\in\Theta}|\varphi_n(\theta) - \varphi(\theta)| \to 0 \text{ as } n \to \infty.$$

Dealing with uniform a.s. convergence of random functions, i.e.,

$$f_n(\theta) \to f(\theta) \text{ a.s. uniformly on } \Theta,$$

a suitable definition is therefore:

$\sup_{\theta\in\Theta}|f_n(\theta) - f(\theta)| \to 0$ a.s. as $n \to \infty$,

However, this has only a probabilistic meaning if the supremum involved is a random variable. If so, then uniform a.s. convergence is equivalent to the following:
There is a null set N and an integer function $n_0(\omega,\varepsilon)$ *both independent of* θ, such that for every $\varepsilon > 0$, every $\omega \in \Omega\backslash N$ and every $\theta \in \Theta$,

$|f_n(\theta,\omega) - f(\theta,\omega)| \leq \varepsilon$ if $n \geq n_0(\omega,\varepsilon)$.

Thus going from pointwise a.s. convergence to uniform a.s. convergence we have to check three things, namely that the null set N is independent of θ, that the integer function $n_0(\omega,\varepsilon)$ is independent of θ, and that

$\sup_{\theta\in\Theta}|f_n(\theta) - f(\theta)|$

is a random variable for each n. Only if so, can we say that $f_n(\theta) \to f(\theta)$ a.s. uniformly on Θ. Nevertheless, if this is not the case but $f_n(\theta,\omega) \to f(\theta,\omega)$ uniformly on Θ for every ω in Ω except in a null set not depending on θ, then we still have a useful property, as will be shown in chapter 4. In this case we can say that $f_n(\theta) \to f(\theta)$ a.s. *pseudo*-uniformly on Θ. Summarizing:

Definition 2.6.1 Let $f(\theta)$ and $f_n(\theta)$ be random functions on a subset Θ of a Euclidean space, and let $\{\Omega,\mathfrak{F},P\}$ be the probability space involved. Then:

(a) $f_n(\theta) \to f(\theta)$ a.s. *pointwise* on Θ if for every $\theta \in \Theta$ there is a null set N_θ in $\mathfrak{F}$ and for every $\varepsilon > 0$ and every $\omega \in \Omega\backslash N_\theta$ a number $n_0(\omega,\theta,\varepsilon)$ such that $|f_n(\theta,\omega) - f(\theta,\omega)| \leq \varepsilon$ if $n \geq n_0(\omega,\theta,\varepsilon)$;
(b) $f_n(\theta) \to f(\theta)$ a.s. *uniformly* on Θ if
(i) $\sup_{\theta\in\Theta}|f_n(\theta) - f(\theta)|$ is a random variable for $n = 1,2,\ldots$, and if
(ii) there is a null set N and an integer function $n_0(\omega,\varepsilon)$, both independent of θ, such that for every $\varepsilon > 0$ and every $\omega \in \Omega\backslash N$, $|f_n(\theta,\omega) - f(\theta,\omega)| \leq \varepsilon$ if $n \geq n_0(\omega,\varepsilon)$.
(c) $f_n(\theta) \to f(\theta)$ a.s. *pseudo-uniformly* on Θ if condition (ii) in (b) holds, but not necessarily condition (i).

Similarly to the case of a.s. uniform convergence of random functions the uniform convergence in probability of $f_n(\theta)$ to $f(\theta)$ can be defined by $\text{plim}_{n\to\infty}\sup_{\theta\in\Theta}|f_n(\theta) - f(\theta)| = 0$, provided that $\sup_{\theta\in\Theta}|f_n(\theta) - f(\theta)|$ is a random variable for $n = 1,2,\ldots$ In that case it follows from theorem 2.1.6 that $f_n(\theta) \to f(\theta)$ in pr. uniformly on Θ if and only if every subsequence (n_k) of (n) contains a further subsequence (n_{k_j}) such that

$f_{n_{k_j}}(\theta) \to f(\theta)$ a.s. uniformly on Θ.

This suggests how to define pseudo-uniform convergence in pr.:

Definition 2.6.2 Let $f_n(\theta)$ and $f(\theta)$ be random functions on a subset Θ of a Euclidean space. Then:

(a) $f_n(\theta) \to f(\theta)$ in pr. uniformly on Θ if $\sup_{\theta\in\Theta}|f_n(\theta) - f(\theta)|$ is a random variable for n = 1,2,... satisfying

$\text{plim}_{n\to\infty}\sup_{\theta\in\Theta}|f_n(\theta) - f(\theta)| = 0$;

(b) $f_n(\theta) \to f(\theta)$ in pr. pseudo-uniformly on Θ if every subsequence (n_k) of (n) contains a further subsequence (n_{k_j}) such that $f_{n_{k_j}}(\theta) \to f(\theta)$ a.s. pseudo-uniformly on Θ.

Remark: In this study we shall often conclude:

$\sup_{\theta\in\Theta}|f_n(\theta) - f(\theta)| \to 0$ a.s. or $\text{plim}_{n\to\infty}\sup_{\theta\in\Theta}|f_n(\theta) - f(\theta)| = 0$

instead of $f_n(\theta) \to f(\theta)$ a.s. or $f_n(\theta) \to f(\theta)$ in pr., uniformly on Θ, respectively. In these cases it will be clear from the context that $\sup_{\theta\in\Theta}|f_n(\theta) - f(\theta)|$ is a random variable for n = 1,2,...

We are now able to generalize theorem 2.1.7 to random functions.

Theorem 2.6.1 Let $(f_n(\theta))$ be a sequence of random functions on a Borel subset Θ of a Euclidean space. Let $f(\theta)$ be an a.s. continuous random function on Θ. Let X_n and X be random vectors in Θ such that $P(X \in \Theta) = 1$ and $P(X_n \in \Theta) = 1$ for n = 1,2,... Moreover, suppose that $f(X)$ is a random variable and that $f_n(X_n)$ is a random variable for n = 1,2,... If

(a) $X_n \to X$ a.s. and $f_n(\theta) \to f(\theta)$ a.s. pseudo-uniformly on Θ, or
(b) $X_n \to X$ in pr. and $f_n(\theta) \to f(\theta)$ in pr. pseudo-uniformly on Θ,

then (a) $f_n(X_n) \to f(X)$ a.s. or (b) $f_n(X_n) \to f(X)$ in pr., respectively.

Proof
(a) Let $(\Omega,\mathfrak{F},P)$ be the probability space. Let N_1 be the null set on which $x_n(\omega) \to x(\omega)$ fails to hold, let N_2 be the null set on which $f(\theta,\omega)$ fails to be continuous, let N_3 and $N_{3,n}$ be null sets on which $x(\omega) \in \Theta$ and $x_n(\omega) \in \Theta$, respectively, fail to hold and finally let N_4 be the null set on which

$\sup_{\theta\in\Theta}|f_n(\theta,\omega) - f(\theta,\omega)| \to 0$

fails to hold. Put $N = N_1 \cup N_2 \cup N_3 \cup \{\cup_{n=1}^{\infty} N_{3,n}\} \cup N_4$. Then $N \in \mathfrak{F}$, $P(N) = 0$ and for $\omega \in \Omega\backslash N$ we have:

$$|f_n(x_n(\omega),\omega) - f(x(\omega),\omega)| \\ \le \sup_{\theta\in\Theta}|f_n(\theta,\omega) - f(\theta,\omega)| + |f(x_n(\omega),\omega) - f(x(\omega),\omega)| \to 0.$$

This proves part (a). Part (b) follows from (a) by using theorem 2.1.6.

Q.E.D.

Exercise

1. Let X be uniformly distributed on [0,1]. Define for $\theta \in [0,1]$,

   $f_n(\theta) = n^{-|X-\theta|}$.

   Show that $f_n(\theta) \to 0$ a.s. pointwise on $\Theta = [0,1]$ while $\sup_{\theta\in\Theta}|f_n(\theta)| = 1$. (This is a counter-example that pointwise a.s. convergence on compact spaces does not imply uniform a.s. convergence.)

2.7 Uniform strong and weak laws of large numbers

Next we shall extend theorems 1 and 2 of Jennrich (1969). We shall closely follow Jennrich's proof, but instead of the Helly–Bray theorem (theorem 2.3.1) we shall now use theorems 2.5.1 and 2.5.5. The extension involved is:

Theorem 2.7.1 Let $X_1,X_2,...$ be a sequence of independent random vectors in R^k with distribution functions $F_1,F_2,...$ respectively. Let $f(x,\theta)$ be a continuous real function on $R^k \times \Theta$, where Θ is a compact Borel set in R^m. If

$$(1/n)\textstyle\sum_{j=1}^{n}F_j \to G \text{ properly pointwise} \tag{2.7.1}$$

and

$$\sup_n(1/n)\textstyle\sum_{j=1}^{n}E[\sup_{\theta\in\Theta}|f(x,\theta)|^{2+\delta}] < \infty \tag{2.7.2}$$

then

$$(1/n)\textstyle\sum_{j=1}^{n}f(X_j,\theta) \to \int f(x,\theta)dG(x) \text{ a.s. uniformly on } \Theta,$$

where the limit function involved is continuous on Θ.

Proof: First we note that by theorem 1.6.1 the supremum in (2.7.2) is a random variable.

For the sake of convenience and clarity we shall label the main steps of the proof.

Step 1: Choose θ_0 arbitrarily in Θ and put for $\delta \geq 0$

$$\Gamma_\delta = \{\theta \in R^m: |\theta - \theta_0| \leq \delta\} \cap \Theta,$$

Then for any $\delta \geq 0$, $\sup_{\theta\in\Gamma_\delta}f(x,\theta)$ and $\inf_{\theta\in\Gamma_\delta}f(x,\theta)$ are continuous functions on R^k, because Γ_δ is a closed subset of a compact set and therefore compact itself. See Rudin (1976, theorem 2.35) and compare theorem 1.6.1. Moreover,

$$|\sup_{\theta\in\Gamma_\delta}f(x,\theta)| \leq \sup_{\theta\in\Theta}|f(x,\theta)|, \tag{2.7.3}$$

$$|\inf_{\theta\in\Gamma_\delta}f(x,\theta)| \leq \sup_{\theta\in\Theta}|f(x,\theta)|. \tag{2.7.4}$$

Thus it follows from theorem 2.5.3 and the conditions (2.7.1) and (2.7.2) that

$$(1/n)\sum_{j=1}^{n}\sup_{\theta\in\Gamma_\delta}f(X_j,\theta) \to \int\sup_{\theta\in\Gamma_\delta}f(x,\theta)dG(x) \to \text{a.s.} \tag{2.7.5}$$

and

$$(1/n)\sum_{j=1}^{n}\inf_{\theta\in\Gamma_\delta}f(X_j,\theta) \to \int\inf_{\theta\in\Gamma_\delta}f(x,\theta)dG(x) \text{ a.s.} \tag{2.7.6}$$

Step 2: By continuity,

$$\sup_{\theta\in\Gamma_\delta}f(x,\theta) - \inf_{\theta\in\Gamma_\delta}f(x,\theta) \to 0 \text{ as } \delta\downarrow 0,$$

pointwise in x. It follows now from the dominated convergence theorem that

$$\lim_{\delta\downarrow 0}\left|\int\sup_{\theta\in\Gamma_\delta}f(x,\theta)dG(x) - \int\inf_{\theta\in\Gamma_\delta}f(x,\theta)dG(x)\right| = 0. \tag{2.7.7}$$

Step 3: Choose $\varepsilon > 0$ arbitrarily. From (2.7.7) it follows that $\delta > 0$ can be chosen so small, say $\delta = \delta(\varepsilon)$, that

$$0 \le \int\sup_{\theta\in\Gamma_{\delta(\varepsilon)}}f(x,\theta)dG(x) - \int\inf_{\theta\in\Gamma_{\delta(\varepsilon)}}f(x,\theta)dG(x) \le \tfrac{1}{2}\varepsilon. \tag{2.7.8}$$

Let $\{\Omega,\mathfrak{F},P\}$ be the probability space involved. From (2.7.5) and (2.7.6) it follows that there is a null set N and for each $\omega \in \Omega\backslash N$ a number $n_0(\omega,\varepsilon)$ such that:

$$\left|(1/n)\sum_{j=1}^{n}\sup_{\theta\in\Gamma_{\delta(\varepsilon)}}f(x_j(\omega),\theta) - \int\sup_{\theta\in\Gamma_{\delta(\varepsilon)}}f(x,\theta)dG(x)\right| \le \tfrac{1}{2}\varepsilon, \tag{2.7.9}$$

$$\left|(1/n)\sum_{j=1}^{n}\inf_{\theta\in\Gamma_{\delta(\varepsilon)}}f(x_j(\omega),\theta) - \int\inf_{\theta\in\Gamma_{\delta(\varepsilon)}}f(x,\theta)dG(x)\right| \le \tfrac{1}{2}\varepsilon, \tag{2.7.10}$$

if $n \ge n_0(\omega,\varepsilon)$. From (2.7.8), (2.7.9) and (2.7.10) it follows now that for every $\omega \in \Omega\backslash N$, every $n \ge n_0(\omega,\varepsilon)$ and every $\theta \in \Gamma_{\delta(\varepsilon)}$:

$$\begin{aligned}
&(1/n)\sum_{j=1}^{n}f(x_j(\omega),\theta) - \int f(x,\theta)dG(x) \\
&\quad\le (1/n)\sum_{j=1}^{n}\sup_{\theta\in\Gamma_{\delta(\varepsilon)}}f(x_j(\omega),\theta) - \int\inf_{\theta\in\Gamma_{\delta(\varepsilon)}}f(x,\theta)dG(x) \\
&\quad\le \left|(1/n)\sum_{j=1}^{n}\sup_{\theta\in\Gamma_{\delta(\varepsilon)}}f(x_j(\omega),\theta) - \int\sup_{\theta\in\Gamma_{\delta(\varepsilon)}}f(x,\Theta)dG(x)\right| \\
&\qquad+ \left|\int\sup_{\theta\in\Gamma_{\delta(\varepsilon)}}f(x,\theta)dG(x) - \int\inf_{\theta\in\Gamma_{\delta(\varepsilon)}}f(x,\theta)dG(x)\right| \le \varepsilon
\end{aligned}$$

and similarly:

$$(1/n)\sum_{j=1}^{n}f(x_j(\omega),\theta) - \int f(x,\theta)dG(x) \ge -\varepsilon.$$

Thus for $\omega \in \Omega\backslash N$ and $n \ge n_0(\omega,\varepsilon)$ we have:

$$\sup_{\theta\in\Gamma_{\delta(\varepsilon)}}\left|(1/n)\sum_{j=1}^{n}f(x_j(\omega),\theta) - \int f(x,\theta)dG(x)\right| \le \varepsilon.$$

We note that the null set N and the number $n_0(\omega,\varepsilon)$ depend on the set $\Gamma_{\delta(\varepsilon)}$, which in its turn depends on θ_0 and ε. Thus the above result should be restated as follows. For every θ_0 in Θ and every $\varepsilon > 0$ there is a null set $N(\theta_0,\varepsilon)$ and an integer function $n_0(.,\varepsilon,\theta_0)$ on $\Omega\backslash N(\theta_0,\varepsilon)$ such that for $\omega \in \Omega\backslash N(\theta_0,\varepsilon)$ and $n \geq n_0(\omega,\varepsilon,\theta_0)$:

$$\sup_{\theta\in\Gamma_{\delta(\varepsilon)}(\theta_0)}|(1/n)\textstyle\sum_{j=1}^{n}f(x_j(\omega),\theta) - \int f(x,\theta)dG(x)| \leq \varepsilon, \tag{2.7.11}$$

where

$$\Gamma_\delta(\theta_0) = \{\theta \in R^k: |\theta - \theta_0| \leq \delta\} \cap \Theta. \tag{2.7.12}$$

Step 4: The collection of sets $\{\theta \in R^k:|\theta-\theta_0| < \delta\}$ with $\theta_0 \in \Theta$ is an open covering of Θ. Since Θ is compact, there exists by definition of compactness a finite covering. Thus there are a finite number of points in Θ, say

$\theta_{\delta,1},\ldots,\theta_{\delta,r_\delta}$ with $r_\delta < \infty$

such that

$\Theta \subset \cup_{i=1}^{r_\delta} \{\theta \in R^k:|\theta - \theta_{\delta,i}| < \delta\}.$

Using (2.7.12) we therefore have:

$$\Theta = \cup_{i=1}^{r_\delta} \Gamma_\delta(\theta_{\delta,i}). \tag{2.7.13}$$

Now put:

$N_\varepsilon = \cup_{i=1}^{r_{\delta(\varepsilon)}} N(\theta_{\delta(\varepsilon),i},\varepsilon)$, $n_*(\omega,\varepsilon) = \max_{1\leq i\leq r_{\delta(\varepsilon)}} n_0(\omega,\varepsilon,\theta_{\delta(\varepsilon),i})$.

Then by (2.7.12) and (2.7.13) we have for $\omega \in \Omega\backslash N_\varepsilon$ and $n \geq n_*(\omega,\varepsilon)$,

$$\begin{aligned}&\sup_{\theta\in\Theta}|(1/n)\textstyle\sum_{j=1}^{n}f(x_j(\omega),\theta) - \int f(x,\theta)dG(x)| \\ &\qquad \leq \max_{1\leq i\leq r_{\delta(\varepsilon)}}\sup_{\theta\in\Gamma_{\delta(\varepsilon)}(\theta_{\delta(\varepsilon),i})}|(1/n)\textstyle\sum_{j=1}^{n}f(x_j(\omega),\theta) \\ &\qquad\qquad - \int f(x,\theta)dG(x)| \leq \varepsilon.\end{aligned}$$

Since it can be shown, similarly to the proof of theorem 2.2.1, that the null set N_ε can be chosen independently of ε, it follows now that

$$(1/n)\textstyle\sum_{j=1}^{n}f(X_j,\theta) \rightarrow \int f(x,\theta)dG(x) \text{ a.s. pseudo-uniformly on } \Theta. \tag{2.7.14}$$

Step 5: From (2.7.7) it follows that $\int f(x,\theta)dG(x)$ is a continuous function on Θ. Using theorem 1.6.1, it is now easy to verify that

$$\sup_{\theta\in\Theta}|(1/n)\textstyle\sum_{j=1}^{n}f(X_j,\theta) - \int f(x,\theta)dG(x)|$$

is a random variable, so that (2.7.14) becomes

$$(1/n)\textstyle\sum_{j=1}^{n}f(X_j,\theta) \rightarrow \int f(x,\theta)dG(x) \text{ a.s. uniformly on } \Theta.$$

This completes the proof. Q.E.D.

If condition (2.7.2) is only satisfied with $1+\delta$ instead of $2+\delta$ then we can no longer apply theorem 2.5.3 for proving (2.7.5) and (2.7.6).

However, applying theorem 2.5.2 we see that (2.7.5) and (2.7.6) still hold in probability. From theorem 2.1.6 it then follows that any subsequence (n_k) of (n) contains further subsequences $(n^{(1)}_{k_m})$ and $(n^{(2)}_{k_m})$, say, such that for $m \to \infty$,

$$(1/n^{(1)}_{k_m})\sum_{j=1}^{n^{(1)}_{k_m}} \sup_{\theta\in\Gamma_\delta} f(X_j,\theta) \to \int \sup_{\theta\in\Gamma_\delta} f(x,\theta)dG(x) \text{ a.s.}$$

$$(1/n^{(2)}_{k_m})\sum_{j=1}^{n^{(2)}_{k_m}} \inf_{\theta\in\Gamma_\delta} f(X_j,\theta) \to \int \inf_{\theta\in\Gamma_\delta} f(x,\theta)dG(x) \text{ a.s.}$$

Note that we may assume without loss of generality that these further subsequences are equal:

$$n_{k_m} = n^{(1)}_{k_m} = n^{(2)}_{k_m}.$$

We now conclude from the argument in the proof of theorem 2.7.1 that

$$\sup_{\theta\in\Theta}|(1/n_{k_m})\sum_{j=1}^{n_{k_m}} f(X_j,\theta) - \int f(x,\theta)dG(x)| \to 0 \text{ a.s.}$$

as $m \to \infty$. Again using theorem 2.1.6 we then conclude:

Theorem 2.7.2 Let the conditions of theorem 2.7.1 be satisfied, except (2.7.2). If

$$\sup_n(1/n)\sum_{j=1}^n E[\sup_{\theta\in\Theta}|f(X_j,\theta)|^{1+\delta}] < \infty \text{ for some } \delta > 0,$$

then

$$(1/n)\sum_{j=1}^n f(X_j,\theta) \to \int f(x,\theta)dG(x) \text{ in pr. uniformly on } \Theta,$$

where the limit function involved is continuous on Θ.

Next, let $f(x,\theta)$ be Borel measurable in both arguments and for each $x \in R^k$ continuous on Θ. Referring to theorems 2.5.6 and 2.5.7 instead of theorems 2.5.2 and 2.5.3, respectively, we have:

Theorem 2.7.3 Let $X_1,X_2,\ldots$ be a sequence of independent random vectors in R^k with distribution functions $F_1,F_2,\ldots$ respectively. Let $f(x,\theta)$ be a Borel measurable function on $R^k \times \Theta$, where Θ is a compact Borel set in R^m, which is continuous in θ for each $x \in R^k$. If

$$(1/n)\sum_{j=1}^n F_j \to G \text{ properly setwise} \tag{2.7.15}$$

and

$$\sup_n(1/n)\sum_{j=1}^n E[\sup_{\theta\in\Theta}|f(X_j,\theta)|^{2+\delta}] < \infty \text{ for some } \delta > 0 \tag{2.7.16}$$

then

$$(1/n)\sum_{j=1}^n f(X_j,\theta) \to \int f(x,\theta)dG(x) \text{ a.s. uniformly on } \Theta,$$

where the limit function involved is continuous on Θ.

Theorem 2.7.4 Let the conditions of theorem 2.7.3 be satisfied, except condition (2.7.16). If

$$\sup_n (1/n)\sum_{j=1}^{n} E[\sup_{\theta\in\Theta}|f(X_j,\theta)|^{1+\delta}] < \infty \text{ for some } \delta > 0 \quad (2.7.17)$$

then

$$(1/n)\sum_{j=1}^{n} f(X_j,\theta) \to \int f(x,\theta)dG(x) \text{ in pr. uniformly on } \Theta,$$

where the limit function involved is continuous on Θ.

Finally, if the sequence (X_j) is i.i.d. we can relax the moment conditions (2.7.16) and (2.7.17) further, due to Kolmogorov's strong law (cf. theorem 2.1.5):

Theorem 2.7.5 Let the conditions of theorem 2.7.3 be satisfied, except condition (2.7.16). If (X_j) is i.i.d. with

$$F_j \equiv G \text{ and } E[\sup_{\theta\in\Theta}|f(X_j,\theta)|] < \infty$$

then the conclusion of theorem 2.7.3 carries over.

Exercise

1. Restate theorems 2.7.2 and 2.7.4 for double arrays $(X_{n,j})$, $j=1,2,...,n$, $n=1,2,...$ of random vectors in R^k (cf. exercise 2 in section 2.5).

3

Introduction to conditioning

The concept of conditional expectation is basic to regression analysis, as regression models essentially represent conditional expectations. The theory of conditioning, however, is one of the most abstract and difficult parts of probability theory. In particular, conditioning relative to a one-sided infinite sequence of random variables requires the concept of conditional expectation relative to a Borel field. We shall need this concept when we deal with time series regression models. However, as long as we deal with independent samples, we only need the concept of a conditional expectation relative to a random vector, and fortunately the latter conditional expectation concept can be defined in a much more transparant way than the former. Therefore we shall discuss the abstract theory of conditioning relative to a Borel field later on. Here we shall confine attention to the easier concept of conditional expectation relative to a random vector.

3.1 Definition of conditional expectation

Most intermediate textbooks on mathematical statistics define conditional expectations by using conditional densities and probabilities. For our purpose this elementary conditional expectation concept is not suitable. In particular, our theory of model specification testing requires a more rigorous conditioning concept. Before we introduce this rigorous concept, however, we illustrate two basic features of the elementary conditional expectation concept. Thus let $(Y,X) \in R \times R^k$ be an absolutely continuously distributed random vector with density $f(y,x)$ and marginal density $h(x)$. Then the conditional density of Y relative to the event $X = x$ is defined as:

$$f(y|x) = f(y,x)/h(x) \text{ if } h(x) > 0,$$
$$f(y|x) = 0 \qquad\qquad \text{ if } h(x) = 0.$$

The conditional expectation of Y relative to the event $X = x$ is

$$E(Y|X = x) = \int_{-\infty}^{+\infty} yf(y|x)dy = g(x),$$

say. Substituting X for x, we get the conditional expectation of Y relative to X:

$$E(Y|X) = g(X).$$

Thus E(Y|X) is a *function* of X. Moreover, we also have

$$E[Y-E(Y|X)]\psi(X) = E[Y\psi(X)] - E[g(X)\psi(X)] = 0$$

for every function ψ for which this expectation is defined, as easily follows from the above elementary definition. These two properties are basic to conditional expectations. In fact they form the defining properties:

> *Definition 3.1.1* Let Y be a random variable satisfying $E(|Y|) < \infty$ and let X be a random vector in R^k. The conditional expectation of Y relative to X, denoted by E(Y|X), is defined as E(Y|X) = g(X), where g is a Borel measurable real function on R^k such that for every bounded Borel measurable real function ψ on R^k,
>
> $$E[Y-g(X)]\psi(X)=0. \quad (3.1.1)$$

Example: Draw randomly a pair (Y,X) from the set

$$\{(1,1),(2,1),(3,2),(4,2)\}.$$

Since X takes only two values, any Borel measurable function ψ of X is a.s. equal to a simple function of X, i.e.

$$\psi(X) = a\cdot I(X=1) + b\cdot I(X=2),\ a,b \in R.$$

Now we have

$$E[Y-g(X)]\psi(X) = \tfrac{1}{4}\{[1-g(1)]a + [2\text{-}g(1)]a + [3\text{-}g(2)]b + [4\text{-}g(2)]b\}$$
$$= [\tfrac{3}{4} - \tfrac{1}{2}g(1)]a + [\tfrac{7}{4} - \tfrac{1}{2}g(2)]b = 0$$

for every $a \in R$, $b \in R$, hence $g(1) = \frac{3}{2}$, $g(2) = \frac{7}{2}$. Thus

$$E(Y|X) = 1.5\cdot I(X=1) + 3.5\cdot I(X=2).$$

Two problems now arise. First, does this function g always exist? The answer is yes, but for the proof we actually need the notion of a conditional expectation relative to a Borel field (see, for example, Chung [1974, ch. 9]), together with the Radon–Nikodym theorem (see Royden [1968, p. 238]). We shall not pursue this point further here. Second, is g(X) unique? The answer to this question is also affirmative, owing to the Radon–Nikodym theorem, in the sense that if there are two Borel measurable real functions g_1 and g_2 on R^k satisfying the definition, then $g_1(X) = g_2(X)$ a.s. An alternative proof of the uniqueness of g(X) is given by the following theorem of Bierens (1982), which is also of intrinsic interest and, moreover, is basic to our theory of model specification testing, described in chapter 5.

> *Theorem 3.1.1* Let g_1 and g_2 be Borel measurable real functions on R^k. Let X be a random vector in R^k such that $E(|g_1(X)|) < \infty$, $E(|g_2(X)|) < \infty$. Let for non-random $t \in R^k$,
>
> $$\varphi_1(t) = E[g_1(X)\exp(i \cdot t'X)],\ \varphi_2(t) = E[g_2(X)\exp(i \cdot t'X)].$$
>
> Then $P(g_1(X) = g_2(X)) < 1$ if and only if $\varphi_1(t) \neq \varphi_2(t)$ for some $t \in R^k$.

Now suppose that there exist two Borel measurable real functions g_1 and g_2 satisfying (3.1.1) for every bounded Borel measurable real function $\psi(x)$ on R^k. Then also

$$E[(g_1(X) - g_2(X))\psi(X)] = 0$$

and consequently

$$E[(g_1(X) - g_2(X))\cos(t'X)] = 0 \text{ for all } t \in R^k,$$

$$E[(g_1(X) - g_2(X))\sin(t'X)] = 0 \text{ for all } t \in R^k.$$

Since $\exp(i \cdot t'x) = \cos(t'x) + i \cdot \sin(t'x)$, it now follows that

$$\varphi_1(t) = \varphi_2(t) \text{ for all } t \in R^k,$$

which by theorem 3.1.1 implies $P(g_1(X) = g_2(X)) = 1$. Thus g(X) is a.s. unique.

A by-product of this argument is:

> *Theorem 3.1.2* Let $Y \in R$ be a random variable satisfying $E(|Y|) < \infty$ and let $X \in R^k$ be a random vector. Let g be a Borel measurable real function on R^k. If $E[(Y - g(X))\psi(X)] = 0$ for all bounded *continuous* functions ψ on R^k then $E(Y|X) = g(X)$.

Proof of theorem 3.1.1: Let

$$r(x) = g_1(x) - g_2(x).$$

Then r is Borel measurable, and so are

$$r_1(x) = \max(r(x),0),\ r_2(x) = \max(-r(x),0).$$

Clearly we have $r = r_1 - r_2$, where r_1 and r_2 are non-negative. Now assume for the moment

$$c_1 = E[r_1(X)] > 0,\ c_2 = E[r_2(X)] > 0. \tag{3.1.2}$$

Then we can define probability measures υ_1 and υ_2 on the Euclidean Borel field $\mathfrak{B}^k$ by (cf. exercise 1a)

$$\upsilon_j(B) = \int_B r_j(x)\upsilon(dx)/c_j,\ j = 1,2, \tag{3.1.3}$$

where υ is the probability measure induced by X (cf. section 1.1) and B is an arbitrary Borel set in R^k. We may now write (cf. exercise 1c)

$$\begin{aligned} E\,[r(X)\exp(i\cdot t'X)] &= \int r(x)\exp(i\cdot t'x)\upsilon(dx) \\ &= \int r_1(x)\exp(i\cdot t'x)\upsilon(dx) - \int r_2(x)\exp(i\cdot t'x)\upsilon(dx) \\ &= c_1\int \exp(i\cdot t'x)\upsilon_1(dx) - c_2\int \exp(i\cdot t'x)\upsilon_2(dx) \\ &= c_1\eta_1(t) - c_2\eta_2(t), \end{aligned}$$

say, where

$$\eta_j(t) = \int \exp(i\cdot t'x)\upsilon_j(dx),\ j = 1,2,$$

is the characteristic function of υ_j, $j = 1,2$. If

$$E\,[r(X)\exp(i\cdot t'X)] \equiv 0$$

then $c_1\eta_1(t) - c_2\eta_2(t) = 0$ for all $t \in R^k$. Substituting $t = 0$ yields:

$$c_1\eta_1(0) - c_2\eta_2(0) = c_1 - c_2 = 0, \tag{3.1.4}$$

hence

$$\eta_1(t) = \eta_2(t) \text{ for all } t \in R^k.$$

The latter implies that the corresponding probability measures are equal, i.e.,

$$\upsilon_1(B) = \upsilon_2(B) \text{ for all Borel sets B in } R^k. \tag{3.1.5}$$

From (3.1.3), (3.1.4), and (3.1.5) it follows now:

$$\int_B r_1(x)\upsilon(dx) = \int_B r_2(x)\upsilon(dx) \text{ for all } B \in \mathfrak{B}^k$$

and consequently

$$\int_B r(x)\upsilon(dx) = 0 \text{ for all } B \in \mathfrak{B}^k. \tag{3.1.6}$$

Now take

$$B_1 = \{x \in R^k: r(x) > 0\}.$$

This is a Borel set, for r is Borel measurable. Hence by (3.1.6), $\int_{B_1} r(x)\upsilon(dx) = 0$. This implies that $\upsilon(B_1) = 0$. Similarly, we have for

$$B_2 = \{x \in R^k: r(x) < 0\}$$

that $\upsilon(B_2) = 0$. Since B_1 and B_2 are disjoint we now have $\upsilon(B_1 \cup B_2) = \upsilon(B_1) + \upsilon(B_2) = 0$ or equivalently:

$P(r(X) \neq 0) = 0.$

This proves that $r(X) = g_1(X) - g_2(X) = 0$ a.s. if (3.1.2) holds. The proof for the case that $E[r_1(X)] = 0$ and/or $E[r_2(X)] = 0$ is left to the reader as an easy exercise. Q.E.D.

Exercises

1. Let υ be a probability measure on $(R^k,\mathfrak{B}^k)$ and let f be a non-negative Borel measurable function on R^k such that $\int f(x)\upsilon(dx) = c$ with $0 < c < \infty$. Define for $B \in \mathfrak{B}^k$,

   $\mu(B) = \int_B f(x)\upsilon(dx)/c.$

   a) Prove that μ is a probability measure on $\{R^k,\mathfrak{B}^k\}$.
   b) Prove that for every simple function φ on R^k,

   $\int\varphi(x)f(x)\upsilon(dx) = c\int\varphi(x)\mu(dx).$

   c) Prove the same for bounded Borel measurable real functions φ on R^k.
2. Check the proof of theorem 3.1.1 for the cases $c_1 = 0; c_2 > 0$, $c_1 > 0; c_2 = 0$; and $c_1 = c_2 = 0$.
3. Prove theorem 3.1.2.

3.2 Basic properties of conditional expectations

All the basic properties of conditional expectations, which are well known from intermediate statistical textbooks, can easily be derived from definition 3.1.1 and theorem 3.1.1. We list them in theorem 3.2.1 below. The proofs are left to the reader as exercises.

Theorem 3.2.1 Let $Y \in R$ and $V \in R$ be random variables satisfying $E(|Y|) < \infty$, $E(|V|) < \infty$, and let $X \in R^k$ and $Z \in R^m$ be random vectors. We have:

(i) $E[E(Y|X,Z)|X] = E(Y|X) = E[E(Y|X)|X,Z]$;

(ii) $E[E(Y|X)] = E(Y)$; $E(Y|Y) = Y$;

(iii) Let $U = Y - E(Y|X)$. Then $E(U|X) = 0$ a.s.;

(iv) $E(Y + V|X) = E(Y|X) + E(V|X)$;

(v) $Y \leq V$ a.s. implies $E(Y|X) \leq E(V|X)$ a.s.;

(vi) $|E(Y|X)| \leq E(|Y||X)$ a.s.;

(vii) $E(Y \cdot f(X)|X) = f(X)E(Y|X)$ a.s. for every Borel measurable real function f on R^k satisfying $E(|f(X)|) < \infty$;

(viii) Let Γ be a Borel measurable mapping from R^k into a subset of R^m. Then $E[E(Y|X)|\Gamma(X)] = E[Y|\Gamma(X)]$ a.s. If Γ is a *one-to-one* mapping then $E(Y|\Gamma(X)) = E(Y|X)$ a.s.

(ix) If X and Y are independent then $E(Y|X) = E(Y)$ a.s.

Hint. For proving (v) apply (3.1.1) with

$\psi(X) = I[E(Y|X) > E(V|X)]$,

where I[.] is the indicator function.

Also Chebishev's, Holder's, Minkowski's, Liapounov's, and Jensen's inequalities easily carry over to conditional expectations:

Theorem 3.2.2 (Chebishev's inequality) Let $Y \in R$, $X \in R^k$ and let φ be a positive monotonic increasing real function on $(0,\infty)$ such that $\varphi(y) = \varphi(-y)$ and $E[\varphi(Y)] < \infty$. Then for every $\delta > 0$,

$E[I(|Y| > \delta)| X] \leq E[\varphi(Y)|X]/\varphi(\delta)$ a.s.

Proof: Let $\psi(X) = I\{E[I(|Y| > \delta)| X] > E[\varphi(Y)|X]/\varphi(\delta)\}$. Applying definition 3.1.1 we find $\psi(X) = 0$ a.s. Q.E.D.

Theorem 3.2.3 (Holder's inequality) Let $Y \in R$, $V \in R$, $E(|Y|^p) < \infty$, $E(|V|^q) < \infty$, $E(|Y{\cdot}V|) < \infty$, and $X \in R^k$, where $p > 1$ and $1/p + 1/q = 1$. Then

$|E(Y{\cdot}V|X)| \leq [E(|Y|^p|X)]^{1/p}[E(|V|^q| X)]^{1/q}$ a.s.

Proof: Similarly to the unconditional case.

Theorem 3.2.4 (Minkowski's inequality) Let $Y \in R$, $V \in R$, $X \in R^k$ and $E(|Y|^p) < \infty$, $E(|V|^p) < \infty$ for some $p \geq 1$. Then

$[E(|Y+V|^p| X)]^{1/p} \leq [E(|Y|^p| X)]^{1/p} + [E(|V|^p| X)]^{1/p}$ a.s.

Proof: Similarly to the unconditional case.

Theorem 3.2.5 (Liapounov's inequality) Let $Y \in R$, $E(|Y|^q) < \infty$ for some $q > 1$, $X \in R^k$ and $1 \leq p < q$. Then

$[E(|Y|^p| X)]^{1/p} \leq [E(|Y|^q | X)]^{1/q}$ a.s.

Proof: Let $V \equiv 1$ in theorem 3.2.3. Q.E.D.

Theorem 3.2.6 (Jensen's inequality) Let φ be a convex real function on R and let $Y \in R$, $X \in R^k$, $E(|Y|) < \infty$, $E(|\varphi(Y)|) < \infty$. Then

$\varphi[E(Y|X)] \leq E[\varphi(Y)|X]$ a.s.

Proof: Similar to the unconditional cse.

The results in section 2.2 also go through for conditional expectations. Although we do not need these generalizations in the sequel we shall state and prove them here for completeness.

Theorem 3.2.7 Let Y_n, Y and Z be random variables and let X be a random vector in R^k. If $\sup_n(|Y_n|) \leq Z$; $E(|Z|^p) < \infty$ for some $p > 0$ and $Y_n \to Y$ in prob., then $E(|Y_n - Y|^p \mid X) \to 0$ in pr.

Proof: The theorem follows easily from theorem 2.2.1, Chebishev's inequality and theorem 3.2.1 (ii). Q.E.D.

Theorem 3.2.8 (*Dominated convergence theorem*) Let the conditions of theorem 3.2.7 with $p = 1$ be satisfied. Then

$E(Y_n|X) \to E(Y|X)$ in pr.

Proof: By theorems 3.2.1 (iv and vi) and 3.2.7 it follows that

$$|E(Y_n|X) - E(Y|X)| = |E[(Y_n - Y)|X]| \leq E(|Y_n - Y||X) \to 0 \text{ in pr.}$$

Q.E.D.

Theorem 3.2.9 (*Fatou's lemma*) Let Y_n be a random variable satisfying $Y_n \geq 0$ a.s. and let X be a random vector in R^k. Then

$E(\liminf_{n\to\infty} Y_n \mid X) \leq \liminf_{n\to\infty} E(Y_n|X)$ a.s.

Proof: Put $Y = \liminf_{n\to\infty} Y_n$, $Z_n = Y_n - Y$, and let $F_n(z \mid x)$ be the conditional distribution function of Z_n, given $X = x$. Then it follows from the unconditional Fatou's lemma (theorem 2.2.3) that pointwise in x,

$$\liminf_{n\to\infty} \int z \, dF_n(z \mid x) \geq 0.$$

Plugging in X for x now yields

$$0 \leq \liminf_{n\to\infty} \int z \, dF_n(z \mid X) = \liminf_{n\to\infty} E(Z_n \mid X)$$
$$= \limsup_{n\to\infty} E(Y_n \mid X) - E(Y \mid X) \text{ a.s.}$$

Q.E.D.

Theorem 3.2.10 (*Monotone convergence theorem*) Let (Y_n) be a non-decreasing sequence of random variables satisfying $E|Y_n| < \infty$ and let X be a random vector in R^k. Then

$$E(\lim_{n\to\infty} Y_n | X) = \lim_{n\to\infty} E(Y_n|X) \le \infty \text{ a.s.}$$

Proof: Similarly to the proof of theorem 2.2.4, using theorem 3.2.9 instead of theorem 2.2.3. Q.E.D.

Exercises

1. Prove theorem 3.2.1.
2. Complete the proof of theorem 3.2.2.
3. Prove theorem 3.2.7.

3.3 Identification of conditional expectations

In parametric regression analysis the conditional expectation E(Y|X) is specified as a member of a parametric family of functions of X. In particular the family of linear functions is often used in empirical research. The question we now ask is how a given specification can be identified as the conditional expectation involved. In other words: given a dependent variable Y, a k-vector X of explanatory variables and a Borel measurable functional specification f(X) of E(Y|X), how can we distinguish between

$$P[E(Y|X) = f(X)] = 1 \tag{3.3.1}$$

and

$$P[E(Y|X) = f(X)] < 1\ ? \tag{3.3.2}$$

An answer is given by theorem 3.1.1, i.e. (3.3.1) is true if

$$E[Y - f(X)]\exp(i \cdot t'X) \equiv 0$$

and (3.3.2) is true if

$$E[Y - f(X)]\exp(i \cdot t'X) \neq 0 \text{ for some } t \in R^k.$$

Verifying this, however, requires searching over the entire space R^k for such a point t. So where should we look? For the case that X is bounded the answer is this:

> *Theorem 3.3.1* Let X be bounded. Then (3.3.2) is true if and only if
>
> $$E[Y - f(X)]\exp(i \cdot t_0'X) \neq 0$$
>
> for some $t_0 \neq 0$ in an arbitrary small neighborhood of the origin of R^k.

Thus in this case we may confine our search to an arbitrary neighborhood of $t = 0$. If we do not find such a t_0 in this neighborhood, then

$E(Y - g(X))\exp(i \cdot t'X) \equiv 0$

and thus (3.3.1) is true.

Proof: Let (3.3.2) be true. According to theorem 3.3.1 there exists a $t_* \in R^k$ for which

$$E[Y - f(X)]\exp(i.t_*'X) \neq 0 \qquad (3.3.3)$$

Let Z be a discrete random variable, *independent* of X and Y, such that $P(Z = j) = (1/j!)e^{-1}$, $j = 0,1,2,\ldots$ Since X is bounded and Z is independent of (X,Y) we can now write (3.3.3) as

$$\begin{aligned} E[Y - f(X)]\exp(i \cdot t_*'X) &= E[Y - f(X)]\textstyle\sum_{j=0}^{\infty}(i^j/j!)(t_*'X)^j \\ &= \exp(1) \cdot E\{E[(Y - f(X))i^Z(t_*'X)^Z|X,Y]\} \\ &= \exp(1) \cdot E[(Y - f(X))i^Z(t_*'X)^Z] \\ &= \exp(1) \cdot E\{E[(Y - f(X))i^Z(t_*'X)^Z|Z]\} \\ &= \textstyle\sum_{j=0}^{\infty}(i^j/j!)E[(Y - f(X))(t_*'X)^j] \neq 0. \end{aligned}$$

Consequently, there exists at least one j_* for which

$$E\,[(Y - f(X))(t_*'X)^{j_*}] \neq 0.$$

Then

$$\begin{aligned} &(d/d\lambda)^{j_*}E[(Y - f(X))\exp[i \cdot \lambda t_*'X)] \\ &\quad = \textstyle\sum_{j=j_*}^{\infty}\{i^j\lambda^{j-j_*}/[(j-j_*)!]\}E[(Y - f(X))(t_*'X)X)^j] \\ &\quad \to i^{j_*}\,E[(Y - f(X))(t_*'X)^{j_*}] \neq 0 \text{ as } \lambda \to 0. \end{aligned}$$

This result implies that there exists an arbitrarily small λ_* such that

$$E[(Y - f(X))\exp(i \cdot \lambda_* t_*'X)\,] \neq 0.$$

Taking $t_0 = \lambda_* t_*$, the theorem follows. Q.E.D.

Now observe from the proof of theorem 3.3.1 that (3.3.2) is true if and only if for a point t_0 in an arbitrarily small neighborhood of the origin of R^k and some non-negative integer j_0,

$$E[(Y - f(X))(t_0'X)^{j_0}] \neq 0.$$

Applying a similar argument as in the proof of theorem 3.3.1 (with i replaced by 1) it is easy to verify:

> *Theorem 3.3.2* Let X be bounded. Then (3.3.2) is true if and only if the function $E[(Y - f(X))\exp(t'X)]$ is nonzero for a t in an arbitrarily small neighborhood of the origin of R^k.

Clearly this theorem is more convenient than theorem 3.3.1, as we no longer have to deal with complex-valued functions. Next, let $t_* \in R^k$ be arbitrary, let

$$Y_* = Y \cdot \exp(t_*'X)$$

and let

$$f_*(X) = f(X)\exp(t_*'X).$$

Then (3.3.2) is true if and only if

$$P[E(Y_*|X) = f_*(X)] < 1.$$

Applying theorem 3.3.2 we see that then

$$E[(Y_* - f_*(X))\exp(t_0'X)] = E\{(Y - f(X))\exp[(t_* + t_0)'X]\} \neq 0$$

for some t_0 in an arbitrary neighborhood of the origin of R^k. Consequently we have:

> *Theorem 3.3.3* Let X be bounded and let $t_* \in R^k$ be arbitrary. Then (3.3.2) is true if and only if $E(Y - f(X))\exp(t_0'X) \neq 0$ for a t_0 in an arbitrarily small neighborhood of t_*.

Thus we may pick an arbitrary neighborhood and check whether there exists a t_0 in this neighborhood for which

$$E[(Y - f(X))\exp(t_0'X)] \neq 0.$$

If so, then (3.3.2) is true, else (3.3.1) is true. This result now leads to our main theorem.

> *Theorem 3.3.4* Let $X \in R^k$ be bounded, and let S be the set of all $t \in R^k$ for which $E[(Y - f(X))\exp(t'X)] = 0$. For any probability measure μ on $\mathfrak{B}^k$ corresponding to an absolutely continuous distribution we have: $\mu(S) = 1$ if (3.3.1) is true and $\mu(S) = 0$ if (3.3.2) is true.

Proof: Let $V = Y - f(X)$ and let t_0 be arbitrary. Suppose for the moment that $X \in R$. If $P[E(V|X) = 0] < 1$, then theorem 3.3.3 implies that for every $t_0 \in R$ there exists a $\delta > 0$ such that

$$E[V \cdot \exp(tX)] \neq 0 \text{ on } (t_0 - \delta, t_0) \cup (t_0, t_0 + \delta).$$

Consequently, we have:

> *Lemma 3.3.1* Let $V \in R$ be a random variable satisfying $E(|V|) < \infty$ and let $X \in R$ be a bounded random variable. If $P[E(V|X) = 0] < 1$ then the set
>
> $$S = \{t \in R : E[V \cdot \exp(tX)] = 0\}$$
>
> is countable.

Using the lemma it is very easy to prove theorem 3.3.4 for the case $k = 1$. So let us turn to the case $k = 2$. Let $P[E(V|X) = 0] < 1$. According to theorem 3.3.3 there exists a $t_* \in R^2$ such that

$$E[V \cdot \exp(t_*'X)] \neq 0.$$

Denote

$$V_* = V \cdot \exp(t_*'X), \ \psi_*(t_1,t_2) = E[V \cdot \exp(t_1X_1 + t_2X_2)]$$

where X_1 and X_2 are the components of X. Moreover, let

$$S_1 = \{t_1 \in R: \psi_*(t_1,0) = 0\}, S_2(t_1) = \{t_2 \in R: \psi_*(t_1,t_2) = 0\} .$$

Since $E(V_*) \neq 0$, we have $P[E(V_*|X_1) = 0] < 1$, hence by lemma 3.3.1 the set S_1 is countable. By the same argument it follows that the set $S_2(t_1)$ is countable if $t_1 \notin S_1$. Now let $(\boldsymbol{t}_1,\boldsymbol{t}_2)$ be a random drawing from an absolutely continuous distribution. We have:

$$\begin{aligned} E\{I[\psi_*(\boldsymbol{t}_1,\boldsymbol{t}_2) = 0]\} &= E\{I[\psi_*(\boldsymbol{t}_1,\boldsymbol{t}_2) = 0] \cdot I(\boldsymbol{t}_1 \in S_1) \\ &\quad + E\{I[\psi_*(\boldsymbol{t}_1,\boldsymbol{t}_2) = 0] \cdot I[\boldsymbol{t}_1 \notin S_1]\} \\ &\leq E[I(\boldsymbol{t}_1 \in S_1)] + E[I(\boldsymbol{t}_1 \notin S_1) \cdot I(\boldsymbol{t}_2 \in S_2(\boldsymbol{t}_1)). \end{aligned}$$

Since the set S_1 is countable and $\boldsymbol{t}_1$ is continuously distributed we have $E[I(\boldsymbol{t}_1 \in S_1)] = 0$. Moreover, since the distribution of $\boldsymbol{t}_2$ conditional on $\boldsymbol{t}_1$ is continuous we have:

$$E[I(\boldsymbol{t}_2 \in S_2(\boldsymbol{t}_1)) \cdot I(\boldsymbol{t}_1 \notin S_1)] = 0 ,$$

for $S_2(t_1)$ is countable if $t_1 \notin S_1$. Thus:

$$P[\psi_*(\boldsymbol{t}_1,\boldsymbol{t}_2) = 0] = 0.$$

Replacing $(\boldsymbol{t}_1,\boldsymbol{t}_2)$ by $(\boldsymbol{t}_1 - t_1^*, \boldsymbol{t}_2 - t_2^*)$, where t_1^* and t_2^* are the compoments of t_*, we now see that theorem 3.3.3 holds too for the case $k = 2$. The proof of the cases $k = 3,4,...$ is similar to the case $k = 2$ and therefore left to the reader. Q.E.D.

Finally we consider the case that X is not bounded. By theorem 3.2.1 (viii) we have $E[Y - f(X)|X] = E[Y - f(X)|\Gamma(X)]$ a.s. for every Borel measurable one-to-one mapping Γ from R^k into R^k. From this result and theorem 3.3.3 it now follows:

Theorem 3.3.5 Let the conditions of theorem 3.3.3 be satisfied, except that X is bounded. Let Γ be an arbitrary bounded Borel measurable one-to-one mapping from R^k into R^k, and let

$$S = \{t \in R^k: E[(Y - f(X))\exp(t'\Gamma(X))] = 0\}.$$

For any probability measure μ on $\mathfrak{B}^k$ corresponding to an absolutely continuous distribution we have: $\mu(S) = 1$ if (3.3.1) is true and $\mu(S) = 0$ if (3.3.2) is true.

Exercises

1. Use the argument in the proof of theorem 3.3.1 to prove the following corollary: Let $X = (X_1,\ldots,X_k)'$. Under the conditions of theorem 3.3.1 it follows that (3.3.2) is true if and only if there exist non-negative integers $m_1,\ldots,m_k$ such that

   $$E[(Y - f(X))\Pi_{j=1}^{k} X_j^{m_j}] \neq 0.$$

   Cf. Bierens (1982, theorem 2).
2. Let Θ be a subset of R^k. A point y in R^k is called a point of closure of Θ if for every $\varepsilon > 0$ we can find an $x \in \Theta$ such that $|x-y| < \varepsilon$. The set of all points of closure of Θ is called the closure of Θ. A subset S of Θ is called *dense* in Θ if $\Theta \subset S^-$, where S^- is the closure of S. Prove that the set S in theorem 3.3.4 and 3.3.4 is *not* dense in R^k.

4

Nonlinear parametric regression analysis and maximum likelihood theory

In this chapter we consider the asymptotic properties, i.e. weak and strong consistency and asymptotic normality, of the least squares estimators of the parameters of a nonlinear regression model. Throughout we assume that the data generating process is independent, but we distinguish between the identically distributed and the non-identically distributed case. Also, we consider maximum likelihood estimation and the Wald, likelihood ratio and Lagrange multiplier tests of (non)linear restrictions on the parameters. Notable work in the area of nonlinear regression has been done by Jennrich (1969), Malinvaud (1970a,b), White (1980b, 1982), Bierens (1981), Burguete, Gallant, and Souza (1982), and Gallant (1987), among others. The present nonlinear regression approach is a further elaboration of the approach in Bierens (1981, section 3.1).

4.1 Nonlinear regression models and the nonlinear least squares estimator

Consider an independent data generating process $\{(Y_j,X_j)\}$, $j=1,2,...$ where $Y_j \in R$ is the dependent variable and $X_j \in R^k$ is a vector of regressors. The central problem in regression analysis is how to determine the conditional expectation functions

$$g_j(X_j) = E(Y_j|X_j),\ j = 1,2,... \tag{4.1.1}$$

We shall call this function g_j the *response function*. Note that this response function exists and is a Borel measurable real function on R^k, provided

$$E(|Y_j|) < \infty \tag{4.1.2}$$

(cf. section 3.1). Defining

$$U_j = Y_j - g_j(X_j),\ j = 1,2,... \tag{4.1.3}$$

we get the tautological regression model

$$Y_j = g_j(X_j) + U_j,\ j = 1,2,... \tag{4.1.4}$$

where by construction the errors U_j satisfy

$$E(U_j|X_j) = 0 \text{ a.s.}, j = 1,2,... \tag{4.1.5}$$

In parametric regression analysis it is assumed that:

(i) g_j does not depend on j:

$$g_j = g \text{ for } j = 1,2,...; \tag{4.1.6}$$

(ii) the function g belongs to a parametric family of functions $f(.,\theta)$;

$$g(.) \in \{f(.,\theta): \theta \in \Theta\}, \tag{4.1.7}$$

where Θ is a subset of a Euclidean space, called the *parameter space*, and $f(x,\theta)$ is known for each $x \in R^k$ and each $\theta \in \Theta$.

Quite often one also assumes that the errors U_j are independent of X_j and even that the U_j's are normally distributed. These assumptions, however, are not necessary for the asymptotic theory of regression analysis and therefore we shall not depend on them.

Condition (i) naturally holds if the data generating process is i.i.d. However, if some or all of the components of X_j are control variables set by the analyst in a statistical experiment, we can no longer assume that the X_j's are identically distributed. In that case the response function may depend on the observation index j.

The condition that the response function belongs to a certain parametric family of known functions is crucial to parametric regression analysis, but is also disputable. In practice we almost never know the exact functional form of a regression model. The choice of the parametric family (4.1.7) is therefore almost always a matter of convenience rather than a matter of precise *a priori* knowledge. For that reason the linear regression model is still the most popular functional specification in empirical research, owing to its convenience in estimating the parameters by ordinary least squares (OLS). So why should we bother about nonlinear regression models?

There are various reasons why nonlinear regression analysis makes sense. First, it is possible to test whether a given (linear) functional specification is correct (see chapter 5). If we have to reject the linear specification we are then forced to look for a nonlinear specification that is closer to the true response function. Second, a linear regression model sometimes is logically inconsistent with the nature of the data. If for example the range of Y_j is $[0,\infty)$ and the range of the components of X_j is $(-\infty,\infty)$, then the linear response function may take negative values, whereas $E(Y_j|X_j) \geq 0$ a.s. (cf. theorem 3.2.1.(v)). Another example is the case where Y_j is a binary variable only taking the values 0 and 1. Then $E(Y_j|X_j)$ is just the conditional probability of the event $Y_j = 1$ relative to X_j, and must therefore lie in the interval [0,1]. A possible specification in this case is a logit-type model:

$$Y_j = 1/[1 + \exp(-\theta_0 - \theta_1' X_j)] + U_j = f(X_j,\theta) + U_j,$$
with $E(U_j|X_j) = 0$ a.s.

where $\theta = (\theta_0,\theta_1')' \in R \times R^k = \Theta$. Note that in this case U_j cannot be independent of X_j.

Third, there are cases where theory is more explicit about the functional form of a model. An example is the CES production function in economics, introduced by Arrow, Chenery, Minhas, and Solow (1961). This production function takes the form

$$y = \{\theta_1 x_1^{-\theta_3} + \theta_2 x_2^{-\theta_3}\}^{-1/\theta_3},$$

where $\theta_1 > 0$, $\theta_2 > 0$, $\theta_3 \geq -1$, y is the output level of an industry, x_1 is the total labor force employed in the industry and x_2 is the stock of capital in the industry. Adding an error term to the right-hand side yields a nonlinear regression model.

Fourth, there are flexible functional specifications that allow the functional form to be partly determined by the data. A typical example of such a flexible functional specification is the Box–Cox (1964) transformation. The Box–Cox transformation of a variable v is given by

$$\eta(v|\lambda) = (v^\lambda - 1)/\lambda.$$

For $\lambda = 0$ we have $\eta(v|0) = \ln(v)$, and clearly $\eta(v|1) = v - 1$. This transformation is particularly suitable when the regressors are positively valued. Consider for example the case $X_j \in R$, $P(X_j > 0) = 1$. Specifying the regression model as

$$Y_j = \theta_1 + \theta_2\, \eta(X_j|\theta_3) + U_j$$

yields a model that contains the linear model and the semi-loglinear model $[Y_j = \theta_1 + \theta_2 \ln(X_j) + U_j]$ as special cases. By estimating the parameters θ_1, θ_2 and θ_3 and testing the hypothesis $\theta_3 = 0$ against $\theta_3 = 1$ we actually let the data choose between these alternatives.

From now on we take the parametric family of functional forms as given (though not necessarily as true). Moreover, we confine ourselves to functions that are Borel measurable in the explanatory variables and the parameters and are continuous in the parameters. Furthermore, the parameter space Θ is assumed to be a compact Borel set.

Assumption 4.1.1 Given the data generating process $\{(Y_j,X_j)\}$,

$j=1,2,\ldots$ in $R \times R^k$ with $E(|Y_j|) < \infty$, the conditional expectation of Y_j relative to X_j equals $f(X_j,\theta_0)$ a.s. for $j=1,2,\ldots$, where $f(x,\theta)$ is a known Borel measurable real function on $R^k \times \Theta$ with Θ a compact Borel set in R^m containing θ_0. For each $x \in R^k$ the function $f(x,\theta)$ is continuous on Θ.

We recall that compactness of a set implies that every open covering contains a finite subcovering, and that a subset of a Euclidean space is compact if and only if it is closed and bounded; cf. Royden (1968). Assuming that the data generating process is observable for $j=1,2,\ldots,n$, the nonlinear least squares estimator for θ_0 is now defined as a measurable solution of the following minimization problem:

$$\theta \in \Theta: \hat{Q}(\hat{\theta}) = \inf_{\theta\in\Theta}\hat{Q}(\theta), \tag{4.1.8}$$

where

$$\hat{Q}(\theta) = (1/n)\sum_{j=1}^{n}[Y_j - f(X_j,\theta)]^2. \tag{4.1.9}$$

By theorem 1.6.1 such a measurable solution always exists. Later in this chapter we shall give further conditions for strong consistency, i.e.

$$\hat{\theta} \rightarrow \theta_0 \text{ a.s. as } n \rightarrow \infty \tag{4.1.10}$$

or weak consistency:

$$\text{plim}_{n\rightarrow\infty}\, \hat{\theta} = \theta_0, \tag{4.1.11}$$

and asymptotic normality, i.e.

$$\surd n(\hat{\theta} - \theta_0) \rightarrow N_m(0,\Omega) \text{ in distr.} \tag{4.1.12}$$

4.2 Consistency and asymptotic normality: general theory

4.2.1 Consistency

The consistency proof contains two main steps. First we set forth conditions such that

$$\hat{Q}(\theta) \rightarrow Q(\theta) \text{ a.s. (in pr.) pseudo-uniformly on } \Theta \tag{4.2.1}$$

where

$$Q(\theta) = \lim_{n\rightarrow\infty}E[\hat{Q}(\theta)] \text{ is continuous on } \Theta \tag{4.2.2}$$

and then we set forth conditions such that

$$\theta_* \in \Theta: Q(\theta_*) = \inf_{\theta\in\Theta}Q(\theta) \Rightarrow \theta_* = \theta_0. \tag{4.2.3}$$

Thus the latter condition says that $Q(\theta)$ has a unique infimum on Θ at θ_0. The conditions (4.2.2) and (4.2.3) guarantee that

$$\hat{\theta} \rightarrow \theta_0 \text{ a.s. (in pr.)},$$

because of the following fundamental theorem.

Theorem 4.2.1 Let $(Q_n(\theta))$ be a sequence of random functions on a compact set $\Theta \subset R^m$ such that for a continuous real function $Q(\theta)$ on Θ,

$$Q_n(\theta) \rightarrow Q(\theta) \text{ a.s. (in pr.) pseudo-uniformly on } \Theta.$$

Let θ_n be any random vector in Θ satisfying

$$Q_n(\theta_n) = \inf_{\theta \in \Theta} Q_n(\theta)$$

and let θ_0 be a unique point in Θ such that

$$Q(\theta_0) = \inf_{\theta \in \Theta} Q(\theta).$$

Then $\theta_n \rightarrow \theta_0$ a.s. (in pr.)

Proof: We consider first the a.s. case. Let $\{\Omega,\mathfrak{F},P\}$ be the probability space and let N be the null set on which the uniform convergence fails to hold. For $\omega \in \Omega \backslash N$ we then have

$$\begin{aligned} 0 \leq Q(\theta_n(\omega)) - Q(\theta_0) &= Q(\theta_n(\omega)) - Q_n(\theta_n(\omega),\omega) + Q_n(\theta_n(\omega),\omega) - Q(\theta_0) \\ &\leq Q(\theta_n(\omega)) - Q_n(\theta_n(\omega),\omega) + Q_n(\theta_0,\omega) - Q(\theta_0) \\ &\leq 2 \cdot \sup_{\theta \in \Theta} |Q_n(\theta,\omega) - Q(\theta)| \rightarrow 0 \text{ as } n \rightarrow \infty, \end{aligned}$$

hence

$$Q(\theta_n(\omega)) \rightarrow Q(\theta_0) \text{ as } n \rightarrow \infty \text{ and } \omega \in \Omega \backslash N. \tag{4.2.4}$$

Now let $\theta^*(\omega)$ be any limit point of the sequence $(\theta_n(\omega))$. Since this sequence lies in a compact set θ, all its limit points lie in θ. Thus, $\theta^*(\omega) \in \Theta$. By definition of a limit point there exists a subsequence $(\theta_{n_j}(\omega))$ such that $\lim_{j \rightarrow \infty} \theta_{n_j}(\omega) = \theta^*(\omega)$. From (4.2.4) and the continuity of $Q(\theta)$ it follows that also

$$\lim_{j \rightarrow \infty} Q(\theta_{n_j}(\omega)) = Q(\lim_{j \rightarrow \infty} \theta_{n_j}(\omega)) = Q(\theta^*(\omega)) = Q(\theta_0),$$

hence $\theta^*(\omega) = \theta_0$ by uniqueness. Thus all the limit points of $\theta_n(\omega)$ are equal to θ_0 and consequently

$$\lim_{n \rightarrow \infty} \theta_n(\omega) = \theta_0 \text{ for } \omega \in \Omega \backslash N.$$

By definition, this implies $\theta_n \rightarrow \theta_0$ a.s. The convergence in probability case follows easily from theorem 2.1.6 and the above argument. Q.E.D.

4.2.2 Asymptotic normality

Next we turn to asymptotic normality. We shall put our argument in a general framework, in order also to use the results for more general cases than considered in this chapter.

Theorem 4.2.2 Let the conditions of theorem 4.2.1 be satisfied (for the convergence in probability case) and assume in addition that:

(i) Θ is convex and θ_0 is an interior point of Θ;

(ii) $(\partial/\partial\theta')Q_n(\theta)$ and $(\partial/\partial\theta)(\partial/\partial\theta')Q_n(\theta)$ are well defined as vector and matrix, respectively, of random functions on Θ;

(iii) $\sqrt{n}(\partial/\partial\theta')Q_n(\theta_0) \to N_m(0,A_1)$ in distr., where A_1 is a positive semi-definite $m \times m$ matrix;

(iv) for $i_1,i_2 = 1,2,\ldots,m$,

$(\partial/\partial\theta_{i_1})(\partial/\partial\theta_{i_2})Q_n(\theta) \to (\partial/\partial\theta_{i_1})(\partial/\partial\theta_{i_2})Q(\theta)$ in pr.

pseudo-uniformly on a neighborhood of θ_0, where the limit function involved is continuous in θ_0;

(v) the matrix $A_2 = (\partial/\partial\theta)(\partial/\partial\theta')Q(\theta_0)$ is nonsingular.

Then $\sqrt{n}(\theta_n-\theta_0) \to N_m(0, A_2^{-1}A_1A_2^{-1})$.

Proof: Consider the following Taylor expansion of $(\partial/\partial\theta_i)Q_n(\theta_n)$ around θ_0:

$$(\partial/\partial\theta_i)Q_n(\theta_n) = (\partial/\partial\theta_i)Q_n(\theta_0) + [(\partial/\partial\theta')(\partial/\partial\theta_i)Q_n(\theta_n^{(i)})]'(\theta_n-\theta_0)$$
$$i = 1,2,\ldots,m \qquad (4.2.5)$$

where $\theta_n^{(i)}$ is a mean value satisfying

$$|\theta_n^{(i)}-\theta_0| \le |\theta_n-\theta_0| \text{ a.s.} \qquad (4.2.6)$$

In the non-random case the existence of such a mean value is proved by Taylor's theorem. In the random case under review, however, we should also ask whether a *measurable* mean value exists. For the moment we shall ignore this problem. At the end of the proof we shall return to this issue.

Note that we have indexed the mean values by i. This indicates that these mean values may be different for different i's. Cf. Don (1986).

Now consider the left member of equation (4.2.5). If θ_n is an interior point of Θ then $(\partial/\partial\theta_i)Q_n(\theta_n) = 0$, owing to the well-known first-order conditions for a minimum of $Q_n(\theta)$ at θ_n. These first-order conditions may not hold if θ_n lies on the boundary of Θ. However, since $\theta_n \to \theta_0$ in pr. and θ_0 is an interior point of Θ, the probability that θ_n is an interior point of Θ will converge to 1, hence

$$\lim_{n\to\infty} P[(\partial/\partial\theta_i)Q_n(\theta_n) = 0] = 1. \quad (4.2.7)$$

Next consider the m × m random matrix

$$\hat{A}_2 = [(\partial/\partial\theta_{i_1})(\partial/\partial\theta_{i_2})Q_n(\theta_n^{(i_2)})] \quad (4.2.8)$$

Then it follows from (4.2.5) and (4.2.7) that

$$\lim_{n\to\infty} P[\surd n(\theta_n - \theta_0) = -\hat{A}_2^{-1}\surd n(\partial/\partial\theta')Q_n(\theta_0)] = 1,$$

hence

$$\text{plim}_{n\to\infty}[\surd n(\theta_n - \theta_0) + (\hat{A}_2^{-1} - A_2^{-1})\surd n(\partial/\partial\theta')Q_n(\theta_0) + A_2^{-1}\surd n(\partial/\partial\theta')Q_n(\theta_0)] = 0. \quad (4.2.9)$$

If

$$\text{plim}_{n\to\infty}(\hat{A}_2^{-1} - A_2^{-1}) = O \quad (4.2.10)$$

then it follows from condition (iii) and theorems 2.3.3 and 2.3.5 that

$$\text{plim}_{n\to\infty}(\hat{A}_2^{-1} - A_2^{-1})\surd n(\partial/\partial\theta')Q_n(\theta_0) = 0. \quad (4.2.11)$$

Combining (4.2.9) and (4.2.11) we then conclude

$$\text{plim}_{n\to\infty}[\surd n(\theta_n - \theta_0) + A_2^{-1}\surd n(\partial/\partial\theta')Q_n(\theta_0)] = 0. \quad (4.2.12)$$

Since condition (iii) implies

$$-A_2^{-1}\surd n(\partial/\partial\theta')Q_n(\theta_0) \to N_m(0, A_2^{-1}A_1A_2^{-1}) \quad (4.2.13)$$

(note that A_2 is symmetric), it follows from (4.2.12) and theorem 2.3.5 that

$$\surd n(\theta_n - \theta_0) \to N_m(0, A_2^{-1}A_1A_2^{-1}) \text{ in distr.}$$

Thus for proving the theorem it remains to show that (4.2.10) holds and that the mean values are indeed properly defined random vectors. For proving (4.2.10), observe from (4.2.6) that $\text{plim}_{n\to\infty}\theta_n = \theta_0$ implies

$$\text{plim}_{n\to\infty}\theta_n^{(i)} = \theta_0,\ i=1,2,\ldots,m. \quad (4.2.14)$$

From (4.2.14), condition (iv), and theorem 2.6.1 it follows now that

$$\text{plim}_{n\to\infty}\hat{A}_2 = A_2 \quad (4.2.15)$$

Finally, since the elements of an inverse matrix are continuous functions of the elements of the inverted matrix, provided the latter is nonsingular, it follows from (4.2.15), condition (v) and theorem 2.1.7 that

$\text{plim}_{n\to\infty}\hat{A}_2^{-1} = A_2^{-1}$,

which proves (4.2.10).

We now conclude our proof with the following lemma of Jennrich:

> *Lemma 4.2.1* Let $f(x,\theta)$ be a real-valued function on $R^k \times \Theta$, where Θ is a convex compact subset of R^m. For each θ in Θ let $f(x,\theta)$ be a Borel measurable function on R^k and for each $x \in R^k$ let $f(x,\theta)$ be a continuously differentiable function on Θ. Let $\theta_1(x)$ and $\theta_2(x)$ be Borel measurable functions from R^k into Θ. Then there exists a Borel measurable function $\theta_*(x)$ from R^k into Θ such that
>
> (i) $f(x,\theta_1(x)) - f(x,\theta_2(x)) = (\partial/\partial\theta)f(x,\theta_*(x))(\theta_1(x) - \theta_2(x))$,
>
> (ii) $\theta_*(x)$ lies on the segment joining $\theta_1(x)$ and $\theta_2(x)$.

Proof: Jennrich (1969, lemma 3).

Thus, it follows from condition (i) and lemma 4.2.1 that the mean values $\theta_n^{(i)}$ are measurable and that

$|\theta_n^{(i)} - \theta_0| \le |\theta_n - \theta_0|$ a.s. Q.E.D.

Exercises

1. Let $Y_1,...,Y_n$ be independent standard normally distributed random variables. Let

   $Q_n(\theta) = (1/n)\sum_{j=1}^{n}|Y_j - \theta|$, $\Theta = [a,b]$, $-\infty < a < 0 < b < \infty$.

   Let θ_n be defined as in theorem 4.2.1. Prove $\theta_n \to 0$ a.s. (Hint: Use theorems 2.7.5 and 4.2.1.)
2. Let $Y_1,...,Y_n$ be i.i.d. random variables satisfying

   $P(Y_j = 1) = P(Y_j = -1) = \frac{1}{2}$.

   Let

   $Q_n(\theta) = (1/n)\sum_{j=1}^{n}(Y_j - \theta)^4$

   and let Θ be as in exercise 1.

   (a) Prove $\theta_n \to 0$ a.s.

   (b) Prove $\sqrt{n}\theta_n \to N(0,\sigma^2)$ in distr.

   (c) Determine σ^2.

4.3 Consistency and asymptotic normality of nonlinear least squares estimators in the i.i.d. case

4.3.1 Consistency

We now consider the case where $(Y_1,X_1),\ldots,(Y_n,X_n),\ldots$ are independent identically distributed random vectors in $R\times R^k$, and we verify the conditions for consistency and asymptotic normality in section 4.2 for the nonlinear least squares estimator. Thus, we augment assumption 4.1.1 with:

> *Assumption 4.3.1* The random vectors (Y_j,X_j), $j=1,2,\ldots,n,\ldots$ are independent random drawings from a $k+1$-variate distribution. Moreover, $E(Y_j^2) < \infty$.

For proving strong consistency we use theorem 2.7.5 in order to show (4.2.1). First,

> *Assumption 4.3.2* Let $E[\sup_{\theta\in\Theta} f(X_1,\theta)^2] < \infty$.

Then

$$E[\sup_{\theta\in\Theta}(Y_1 - f(X_1,\theta))]^2] \leq 2E(Y_1^2)+2E[\sup_{\theta\in\Theta} f(X_1,\theta)^2] < \infty, \quad (4.3.1)$$

hence by theorem 2.7.5

$$\sup_{\theta\in\Theta}|\hat{Q}(\theta)-Q(\theta)| \to 0 \text{ a.s.}, \quad (4.3.2)$$

where

$$Q(\theta) = E\{[Y_1-f(X_1,\theta)]^2\}. \quad (4.3.3)$$

From assumption 4.1.1 it follows that

$$Y_1 = f(X_1,\theta_0) + U_1, \text{ with } E(U_1|X_1) = 0 \text{ a.s.} \quad (4.3.4)$$

hence

$$\begin{aligned} Q(\theta) &= E(U_1^2)+2E[U_1(f(X_1,\theta_0)-f(X_1,\theta))]+E[(f(X_1,\theta_0)-f(X_1,\theta))^2] \\ &= E(U_1^2)+E[(f(X_1,\theta_0)-f(X_1,\theta))^2]. \end{aligned} \quad (4.3.5)$$

Note that $E(Y_1^2)<\infty$ implies $E(U_1^2)<\infty$. Since $f(x,\theta)$ is continuous in θ for each $x \in R^k$ (cf. assumption 4.1.1), Q is continuous on Θ. Now assume:

> *Assumption 4.3.3* $Q(\theta)$ takes a unique global minimum on Θ at $\theta = \theta_0$,

Referring to theorem 4.2.1 we then conclude:

Theorem 4.3.1. Under assumptions 4.1.1 and 4.3.1-4.3.3,$\hat{\theta} \to \theta_0$ a.s.

4.3.2 Asymptotic normality

Next we set forth the conditions for asymptotic normality by specializing the conditions of theorem 4.2.2. First,

> *Assumption 4.3.4* Let Θ be convex, let θ_0 be an interior point of Θ and let $f(x,\theta)$ be twice continuously differentiable in θ for each $x \in R^k$.

Then the conditions (i) and (ii) of theorem 4.2.2 hold. Now consider the first and second derivatives of $\hat{Q}(\theta)$:

$$(\partial/\partial\theta')\hat{Q}(\theta) = (-2)(1/n)\textstyle\sum_{j=1}^{n}[Y_j - f(X_j,\theta)](\partial/\partial\theta'))f(X_j,\theta), \tag{4.3.6}$$

$$\begin{aligned}(\partial/\partial\theta)(\partial/\partial\theta')\hat{Q}(\theta) = {} & (-2)(1/n)\textstyle\sum_{j=1}^{n}[Y_j - f(X_j,\theta)](\partial/\partial\theta)(\partial/\partial\theta')f(X_j,\theta) \\ & + 2(1/n)\textstyle\sum_{j=1}^{n}[(\partial/\partial\theta')f(X_j,\theta)][(\partial/\partial\theta)f(X_j,\theta)].\end{aligned} \tag{4.3.7}$$

> *Assumption 4.3.5* Let for $i,i_1,i_2 = 1,2,...,m$,
> $E\{\sup_{\theta\in\Theta}[(\partial/\partial\theta_i)f(X_1,\theta)]^2\} < \infty$;
> $E\{\sup_{\theta\in\Theta}[\partial/\partial\theta_{i_1})(\partial/\partial\theta_{i_2})f(X_1,\theta)]^2\} < \infty$.

Then by the Cauchy–Schwarz inequality,

$$\begin{aligned}&E\{\sup_{\theta\in\Theta}|[(\partial/\partial\theta_{i_1})f(X_1,\theta)][(\partial/\partial\theta_{i_2})f(X_1,\theta)]|\} \\ &\quad \le (E\{\sup_{\theta\in\Theta}[(\partial/\partial\theta_{i_1})f(X_1,\theta)]^2\})^{1/2} \\ &\quad \times (E\{\sup_{\theta\in\Theta}[(\partial/\partial\theta_{i_2})f(X_1,\theta)]^2\})^{1/2} < \infty\end{aligned} \tag{4.3.8}$$

and

$$\begin{aligned}&E\{\sup_{\theta\in\Theta}|[Y_1 - f(X_1,\theta)](\partial/\partial\theta_{i_1})(\partial/\partial\theta_{i_2})f(X_1,\theta)|\} \\ &\quad \le \{E[\sup_{\theta\in\Theta}(Y_1 - f(X_1,\theta)])^2]\}^{1/2} \\ &\quad \times \{E[\sup_{\theta\in\Theta}((\partial/\partial\theta_{i_1})(\partial/\partial\theta_{i_2})f(X_1,\theta)]^2\}^{1/2} < \infty\end{aligned} \tag{4.3.9}$$

where the last inequality follows partly from (4.3.1). Using theorem 2.7.5 we now conclude from (4.3.8) and (4.3.9) that for $i_1,i_2 = 1,2,...,m$.

$$\sup_{\theta\in\Theta}|(\partial/\partial\theta_{i_1})(\partial/\partial\theta_{i_2})\hat{Q}(\theta) - E[(\partial/\partial\theta_{i_1})(\partial/\partial\theta_{i_2})\hat{Q}(\theta)]| \to 0 \text{ a.s.} \tag{4.3.10}$$

which proves condition (iv) of theorem 4.2.2. Now consider the matrix A_2:

$$\begin{aligned}A_2 = (\partial/\partial\theta)(\partial/\partial\theta')Q(\theta_0) &= E(\partial/\partial\theta)(\partial/\partial\theta')\hat{Q}(\theta_0) \\ &= -2\,E[Y_1 - f(X_1,\theta_0)](\partial/\partial\theta)(\partial/\partial\theta')f(X_1,\theta_0) \\ &\quad + 2\,E[(\partial/\partial\theta')f(X_1,\theta_0)][(\partial/\partial\theta)f(X_1,\theta_0)].\end{aligned} \tag{4.3.11}$$

Since $E[Y_1 - f(X_1,\theta_0)|X_1] = E(U_1|X_1) = 0$ a.s., the first term vanishes. Thus:

$$A_2 = 2\Omega_2, \tag{4.3.12}$$

where

$$\Omega_2 = E[(\partial/\partial\theta')f(X_1,\theta_0)][(\partial/\partial\theta)f(X_1,\theta_0)]. \tag{4.3.13}$$

Assumption 4.3.6 Let Ω_2 be nonsingular.

Then condition (v) of theorem 4.2.2 is satisfied. So it remains to show that condition (iii) of theorem 4.2.2 holds. Observe from (4.3.4) and (4.3.6) that

$$(\partial/\partial\theta')\hat{Q}(\theta_0) = -2(1/n)\textstyle\sum_{j=1}^n U_j(\partial/\partial\theta')f(X_j,\theta_0) = -2(1/n)\sum_{j=1}^n Z_j, \tag{4.3.14}$$

say, where (Z_j), $j=1,2,...$, is a sequence of i.i.d. random vectors in R^k with

$$E(Z_1) = E[U_1(\partial/\partial\theta')f(X_1,\theta_0)] = E\{E[(U_1|X_1)(\partial/\partial\theta')f(X_1,\theta_0)]\} = 0 \tag{4.3.15}$$

(for $E(U_1|X_1) = 0$ a.s.). Moreover,

$$E(Z_1Z_1') = E(U_1^2\{(\partial/\partial\theta')f(X_1,\theta_0)\}\{(\partial/\partial\theta)f(X_1,\theta_0)\}) = \Omega_1, \tag{4.3.16}$$

say. If

Assumption 4.3.7 For $i_1,i_2=1,2,...,m$,
$E\{\sup_{\theta\in\Theta}[Y_1 - f(X_1,\theta)]^2|(\partial/\partial\theta_{i_1})f(X_1,\theta)||(\partial/\partial\theta_{i_2})f(X_1,\theta)|\} < \infty$,

then the elements of the matrix Ω_1 are finite, hence we may apply theorem 2.4.1 to arbitrary linear combinations $\xi'Z_j$ ($\xi \in R^m$):

$$(1/\sqrt{n})\textstyle\sum_{j=1}^n \xi'Z_j \to N(0,\xi'\Omega_1\xi) \text{ in distr.} \tag{4.3.17}$$

From theorem 2.3.7 we then conclude:

$$(1/\sqrt{n})\textstyle\sum_{j=1}^n Z_j \to N_m(0,\Omega_1) \text{ in distr.} \tag{4.3.18}$$

Thus

$$\sqrt{n}(\partial/\partial\theta')\hat{Q}(\theta_0) \to N_m(0,4\Omega_1) \text{ in distr.}$$

This proves condition (iii) of theorem 4.2.2 with $A_1 = 4\Omega_1$. Summarizing, we have shown:

Theorem 4.3.2. Under the conditions of theorem 4.3.1 and the additional assumptions 4.3.4–4.3.7 we have:

$$\sqrt{n}(\hat{\theta} - \theta_0) \to N_m(0,\Omega_2^{-1}\Omega_1\Omega_2^{-1}) \text{ in distr.,}$$

where Ω_1 and Ω_2 are defined by (4.3.16) and (4.3.13), respectively.

Cf. White (1980b). Quite often it is assumed that U_j is independent of X_j or that

Assumption 4.3.8. $E(U_1^2|X_1) = E(U_1^2) = \sigma^2$ a.s.

Then $\Omega_1 = \sigma^2\Omega_2$, and moreover assumption 4.3.7 then follows from assumption 4.3.5 and the condition $E(Y_1^2) < \infty$. Thus:

Theorem 4.3.3. Under the conditions of theorem 4.3.2, with assumption 4.3.7 replaced by assumption 4.3.8, we have:

$\surd n(\hat{\theta} - \theta_0) \to N_m[0,\sigma^2\Omega_2^{-1}]$ in distr.

4.3.3 *Consistent estimation of the asymptotic variance matrix*

Finally, we turn to the problem of how to consistently estimate the asymptotic variance matrices in theorems 4.3.2 and 4.3.3. Let

$$\hat{\Omega}_1(\theta) = (1/n)\sum_{j=1}^{n}[Y_j - f(X_j,\theta)]^2[(\partial/\partial\theta')f(X_j,\theta)][(\partial/\partial\theta)f(X_j,\theta)] \quad (4.3.19)$$

$$\hat{\Omega}_2(\theta) = (1/n)\sum_{j=1}^{n}[(\partial/\partial\theta')f(X_j,\theta)][\partial/\partial\theta)f(X_j,\theta)] \quad (4.3.20)$$

$$\hat{\Omega}_1 = \hat{\Omega}_1(\hat{\theta}),\ \hat{\Omega}_2 = \hat{\Omega}_2(\hat{\theta}),\ \hat{\sigma}^2 = \hat{Q}(\hat{\theta}) \quad (4.3.21)$$

We have shown that under the conditions of theorem 4.3.2:

$$\hat{\Omega}_1(\theta) \to E[\hat{\Omega}_1(\theta)] \text{ a.s. uniformly on } \Theta, \quad (4.3.22)$$

$$\hat{\Omega}_2(\theta) \to E[\hat{\Omega}_2(\theta)] \text{ a.s. uniformly on } \Theta, \quad (4.3.23)$$

$$\hat{Q}(\theta) \to E[\hat{Q}(\theta)] \text{ a.s. uniformly on } \Theta, \quad (4.3.24)$$

and

$$\Omega_1 = E[\hat{\Omega}_1(\theta_0)],\ \Omega_2 = E[\hat{\Omega}_2(\theta_0)],\ \sigma^2 = E(U_1^2) = E[\hat{Q}(\theta_0)]$$

From theorems 2.6.1 and 4.3.1 it therefore follows:

$$\hat{\Omega}_1 \to \Omega_1 \text{ a.s.};\ \hat{\Omega}_2 \to \Omega_2 \text{ a.s.};\ \hat{\sigma}^2 \to \sigma^2 \text{ a.s.}; \quad (4.3.25)$$

hence, using theorem 2.1.7, we have:

Theorem 4.3.4 Under the conditions of theorem 4.3.2,
$\hat{\Omega}_2^{-1}\hat{\Omega}_1\hat{\Omega}_2^{-1} \to \Omega_2^{-1}\Omega_1\Omega_2^{-1}$ a.s.,
and under the conditions of theorem 4.3.3 we have:

$\hat{\sigma}^2\hat{\Omega}_2^{-1} \to \sigma^2\Omega_2^{-1}$ a.s.

Exercises

1. Verify the conditions for strong consistency and asymptotic normality of $\hat{\theta}$ for the standard linear regression model $Y_j = \theta_0'X_j + U_j$, where U_j and X_j are mutually independent.
2. Suppose that $f(x,\theta)$ is *incorrectly* specified as $\theta'x$, with $\theta \in \Theta \subset R^k$, $x \in R^k$. Set forth conditions such that $\hat{\theta} \to \theta_0$ a.s. and

   $$\sqrt{}n(\hat{\theta}-\theta_0) \to N_k(0,[E(X_1X_1')]^{-1}\{E[(Y_1-\theta_0'X_1)X_1X_1'][E(X_1X_1')]^{-1})$$

   in distr., where $\theta_0 = [E(X_1X_1')]^{-1}E(X_1Y_1)]$. Cf. White (1980a).

4.4 Consistency and asymptotic normality of nonlinear least squares estimators under data heterogeneity

4.4.1 Data heterogeneity

In medicine, biology, psychology, and physics the source of the data set $\{(Y_j,X_j)\}$, $j=1,\ldots,n$, is quite often a statistical experiment, where Y_j is the outcome of the experiment and X_j is a vector of control variables set by the analyst. In this case the vector X_j is in fact non-random. However, non-random variables or vectors may be considered as random variables or vectors, respectively, taking a value with probability 1. Thus, if (x_j), $j=1,2,\ldots$ is a sequence of control vectors then we define:

$$X_j = x_j \text{ a.s.}$$

The distribution function of X_j is then

$$H_j(x) = \prod_{\ell=1}^{k} I(X_{\ell j} \leqslant x^{(\ell)}),$$

where $I(.)$ is the indicator function and $X_{\ell j}$ and $x^{(\ell)}$ are the ℓ-th components of X_j and x, respectively. Moreover, suppose

$$E(Y_j) = g(x_j),\ U_j = Y_j - g(x_j).$$

Then

$$Y_j = g(X_j) + U_j \text{ a.s.},$$

where $E(U_j) = 0$ and U_j is independent of X_j. The joint distribution function $F_j(y,x)$ of (Y_j,X_j) is now:

$$F_j(y,x) = P[U_j \leq y - g(x_j)]H_j(x).$$

These kind of data-generating processes will be called *heterogeneous*. Data heterogeneity also occurs when the sample is stratified. For example, let Y_j be the expenditures of household j on a certain commodity and let X_j be the disposable income of household j. We wish to estimate the Engel curve $E(Y_j|X_j)$ (cf. Cramer [1969]) on the basis of a stratified sample of size n with q strata of different sizes n_i $(i=1,\ldots,q, n=n_1+\ldots+n_q)$, corresponding to q income classes. Then the distribution of (Y_j,X_j) depends on the stratum to which j belongs. See further White (1980b). In order to cover data heterogeneity as well, we now augment assumption 4.1.1 with:

Assumption 4.4.1 The random vectors (Y_j,X_j), $j=1,2,\ldots,n,\ldots$ are independent with joint distribution functions $F_j(y,x)$, $j=1,2,\ldots,n,\ldots$, respectively. Moreover, denoting

$$F^{(n)}(y,x) = (1/n)\sum_{j=1}^{n}F_j(y,x),$$

one of the following alternative conditions holds:
(a) $F^{(n)} \to F$ properly setwise,
(b) $F^{(n)} \to F$ properly pointwise, and $f(x,\theta)$ is continuous in both of its arguments.

The distinction between the alternatives (a) and (b) is due to the distinction between the conditions of theorems 2.7.1–2.7.4, i.e., under assumption 4.4.1a we shall apply theorems 2.7.3 and 2.7.4 and under assumption 4.4.1b we shall apply theorems 2.7.1 and 2.7.2.

4.4.2 Strong and weak consistency

Now let us modify the assumptions of section 4.3 to the case under consideration. Depending on whether we wish to prove weak consistency, i.e..

$$\text{plim}_{n\to\infty}\hat{\theta} = \theta_0,$$

or strong consistency, i.e.,

$$\hat{\theta} \to \theta_0 \text{ a.s.}$$

we assume either

Assumption 4.4.2(i). Let, for some $\delta > 0$,

$$\sup_n(1/n)\sum_{j=1}^{n}E[\sup_{\theta\in\Theta}|Y_j - f(X_j,\theta)|^{2+\delta}] < \infty,$$

or

Assumption 4.4.2(ii). Let, for some $\delta > 0$,

$$\sup_n(1/n)\sum_{j=1}^{n}E[\sup_{\theta\in\Theta}|Y_j - f(X_j,\theta)|^{4+\delta}] < \infty.$$

Denoting

$$Q(\theta) = \int(y-f(x,\theta))^2dF(y,x), \tag{4.4.1}$$

it follows from assumptions 4.1.1, 4.4.1, and 4.4.2(i) and theorems 2.7.2 and 2.7.4 that

$$\text{plim}_{n\to\infty}\sup_{\theta\in\Theta}|\hat{Q}(\theta) - Q(\theta)| = 0, \tag{4.4.2}$$

whereas from assumptions 4.1.1, 4.4.1, 4.4.2.(ii) and theorems 2.7.1 and 2.7.3 it follows that:

$$\sup_{\theta\in\Theta}|\hat{Q}(\theta) - Q(\theta)| \to 0 \text{ a.s.} \tag{4.4.3}$$

Moreover, in both cases the limit function $Q(\theta)$ is continuous. Furthermore, it follows from theorems 2.5.1 and 2.5.4 that

$$\begin{aligned} Q(\theta) &= \lim_{n\to\infty}E[\hat{Q}(\theta)] = \lim_{n\to\infty}(1/n)\sum_{j=1}^{n}E\{[U_j + f(X_j,\theta_0) - f(X_j,\theta)]^2\} \\ &= \lim_{n\to\infty}(1/n)\sum_{j=1}^{n}E(U_j^2) + \lim_{n\to\infty}(1/n)\sum_{j=1}^{n}E\{[f(X_j,\theta_0) - f(X_j,\theta)]^2\}; \end{aligned} \tag{4.4.4}$$

hence

$$Q(\theta_0) = \inf_{\theta\in\Theta}Q(\theta). \tag{4.4.5}$$

Thus, if

Assumption 4.4.3 $Q(\theta)$ takes a unique minimum on Θ,

then by theorem 4.2.1

Theorem 4.4.1.

(i) Under assumptions 4.1.1, 4.4.1, 4.4.2(i) and 4.4.3, $\text{plim}_{n\to\infty}\hat{\theta} = \theta_0$.

(ii) Under assumptions 4.1.1, 4.4.1, 4.4.2(ii) and 4.4.3, $\hat{\theta} \to \theta_0$ a.s.

4.4.3 Asymptotic normality

Next we shall modify the assumptions 4.3.4–4.3.8 such that we may replace the reference to theorem 2.7.5 by references to theorems 2.7.2 and 2.7.4, and the reference to theorem 2.4.1 by a reference to theorem 2.4.3.

Assumption 4.4.4 Let assumption 4.3.4 hold. If part (b) of assumption 4.4.1 holds then the first and second partial derivatives of $f(x,\theta)$ to θ are continuous in both arguments.

Assumption 4.4.5 Let for some $\delta > 0$ and $i,i_1,i_2 = 1,2,\ldots,m$,

$$\sup_n(1/n)\sum_{j=1}^{n}E[\sup_{\theta\in\Theta}|(\partial/\partial\theta_i)f(X_j,\theta)|^{2+\delta}] < \infty;$$
$$\sup_n(1/n)\sum_{j=1}^{n}E[\sup_{\theta\in\Theta}|(\partial/\partial\theta_{i_1})(\partial/\partial\theta_{i_2})f(X_j,\theta)|^{2+\delta}] < \infty.$$

Assumption 4.4.6 The matrix

$$\Omega_2 = \int[(\partial/\partial\theta')f(x,\theta_0)][(\partial/\partial\theta)f(x,\theta_0)]dF(y,x)$$

is nonsingular.

Assumption 4.4.7 Let for some $\delta > 0$ and $i_1,i_2 = 1,2,...,m$,

$$\sup_n(1/n)\sum_{j=1}^n E[\sup_{\theta\in\Theta}|Y_j - f(X_j,\theta)|^{2+\delta}|(\partial/\partial\theta_{i_1})f(X_j,\theta)|^{1+\delta} \times |(\partial/\partial\theta_{i_2})f(X_j,\theta)|^{1+\delta}] < \infty.$$

Assumption 4.4.8 For $j = 1,2,...$, $E(U_j^2|X_j) = E(U_j^2) = \sigma^2$ a.s.

Moreover, let

$$\Omega_1 = \int[y - f(x,\theta_0)]^2[(\partial/\partial\theta')f(x,\theta_0)][(\partial/\partial\theta)f(x,\theta_0)]dF(y,x).$$

Then similarly to theorems 4.3.2, 4.3.3, and 4.3.4 we have:

Theorem 4.4.2 Let the conditions of theorem 4.4.1(i) be satisfied.

(i) Under the additional assumptions 4.4.4–4.4.7 we have:

$$\sqrt{n}(\hat{\theta} - \theta_0) \to N_m[0,\Omega_2^{-1}\Omega_1\Omega_2^{-1}] \text{ in distr.},$$
$$\text{plim}_{n\to\infty}\hat{\Omega}_2^{-1}\hat{\Omega}_1\hat{\Omega}_2^{-1} = \Omega_2^{-1}\Omega_1\Omega_2^{-1}.$$

(ii) Under the additional asumptions 4.4.4–4.4.6 and 4.4.8 we have:

$$\sqrt{n}(\hat{\theta} - \theta_0) \to N_m(0,\sigma^2\Omega_2^{-1}) \text{ in distr. and}$$
$$\text{plim}_{n\to\infty}\hat{\sigma}^2\hat{\Omega}_2^{-1} = \sigma^2\Omega_2^{-1}.$$

4.5 Maximum likelihood theory

The theory in section 4.2 is straightforwardly applicable to maximum likelihood (ML) estimation as well. Although we assume that the reader is familiar with the basics of ML theory, say on the level of Hogg and Craig (1978), we shall briefly review here the asymptotic properties of ML estimators, for the case of a random sample from a continuous distribution.

Let $Z_1,...,Z_n$ be a random sample from an absolutely continuous k-variate distribution with density function $h(z|\theta_0)$, where θ_0 is an unknown parameter vector in a known parameter space $\Theta \subset R^m$. We assume that

Assumption 4.5.1 The parameter space Θ is convex and compact. For each $z \in R^k$, $h(z|\theta)$ is twice continuously differentiable on Θ. Moreover, the following conditions hold for *each* interior point θ_0 of Θ:

(i) $\int \sup_{\theta\in\Theta}|\ln(h(z|\theta))|h(z|\theta_0)dz < \infty$;

(ii) For i,r,s = 1,...,m,

$\int \sup_{\theta\in\Theta}|(\partial/\partial\theta_i)\ln(h(z|\theta))|^2 h(z|\theta_0)dz < \infty$,
$\int \sup_{\theta\in\Theta}|(\partial/\partial\theta_i)h(z|\theta)|dz < \infty$,
$\int \sup_{\theta\in\theta}|(\partial/\partial\theta_r)(\partial/\partial\theta_s)\ln(h(z|\theta))|h(z|\theta_0)dz < \infty$,
$\int \sup_{\theta\in\Theta}|(\partial/\partial\theta_r)(\partial/\partial\theta_s)h(z|\theta)|dz < \infty$.

(iii) The function

$$\ell(\theta|\theta_0) = \int \ln(h(z|\theta))h(z|\theta_0)dz \tag{4.5.1}$$

has a *unique* supremum on Θ.

(iv) The matrix

$$H(\theta_0) = \int\{(\partial/\partial\theta_0')\ln(h(z|\theta_0))\}\{(\partial/\partial\theta_0)\ln(h(z|\theta_0))\}h(z|\theta_0)dz \tag{4.5.2}$$

is nonsingular.

Assumptions 4.5.1(i)–(iii) are just what are often termed in intermediate statistics and econometrics textbooks "some mild regularity conditions." In particular, condition (ii) allows us to take derivatives of integrals by integrating the corresponding derivatives:

Lemma 4.5.1 Let assumption 4.5.1(ii) hold. For i,r,s = 1,...,m and every pair of interior points θ and θ_0 of Θ,

(a) $\int(\partial/\partial\theta_i)\ln(h(z|\theta))h(z|\theta_0)dz = (\partial/\partial\theta_i)\int\ln(h(z|\theta))h(z|\theta_0)dz$;

(b) $\int(\partial/\partial\theta_r)(\partial/\partial\theta_s)\ln(h(z|\theta)h(z|\theta_0)dz$
$= (\partial/\partial\theta_r)(\partial/\partial\theta_s)\int\ln(h(z|\theta))h(z|\theta_0)dz$;

(c) $\int(\partial/\partial\theta_i)h(z|\theta)dz = \int(\partial/\partial\theta_r)(\partial/\partial\theta_s)h(z|\theta)dz = 0$.

Proof: Let e_i be the i-th unit vector in R^m. Then

$$(\partial/\partial\theta_i)\ln(h(z|\theta)) = \lim_{\delta\to 0}\delta^{-1}[\ln(h(z|\theta+\delta e_i)) - \ln(h(z|\theta))],$$

whereas by the mean value theorem

$$|\delta^{-1}[\ln(h(z|\theta+\delta e_i)) - \ln(h(z|\theta))]| \leq \delta^{-1}\sup_{\theta\in\Theta}|(\partial/\partial\theta_i)(\partial/\partial\theta)\ln(h(z|\theta))|.$$

The result (a) therefore follows from the dominated convergence theorem 2.2.2. Similarly, so do (b) and (c). Q.E.D.

A direct corollary of lemma 4.5.1 is that

$$(\partial/\partial\theta')\int \ln(h(z|\theta))h(z|\theta_0)dz = 0 \text{ at } \theta = \theta_0; \quad (4.5.3)$$

$$(\partial/\partial\theta)(\partial/\partial\theta')\int \ln(h(z|\theta))h(z|\theta_0)dz = -H(\theta_0) \text{ at } \theta = \theta_0; \quad (4.5.4)$$

hence the first- and second-order conditions for a maximum of $\int \ln(h(z|\theta))h(z|\theta_0)dz$ in θ_0 are satisfied:

Lemma 4.5.2 Under assumption 4.5.1, the function $\ell(\theta|\theta_0)$ [cf. (4.5.1)]) takes a unique supremum on Θ at $\theta = \theta_0$.

The ML estimator $\hat{\theta}$ of θ_0 is now defined as a measurable solution of the maximization problem $\sup_{\theta\in\Theta} L_n(Z|\theta)$, or equivalently $\sup_{\theta\in\Theta}\ln(L_n(Z|\theta))$, where

$$L_n(Z|\theta) = \prod_{j=1}^{n} h(Z_j|\theta), \text{ with } Z = (Z_1',...,Z_n')', \quad (4.5.5)$$

is the likelihood function. Denoting $Q_n(\theta) = \ln(L_n(Z|\theta))/n$ and

$$\hat{H} = (1/n)\sum_{j=1}^{n}[(\partial/\partial\theta')\ln(h(Z_j|\hat{\theta}))\}\{(\partial/\partial\theta)\ln(h(Z_j|\hat{\theta}))], \quad (4.5.6)$$

it follows straightforwardly from theorems 4.2.1–4.2.2 that:

Theorem 4.5.1 Under assumption 4.5.1, $\hat{\theta} \to \theta_0$ a.s., $\sqrt{n}(\hat{\theta} - \theta_0) \to N_m(0,H(\theta_0)^{-1})$ in distribution and $\hat{H} \to H(\theta_0)$ a.s.

Proof: Exercise 1.

Least squares estimators and ML estimators are members of the class of so-called M-estimators. A typical M-estimator $\tilde{\theta}$ is obtained by maximizing an objective function of the form

$$Q_n(\theta) = (1/n)\sum_{j=1}^{n}\varphi(Z_j,\theta). \quad (4.5.7)$$

For example, in the case of least squares estimation of a nonlinear regression model $Y_j = g(X_j,\theta_0) + U_j$, we have $-\varphi(Z_j,\theta) = (Y_j - g(X_j,\theta))^2$, with $Z_j = (Y_j,X_j')'$. Moreover, if U_j is independent of X_j and the distribution of U_j is symmetric unimodal, one may choose $\varphi(Z_j,\theta) = \rho(Y_j - g(X_j,\theta))$ with $\rho(.)$ a symmetric unimodal density. Cf. Bierens (1981).

Now let the Z_j's be the same as before, and assume in addition to assumption 4.5.1:

Assumption 4.5.2 For each $z \in R^k$, $\varphi(z,\theta)$ is twice continuously differentiable on $\Theta \subset R^m$, and for each $\theta \in \Theta$, $\varphi(z,\theta)$ is Borel measurable in z. Moreover, the following conditions (i)–(iv) hold for *each* interior point θ_0 of Θ:

(i) $\int \sup_{\theta\in\Theta}|\varphi(z,\theta)|h(z|\theta_0)dz < \infty$;

(ii) The function

$$\psi(\theta|\theta_0) = \int\varphi(z,\theta)h(z|\theta_0)dz \tag{4.5.8}$$

has a *unique* supremum on Θ at $\theta = \theta_0$.

(iii) For i,r,s = 1,...,m,

$\int\sup_{\theta\in\Theta}|(\partial/\partial\theta_i)\varphi(z,\theta)|^2h(z|\theta_0)dz < \infty$,
$\int\sup_{\theta\in\Theta}|(\partial/\partial\theta_r)(\partial/\partial\theta_s)\varphi(z,\theta)|h(z|\theta_0)dz < \infty$,
$\int\sup_{\theta\in\Theta}|[(\partial/\partial\theta_r)\varphi(z,\theta)][(\partial/\partial\theta_s)h(z|\theta)]|dz < \infty$.
$\int\sup_{\theta\in\Theta}|\varphi(z,\theta)(\partial/\partial\theta_r)(\partial/\partial\theta_s)h(z|\theta)|dz < \infty$.

(iv) The matrix

$$B(\theta_0) = \int[(\partial/\partial\theta_0)(\partial/\partial\theta_0')\varphi(z,\theta_0)]h(z|\theta_0)dz. \tag{4.5.9}$$

is nonsingular.

Denoting

$$A(\theta) = \int[(\partial/\partial\theta')\varphi(z,\theta)][(\partial/\partial\theta)\varphi(z,\theta)]h(z|\theta)dz, \tag{4.5.10}$$

it follows now that:

Theorem 4.5.2 Under assumptions 4.5.1–4.5.2, $\tilde{\theta} \to \theta_0$ a.s. and $\sqrt{n}(\tilde{\theta} - \theta_0) \to N_m(0,B(\theta_0)^{-1}A(\theta_0)B(\theta_0)^{-1})$ in distribution.

Proof: Exercise 2.

The position of the ML estimator within the class of M-estimators is a very special one, namely that of the asymptotic efficient estimator, i.e., the asymptotic variance matrix of the ML estimator is always "smaller" (or at least not "greater") than the asymptotic variance matrix of the typical M-estimator, in the following sense:

Theorem 4.5.3. Under assumptions 4.5.1–4.5.2, the matrix

$$B(\theta_0)^{-1}A(\theta_0)B(\theta_0)^{-1} - H(\theta_0)^{-1} \tag{4.5.11}$$

is positive semi-definite.

Proof: The first-order condition for a maximum of $\psi(\theta^*|\theta)$ in $\theta^* = \theta$ is: $\int[(\partial/\partial\theta')\varphi(z,\theta)]h(z|\theta)dz = 0$, for each interior point θ of Θ. Taking derivatives again it follows that

$$\begin{aligned} O &= (\partial/\partial\theta)\int[(\partial/\partial\theta')\varphi(z,\theta)]h(z|\theta)dz \\ &= \int[(\partial/\partial\theta)(\partial/\partial\theta')\varphi(z,\theta)]h(z|\theta)dz + \int[(\partial/\partial\theta')\varphi(z,\theta)][(\partial/\partial\theta)h(z|\theta)]dz, \end{aligned} \tag{4.5.12}$$

where assumptions 4.5.1–4.5.2 allow us to take the derivatives inside the integrals. Consequently, we have

$$\int[(\partial/\partial\theta')\varphi(z,\theta)][(\partial/\partial\theta)\ln(h(z|\theta))]h(z|\theta)dz = -B(\theta). \tag{4.5.13}$$

This is the main key for the proof of the asymptotic efficiency of ML estimation. The rest of the proof below is quite similar to the derivation of the Cramer–Rao lower bound of the variance of an unbiased estimator.

It is not hard to show (cf. exercise 2) that

$$\sqrt{n}(\tilde{\theta} - \theta_0) = V_n + o_p(1), \tag{4.5.14}$$

where

$$V_n = B(\theta_0)^{-1}(1/\sqrt{n})\sum_{j=1}^{n}(\partial/\partial\theta')\varphi(Z_j,\theta_0) \tag{4.5.15}$$

and $o_p(1)$ denotes a random variable that converges in probability to zero. Moreover, denote

$$W_n = (1/\sqrt{n})\sum_{j=1}^{n}(\partial/\partial\theta')\ln(h(Z_j|\theta_0)). \tag{4.5.16}$$

Then

$$\mathrm{var}(V_n) = B(\theta_0)^{-1}A(\theta_0)B(\theta_0)^{-1} \text{ and } \mathrm{var}(W_n) = H(\theta_0), \tag{4.5.17}$$

whereas by (4.5.13) and (4.5.14),

$$\mathrm{covar}(V_n,W_n) = \mathrm{covar}(W_n,V_n) = -I. \tag{4.5.18}$$

It follows now from (4.5.17) and (4.5.18) that

$$M = \begin{pmatrix} B(\theta_0)^{-1}A(\theta_0)B(\theta_0)^{-1} & -I \\ -I & H(\theta_0) \end{pmatrix} \tag{4.5.19}$$

is the variance matrix of $(V_n',W_n')'$; hence M is positive semi-definite, and so is $SMS' = B(\theta_0)^{-1}A(\theta_0)B(\theta_0)^{-1} - H(\theta_0)^{-1}$, with $S=(I,H(\theta_0)^{-1})$.

Q.E.D.

Since the ML estimator is the efficient estimator, one may wonder why somebody would consider other, less efficient, estimators. The reason is robustness. ML estimation requires complete specification of the density $h(z|\theta)$. Only if $h(z|\theta) = h(z_1,z_2|\theta)$ can be written as $h_1(z_1|z_2,\theta)h_2(z_2)$, with h_1 the conditional density of h given z_2, and h_2 the marginal density, where only h_1 depends on θ, do we not need to know the functional form of h_2. For example, ML estimation of the regression model $Y_j = f(X_j,\theta_0) + U_j$ requires full specification of the conditional density of U_j relative to the event $X_j = x$, whereas least squares estimation requires the much weaker condition that $E(U_j|X_j) = 0$ a.s. Thus, since ML estimation employs more *a priori* information about the data-generating process than say least squares, it is not suprising that ML estimators are more efficient. However, this virtue also makes ML estimators vulnerable to deviations from the assumed distributions. For example, if the errors U_j of the regression model $Y_j = f(X_j,\theta_0) + U_j$ are independent of X_j but their distribution is non-normal with fat tails, while ML estimation is conducted under the assumption of normality of U_j, the "pseudo" ML estimator involved will be asymptotically less efficient than many alternative robust M-estimators. See Bierens (1981).

Often the ML estimator is more complicated to calculate than some alternative non-efficient M-estimators. Take, for example, the case of a linear regression model $Y_j = \alpha + \beta X_j + U_j$, where X_j and U_j are independent and the distribution of U_j is a mixture of two normal distributions, say N(0,1) and N(0,2), with mixture coefficient λ. Thus we assume that the density of U_j is

$$f(u) = \lambda \exp(-\tfrac{1}{2}u^2)/\surd(2\pi) + (1-\lambda)\exp(-\tfrac{1}{2}u^2/2)/\surd(4\pi), \qquad (4.5.20)$$

where $\lambda \in [0,1]$ is the mixture coefficient. Potscher and Prucha (1986) consider the similar but even more complicated problem of efficient estimation of a nonlinear time series regression model with t-distributed errors, and they propose the adaptive one-step M-estimator discussed below.

Denoting the possibly unknown density of X_j by g(x), the joint density of $(Y_j,X_j)'$ is now:

$$h(y,x|\alpha,\beta,\lambda) = \{\lambda \exp[-\tfrac{1}{2}(y-\alpha-\beta x)^2]/\surd(2\pi) \\ + (1-\lambda)\exp[-\tfrac{1}{2}(y-\alpha-\beta x)^2/2]/\surd(4\pi)\}g(x), \qquad (4.5.21)$$

hence the log-likelihood function takes the form

$$\ln(L_n(Z|\theta)) = \textstyle\sum_{j=1}^n \ln\{\lambda \exp[-\tfrac{1}{2}(Y_j-\alpha-\beta X_j)^2]/\surd(2\pi) \\ + (1-\lambda)\exp[-\tfrac{1}{2}(Y_j-\alpha-\beta X_j)^2/2]/\surd(4\pi)\} + \textstyle\sum_{j=1}^n \ln(g(X_j)), \quad (4.5.22)$$

where $Z = (Y_1,X_1,\ldots,Y_n,X_n)'$ and $\theta = (\alpha,\beta,\lambda)'$. Note that the term $\sum_{j=1}^n \ln(g(X_j))$ does not matter for the solution of $\sup_\theta \ln(L_n(Z|\theta))$.

Clearly, maximizing (4.5.22) with respect to θ is a highly nonlinear optimization problem. However, in the present case it is easy to obtain an asymptotically efficient estimator of θ by conducting a single Newton step starting from an initial estimator $\tilde{\theta}$ of θ for which $\surd n(\tilde{\theta}-\theta) = O_p(1)$, as follows.

Let $\tilde{\alpha}$ and $\tilde{\beta}$ be the OLS estimators of α and β, respectively, and let $\tilde{\sigma}^2 = (1/n)\sum_{j=1}^n (Y_j-\tilde{\alpha}-\tilde{\beta}X_j)^2$ be the usual estimator of the variance σ^2 of U_j. Since in the case under consideration $\sigma^2 = \lambda + 2(1-\lambda) = 2-\lambda$, we estimate λ by $\tilde{\lambda} = 2-\tilde{\sigma}^2$. Now let

$$\tilde{\theta} = (\tilde{\alpha},\tilde{\beta},\tilde{\lambda})'. \qquad (4.5.23)$$

It can be shown that if the (Y_j,X_j)'s are independent and $0 < E[|X_j-E(X_j)|^2] < \infty$, then $\surd n(\tilde{\theta}-\theta)$ converges in distribution to $N_3(0,\Omega)$, hence $\surd n(\tilde{\theta}-\theta) = O_p(1)$. Cf. theorem 2.5.9 and exercise 5.

The Newton method for finding a maximum or minimum of a twice differentiable function $\Phi(\theta)$ on R^m is based on the second-order Taylor approximation of $\Phi(\theta)$ about an initial point θ_1:

$$\Phi(\theta) \approx \Phi(\theta_1) + (\theta-\theta_1)'\Delta\Phi(\theta_1) + \tfrac{1}{2}(\theta-\theta_1)'\Delta^2\Phi(\theta_1)(\theta-\theta_1), \qquad (4.5.24)$$

where $\Delta\Phi(\theta) = (\partial/\partial\theta')\Phi(\theta)$ and $\Delta^2\Phi(\theta) = (\partial/\partial\theta)(\partial/\partial\theta')\Phi(\theta)$. Differentiating the right-hand side of (4.5.24) to θ and equating the results to zero yield the Newton step:

$$\theta_2 = \theta_1 - (\Delta^2\Phi(\theta_1))^{-1}\Delta\Phi(\theta_1). \qquad (4.5.25)$$

In the present case $\Phi(\theta) = \ln(L_n(Z|\theta))$ and $\theta_1 = \tilde{\theta}$, so the single Newton step estimator involved is:

$$\tilde{\tilde{\theta}} = \tilde{\theta} - [(\partial/\partial\theta)(\partial/\partial\theta')\ln(L_n(Z|\tilde{\theta}))]^{-1}(\partial/\partial\theta')\ln(L_n(Z|\tilde{\theta})). \qquad (4.5.26)$$

Theorem 4.5.4 Let the conditions of theorem 4.5.1 hold, and let $\tilde{\tilde{\theta}}$ be the single Newton step estimator (4.5.26), where the initial estimator $\tilde{\theta}$ is such that $\sqrt{n}(\tilde{\theta} - \theta_0) = O_p(1)$. Then $\sqrt{n}(\tilde{\tilde{\theta}} - \theta_0) \to N_m(0, H(\theta_0)^{-1})$.

Proof: We leave the details of the proof as an exercise (exercise 6). Here we shall only give some hints. First, let

$$\tilde{H} = -(1/n)(\partial/\partial\theta)(\partial/\partial\theta')\ln(L_n(Z|\tilde{\theta})) \qquad (4.5.27)$$

and prove that

$$\text{plim}_{n\to\infty}\tilde{H} = H(\theta_0). \qquad (4.5.28)$$

Next, using the mean value theorem, show that there exists a matrix $\tilde{\tilde{H}}$ such that

$$(1/\sqrt{n})(\partial/\partial\theta')\ln(L_n(Z|\tilde{\theta})) = (1/\sqrt{n})(\partial/\partial\theta')\ln(L_n(Z|\theta_0)) - \tilde{\tilde{H}}\sqrt{n}(\tilde{\theta} - \theta_0) \qquad (4.5.29)$$

and

$$\text{plim}_{n\to\infty}\tilde{\tilde{H}} = H(\theta_0). \qquad (4.5.30)$$

Then

$$\begin{aligned}\sqrt{n}(\tilde{\tilde{\theta}} - \theta_0) &= \sqrt{n}(\tilde{\theta} - \theta_0) + \tilde{H}^{-1}[(1/\sqrt{n})(\partial/\partial\theta')\ln(L_n(Z|\theta_0)) - \tilde{\tilde{H}}\sqrt{n}(\tilde{\theta} - \theta_0)] \\ &= (I - \tilde{H}^{-1}\tilde{\tilde{H}})\sqrt{n}(\tilde{\theta} - \theta_0) + \tilde{H}^{-1}[(1/\sqrt{n})(\partial/\partial\theta')\ln(L_n(Z|\theta_0))].\end{aligned} \qquad (4.5.31)$$

Finally, show that

$$\text{plim}_{n\to\infty}(I - \tilde{H}^{-1}\tilde{\tilde{H}})\sqrt{n}(\tilde{\theta} - \theta_0) = 0 \qquad (4.5.32)$$

and

$$\tilde{H}^{-1}[(1/\sqrt{n})(\partial/\partial\theta')\ln(L_n(Z|\theta_0))] \to N_m(0,H(\theta_0)^{-1}). \tag{4.5.33}$$

Q.E.D.

Exercises

1. Prove theorem 4.5.1.
2. Prove theorem 4.5.2.
3. Verify (4.5.18).
4. Let $Z_j = (Y_j, X_j)' \in R^2$, $j=1,..,.n$, be a random sample from a bivariate distribution, where $Y_j = \alpha + \beta X_j + \sigma U_j$ with U_j standard normally distributed and independent of X_j. The distribution of X_j is unknown. Let $\theta = (\alpha,\beta,\sigma^2)$. Derive the ML estimator $\hat{\theta}$ of θ and the asymptotic distribution of $\sqrt{n}(\hat{\theta}-\theta)$.
5. Prove that for the estimator (4.5.23), $\sqrt{n}(\tilde{\theta}-\theta) \to N_3(0,\Omega)$, and derive Ω.
6. Complete the details of the proof of theorem 4.5.4.

4.6 Testing parameter restrictions

4.6.1 The Wald test

Estimation of a regression model is usually not the final stage of regression analysis. What we actually want to know are the properties of the true model rather than those of the estimated model. Given the truth of the functional form, we thus want to make inference about the true parameter vector θ_0. Various restrictions on θ_0 may correspond to various theories about the phenomenon being studied. In particular, the theory of interest may correspond to a set of q (non)linear restrictions in θ_0, i.e.,

$$H_0\colon \eta_i(\theta_0) = 0 \text{ for } i=1,2,...,q \leq m \tag{4.6.1}$$

Throughout we assume that the functions η_i are continuously differentiable in a neighborhood of θ_0 and that the $q \times m$ matrix

$$\Gamma = [(\partial/\partial\theta_{i_2})\eta_{i_1}(\theta_0)] \tag{4.6.2}$$

has rank q. We now derive the limiting distribution of

$$\hat{\eta} = (\eta_1(\hat{\theta}),...,\eta_q(\hat{\theta}))'$$

under H_0, given that

$$\sqrt{n}(\hat{\theta}-\theta_0) \to N_m(0,\Omega), \tag{4.6.3}$$

where Ω is nonsingular, and that $\hat{\Omega}$ is a consistent estimator of Ω:

$$\text{plim}_{n\to\infty}\, \hat{\Omega} = \Omega. \tag{4.6.4}$$

Note that if $\hat{\theta}$ is a ML estimator, $\Omega = H(\theta_0)^{-1}$ and $\hat{\Omega} = \hat{H}^{-1}$.

Observe from the mean value theorem that

$$\sqrt{n}(\eta_i(\hat{\theta}) - \eta_i(\theta_0)) = [(\partial/\partial\theta)\eta_i(\hat{\theta}^{(i)})]\sqrt{n}(\hat{\theta} - \theta_0), \tag{4.6.5}$$

where $\hat{\theta}^{(i)}$ satisfies

$$|\hat{\theta}^{(i)} - \theta_0| \leq |\hat{\theta} - \theta_0| \text{ a.s.} \tag{4.6.6}$$

Since (4.6.3) and (4.6.6) imply $\text{plim}_{n\to\infty}\hat{\theta}^{(i)} = \theta_0$, it follows from theorem 2.1.7 that

$$\text{plim}_{n\to\infty}(\partial/\partial\theta)\eta_i(\hat{\theta}^{(i)}) = (\partial/\partial\theta)\eta_i(\theta_0) \tag{4.6.7}$$

and consequently, by (4.6.3) and theorems 2.3.3 and 2.3.5,

$$\text{plim}_{n\to\infty}[(\partial/\partial\theta)\eta_i(\hat{\theta}^{(i)}) - (\partial/\partial\theta)\eta_i(\theta_0)]\sqrt{n}(\hat{\theta} - \theta_0) = 0 \tag{4.6.8}$$

Combining (4.6.5) and (4.6.8) it follows that

$$\text{plim}_{n\to\infty}[\sqrt{n}(\eta_i(\hat{\theta}) - \eta_i(\theta_0)) - (\partial/\partial\theta)\eta_i(\theta_0)\sqrt{n}(\hat{\theta} - \theta_0)] = 0 \tag{4.6.9}$$

and consequently

$$\text{plim}_{n\to\infty}[\sqrt{n}(\hat{\eta} - \eta) - \Gamma\sqrt{n}(\hat{\theta} - \theta_0)] = 0, \tag{4.6.10}$$

where

$$\eta = (\eta_1(\theta_0),\ldots,\eta_q(\theta_0))' \tag{4.6.11}$$

Since (4.6.3) implies that

$$\Gamma\sqrt{n}(\hat{\theta} - \theta_0) \to N_q(0,\Gamma\Omega\Gamma') \text{ in distr.},$$

it follows now from (4.6.10) that,

$$\sqrt{n}(\hat{\eta} - \eta) \to N_q(0,\Gamma\Omega\Gamma']) \text{ in distr.} \quad 4.6.12)$$

Note that $\Gamma\Omega\Gamma'$ has rank q and is therefore nonsingular. Now let

$$\hat{\Gamma} = [(\partial/\partial\theta_{i_2})\eta_{i_1}(\hat{\theta})] \tag{4.6.13}$$

Then $\text{plim}_{n\to\infty}\hat{\theta} = \theta_0$ implies

$$\text{plim}_{n\to\infty}\hat{\Gamma} = \Gamma \tag{4.6.14}$$

and thus

$$\text{plim}_{n\to\infty}\hat{\Gamma}\hat{\Omega}\hat{\Gamma}' = \Gamma\Omega\Gamma'. \tag{4.6.15}$$

Using theorem 2.3.5 we conclude from (4.6.12) and (4.6.15) that

$$(\hat{\Gamma}\hat{\Omega}\hat{\Gamma}')^{-1/2}\sqrt{n}(\hat{\eta} - \eta) \to N_q(0,I) \text{ in distr.} \tag{4.6.16}$$

and consequently by theorem 2.3.4,

$$n(\hat{\eta}-\eta)'(\hat{\Gamma}\hat{\Omega}\hat{\Gamma}')^{-1}(\hat{\eta}-\eta) \to \chi^2_q \text{ in distr.} \tag{4.6.17}$$

The Wald statistic for testing $H_0 : \eta = 0$ is now

$$W_n = n\hat{\eta}'(\hat{\Gamma}\hat{\Omega}\hat{\Gamma}')^{-1}\hat{\eta}. \tag{4.6.18}$$

Clearly,

$$W_n \to \chi^2_q \text{ in distr. if } H_0 \text{ is true.} \tag{4.6.19}$$

If H_0 is false, i.e., $\eta \neq 0$, then

$$\text{plim}_{n\to\infty} W_n/n = \eta'(\Gamma\Omega\Gamma')^{-1}\eta > 0, \tag{4.6.20}$$

hence

$$\text{plim}_{n\to\infty} W_n = \infty. \tag{4.6.21}$$

Remark: A drawback of the Wald test is that changing the form of the nonlinear restrictions $\eta_i(\theta_0) = 0$ to a form which is algebraically equivalent under the null hypothesis will change the Wald statistic W_n. See Gregory and Veall (1985) and Phillips and Park (1988). The former authors show on the basis of Monte Carlo experiments that differences in functional form of the restrictions are likely to be important in small samples, and the latter two authors investigate this phenomenon analytically.

Note that the result in this section is in fact a straightforward corollary of the following general theorem.

> *Theorem 4.6.1* Let (θ_n) be a sequence of random vectors in R^k satisfying $r_n(\theta_n-\theta_0) \to N_k(0,\Omega)$, where (r_n) is a sequence of real numbers converging to infinity and $\theta_0 \in R^k$ is non-random. Let $\eta_1(\theta),\ldots,\eta_m(\theta)$ be Borel measurable real functions on R^k such that for $j=1,\ldots,m$, $\eta_j(\theta)$ is continuously differentiable in θ_0. Let $\eta(\theta) = (\eta_1(\theta),\ldots,\eta_m(\theta))'$ and let Γ be the $q \times m$ matrix
>
> $$\Gamma = [(\partial/\partial\theta_{i_2})\eta_{i_1}(\theta_0)] \tag{4.6.22}$$
>
> Then $r_n(\eta(\theta_n)-\eta(\theta_0)) \to N_m(0,\Gamma\Omega\Gamma')$ in distr. (N.B. m may be larger than k.)

4.6.2 The likelihood ratio test

Suppose that $\hat{\theta}$ is the ML estimator of θ_0, and consider again the problem of testing the null hypothesis (4.6.1). We recall that the null hypothesis involved is

$$H_0: \eta(\theta_0) = 0, \tag{4.6.23}$$

where

$$\eta(\theta) = (\eta_1(\theta),...,\eta_q\theta))'. \tag{4.6.24}$$

Cf. (4.6.1). The likelihood ratio (LR) test is based on the ratio of the constrained and the unconstrained maximum likelihood:

$$\lambda_n = \sup_{\theta\in\Theta,\eta(\theta)=0} L_n(Z|\theta) \ / \ \sup_{\theta\in\Theta} L_n(Z|\theta). \tag{4.6.25}$$

Note that $0 \leq \lambda_n \leq 1$. If H_0 is true one may expect λ_n to be close to 1, whereas if H_0 is false λ_n will tend to zero. Therefore the LR test is one-sided: H_0 is rejected if λ_n is less than the α-critical value λ_α, which under H_0 is such that $P(\lambda_n \leq \lambda_\alpha) = \alpha$, with α the significance level.

In the further discussion of the LR test it will be convenient to reparameterize the parameter space by augmenting the vector function $\eta(\theta)$ with a (m-q) × 1 vector function $\eta_*(\theta)$ such that

$$\Psi(\theta) = \begin{bmatrix} \eta_*(\theta) \\ \eta(\theta) \end{bmatrix} \tag{4.6.26}$$

is a continuously differentiable one-to-one mapping. Let

$$\Theta^* = \{\theta^*: \Psi^{-1}(\theta^*)\in\Theta\} \tag{4.6.27}$$

be the new parameter space, and let

$$L_n^*(Z|\theta^*) = L_n(Z|\Psi^{-1}(\theta^*)) \tag{4.6.28}$$

be the reparameterized likelihood function. The null hypothesis (4.6.23) now simplifies to

$$H_0\text{: The last q components of } \theta_0^* = \Psi(\theta_0) \text{ are zero,} \tag{4.6.29}$$

and the LR test involved becomes

$$\lambda_n = \sup_{(\theta_1,\theta_2)\in\Theta^*,\theta_2=0} L_n^*(Z|(\theta_1,\theta_2))/\sup_{\theta\in\Theta^*} L_n^*(Z|\theta), \tag{4.6.30}$$

where θ_2 is a q-component subvector. Thus without loss of generality we may confine our attention to testing the simple null hypothesis:

$$H_0\text{: } \theta_0 = (\theta_{01}',0')'\text{, with } 0' \text{ a } 1 \times q \text{ zero vector.} \tag{4.6.31}$$

Let

$$\tilde{\theta} = (\tilde{\theta}_1,0')' \tag{4.6.32}$$

be the constrained ML estimator. Then the LR test statistic is:

$$\lambda_n = L_n(Z|\tilde{\theta})/L_n(Z|\hat{\theta}). \tag{4.6.33}$$

In practice the distribution of λ_n under H_0 is often unknown, so that the critical value λ_α cannot be calculated. However, λ_α can be approximated using the following asymptotic result:

Theorem 4.6.2 Let the conditions of theorem 4.5.1 hold. Under the null hypothesis (4.6.31), $-2.\ln(\lambda_n) \to \chi^2_q$ in distribution.

Proof: We leave the details of the proof as an exercise. Here we shall only give some hints. Consider the second-order Taylor expansion

$$\ln(L_n(Z|\tilde{\theta})) - \ln(L_n(Z|\hat{\theta})) = (\tilde{\theta} - \hat{\theta})(\partial/\partial\theta')\ln(L_n(Z|\hat{\theta})) + \tfrac{1}{2}(\tilde{\theta} - \hat{\theta})'[(\partial/\partial\theta/)(\partial/\partial\theta)\ln(L_n(Z|\hat{\theta}_*))](\tilde{\theta} - \hat{\theta}), \qquad (4.6.34)$$

with $\hat{\theta}_*$ a mean value. Conclude from (4.6.34) that

$$-2.\ln(\lambda_n) = \sqrt{n}(\tilde{\theta} - \hat{\theta})'H(\theta_0)\sqrt{n}(\tilde{\theta} - \hat{\theta}) + o_p(1), \qquad (4.6.35)$$

where we recall that $o_p(1)$ stands for a random variable that converges in probability to zero. Next, observe that

$$\sqrt{n}(\tilde{\theta}_1 - \theta_{01}) = H_{11}(\theta_0)^{-1}[(1/\sqrt{n})\textstyle\sum_{j=1}^{n}(\partial/\partial\theta_{01}')\ln(h(Z_j|\theta_0))] + o_p(1) \qquad (4.6.36)$$

and

$$\sqrt{n}(\hat{\theta} - \theta_0) = H(\theta_0)^{-1}[(1/\sqrt{n})\textstyle\sum_{j=1}^{n}(\partial/\partial\theta')\ln(h(Z_j|\theta_0))] + o_p(1), \qquad (4.6.37)$$

where $H_{11}(\theta_0)$ is the upper-left $(m\text{-}q)\times(m\text{-}q)$ submatrix of $H(\theta_0)$. Denoting $H = H(\theta_0)$, $H_{11} = H_{11}(\theta_0)$ and

$$S = S_0 - H^{-1} \text{ with } S_0 = \begin{pmatrix} H_{11}^{-1} & O \\ O & O \end{pmatrix}, \qquad (4.6.38)$$

we conclude from (4.6.36) and (4.6.37) that

$$\sqrt{n}(\tilde{\theta} - \hat{\theta}) \to N_m(0, SHS'), \qquad (4.6.39)$$

which implies that

$$H^{1/2}\sqrt{n}(\tilde{\theta} - \hat{\theta}) \to N_m(0, I - H^{1/2}S_0H^{1/2}). \qquad (4.6.40)$$

Since the matrix $I - H^{\frac{1}{2}}S_0H^{\frac{1}{2}}$ is idempotent with rank q, the theorem under consideration follows. Q.E.D.

We have seen in section 4.6.1 that the Wald test is not invariant with respect to possible mathematically equivalent functional specifications of the parameter restrictions under the null hypothesis. This does not apply to the LR test, owing to the fact that the LR test statistic λ_n is invariant with respect to reparameterization. In particular, the null hypothesis (4.6.31) is mathematically equivalent to (4.6.23). This implies that:

Theorem 4.6.3 The result of theorem 4.6.2 carries over if the null hypothesis is replaced by (4.6.23). Moreover, the LR test is invariant with respect to possible mathematically equivalent functional specifications of the restrictions in (4.6.23).

This invariance property distinguishes the LR test favorably from the Wald test. On the other hand, the LR test requires full specification of the likelihood function (up to a possible factor that does not depend on the parameters), and two different ML estimators, the constrained and the unconstrained ML estimators. The Wald test employs only one unconstrained estimator and does not require full specification of the likelihood function. Thus the Wald test is more robust with respect to possible misspecification of the model and has the advantage of computational simplicity.

Finally, we note that the LR test is a consistent test. If the null hypothesis is false then asymptotically we will always reject the null hypothesis:

Theorem 4.6.4 Let the conditions of theorem 4.5.1 hold. If H_0 is false then $\text{plim}_{n\to\infty} -2.\ln(\lambda_n) = \infty$.

Proof: Exercise 2.

4.6.3 The Lagrange multiplier test

Maximization of the likelihood function under the restrictions (4.6.23) can be done using the well-known Lagrange technique. Consider the Lagrange function

$$F(\theta,\mu) = \ln(L_n(Z|\theta)) - \mu'\eta(\theta). \tag{4.6.41}$$

The first-order conditions for an optimum in $(\tilde{\theta}, \tilde{\mu})$ are:

$$(\partial/\partial\theta')\ln(L_n(Z|\hat{\theta})) - \Gamma(\tilde{\theta})'\tilde{\mu} = 0; \tag{4.6.42}$$

$$\eta(\tilde{\theta}) = 0; \tag{4.6.43}$$

where $\Gamma(\theta)$ is the $q \times m$ matrix

$$\Gamma(\theta) = [(\partial/\partial\theta_{i_2})\eta_{i_1}(\theta)],\ i_1 = 1,\ldots,q,\ i_2 = 1,\ldots,m. \tag{4.6.44}$$

Cf. (4.6.2).

The Lagrange multiplier (LM) test is based on the vector $\tilde{\mu}$ of Lagrange multipliers:

$$\ell_n = (\tilde{\mu}/\sqrt{n})\tilde{\Gamma}\tilde{H}^{-1}\tilde{\Gamma}'(\tilde{\mu}/\sqrt{n}), \tag{4.6.45}$$

where $\tilde{\Gamma} = \Gamma(\tilde{\theta})$ and

$$\tilde{H} = (1/n)\textstyle\sum_{j=1}^{n}[(\partial/\partial\theta')\ln(h(Z_j|\tilde{\theta}))][(\partial/\partial\theta)\ln(h(Z_j|\tilde{\theta}))]. \tag{4.6.46}$$

Theorem 4.6.5 Let the conditions of theorem 4.5.1 hold. Under the null hypothesis (4.6.23), $\ell_n \rightarrow \chi^2_q$, whereas if (4.6.23) is false, $\text{plim}_{n\rightarrow\infty}\, \ell_n = \infty$.

Also the LM test is invariant with respect to possible mathematically equivalent formulations of the null hypothesis, although this is not so obvious as in the case of the LR test. Moreover, we note that the LM test is a special case of Neyman's (1959) C(α) test. See Dagenais and Dufour (1991).

In the first instance the test statistics of the Wald, LR and LM tests look quite different, but they are in fact asymptotically equivalent under the null hypothesis, in the sense that:

Theorem 4.6.6. Under the conditions of theorem 4.5.1 and the null hypothesis (4.6.23),

(a) $\text{plim}_{n\rightarrow\infty}\{\ell_n + 2.\ln(\lambda_n)\} = 0$,

(b) $\text{plim}_{n\rightarrow\infty}\{W_n + 2.\ln(\lambda_n)\} = 0$.

Proof: Exercise 3. (Hint: Show by using the mean value theorem that

$$(1/\surd n)(\partial/\partial\theta')\ln(L_n(Z|\tilde{\theta})) = H(\theta_0)\surd n(\tilde{\theta}-\hat{\theta}) + o_p(1), \qquad (4.6.47)$$

and then use (4.6.40) and (4.6.42). This proves part (a). The proof of part (b) goes similarly.) Q.E.D.

Thus, the first part of theorem 4.6.5 follows from theorems 4.6.3 and 4.6.6a. The second part is left as exercise 4.

Exercises

1. Complete the details of the proof of theorem 4.6.2.
2. Prove theorem 4.6.4.
3. Prove theorem 4.6.6.
4. Prove the consistency of the LM test.

5

Tests for model misspecification

In the literature on model specification testing two trends can be distinguished. One trend consists of tests using one or more well-specified non-nested alternative specifications. See Cox (1961, 1962), Atkinson (1969, 1970), Quandt (1974), Pereira (1977, 1978), Pesaran and Deaton (1978), Davidson and MacKinnon (1981), among others. The other trend consists of tests of the orthogonality condition, i.e. the condition that the conditional expectation of the error relative to the regressors equals zero a.s., without employing a well-specified alternative. Notable work on this problem has been done by Ramsey (1969, 1970), Hausman (1978), White (1981), Holly (1982), Bierens (1982, 1991a), Newey (1985), and Tauchen (1985), among others.

A pair of models is called non-nested if it is not possible to construct one model out of the other by fixing some parameters. The non-nested models considered in the literature usually have different vectors of regressors, for testing non-nested models with common regressors makes no sense. In the latter case one may simply choose the model with the minimum estimated error variance, and this choice will be consistent in the sense that the probability that we pick the wrong model converges to zero. A serious point overlooked by virtually all authors is that non-nested models with different sets of regressors may all be correct. This is obvious if the dependent variable and all the regressors involved are jointly normally distributed and the non-nested models are all linear, for conditional expectations on the basis of jointly normally distributed random variables are always linear functions of the conditioning variables. Moreover, in each model involved the errors are independent of the regressors. In particular, in this case, the tests of Davidson and MacKinnon (1981) will likely reject each of these true models, as these tests are based on combining linearly the non-nested models into a compound regression model. Since other tests of non-nested hypotheses are basically in the same spirit one may expect this flaw to be a pervasive phenomenon. Consequently, these tests are only valid if either the null or only one of the alternatives is true. Moreover, tests of non-nested hypotheses may have low power against nonspecified alternatives, as pointed out by Bierens (1982). Therefore we shall not review these tests further. In this chapter we only consider tests of the orthogonality condition, without employing a specific alternative. First we discuss White's version of Hausman's test in section 5.1 and then, in section 5.2, the more general M-test of Newey. In section 5.3 we modify the M-test to a consistent test and in section 5.4 we consider a further elaboration of Bierens' integrated M-test.

5.1 White's version of Hausman's test

In an influential paper, Hausman (1978) proposed to test for model misspecification by comparing an efficient estimator with a consistent but inefficient estimator. Under the null hypothesis that the model is correctly specified the difference of these estimators times the square root of the sample size, will converge in distribution to the normal with zero mean, whereas under the alternative that the model is misspecified it is likely that these two estimators have different probability limits. White (1981) has extended Hausman's test to nonlinear models, using the nonlinear least squares estimator as the efficient estimator and a weighted nonlinear least squares estimator as the nonefficient consistent estimator.

The null hypothesis to be tested is that assumption 4.1.1 holds:

$$H_0\text{: } E(Y_j|X_j) = f(X_j,\theta_0) \text{ a.s. for some } \theta_0 \in \Theta,$$

where $f(x,\theta)$ is a given Borel measurable real function on $R^k \times \Theta$ which for each $x \in R^k$ is continuous on the compact Borel set $\theta \subset R^m$.

The weighted nonlinear least squares estimator is a measurable solution $\hat{\theta}$ of:

$$\hat{\theta}^* \in \Theta \text{ a.s., } \hat{Q}^*(\hat{\theta}^*) = \inf_{\theta\in\Theta}\hat{Q}^*(\theta),$$

where

$$Q^*(\theta) = (1/n)\textstyle\sum_{j=1}^{n}(Y_j - f(X_j,\theta))^2 w(x_j),$$

with w(.) a positive Borel measurable real weight function on R^k. Following White (1981), we shall now set forth conditions such that under the null hypothesis,

$$\sqrt{n}(\hat{\theta} - \hat{\theta}^*) \rightarrow N_m(0,\Omega) \text{ in distr.},$$

with $\hat{\theta}$ the nonlinear least squares estimator, whereas if H_0 is false,

$$\text{plim}_{n\rightarrow\infty}\hat{\theta} \neq \text{plim}_{n\rightarrow\infty}\hat{\theta}^*.$$

Given a consistent estimator $\hat{\Omega}$ of the asymptotic variance matrix Ω the test statistic of White's version of Hausman's test is now

$$\hat{W}^* = n(\hat{\theta} - \hat{\theta}^*)'\hat{\Omega}^{-1}(\hat{\theta} - \hat{\theta}^*),$$

which is asymptotically χ^2_m distributed under H_0 and converges in probability to infinity if H_0 is false.

Let us now list the maintained hypotheses which are assumed to hold regardless whether or not the model is correctly specified.

Assumption 5.1.1. Assumption 4.3.1 holds and $E[Y_j^2 w(X_j)] < \infty$.

Assumption 5.1.2 Assumption 4.3.2 holds and

$$E[\sup_{\theta\in\Theta} f(X_1,\theta)^2\, w(X_1)] < \infty.$$

Assumption 5.1.3 There are unique vectors θ_* and θ_{**} in Θ such that

$$E\{[E(Y_1|X_1) - f(X_1,\theta_*)]^2\} = \inf_{\theta\in\Theta} E\{[E(Y_1|X_1) - f(X_1,\theta)]^2\}$$

and

$$E\{[E(Y_1|X_1) - f(X_1,\theta_{**})]^2 w(X_1)\} = \inf_{\theta\in\Theta} E\{[E(Y_1|X_1) - f(X_1,\theta)]^2 w(X_1)\}.$$

If H_0 is false then $\theta_* \neq \theta_{**}$.

Assumption 5.1.4 The parameter space Θ is convex and $f(x,\theta)$ is for each $x \in R^k$ twice continuously differentiable on Θ. If H_0 is true then θ_0 is an interior point of Θ.

Assumption 5.1.5 Let assumption 4.3.5 hold. Moreover, let for $i,i_1,i_2 = 1,\ldots,m$,

$$E\{\sup_{\theta\in\Theta}[(\partial/\partial\theta_i)f(X_1,\theta)]^2\, w(X_1)\} < \infty,$$
$$E\{\sup_{\theta\in\Theta}[(\partial/\partial\theta_{i_1})(\partial/\partial\theta_{i_2})f(X_1,\theta)]^2\, w(X_1)\} < \infty.$$

Assumption 5.1.6 The matrices

$$\Omega_{ij} = E\{[Y_1 - f(X_1,\theta_*)]^{2i}\, w(X_1)^j\, [(\partial/\partial\theta')f(X_1,\theta_*)][(\partial/\partial\theta)f(X_1,\theta_*)]\}$$

are nonsingular for $i = 0,1$; $j = 0,1$.

Assumption 5.1.7 Let assumption 4.3.7 hold and let for $i_1,i_2 = 1,\ldots,m$,

$$E\{\sup_{\theta\in\Theta}[Y_1 - f(X_1,\theta)]^2\, w(X_1)^2\, |(\partial/\partial\theta_{i_1})f(X_1,\theta)| \times |(\partial/\partial\theta_{i_2})f(X_1,\theta)|\} < \infty.$$

Finally, denoting

$$\Omega = \Omega_{00}^{-1}\Omega_{10}\Omega_{00}^{-1} - \Omega_{00}^{-1}\Omega_{11}\Omega_{01}^{-1} - \Omega_{01}^{-1}\Omega_{11}\Omega_{00}^{-1} + \Omega_{01}^{-1}\Omega_{12}\Omega_{01}^{-1},$$

we assume:

Assumption 5.1.8 The matrix Ω is nonsingular.

Now observe that under assumptions 5.1.1 and 5.1.2,

$\hat{Q}(\theta) \rightarrow Q(\theta)$ a.s. uniformly on Θ,
$\hat{Q}^*(\theta) \rightarrow Q^*(\theta)$ a.s. uniformly on Θ,

where $\hat{Q}(\theta)$ and $Q(\theta)$ are defined in (4.1.9) and (4.3.3), respectively, and

$Q^*(\theta) = E\{[Y_1 - f(X_1,\theta)]^2 w(X_1)\}$.

Together with assumption 5.1.3 these results now imply:

Theorem 5.1.1 Under assumptions 5.1.1–5.1.3, $\hat{\theta} \rightarrow \theta_*$ a.s. and $\hat{\theta}^* \rightarrow \theta_{**}$ a.s.

(cf. theorem 4.2.1). Moreover, if H_0 is true then clearly

$\theta_* = \theta_{**} = \theta_0$.

Now assume that H_0 is true, and denote

$U_j = Y_j - f(X_j,\theta_0)$.

Then it follows from assumptions 5.1.1–5.1.8, similarly to (4.2.12), that

$$\text{plim}_{n\rightarrow\infty}[\sqrt{n}(\hat{\theta}-\theta_0) - \Omega_{00}^{-1}(1/\sqrt{n})\textstyle\sum_{j=1}^{n} U_j(\partial/\partial\theta')f(X_j,\theta_0)] = 0, \quad (5.1.1)$$

$$\text{plim}_{n\rightarrow\infty}[\sqrt{n}(\hat{\theta}^*-\theta_0) - \Omega_{01}^{-1}(1/\sqrt{n})\textstyle\sum_{j=1}^{n} U_j w(X_j)(\partial/\partial\theta')f(X_j,\theta_0)] = 0, \quad (5.1.2)$$

hence

$$\text{plim}_{n\rightarrow\infty}[(\sqrt{n}(\hat{\theta}-\theta_0)', \sqrt{n}(\hat{\theta}^*-\theta_0)')' - (1/\sqrt{n})\textstyle\sum_{j=1}^{n} Z_j] = 0,$$

where

$$Z_j = U_j[\Omega_{00}^{-1}(\partial/\partial\theta)f(X_j,\theta_0), \Omega_{01}^{-1}w(X_j)(\partial/\partial\theta)f(X_j,\theta_0)]'.$$

Moreover, from the central limit theorem it follows

$$(1/\sqrt{n})\textstyle\sum_{j=1}^{n} Z_j \rightarrow N_{2m}(0,A),$$

where

$$A = E(Z_jZ_j') = \begin{pmatrix} \Omega_{00}^{-1}\Omega_{10}\Omega_{00}^{-1} & \Omega_{00}^{-1}\Omega_{11}\Omega_{01}^{-1} \\ \Omega_{01}^{-1}\Omega_{11}\Omega_{00}^{-1} & \Omega_{01}^{-1}\Omega_{12}\Omega_{01}^{-1} \end{pmatrix}.$$

From these results it easily follows that

Theorem 5.1.2 Under H_0 and assumptions 5.1.1–5.1.8,

$\sqrt{n}(\hat{\theta} - \hat{\theta}^*) \to N_m(0,\Omega)$ in distr.

A consistent estimator of Ω can be constructed as follows. Let for $i=0,1$, $j=0,1,2,\ldots$,

$$\hat{\Omega}_{ij} = (1/n)\sum_{j=1}^{n}(Y_j - f(X_j,\hat{\theta}))^{2i}\, w(X_j)^j \times [(\partial/\partial\theta')f(X_j,\hat{\theta})][(\partial/\partial\theta)f(X_j,\hat{\theta})]$$

and define $\hat{\Omega}$ analogously to Ω. Then

Theorem 5.1.3 Under assumptions 5.1.1–5.1.7, $\hat{\Omega} \to \Omega$ a.s., regardless whether or not the null is true.

Combining theorems 5.1.1–5.1.3 we now have

Theorem 5.1.4 Under assumptions 5.1.1–5.1.8,

$\hat{W}^* \to \chi^2_m$ if H_0 is true and
$\hat{W}^*/n \to (\theta_* - \theta_{**})'\Omega^{-1}(\theta_* - \theta_{**}) > 0$ a.s. if H_0 is false.

The latter implies, of course, that $\text{plim}_{n\to\infty}\hat{W}^* = \infty$.

The power of the Hausman–White test depends heavily on the condition that under misspecification $\theta_* \neq \theta_{**}$, and for that the choice of the weight function w(.) is crucial. Take for example the true model

$$Y_j = X_{1j} + X_{2j} + X_{1j}X_{2j} + U_j$$

where the X_{1j}'s, X_{2j}'s and U_j's are independent and N(0,1) distributed, and let $f(x,\theta) = \theta_1 x_1 + \theta_2 x_2$, $w(x) = x_1^2 + x_2^2$. Then

$$E\{[Y_1 - f(X_1,\theta)]^2\} = (1-\theta_1)^2 + (1-\theta_2)^2 + 2 \qquad (5.1.3)$$

and

$$E\{[Y_1 - f(X_1,\theta)]^2 w(X_1)\} = 4(1-\theta_1)^2 + 4(1-\theta_2)^2 + 8, \qquad (5.1.4)$$

hence $\theta_* = \theta_{**} = (1,1)'$. Moreover, in this case we still have

$$\hat{W}^* \to \chi^2_2 \text{ in distr.}, \qquad (5.1.5)$$

although the model is misspecified. Thus Hausman's test is not consistent against all alternatives, a result also confirmed by Holly (1982).

Remark: If under the null hypothesis H_0 the model is also homoskedastic, i.e.,

Assumption 5.1.9 Under H_0, $E(U_j^2|X_j) = E(U_j^2) = \sigma^2$ a.s., where $U_j = Y_j - f(X_j,\theta_0)$,

then

$$\Omega_{10} = \sigma^2\Omega_{00}, \quad \Omega_{11} = \sigma^2\Omega_{01}, \quad \Omega_{12} = \sigma^2\,\Omega_{02},$$

where

$$\sigma^2 = E[Y_1 - f(X_1,\theta_*)]^2 .$$

Cf. assumption 5.1.6. Hence

$$\Omega = \sigma^2\Omega_{01}^{-1}\Omega_{02}\Omega_{01}^{-1} - \sigma^2\Omega_{00}^{-1} .$$

It is easy to verify that now Ω is just the difference of the asymptotic variance matrix of the weighted nonlinear least squares estimator $\hat{\theta}^*$ and the asymptotic variance matrix of the least squares estimator $\hat{\theta}$. Thus we have:

> *Theorem 5.1.5.* Under H_0 and the assumptions 5.1.1-5.1.9,
>
> $$\sqrt{n}(\hat{\theta}^* - \theta_0) \rightarrow N_m(0,\sigma^2\Omega_{01}^{-1}\Omega_{02}\Omega_{01}^{-1}) \text{ in distr,}$$
> $$\sqrt{n}(\hat{\theta} - \theta_0) \rightarrow N_m(0,\sigma^2\Omega_{00}^{-1}) \text{ in distr., and}$$
> $$\sqrt{n}(\hat{\theta}^* - \hat{\theta}) \rightarrow N_m(0,\sigma^2\Omega_{01}^{-1}\Omega_{02}\Omega_{01}^{-1} - \sigma^2\Omega_{00}^{-1}) \text{ in distr.}$$

Consequently, denoting

$$\hat{\Omega} = \hat{\sigma}^2\hat{\Omega}_{01}^{-1}\hat{\Omega}_{02}\hat{\Omega}_{01}^{-1} - \hat{\sigma}^2\Omega_{00}^{-1}$$

with

$$\hat{\sigma}^2 = (1/n)\textstyle\sum_{j=1}^{n}(Y_j - f(X_j,\hat{\theta}))^2 ,$$

we have:

> *Theorem 5.1.6* Under assumptions 5.1.1–5.1.9 the results in theorem 5.1.4 carry over.

Actually, this is the form of the Hausman–White test considered by White (1981).

Exercises

1. Prove (5.1.2).
2. Prove theorem 5.1.2.
3. Prove theorem 5.1.3.
4. Prove (5.1.3) and (5.1.4), using the fact that the fourth moment of a standard normally distributed random variable equals 3.
5. Prove (5.1.5).

5.2 Newey's M-test

5.2.1 Introduction

Newey (1985) argues that testing model correctness usually amounts to testing a null hypothesis of the form

$$H_0: E[M(Y_j,X_j,\theta_0)] = 0, \tag{5.2.1}$$

where $M(y,x,\theta) = (M_1(y,x,\theta),\ldots,M_p(y,x,\theta))'$ is a vector-valued function on $R\times R^k \times \Theta$ (with Borel measurable components). A specification test can then be based on the sample moment vector

$$\hat{M}(\hat{\theta}) = (1/n)\textstyle\sum_{j=1}^{n} M(Y_j,X_j,\hat{\theta}), \tag{5.2.2}$$

where $\hat{\theta}$ is, under H_0, a consistent and asymptotically normally distributed estimator of θ_0.

A similar class of M-tests has been developed independently by Tauchen (1985), under weaker conditions on the function M(.) than in Newey (1985). See also Pagan and Vella (1989) for a survey of various M-tests and their application.

We show now that the Hausman–White test is indeed asymptotically equivalent under H_0 to a particular M-test. Let

$$M(y,x,\theta) = (y-f(x,\theta))(\partial/\partial\theta')f(x,\theta)w(x). \tag{5.2.3}$$

Then the i-th component of $\hat{M}(\theta)$ is:

$$\hat{M}_i(\theta) = (1/n)\textstyle\sum_{j=1}^{n}(Y_j-f(X_j,\theta))(\partial/\partial\theta_i)f(X_j,\theta)w(X_j).$$

Let $\hat{\theta}$ be the nonlinear least squares estimator. It follows from the mean value theorem that there exists a mean value $\hat{\theta}^{(i)}$ satisfying $|\hat{\theta}^{(i)}-\theta_0| \le |\hat{\theta}-\theta_0|$ a.s. such that

$$\sqrt{n}\hat{M}_i(\hat{\theta}) = \sqrt{n}\hat{M}_i(\theta_0) + [(\partial/\partial\theta)\hat{M}_i(\hat{\theta}^{(i)})]\sqrt{n}(\hat{\theta}-\theta_0).$$

We leave it as an exercise (cf. exercise 1) to show that under the conditions of theorem 5.1.2,

$$\text{plim}_{n\to\infty}[(\partial/\partial\theta')\hat{M}_1(\hat{\theta}^{(1)}),\ldots,(\partial/\partial\theta')\hat{M}_m(\hat{\theta}^{(m)})]' = -\Omega_{01},$$

hence

$$\text{plim}_{n\to\infty}[\sqrt{n}\,\hat{M}(\hat{\theta})-(1/\sqrt{n})\textstyle\sum_{j=1}^{n}U_j(\partial/\partial\theta')f(X_j,\theta_0)w(X_j) + \Omega_{01}\sqrt{n}(\hat{\theta}-\theta_0)] = 0. \tag{5.2.4}$$

Comparing this result with (5.1.2) we now see that

$$\text{plim}_{n\to\infty}[\sqrt{n}\,\hat{M}(\hat{\theta}) - \Omega_{01}\sqrt{n}(\hat{\theta}^{*}-\hat{\theta})] = 0,$$

hence the chi-square test based on $\sqrt{n}\hat{M}(\hat{\theta})$ is the same as the chi-square test based on $\sqrt{n}(\hat{\theta}-\hat{\theta}^*)$. This result demonstrates the asymptotic equivalence under H_0 of this special case of the M-test and the Hausman–White test.

Next, consider the case that H_0 is false. Under the conditions of theorem 5.1.4 we have

$$\text{plim}_{n\to\infty}\hat{M}(\hat{\theta}) = E[E(Y_1|X_1) - f(X_1,\theta_*)](\partial/\partial\theta')f(X_1,\theta_*)w(X_1) \tag{5.2.5}$$

as is not hard to verify. Cf. exercise 2. Now assume that the function

$$[E(Y_1|X_1) - f(X_1,\theta)]^2 w(X_1)$$

has no local extremum at $\theta=\theta_*$. This condition is only a minor augmentation of assumption 5.1.3. Then the right-hand side of (5.2.5) is unequal to the zero vector, i.e.,

$$\text{plim}_{n\to\infty}\hat{M}(\hat{\theta}) \neq 0.$$

This establishes the asymptotic power of the M-test under review. However, also the M-test is not generally watertight. It is not hard to verify that for the example at the end of section 5.1 this version of the M-test also has low power.

Another example of an M-test is the Wald test in section 4.6.1, with $M(y,x,\theta) = \eta(\theta)$. Also, Ramsey's (1969, 1970) RESET test may be considered as a special case of the M-test.

5.2.2 The conditional M-test

In regression analysis, where we deal with conditional expectations, model correctness usually corresponds to a null hypothesis of the form

$$H_0 : E[r(Y_j,X_j,\theta)|X_j] = 0 \text{ a.s. if and only if } \theta = \theta_0. \tag{5.2.6}$$

For example in the regression case considered in section 4.3 an obvious candidate for this function r is $r(y,x,\theta) = y-f(x,\theta)$. Also, we may choose

$$r(y,x,\theta) = (y-f(x,\theta))(\partial/\partial\theta')f(x,\theta). \tag{5.2.7}$$

In this case we have:

$$E[r(Y_j,X_j,\theta)|X_j] = [E(Y_j|X_j)-f(X_j,\theta)](\partial/\partial\theta')f(X_j,\theta) = 0 \text{ a.s.}$$
$$\text{if and only if } E(Y_j|X_j) = f(X_j,\theta_0) \text{ a.s. and } \theta = \theta_0. \tag{5.2.8}$$

Furthermore, observe that in the case (5.2.7) the least squares estimator $\hat{\theta}$ of θ_0 is such that

$$P[(1/n)\textstyle\sum_{j=1}^{n} r(Y_j,X_j,\hat{\theta}) = 0] \to 1. \tag{5.2.9}$$

Cf. (4.2.7). This is true even if the model is misspecified, provided that $\hat{\theta}$ converges in probability to an interior point of the parameter space Θ.

Consequently we cannot choose M = r, for then $P(\hat{M}(\hat{\theta})=0) \rightarrow 1$ anyhow and thus any test based on $\hat{M}(\hat{\theta})$ will have no power at all.

In order to cure this problem we need to use a weight function, similarly to (5.2.3), i.e., let $r_i(y,x,\theta)$ be the i-th component of the vector $r(y,x,\theta)$, and let $w_i(x,\theta)$ be a weight function. Then

$$M_i(y,x,\theta) = r_i(y,x,\theta)w_i(x,\theta),\ i=1,2,...,m. \quad (5.2.10)$$

Note that in the case (5.2.3),

$$w_i(x,\theta) \equiv w(x),\ r_i(y,x,\theta) = (y-f(x,\theta))(\partial/\partial\theta_i)f(x,\theta),\ i=1,2,...,k.$$

In view of the above argument, we can now state the basic ingredients of the conditional M-test. First, let us assume that:

Assumption 5.2.1 The data-generating process $\{(Y_j,X_j)\}$ with $Y_j \in R$, $X_j \in R^k$ is i.i.d.

The model is implicitly specified by the functions $r_i(y,x,\theta)$:

Assumption 5.2.2 For $i=1,2,...,m$ the functions $r_i(y,x,\theta)$ are Borel measurable real functions on $R \times R^k \times \Theta$, where Θ is a compact Borel subset of R^m. Moreover, for each $(y,x) \in R \times R^k$ the functions $r_i(y,x,\theta)$ are continuously differentiable on θ. Let

$$r(y,x,\theta) = (r_1(y,x,\theta),...,r_m(y,x,\theta))'.$$

There exists a unique interior point θ_0 of Θ such that

$$E[r(Y_j,X_j,\theta_0)] = 0\ (\in R^m).$$

Note that the latter condition does not say anything about model correctness. For example in the case of the regression model in section 4.3 this condition merely says that the function

$$E\{[Y_j-f(X_j,\theta)]^2\} = E\{[Y_j-E(Y_j|X_j)]^2\} + E\{[E(Y_j|X_j)-f(X_j,\theta)]^2\}$$

takes a unique minimum on θ at an interior point θ_0, *without* saying that

$$E\{[E(Y_j|X_j)-f(X_j,\theta_0)]^2\} = 0.$$

Next, we consider a consistent estimator θ_n of θ_0, satisfying (5.2.9):

Assumption 5.2.3 Let (θ_n) be a sequence of random vectors in Θ such that,

(i) $\text{plim}_{n\rightarrow\infty}\theta_n = \theta_0$,

(ii) $\lim_{n\rightarrow\infty}P[(1/n)\sum_{j=1}^{n}r(Y_j,X_j,\theta_n) = 0] = 1$.

We may think of θ_n as an estimator obtained by solving an optimization problem with first-order condition

$(1/n)\sum_{j=1}^{n} r(Y_j,X_j,\theta) = 0.$

Estimators based on such moment conditions are called Method of Moment (MM) estimators. Cf. Hansen (1982).

We show now that assumption 5.2.3 implies asymptotic normality. By the mean value theorem we have

$$(1/\sqrt{n})\sum_{j=1}^{n} r_i(Y_j,X_j,\theta_n) = (1/\sqrt{n})\sum_{j=1}^{n} r_i(Y_j,X_j,\theta_0) + [(1/n)\sum_{j=1}^{n}(\partial/\partial\theta')r_i(Y_j,X_j,\theta_n^{(i)})]'\sqrt{n}(\theta_n-\theta_0), \tag{5.2.11}$$

where $\theta_n^{(i)}$ is a mean value satisfying $|\theta_n^{(i)} - \theta_0| \leq |\theta_n-\theta_0|$. Now assume

Assumption 5.2.4 For $i,\ell=1,2,...,m$, let

$$E[\sup_{\theta\in\Theta}|(\partial/\partial\theta_\ell)r_i(Y_1,X_1,\theta)|] < \infty$$

Then by theorem 2.7.5,

$$(1/n)\sum_{j=1}^{n}(\partial/\partial\theta')r_i(Y_j,X_j,\theta) \to E[(\partial/\partial\theta')r_i(Y_1,X_1,\theta)] \text{ a.s.} \tag{5.2.12}$$

uniformly on Θ, hence by theorem 2.6.1 and the consistency of θ_n,

$$\text{plim}_{n\to\infty}\theta_n^{(i)} = \theta_0,$$
$$\text{plim}_{n\to\infty}(1/n)\sum_{j=1}^{n}(\partial/\partial\theta')r_i(Y_j,X_j,\theta_n^{(i)}) = E[(\partial/\partial\theta')r_i(Y_1,X_1,\theta_0)]$$

Denoting

$$\hat{\Gamma}^* = [(1/n)\sum_{j=1}^{n}(\partial/\partial\theta')r_1(Y_j,X_j,\theta_n^{(1)}),...,(1/n)\sum_{j=1}^{n}(\partial/\partial\theta')r_m(Y_j,X_j,\theta_n^{(m)})]'$$

and

$$\Gamma = \left(E[(\partial/\partial\theta')r_1(Y_1,X_1,\theta_0)],...,E[(\partial/\partial\theta')r_m(Y_1,X_1,\theta_0)]\right)' \tag{5.2.13}$$

we thus have

$$\text{plim}_{n\to\infty}\hat{\Gamma}^* = \Gamma. \tag{5.2.14}$$

Next assume:

Assumption 5.2.5 The $(m\times m)$ matrix Γ is nonsingular.

Then

$$\text{plim}_{n\to\infty}\hat{\Gamma}^{*-1} = \Gamma^{-1} \tag{5.2.15}$$

(Cf. exercise 3), whereas by (5.2.11) and assumption 5.2.3

$$\text{plim}_{n\to\infty}[(1/\sqrt{n})\sum_{j=1}^{n}\hat{\Gamma}^{*-1}r(Y_j,X_j,\theta_0) + \sqrt{n}(\theta_n-\theta_0)] = 0. \tag{5.2.16}$$

This result, together with (5.2.15), implies

$$\text{plim}_{n\to\infty}[(1/\sqrt{n})\sum_{j=1}^{n}\Gamma^{-1}r(Y_j,X_j,\theta_0) + \sqrt{n}(\theta_n-\theta_0)] = 0, \tag{5.2.17}$$

provided that $(1/\sqrt{n})\sum_{j=1}^{n}r(Y_j,X_j,\theta_0)$ converges in distribution. Cf. exercise 4. A sufficient additional condition for the latter is:

Assumption 5.2.6 For $i=1,2,...,m$, $E[\sup_{\theta\in\Theta}(r_i(Y_1,X_1,\theta))^2] < \infty$,

as then the $(m \times m)$ variance matrix

$$\Delta = E[r(Y_1,X_1,\theta_0)r(Y_1,X_1,\theta_0)'] \quad (5.2.18)$$

has finite elements. Since the random vectors $r(Y_j,X_j,\theta_0)$ are i.i.d. with zero mean vectors and finite variance matrix Δ it follows now from the central limit theorem

$$(1/\sqrt{n})\sum_{j=1}^{n}r(Y_j,X_j,\theta_0) \to N_m(0,\Delta) \text{ in distr.} \quad (5.2.19)$$

Combining (5.2.17) and (5.2.19) yields:

Theorem 5.2.1 Under assumptions 5.2.1–5.2.6,

$$\sqrt{n}(\theta_n-\theta_0) \to N_m(0,\Omega) \text{ in distr., where } \Omega = (\Gamma)^{-1}\Delta(\Gamma')^{-1}.$$

Note that this result holds regardless of whether or not the underlying model is correctly specified. A similar result has been obtained by White (1980a, 1982) for misspecified linear models and maximum likelihood under misspecification. Moreover, if the underlying model is correctly specified, r is defined by (5.2.7) and θ_n is the nonlinear least squares estimator then Ω reduces to $\Omega_{00}^{-1}\,\Omega_{10}\Omega_{00}^{-1}$. Cf. theorem 4.3.2 and exercise 5.

A consistent estimator of Ω can be obtained as follows. Let

$$\hat{\Gamma} = [(1/n)\sum_{j=1}^{n}(\partial/\partial\theta')r_1(Y_j,X_j,\theta_n), \;....\; ,(1/n)\sum_{j=1}^{n}(\partial/\partial\theta')r_m(Y_j,X_j,\theta_n)]' \quad (5.2.20)$$

$$\hat{\Delta} = (1/n)\sum_{j=1}^{n}r(Y_j,X_j,\theta_n)r(Y_j,X_j,\theta_n)' \quad (5.2.21)$$

$$\hat{\Omega} = \hat{\Gamma}^{-1}\hat{\Delta}(\hat{\Gamma}')^{-1} \quad (5.2.22)$$

Then

Theorem 5.2.2 Under assumptions 5.2.1–5.2.6, $\text{plim}_{n\to\infty}\hat{\Omega} = \Omega$.

Proof: Exercise 6.

We now come to the null hypothesis to be tested. As said before, the null hypothesis $E(Y_j|X_j) = f(X_j,\theta_0)$ a.s. is equivalent to (5.2.6), where r is defined by (5.2.7). If H_0 is true then for $i=1,2,...,m$,

$$E[r_i(Y_j,X_j,\theta_0)w_i(X_j,\theta_0)] = E\{E[r_i(Y_j,X_j,\theta_0)|X_j]w_i(X_i,\theta_0)\} = 0 \quad (5.2.23)$$

for all weight functions w_i for which the expectation involved is defined.

If H_0 is false there exist continuous weight functions w_i for which (5.2.23) does not hold. Cf. theorem 3.1.2. Now let us specify these weight functions.

Assumption 5.2.7 The weight functions $w_i(x,\theta)$, $i=1,2,...,m$, are Borel measurable real functions on $R^k \times \Theta$ such that for $i=1,2,...,m$,

(i) for each $x \in R^k$, $w_i(x,\theta)$ is continuously differentiable on Θ;

(ii) $E[\sup_{\theta\in\Theta}|r_i(Y_1,X_1,\theta)|^2\,|w_i(X_1,\theta)|] < \infty$;

(iii) $E[\sup_{\theta\in\Theta}(r_i(Y_1,X_1,\theta)w_i(X_1,\theta))^2] < \infty$;

(iv) for $\ell=1,2,...,m$, $E[\sup_{\theta\in\Theta}|(\partial/\partial\theta_\ell)(r_i(Y_1,X_1,\theta)w_i(X_1,\theta))|] < \infty$;

(v) if H_0 is false then $E[r_i(Y_1,X_1,\theta_0)w_i(X_1,\theta_0)] \neq 0$ for at least one i.

The conditions (i)–(iv) are regularity conditions. Condition (v), however, is the crux of the conditional M-test, because it determines the power of the test. It says that the random vector function

$$\hat{M}(\theta) = (1/n)\textstyle\sum_{j=1}^{n} M(Y_j,X_j,\theta) \qquad (5.2.24)$$

with

$$\begin{aligned} M(Y_j,X_j,\theta) &= (r_1(Y_j,X_j,\theta)w_1(X_j,\theta),...,r_m(Y_j,X_j,\theta)w_m(X_j,\theta))' \\ &= (M_1(Y_j,X_j,\theta),...,M_m(Y_j,X_j,\theta))' \end{aligned} \qquad (5.2.25)$$

say, has nonzero mean at $\theta=\theta_0$ if H_0 is false. Thus, we actually test the null hypothesis

$$H_0^*\colon E[\hat{M}(\theta_0)]=0 \qquad (5.2.26)$$

against the alternative hypothesis

$$H_1^*\colon E[\hat{M}(\theta_0)] \neq 0. \qquad (5.2.27)$$

However, it may occur that the choice of the weight functions is inappropriate in that H_0^* holds while H_0 is false. The choice of the weight functions is therefore more or less a matter of guesswork, as a watertight choice would require knowledge of the true model. In the next section it will be shown how the conditional M-test can be modified to a consistent test.

We are now going to construct a test statistic on the basis of the statistic $\hat{M}(\theta_n)$. Consider its i-th component $\hat{M}_i(\theta_n)$. By the mean value theorem we have

$$\sqrt{n}\hat{M}_i(\theta_n) = \sqrt{n}\hat{M}_i(\theta_0) + (1/n)\textstyle\sum_{j=1}^{n}(\partial/\partial\theta)M_i(Y_j,X_j,\theta_n^{(i)})\sqrt{n}(\theta_n-\theta_0) \qquad (5.2.28)$$

where $|\theta_n^{(i)} - \theta_0| \leq |\theta_n - \theta_0|$. Denoting

$$A = (E[(\partial/\partial\theta')r_1(Y_1,X_1,\theta_0)w_1(X_1,\theta_0)],\ldots ,E[(\partial/\partial\theta')r_m(Y_1,X_1,\theta_0)w_m(X_1,\theta_0)])' \tag{5.2.29}$$

it is not hard to show, similarly to (5.2.17), that (5.2.28) implies

$$\text{plim}_{n\to\infty}(\sqrt{n}\hat{M}(\theta_n) - \sqrt{n}\hat{M}(\theta_0) - A\sqrt{n}(\theta_n - \theta_0)) = 0 \tag{5.2.30}$$

Cf. exercise 7. Substituting $-(1/\sqrt{n})\sum_{j=1}^n \Gamma^{-1}r(Y_j,X_j,\theta_0)$ for $\sqrt{n}(\theta_n - \theta_0)$ (cf. (5.2.17)) it follows from (5.2.30) and (5.2.24) that

$$\text{plim}_{n\to\infty}(\sqrt{n}\hat{M}(\theta_n) - (1/\sqrt{n})\sum_{j=1}^n Z_j) = 0, \tag{5.2.31}$$

where

$$Z_j = M(Y_j,X_j,\theta_0) - A\Gamma^{-1} r(Y_j,X_j,\theta_0).$$

If H_0 is true then $E(Z_j) = 0$, and moreover it follows from assumption 5.2.7 that $E(Z_jZ_j') = \Delta_*$, where

$$\Delta_* = E[M(Y_1,X_1,\theta_0)M(Y_1,X_1,\theta_0)'] - E[M(Y_1,X_1,\theta_0)r(Y_1,X_1,\theta_0)'(\Gamma')^{-1} A'] - A\Gamma^{-1}E[r(Y_1,X_1,\theta_0)M(Y_1,X_1,\theta_0)'] + A\Gamma^{-1}\Delta(\Gamma')^{-1}A', \tag{5.2.32}$$

is well-defined. By the central limit theorem and (5.2.31) we now have

$$\sqrt{n}M(\theta_n) \to N_m(0,\Delta_*) \text{ in distr. under } H_0. \tag{5.2.33}$$

Moreover, under H_1^* we have

$$\text{plim}_{n\to\infty}\hat{M}(\hat{\theta}_n) = E[M(Y_1,X_1,\theta_0)] \neq 0. \tag{5.2.34}$$

A consistent estimator of Δ_* can be obtained as follows. Let $\hat{\Gamma}$, $\hat{\Delta}$ and $\hat{\Omega}$ be defined by (5.2.19)–(5.2.21), let

$$\hat{A} = ((1/n)\sum_{j=1}^n(\partial/\partial\theta')[r_1(Y_j,X_j,\theta_n)w_1(X_j,\theta_n)]',\ldots ,(1/n)\sum_{j=1}^n(\partial/\partial\theta')[r_m(Y_j,X_j,\theta_n)w_m(X_j,\theta_n)]')$$

$$\hat{B} = (1/n)\sum_{j=1}^n M(Y_j,X_j,\theta_n)M(Y_j,X_j,\theta_n)'$$

$$\hat{C} = (1/n)\sum_{j=1}^n M(Y_j,X_j,\theta_n)r(Y_j,X_j,\theta_n)'$$

and

$$\hat{\Delta}_* = \hat{B} - \hat{C}(\hat{\Gamma}')^{-1}\hat{A}' - \hat{A}\hat{\Gamma}^{-1}\hat{C}' + \hat{A}\hat{\Omega}\hat{A}'. \tag{5.2.35}$$

Then:

Theorem 5.2.3 Under assumptions 5.2.1–5.2.7, $\text{plim}_{n\to\infty}\Delta_* = \Delta_*$.

Proof: Exercise 8.

Note that this result also holds if H_0 is false, although in that case Δ_* is no longer the asymptotic variance matrix of $\sqrt{n}\hat{M}(\theta_n)$.

Finally, assume

Assumption 5.2.8 The matrix Δ_* is nonsingular,

and let

$$\hat{H} = n\hat{M}(\theta_n)'\hat{\Delta}_*^{-1}\hat{M}(\theta_n)$$

be the ultimate test statistic. Then

Theorem 5.2.4 Under assumptions 5.2.1–5.2.8,

(i) $\hat{H} \to \chi^2_m$ in distr. if H_0 is true,

(ii) $\text{plim}_{n\to\infty}\hat{H}/n = \{E[M(Y_1,X_1,\theta_0)]\}'\Delta_*^{-1}\{EM(Y_1,X_1,\theta_0)]\} > 0$ if H_0 is false.

Exercises

1. Prove (5.2.4).
2. Prove (5.2.5).
3. Why does (5.2.15) follow from (5.2.14)?
4. Prove (5.2.17).
5. Prove that under the conditions in section 4.3,

   $$\Omega = \Omega_{00}^{-1}\Omega_{10}\Omega_{00}^{-1}.$$

6. Prove theorem 5.2.2.
7. Prove (5.2.30).
8. Prove theorem 5.2.3. In particular, check which parts of assumption 5.2.7 have been used here.

5.3 A consistent randomized conditional M-test

As mentioned before, the power of the conditional M-test heavily depends on the choice of the weight functions. Quoting Newey (1985, p. 1054): "An important property of specification tests based on a finite set of moment conditions is that they may not be consistent. This inconsistency has been noted in particular examples by Bierens (1982) and Holly (1982) and is a pervasive phenomenon." Thus, the solution of the inconsistency problem is to use an *infinite* set of moment conditions. Theorem 3.3.5 suggests how to do that. Let ψ be a bounded Borel measurable one-to-one mapping from R^k into R^k, and replace $w_i(x,\theta)$ by $\exp(\xi'\psi(x))$. Then theorem 3.3.5 says that the null hypothesis is false, i.e.,

$$H_1: P\{E[r(Y_j,X_j,\theta_0)|X_j] = 0\} < 1,$$

if and only if $E[r(Y_j,X_j,\theta_0)\exp(\xi'\psi(X_j))] \neq 0$, except on a set S with $\mu(S) = 0$, where μ is a probability measure induced by an absolutely continuous k-variate distribution. Note that in general the complement of the set S is infinite, so that we have to check the inequality involved over an infinite (and usually also uncountable) set of ξ's. Denoting

$$M(y,x,\theta,\xi) = r(y,x,\theta)\exp(\xi'\psi(x)) \tag{5.3.1}$$

we now have

$$E[M(Y_j,X_j,\theta_0,\xi)] \neq 0 \text{ for all } \xi \notin S \text{ if } H_0 \text{ is false} \tag{5.3.2}$$

whereas clearly

$$E[M(Y_j,X_j,\theta_0,\xi)] = 0 \text{ for all } \xi \in R^k \text{ if } H_0 \text{ is true.} \tag{5.3.3}$$

Next, let

$$\hat{M}(\theta_n,\xi) = (1/n)\textstyle\sum_{j=1}^{n} M(Y_j,X_j,\theta_n,\xi) \tag{5.3.4}$$

$$\hat{H}(\xi) = n\hat{M}(\theta_n,\xi)'\hat{\Delta}_*(\xi)^{-1}\, M(\theta_n,\xi), \tag{5.3.5}$$

where $\hat{\Delta}_*(\xi)$ is defined in (5.2.35) with $w_i(x,\theta)$ replaced by $\exp(\xi'\psi(x))$, and assume that in particular assumption 5.2.8 holds for every $\xi \in R^k\backslash\{0\}$. Then we have

$$\hat{H}(\xi) \to \chi^2_m \text{ in distr. for every } \xi \in R^k\backslash\{0\} \text{ if } H_0 \text{ is true.} \tag{5.3.6}$$

and

$$\text{plim}_{n\to\infty}\hat{H}(\xi)/n = \{E[M(Y_1,X_1,\theta_0,\xi)]\}'\Delta_*(\xi)^{-1}\{E[M(Y_1,X_1,\theta_0,\xi)]\} > 0$$
$$\text{for all } \xi \in R^k\backslash S \text{ if } H_0 \text{ is false,} \tag{5.3.7}$$

where $\Delta_*(\xi)$ is defined in (5.2.31).

The latter result indicates that this version of the conditional M-test is "almost surely" consistent (i.e., has asymptotic power 1 against all deviations from the null), as consistency only fails for ξ in a null set S of the measure μ. Also, note that we actually have imposed an infinite number of moment restrictions, namely the restrictions (5.3.3). Furthermore, observe that the exclusion of $\xi = 0$ is essential for (5.3.6) and (5.3.7), because by assumption 5.2.3,

$$P[\hat{M}(\theta_n,0) = 0] \to 1,$$

hence

$$\hat{H}(0) \to 0 \text{ in pr.}$$

regardless of whether or not H_0 is true. Thus, the set S contains at least the origin of R^k.

One might argue now that the problem of how to choose the weight function $w(x,\theta)$ has not been solved but merely been shifted to the problem of how to choose the vector ξ in the weight function $\exp(\xi'\psi(x))$. Admittedly, in the present approach, one has still to make a choice, but the point is that our choice will now be far less crucial for the asymptotic power of the test, for the asymptotic power will be equal to 1 for "almost" any $\xi \in R^k$, namely all ξ outside a null set with respect to an absolutely continuous k-variate distribution. If one would pick ξ randomly from such a distribution then ξ will be an admissible choice with probability 1. In fact, the asymptotic properties of the test under H_0 will not be affected by choosing ξ randomly, whereas the asymptotic power will be 1 without worrying about the null set S:

> *Theorem 5.3.1* Let $H(\xi)$ be the test statistic of the conditional M-test with weight functions $w_i(x,\theta) = \exp(\xi'\psi(x))$, where ψ is a bounded Borel measurable one-to-one mapping from R^k into R^k. Suppose that the conditions of theorem 5.2.4 hold for $\xi \in R^k\backslash\{0\}$, possibly except assumption 5.2.7(v). Let ξ be a random drawing from an arbitrary absolutely continuous k-variate distribution. Then
>
> $$\hat{H}(\xi) \rightarrow \chi^2_m \text{ if } H_0 \text{ is true} \tag{5.3.8}$$
>
> and
>
> $$\text{plim}_{n\rightarrow\infty}\hat{H}(\xi) = \infty \text{ if } H_0 \text{ is false} \tag{5.3.9}$$

Proof: First, assume that H_0 is true, so that for every $\xi \in R^k\backslash\{0\}$, $\hat{H}(\xi) \rightarrow \chi^2_m$ in distr. Then by theorem 2.3.6

$$E[\exp(i\cdot t\hat{H}(\xi))] \rightarrow (1-2it)^{-m/2} = \varphi_m(t) \tag{5.3.10}$$

for every $t \in R$ and every fixed $\xi \in R^k\backslash\{0\}$, where $\varphi_m(t)$ is the characteristic function of the χ^2_m distribution. (Cf. section 2.3, exercise 3). Now let ξ be a random drawing from an absolutely continuous k-variate distribution with density $h(\xi)$. Then for every $t \in R$,

$$\begin{aligned} E[\exp(i\cdot t\hat{H}(\xi))] &= \int E[\exp(i\cdot tH(\xi))]h(\xi)d\xi \\ &\rightarrow \int\varphi_m(t)h(\xi)d\xi = \varphi_m(t) \end{aligned} \tag{5.3.11}$$

by bounded convergence (cf. theorem 2.2.2). Theorem 2.3.6 says that this result implies that $\hat{H}(\xi) \rightarrow \chi^2_m$ in distr.

Second, assume that H_0 is false. Then there exists a null set S of the distribution of ξ such that for every $\xi \in R^k\backslash S$,

$$E[M(Y_1,X_1,\theta_0,\xi)] \neq 0.$$

Hence

$$\text{plim}_{n\to\infty}\hat{H}(\xi)/n = \{E[M(Y_1,X_1,\theta_0,\xi)]\}'\Delta_*(\xi)^{-1}\{E[M(Y_1,X_1,\theta_0,\xi)]\} = T(\xi), \quad (5.3.12)$$

say, where

$$T(\xi) > 0 \text{ if } \xi \in R^k\backslash S,\ T(\xi) = 0 \text{ if } \xi \in S. \quad (5.3.13)$$

Again using theorem 2.3.6 we see that

$$\hat{H}(\xi)/n \to T(\xi) \text{ in distr.} \quad (5.3.14)$$

and since S is a null set of the distribution of ξ we have

$$P[T(\xi) > 0] = 1. \quad (5.3.15)$$

It is not hard to show now that (5.3.14) and (5.3.15) imply (5.3.9).
Q.E.D.

Remark: The randomization of the test parameter ξ involved can be avoided by using the more complicated approach in Bierens (1991a). The present approach has been choosen for its simplicity.

Next, we have to deal with a practical problem regarding the choice of the bounded Borel measurable mapping ψ. Suppose for example that we would have chosen

$$\psi(x^{(1)},...,x^{(k)}) = (tg^{-1}(x^{(1)}),...,tg^{-1}(x^{(k)}))'.$$

This mapping is clearly admissible. However, if the components X_{ij} of X_j are large then $tg^{-1}(X_{ij})$ will be close to the upperbound $\frac{1}{2}\pi$, hence $\exp(\xi'\psi(X_j))$ will be almost constant, i.e.,

$$\exp(\xi'\psi(X_j)) \approx \exp(\tfrac{1}{2}\pi\textstyle\sum_{i=1}^k\xi_i)$$

and consequently

$$M(\theta_n,\xi) \approx [(1/n)\textstyle\sum_{j=1}^n r(Y_j,X_j,\theta_n)]\exp(\tfrac{1}{2}\pi\sum_{i=1}^k\xi_i).$$

Since the mean between the square brackets equals the zero vector with probability converging to 1 (cf. assumption 5.2.3), $M(\theta_n,\xi)$ will be close to the zero vector and consequently $H(\xi)$ will be close to zero. This will obviously destroy the power of the test. A cure for this problem is to standardize the X_j's in $\psi(X_j)$. Thus let $\bar{X}_i$ be the sample mean of the X_{ij}'s, let S_i be the sample standard deviation of the X_{ij}'s ($i=1,2,...,k$), and let

$$\hat{Z}_j = (tg^{-1}[(X_{1j}-\bar{X}_1)/S_1],...,tg^{-1}[(X_{kj}-\bar{X}_k)/S_k])'. \quad (5.3.16)$$

Then the proposed weight function is:

$$\exp(\xi'\hat{Z}_j). \quad (5.3.17)$$

It can be shown (cf. exercise 3) that using this weight function is asymptotically equivalent to using the weight function

$$\exp(\xi' Z_j) \tag{5.3.18}$$

where

$$Z_j = (tg^{-1}[(X_{ij}-E(X_{ij}))/\sqrt{var(X_{ij})}],\ldots \\ ,tg^{-1}[(X_{kj}-E(X_{kj}))/\sqrt{var(X_{kj})}])' \tag{5.3.19}$$

Exercises

1. Check the conditions in section 5.2.2 for the weight function $\exp(\xi'\psi(x))$, and in particular verify that only assumption 5.2.8 is of concern.
2. Show that (5.3.12) holds uniformly on any compact subset of R^k.
3. Verify that using the weight function (5.3.17) is asymptotically equivalent to using the weight function (5.3.18), provided that for $i=1,2,\ldots,k$,

   $$\text{plim}_{n\to\infty}\bar{X}_i = E(X_{i1}) \text{ and } \text{plim}_{n\to\infty}S_i = \sqrt{var(X_{i1})} > 0.$$

5.4 The integrated M-test

An alternative to plugging a random ξ into the test statistic $\hat{H}(\xi)$ defined in (5.3.5) is to take a weighted integral of $\hat{H}(\xi)$, say

$$\hat{b} = \int \hat{H}(\xi)h(\xi)d\xi, \tag{5.4.1}$$

where $h(\xi)$ is a k-variate density function. This is the approach in Bierens (1982). This idea seems attractive because under H_1 it is possible to draw a ξ for which the function

$$T(\xi) = \text{plim}_{n\to\infty}\hat{H}(\xi)/n$$

(cf.(5.3.12)) is close to zero, despite the fact that

$$P[T(\xi) > 0] = 1.$$

In that case the small sample power of the test may be rather poor. By integrating over a sufficient large domain of $T(\xi)$ we will likely cover the areas for which $T(\xi)$ is high, hence we may expect that a test based on $\hat{b}$ will in general have higher small sample power than the test in section 5.3. A disadvantage of this approach, however, is firstly that the limiting distribution of $\hat{b}$ under H_0 is of an unknown type, and secondly that calculating $\hat{b}$ can be quite laborious.

It will be shown that under H_0 the test statistic $\hat{b}$ is asymptotically equivalent to an integral of the form

$$\hat{b}^* = \int[(1/\sqrt{n})\sum_{j=1}^{n}Z_j(\xi)]'[(1/\sqrt{n})\sum_{j=1}^{n}Z_j(\xi)]h(\xi)d\xi, \tag{5.4.2}$$

provided $h(\xi)$ vanishes outside a compact set, where the $Z_j(\xi)$'s are for each $\xi \in R^k \setminus\{0\}$ independent random vectors in R^m with zero mean vector and unit variance matrix:

$$E[Z_j(\xi)] = 0,\ E[Z_j(\xi)Z_j(\xi)'] = I_m. \tag{5.4.3}$$

Although

$$[(1/\sqrt{n})\sum_{j=1}^{n}Z_j(\xi)]'[(1/\sqrt{n})\sum_{j=1}^{n}Z_j(\xi)] \rightarrow \chi_m^2 \text{ in distr.}$$

for each $\xi \in R^k \setminus\{0\}$, this result does *not* imply that

$$\hat{b}^* \rightarrow \chi_m^2 \text{ in distr.}$$

On the other hand, the first moment of $\hat{b}^*$ equals m, hence by Chebishev's inequality

$$P(\hat{b}^* \geq m/\varepsilon) \leq E[\hat{b}^*/(m/\varepsilon)] = \varepsilon \tag{5.4.4}$$

for every $\varepsilon > 0$. Since under H_0, $\text{plim}_{n\rightarrow\infty}(\hat{b} - \hat{b}^*) = 0$, we may conclude that for every $\varepsilon > 0$,

$$\text{limsup}_{n\rightarrow\infty}P(\hat{b} \geq m/\varepsilon) \leq \varepsilon \text{ under } H_0. \tag{5.4.5}$$

Moreover, if H_0 is false then $\text{plim}_{n\rightarrow\infty}\hat{b} = \infty$, hence

$$\lim_{n\rightarrow\infty}P(\hat{b} \geq m/\varepsilon) = 1 \text{ under } H_1. \tag{5.4.6}$$

These results suggest to use m/ε as a critical value for testing H_0 at the $\varepsilon \times 100$ per cent significance level, i.e.,

reject H_0 if $\hat{b} \geq m/\varepsilon$ and accept H_0 if $\hat{b} < m/\varepsilon$.

Admittedly, the actual type I error will be (much) smaller than ε, because Chebishev's inequality is not very sharp an inequality, but this is the price we have to pay for possible gains of small sample power.

The problem regarding the calculation of the integral (5.4.1) can be solved by drawing a sample $\{\xi_1,...,\xi_{N_n}\}$ of size N_n ($N_n \rightarrow \infty$ as $n \rightarrow \infty$) from $h(\xi)$ and to use

$$\tilde{b} = (1/N_n)\sum_{\ell=1}^{N_n}\hat{H}(\xi_\ell) \tag{5.4.7}$$

instead of $\hat{b}$. This will be asymptotically equivalent, i.e.,

$$\text{plim}_{n\rightarrow\infty}(\hat{b} - \tilde{b}) = 0 \text{ under } H_0 \tag{5.4.8}$$

and

$$\text{plim}_{n\rightarrow\infty}\tilde{b}_n = \int T(\xi)h(\xi)d\xi > 0 \text{ under } H_1. \tag{5.4.9}$$

Now let us turn to the proof of the asymptotic equivalence of b and b^* under H_0. Observe that similarly to (5.2.28)

$$\sqrt{n}\hat{M}_i(\theta_n,\xi) = \sqrt{n}\hat{M}_i(\theta_0,\xi) + [(1/n)\textstyle\sum_{j=1}^n(\partial/\partial\theta)M_i(Y_j,X_j,\theta_n^{(i)}(\xi),\xi)]\sqrt{n}(\theta_n-\theta_0), \qquad (5.4.10)$$

where $\hat{M}_i(\theta,\xi)$ is the i-th component of $\hat{M}(\theta,\xi)$ defined in (5.3.4) and $\theta_n^{(i)}(\xi)$ is a mean value satisfying

$$|\theta_n^{(i)}(\xi)-\theta_0| \leq |\theta_n-\theta_0| \text{ a.s., for all } \xi \in R^k. \qquad (5.4.11)$$

Let Ξ be a compact subset of R^k . Under the conditions of theorem 5.3.1 we have

$$(1/n)\textstyle\sum_{j=1}^n(\partial/\partial\theta')M_i(Y_j,X_j,\theta,\xi) \rightarrow E[(\partial/\partial\theta')M_i(Y_1,X_1,\theta,\xi)] \qquad (5.4.12)$$

a.s., uniformly on $\Theta \times \Xi$. Cf. theorem 2.7.5. Denoting

$$a_i(\theta,\xi) = E[(\partial/\partial\theta')M_i(Y_1,X_1,\theta,\xi)] \qquad (5.4.13)$$

we thus have

$$\text{plim}_{n\rightarrow\infty}\text{sup}_{\xi\in\Xi}|(1/n)\textstyle\sum_{j=1}^n(\partial/\partial\theta')M_i(Y_j,X_j,\theta_n^{(i)}(\xi),\xi)-a_i(\theta_0,\xi)|$$
$$= \text{plim}_{n\rightarrow\infty}\text{sup}_{\xi\in\Xi}|a_i(\theta_n^{(i)}(\xi),\xi)-a_i(\theta_0,\xi)|$$
$$\leq \text{plim}_{n\rightarrow\infty}\text{sup}_{\xi\in\Xi}\text{sup}_{|\theta_*-\theta_0|\leq|\theta_n-\theta_0|}|a_i(\theta_*,\xi)-a_i(\theta_0,\xi)| = 0, \qquad (5.4.14)$$

where the last step follows from the continuity of $a_i(\theta,\xi)$ on the compact set $\Theta\times\Xi$ (hence $a_i(\theta,\xi)$ is *uniformly* continuous on $\Theta\times\Xi$), and the consistency of θ_n. Consequently, denoting

$$A(\xi) = (a_1(\theta_0,\xi),\ldots,a_m(\theta_0,\xi))', \qquad (5.4.15)$$

(cf. (5.2.29)), we have

$$\text{plim}_{n\rightarrow\infty}\text{sup}_{\xi\in\Xi}|\sqrt{n}\hat{M}(\theta_n,\xi)-\sqrt{n}\hat{M}(\theta_0,\xi) + A(\xi)\sqrt{n}(\theta_n-\theta_0)| = 0. \qquad (5.4.16)$$

Next, let

$$c_j(\xi) = M(Y_j,X_j,\theta_0,\xi) + A(\xi)\Gamma^{-1}r(Y_j,X_j,\theta_0). \qquad (5.4.17)$$

Then it follows from (5.2.17) and (5.4.16) that

$$\text{plim}_{n\rightarrow\infty}\text{sup}_{\xi\in\Xi}|\sqrt{n}\hat{M}(\theta_n,\xi) -(1/\sqrt{n})\textstyle\sum_{j=1}^n c_j(\xi)| = 0. \qquad (5.4.18)$$

Moreover, we have shown in section 5.2 that under H_0,

$$E[c_j(\xi)] = 0,\ E[c_j(\xi)c_j(\xi)'] = \Delta_*(\xi). \qquad (5.4.19)$$

Furthermore, it is not hard to show that the consistent estimator $\hat{\Delta}_*(\xi)$ of $\Delta_*(\xi)$ is also uniformly consistent on Ξ, and thus (cf. exercise 1)

$$\hat{\Delta}_*(\xi)^{-1} \to \Delta_*(\xi)^{-1} \text{ in pr., uniformly on } \Xi. \tag{5.4.20}$$

Denoting

$$Z_j(\xi) = \Delta_*(\xi)^{-1/2} c_j(\xi) \tag{5.4.21}$$

it is now not too hard to show (exercise 2) that

$$\text{plim}_{n\to\infty} \int_\Xi |\hat{H}(\xi) - [(1/\sqrt{n})\textstyle\sum_{j=1}^n Z_j(\xi)]'[(1/\sqrt{n})\sum_{j=1}^n Z_j(\xi)]| h(\xi) d\xi = 0. \tag{5.4.22}$$

Moreover, we leave it to the reader (exercise 3) to show that under H_1,

$$\text{plim}_{n\to\infty} \sup_{\xi \in \Xi} |\hat{H}(\xi)/n - T(\xi)| = 0. \tag{5.4.23}$$

Cf. (5.3.12).

Summarizing, we now have shown:

Theorem 5.4.1 Let the conditions of theorem 5.3.1 hold and let $h(\xi)$ be a k-variate density vanishing outside a compact subset Ξ of R^k.

(i) Under H_0 we have $\text{plim}_{n\to\infty}(\hat{b} - \hat{b}^*) = 0$, where $E(b^*) = m$.

(ii) Under H_1 we have $\text{plim}_{n\to\infty}\hat{b}/n = \int T(\xi)h(\xi)d\xi > 0$.

(iii) Replacing $\hat{b}$ by $\tilde{b}$ defined in (5.4.7), the above results go through.

Exercises

1. Prove (5.4.20).
2. Prove (5.4.22).
3. Prove (5.4.23).
4. Prove part iii of theorem 5.4.1.

6

Conditioning and dependence

Time series models usually aim to represent, directly or indirectly, the conditional expectation of a time series variable relative to the entire past of the time series process involved. The reason is that this conditional expectation is the best forecasting scheme; best in the sense that it yields forecasts with minimal mean square forecast error. The concept of a conditional expectation relative to a one-sided infinite sequence of "past" variables cannot be made clear on the basis of the elementary notion of conditional expectation known from intermediate mathematical-statistical textbooks. Even the more general approach in chapter 3 is not suitable. What we need here is the concept of a conditional expectation relative to a Borel field. We shall discuss this concept and its consequences (in particular martingale theory) in section 6.1. In section 6.2 we consider various measures of dependence as some, though rather weak, conditions have to be imposed on the dependence of a time series process to prove weak (uniform) laws of large numbers. These weak laws are the topics of sections 6.3 and 6.4.

Throughout we assume that the reader is familiar with the basic elements of linear time series analysis, say on the level of Harvey's (1981) textbook.

6.1 Conditional expectations relative to a Borel field

6.1.1 Definition and basic properties

In section 3.1 we have defined the conditional expectation of a random variable Y relative to a random vector $X \in R^k$ as a Borel measurable real function g on R^k such that

$$E[Y - g(X)]\psi(X) = 0$$

for all bounded Borel measurable real functions ψ on R^k. Approximating ψ by simple functions (cf. definition 1.3.2 and theorem 1.3.5) it follows that $g(X) = E(Y|X)$ a.s. if and only if

$$E[Y - g(X)]I(X \in B) = 0 \qquad (6.1.1)$$

for all Borel sets B in R^k, where I(.) is the indicator function. Now let $\{\Omega,\mathfrak{F},P\}$ be the probability space on which (Y,X) is defined and let $\mathfrak{F}_X$ be the Borel field generated by X, i.e. $\mathfrak{F}_X$ is the collection of all sets of the type

$$\{\omega \in \Omega: x(\omega) \in B\},\ B \in \mathfrak{B}^k.$$

Cf. theorem 1.1.1. Then condition (6.1.1) is equivalent to

$$\int_\Lambda [y(\omega) - g(x(\omega))]P(d\omega) = 0$$

for all $\Lambda \in \mathfrak{F}_X$. This justifies the notation

$$E(Y|X) = E(Y|\mathfrak{F}_X).$$

Note that $\mathfrak{F}_X$ is a Borel field contained in $\mathfrak{F}$:

$$\mathfrak{F}_X \subset \mathfrak{F}.$$

Following this line we can define conditional expectations relative to an arbitrary sub-Borel field $\mathfrak{G}$ of $\mathfrak{F}$ without reference to the random variable or vector which generates $\mathfrak{G}$:

> *Definition 6.1.1* Let Y be a random variable defined on the probability space $\{\Omega,\mathfrak{F},P\}$ satisfying $E(|Y|) < \infty$, and let $\mathfrak{G}$ be a Borel field contained in $\mathfrak{F}$. Then the conditional expectation of Y relative to $\mathfrak{G}$ is a random variable Z defined on $\{\Omega,\mathfrak{G},P\}$ such that for every $\Lambda \in \mathfrak{G}$,
>
> $$\int_\Lambda (y(\omega) - z(\omega))P(d\omega) = 0.$$

The existence of $Z = E(Y|\mathfrak{G})$ is guaranteed by the condition $E(|Y|) < \infty$, i.e. if E(Y) exists, so does $E(Y|\mathfrak{G})$. Cf. Chung (1974, theorem 6.1.1.) Moreover, the uniqueness of Z follows from the Radon-Nikodym theorem (cf. Royden [1968, p.238]), i.e. if both Z_1 and Z_2 satisfy the conditions in definition 6.1.1 then $P(Z_1 = Z_2) = 1$. We then say that Z_1 and Z_2 belong to the same equivalence class. Thus, $E(Y|\mathfrak{G})$ is almost surely unique.

Next, we define the Borel field generated by a one-sided infinite sequence (X_t), $t=1,2,\ldots$, of random vectors in R^k. First, let $\mathfrak{F}_n$ be the Borel field generated by $X_1,\ldots,X_n$, i.e. $\mathfrak{F}_n$ is the collection of sets

$$\{\omega \in \Omega: x_1(\omega) \in B_1,\ldots,x_n(\omega) \in B_n\},$$

where $B_1,\ldots,B_n$ are arbitrary Borel sets in R^k. Now $(\mathfrak{F}_n)$ is an increasing sequence of Borel fields:

$$\mathfrak{F}_n \subset \mathfrak{F}_{n+1} \tag{6.1.2}$$

If $\cup_{n\geq 1}\mathfrak{F}_n$ is a Borel field itself, it is just the Borel field generated by (X_t), $t=1,2,\ldots$ However, it is in general not a Borel field, for

$\Lambda_t \in \cup_{n\geq 1}\mathfrak{F}_n$, $t=1,2,\ldots$

does *not* imply

$\cup_{t\geq 1}\Lambda_t \in \cup_{n\geq 1}\mathfrak{F}_n$.

Therefore we define the Borel field $\mathfrak{F}_\infty$ generated by (X_t), $t=1,2,..$, as the minimum Borel field containing $\cup_{n\geq 1}\mathfrak{F}_n$.

> *Definition 6.1.2* Let (X_t), $t=1,2,\ldots$, be a one-sided infinite sequence of random vectors defined on a common probability space $\{\Omega,\mathfrak{F},P\}$, and let $\mathfrak{F}_n$ be the Borel field generated by $X_1,\ldots,X_n$. Then the Borel field generated by (X_t), $t=1,2,\ldots$ is the minimum Borel field containing $\cup_{n\geq 1}\mathfrak{F}_n$, which is denoted by $\mathfrak{F}_\infty = \vee_{n\geq 1}\mathfrak{F}_n$.

Consequently, for every Y defined on $(\Omega,\mathfrak{F},P)$ satisfying $E(|Y|) < \infty$ we have

$E(Y|X_1,X_2,X_3,\ldots]) = E(Y|\mathfrak{F}_\infty)$.

The properties of conditional expectations relative to a Borel field are quite similar to those in section 3.2. In particular, theorem 3.2.1 now reads as:

> *Theorem 6.1.1* Let Y and Z be random variables defined on a probability space $\{\Omega,\mathfrak{F},P\}$ satisfying $E(|Y|) < \infty$, $E(|Z|) < \infty$. Let $\mathfrak{G}$ and $\mathfrak{H}$ be Borel fields satisfying $\mathfrak{G} \subset \mathfrak{H} \subset \mathfrak{F}$. We have:
>
> (i) $E[E(Y|\mathfrak{H})|\mathfrak{G}] = E(Y|\mathfrak{G}) = E[E(Y|\mathfrak{G})|\mathfrak{H}]$;
>
> (ii) (a) $E[E(Y|\mathfrak{G})] = E(Y)$; (b) $E(Y|\mathfrak{F}) = Y$ a.s.;
>
> (iii) $U = Y - E(Y|\mathfrak{G}) \Rightarrow E(U|\mathfrak{G}) = 0$ a.s.;
>
> (iv) $E(Y + Z|\mathfrak{G}) = E(Y|\mathfrak{G}) + E(Z|\mathfrak{G})$ a.s.;
>
> (v) $Y \leq Z \Rightarrow E(Y|\mathfrak{G}) \leq E(Z|\mathfrak{G})$ a.s.;
>
> (vi) $|E(Y|\mathfrak{G})| \leq E[|Y|\,|\mathfrak{G}]$ a.s.;
>
> (vii) If X is defined on $\{\Omega,\mathfrak{G},P\}$ and $E(|X|) < \infty$ then $E(X\cdot Y|\mathfrak{G}) = X\cdot E(Y|\mathfrak{G})$;
>
> (viii) If every random variable defined on $\{\Omega,\mathfrak{G},P\}$ is independent of Y, i.e., $\Lambda_1 \in \mathfrak{F}_Y$, $\Lambda_2 \in \mathfrak{G} \Rightarrow P(\Lambda_1 \cap \Lambda_2) = P(\Lambda_1)\cdot P(\Lambda_2)$, where $\mathfrak{F}_Y$ is the Borel field generated by Y, then $E(Y|\mathfrak{G}) = E(Y)$.

Proof: Exercise 2.

Note that part (viii) of theorem 3.2.1 does not apply anymore. The Borel field generated by $\Gamma(X)$ is contained in the Borel field generated by X, so that the first result of theorem 3.2.1 (viii) is just part (i) of theorem 6.1.1. Moreover, if Γ is a one-to-one mapping the aforementioned Borel fields are the same, and so are the corresponding conditional expectations.

6.1.2 Martingales

A fundamental concept in the theory of stochastic processes is the martingale concept. This concept is particularly important in regression analysis, as the errors of a properly specified time series regression model are, by construction, martingale differences and martingale differences obey central limit theorems similar to those obeyed by independent random variables.

Consider a sequence (X_j) of independent random variables defined on a common probability space, satisfying $E(|X_j|) < \infty$, $E(X_j) = 0$, and let

$$Y_n = \sum_{j=1}^{n} X_j.$$

Moreover, let $\mathfrak{F}_n$ be the Borel field generated by $(X_1,\ldots,X_n)$. Then

$$E(Y_n|\mathfrak{F}_{n-1}) = E(X_n + Y_{n-1}|\mathfrak{F}_{n-1}) = E(X_n|\mathfrak{F}_{n-1}) + E(Y_{n-1}|\mathfrak{F}_{n-1})$$
$$= Y_{n-1} \text{ a.s.,} \qquad (6.1.3)$$

for $E(X_n|\mathfrak{F}_{n-1}) = 0$ by independence and the condition $E(X_n) = 0$ (cf. theorem 6.1.1(viii)]) whereas by theorem 6.1.1 (iib) and the fact that

$$Y_n \text{ is defined on } \{\Omega,\mathfrak{F}_n,P\}, \qquad (6.1.4)$$

we have $E(Y_{n-1}|\mathfrak{F}_{n-1}) = Y_{n-1}$ a.s. Furthermore, observe that

$$E(|Y_n|) < \infty \qquad (6.1.5)$$

and

$$\mathfrak{F}_n \supset \mathfrak{F}_{n-1} \qquad (6.1.6)$$

The properties (6.1.3) through (6.1.6) are just the defining conditions for a martingale:

> *Definition 6.1.3* Let (Y_n) be a sequence of random variables satisfying (a) $E(|Y_n|) < \infty$ (b) Y_n is defined on $\{\Omega,\mathfrak{F}_n,P\}$, (c) $\mathfrak{F}_n \subset \mathfrak{F}_{n+1}$ and (d) $Y_n = E(Y_{n+1}|\mathfrak{F}_n)$ a.s. Then Y_n is called a martingale.

Next, let

$$U_n = Y_n - Y_{n-1}.$$

Then by (d),

$E(U_n|\mathfrak{F}_{n-1}) = 0$ a.s.,

whereas conditions (a), (b), and (c) in definition 6.1.3 hold with Y_n replaced by U_n. Such a sequence (U_n) is called a martingale difference sequence. Conversely, let (U_n) be such that

$$E(|U_n|) < \infty, U_n \text{ is defined on } \{\Omega,\mathfrak{F}_n,P\}, \text{ with } \mathfrak{F}_n \subset \mathfrak{F}_{n+1}, \text{ and } E(U_n|\mathfrak{F}_{n-1}) = 0 \text{ a.s.} \quad (6.1.7)$$

Can we construct a martingale (Y_n) such that

$U_n = Y_n - Y_{n-1}$?

In general the answer is no. The only possible candidate for Y_n is

$Y_n = \sum_{j\leq n} U_j$,

but in general $E(Y_n)$ is not defined. For example, if the U_n's are independent random drawings from the standard normal distribution then $E(|Y_n|) = \infty$. However, for every one-sided infinite sequence (U_n), $n=1,2,...$, satisfying (6.1.7) we can define a martingale (Y_n) such that $U_n = Y_n - Y_{n-1}$ for $n \geq 1$, namely

$$Y_n = \sum_{j=1}^{k} U_j \text{ for } n \geq 1, \ Y_n = 0 \text{ for } n < 1. \quad (6.1.8)$$

Therefore we restrict the martingale difference concept to one-sided infinite sequences:

> *Definition 6.1.4* Let (U_n), $n=1,2,...$, be a sequence of random variables such that for $n \geq 1$ (a) $E(|U_n|) < \infty$ (b) U_n is defined on $\{\Omega,\mathfrak{F}_n,P\}$ (c) $\mathfrak{F}_n \subset \mathfrak{F}_{n+1}$, $\mathfrak{F}_0 = \{\Omega,\emptyset\}$ (d) $E(U_n|\mathfrak{F}_{n-1}) = 0$ a.s. Then (U_n), $n=1,2,...$, is called a martingale difference sequence.

Note that for $n = 1$ condition (d) follows from the definition of $\mathfrak{F}_0$, which is called a *trivial* Borel field, and the condition $E(U_1) = 0$, for

$$E(U_1|\mathfrak{F}_0) = E(U_1) \quad (6.1.9)$$

6.1.3 Martingale convergence theorems

Given a random variable X defined on $\{\Omega,\mathfrak{F},P\}$, with $E(|X|) < \infty$, a martingale (Y_n) can be constructed as follows: let $(\mathfrak{F}_n)$ be any increasing sequence of Borel fields contained in $\mathfrak{F}$ and let

$$Y_n = E(X|\mathfrak{F}_n) \quad (6.1.10)$$

Then by theorem 6.1.1(vi),

$|Y_n| = |E(X|\mathfrak{F}_n)| \leq E(|X|\,|\mathfrak{F}_n)$, hence by theorem 6.1.1(iia),

$E(|Y_n|) \leq E(|X|) < \infty$

Moreover, by definition 6.1.1, Y_n is defined on $\{\Omega,\mathfrak{F}_n,P\}$. Finally,

$E(Y_{n+1}|\mathfrak{F}_n) = E[E(X|\mathfrak{F}_{n+1})|\mathfrak{F}_n] = E(X|\mathfrak{F}_n) = Y_n$

by theorem 6.1.1(i). Thus (Y_n) is a martingale. This construction is important because it enables us to prove the existence of

$\lim_{n\to\infty}E(X|\mathfrak{F}_n)$,

on the basis of the following dominated convergence theorem for martingales.

> *Theorem 6.1.2* Let (Y_n) be a martingale satisfying
>
> $\sup_n E(|Y_n|) < \infty$.
>
> Then Y_n converges a.s. to an a.s. finite limit Y_∞

Proof: Chung (1974, theorem 9.4.4).

Thus the martingale (Y_n) defined in (6.1.10) satisfies:

$\lim_{n\to\infty}E(X|\mathfrak{F}_n) = Y_\infty$ a.s., with $|Y_\infty| < \infty$ a.s.

Moreover, we can identify Y_∞ as a conditional expectation of X:

> *Theorem 6.1.3* Let X be a random variable defined on $\{\Omega,\mathfrak{F},P\}$, satisfying $E(|X|) < \infty$, and let $\mathfrak{F}_n$ be an increasing sequence of Borel fields contained in $\mathfrak{F}$. Then $\lim_{n\to\infty}E(X|\mathfrak{F}_n) = E(X|\mathfrak{F}_\infty)$, where $\mathfrak{F}_\infty = \vee_{n\geq 1}\mathfrak{F}_n$.

Proof: Chung (1974, theorem 9.4.8).

A direct consequence of theorem 6.1.3 and definition 6.1.2 is:

> *Theorem 6.1.4* Let X be defined as in theorem 6.1.3 and let (Z_t), $t=1,2,...$, be a sequence of random variables or vectors defined on $\{\Omega,\mathfrak{F},P\}$. Then
>
> $\lim_{n\to\infty}E(X|Z_1,Z_2,...,Z_n) = E(X|Z_1,Z_2,...)$ a.s.

Another application of theorem 6.1.3 we need later on is the following:

> *Theorem 6.1.5* Let the conditions of theorem 6.1.4 hold. Let $Z_t^{(\ell)}$ be the random vector consisting of the components of Z_t truncated to ℓ decimal digits. Then
>
> $\lim_{\ell\to\infty}E(X|Z_1^{(\ell)},Z_2^{(\ell)},...) = E(X|Z_1,Z_2,...)$ a.s.

Proof: Let $\mathfrak{G}_\ell$ be the Borel field generated by $(Z_t^{(\ell)})$, $t=1,2,...$ and let $\mathfrak{G}_\infty = \vee_{\ell\geq 1}\mathfrak{G}_\ell$. Since for each ℓ, $\mathfrak{G}_\ell \subset \mathfrak{F}_\infty$, we have $\mathfrak{G}_\infty \subset \mathfrak{F}_\infty$. Moreover, since for each ℓ, $\mathfrak{G}_\ell \subset \mathfrak{G}_{\ell+1}$, it follows from theorem 6.1.3 that

$$\lim_{\ell\to\infty} E(X|Z_1^{(\ell)},Z_2^{(\ell)},...) = E(X|\mathfrak{G}_\infty) \text{ a.s.}$$

The theorem can now be proved by showing

$$\mathfrak{F}_\infty \subset \mathfrak{G}_\infty, \tag{6.1.11}$$

as then $\mathfrak{F}_\infty = \mathfrak{G}_\infty$. To prove (6.1.11), assume first that the Z_t $(= z_t(\omega))$ are scalar random variables defined on a common probability space $\{\Omega,\mathfrak{F},P\}$. Next, prove, following the line of the proof of theorem 1.3.2, that for arbitrary $\xi \in R$,

$$\{\omega \in \Omega: z_t(\omega) \leq \xi\} = \{\omega \in \Omega: \limsup_{\ell\to\infty} z_t^{(\ell)}(\omega) \leq \xi\} \in \mathfrak{G}_\infty$$

and conclude from this (cf. theorem 1.1.1) that for every Borel set B_t in R,

$$\{\omega \in \Omega: z_t(\omega) \in B_t\} \in \mathfrak{G}_\infty.$$

See further, exercise 4. Q.E.D.

The importance of theorem 6.1.5 is that the sequence $(Z_t^{(\ell)})$ is rational-valued, hence countably-valued. Cf. Royden (1968, proposition 6, p. 21). This property will enable us to identify $E(X|Z_1,Z_2,...)$ in terms of unconditional expectations, similarly to theorem 3.3.5. See Bierens (1987a, 1988a) and chapter 7.

6.1.4 A martingale difference central limit theorem

The martingale difference central limit theorem we consider here is an extension of theorem 2.4.3 to double arrays $(X_{n,j})$ of martingale differences, based on the following theorem of McLeish (1974).

Theorem 6.1.6 Let $(X_{n,j})$ be a martingale difference array, i.e.

$$E(X_{n,j}|X_{n,j-1},...,X_{n,1}) = 0 \text{ for } j \geq 2,\ E(X_{n,1}) = 0,$$

satisfying

(a) $\sup_{n\geq 1} E[(\max_{j\leq k_n}|X_{n,j}|)^2] < \infty$

(b) $\max_{j\leq k_n}|X_{n,j}| \to 0$ in pr.

(c) $\sum_{j=1}^{k_n} X_{n,j}^2 \to 1$ in pr.,

where $k_n \to \infty$ as $n \to \infty$. Then

$$\sum_{j=1}^{k_n} X_{n,j} \to N(0,1) \text{ in distr.}$$

Proof: McLeish (1974, theorem 2.3)

Using this theorem it is not too hard to prove the following generalization of theorem 2.4.3.

Theorem 6.1.7 Let $(X_{n,j})$ be a double array of martingale differences. If

$$\text{plim}_{n\to\infty}(1/n)\sum_{j=1}^{n}X_{n,j}^2 = \lim_{n\to\infty}(1/n)\sum_{j=1}^{n}E(X_{n,j}^2) = \sigma^2 \in (0,\infty) \quad (6.1.12)$$

and

$$\lim_{n\to\infty}\sum_{j=1}^{n}E(|X_{n,j}/\surd n|^{2+\delta}) = 0 \text{ for some } \delta > 0 \quad (6.1.13)$$

then $(1/\surd n)\sum_{j=1}^{n}X_{n,j} \to N(0,\sigma^2)$ in distr.

Proof: Let

$$Y_{n,j} = X_{n,j} / [\sum_{j=1}^{n}E(X_{n,j}^2)]^{1/2}$$

Verify that $(Y_{n,j})$ satisfies the conditions of theorem 6.1.6 Cf. exercise 5.
Q.E.D.

Remark: Note that condition (6.1.13) is implied by condition

$$\sup_n(1/n)\sum_{j=1}^{n}E(|X_{n,j}|)^{2+\delta} < \infty \text{ for some } \delta > 0. \quad (6.1.14)$$

Exercises

1. Prove that (6.1.1) for arbitrary Borel sets B in R^k implies

   $E(Y|X) = g(X)$ a.s.

2. Prove theorem 6.1.1.
3. Prove (6.1.9).
4. Prove (6.1.11).
5. Prove theorem 6.1.7.

6.2 Measures of dependence

6.2.1 Mixingales

To prove laws of large numbers for sequences of dependent random variables we need some conditions on the extent of dependence of the random variables involved. For example, let (X_t) be a sequence of dependent random variables with $E(X_t^2) < \infty$ for each t. Then

$$\text{var}[(1/n)\sum_{t=1}^{n}X_t] = (1/n^2)\sum_{t=1}^{n}\text{var}(X_t) + 2(1/n^2)\sum_{t=1}^{n-1}\sum_{m=1}^{n-t}\text{cov}(X_{t+m},X_t). \quad (6.2.1)$$

If

$$\sup_{n\geq 1}(1/n)\sum_{t=1}^{n}\mathrm{var}(X_t) = M < \infty \tag{6.2.2}$$

then the first term in (6.2.1) is O(1/n). So for showing that (6.2.1) converges to zero, and hence by Chebishev's inequality,

$$\mathrm{plim}_{n\to\infty}(1/n)\sum_{t=1}^{n}[X_t - E(X_t)] = 0,$$

we need a condition that ensures that the second term in (6.2.1) is o(1). So let us have a closer look at the covariances in (6.2.1).

First we introduce some notation, which will be maintained throughout this section. For $-\infty \leq n \leq m \leq \infty$,

$\mathfrak{F}_n^m$ is the Borel field generated by $X_n, X_{n+1}, X_{n+2}, \ldots, X_m$.

Now by theorem 6.1.1(ii,vii) and Cauchy–Schwarz inequality,

$$\begin{aligned}|\mathrm{cov}(X_{t+m}, X_t)| &= |E(\{[X_{t+m} - E(X_{t+m})][(X_t - E(X_t)]\}| \\ &= |E\{[E(X_{t+m}|\mathfrak{F}_{-\infty}^t) - E(X_{t+m})][X_t - E(X_t)]\}| \\ &\leq \left(E\{[E(X_{t+m}|\mathfrak{F}_{-\infty}^t) - E(X_{t+m})]^2\}\right)^{1/2}(\mathrm{var}(X_t))^{1/2}.\end{aligned} \tag{6.2.3}$$

Denoting

$$\eta(m) = \sup_{t\geq 1}\left(E\{[E(X_{t+m}|\mathfrak{F}_{-\infty}^t) - E(X_{t+m})]^2\right)^{1/2} \tag{6.2.4}$$

it follows now from (6.2.1)–(6.2.3) and Liapounov's inequality

$$\begin{aligned}\mathrm{var}[(1/n)\textstyle\sum_{t=1}^{n}X_t] &\leq (1/n)M + 2(1/n)\textstyle\sum_{t=1}^{n}(\mathrm{var}(X_t))^{1/2}(1/n)\textstyle\sum_{m=1}^{n}\eta(m) \\ &\leq (1/n)M + 2[(1/n)\textstyle\sum_{t=1}^{n}\mathrm{var}(X_t)]^{1/2}(1/n)\textstyle\sum_{m=1}^{n}\eta(m) \\ &\leq (1/n)M + 2M^{1/2}(1/n)\textstyle\sum_{m=1}^{n}\eta(m) \to 0\end{aligned} \tag{6.2.5}$$

if

$$\lim_{m\to\infty}\eta(m) = 0. \tag{6.2.6}$$

Condition (6.2.6), together with (6.2.2), is therefore a sufficient condition for a weak law of large numbers. Sequences satisfying condition (6.2.6) are called *mixingales* (cf. McLeish [1975]).

> *Definition 6.2.1.* Let (X_t) be a sequence of random variables defined on a common probability space, satisfying $E(X_t^2) < \infty$ for each $t \geq 1$. Then (X_t) is called a mixingale if there exists non-negative constants c_t, ψ_m, with $\psi_m \to 0$ as $m \to \infty$, such that for all $t \geq 1$, $m \geq 0$,
>
> $$\left(E\{[E(X_{t+m}|\mathfrak{F}_{-\infty}^t) - E(X_{t+m})]^2\}\right)^{1/2} \leq c_{t+m}\psi_m.$$

Thus, condition (6.2.6) now holds if $\sup_{t\geq 1}c_t < \infty$, as then $\eta(m) = O(\psi_m)$.

Examples of mixingales

(1) *Independent sequences.* If the X_t's are independent then by theorem 6.1.1(viii),

$$E(X_{t+m}|\mathfrak{F}^t_{-\infty}) = E(X_{t+m}) \text{ for } m \geq 1,$$

hence $\psi_m = 0$ for $m \geq 1$. For $m = 0$ we have

$$E(X_t|\mathfrak{F}^t_{-\infty}) = X_t$$

(cf. theorem 6.1.1(iib)), hence we may choose

$$c_t = (\text{var}(X_t)])^{1/2}, \psi_0 = 1.$$

(2) *Finite dependent sequences.* The sequence (X_t) is finite dependent if for some non-negative integer ℓ, $X_{t+\ell}$, $X_{t+\ell+1}$, ... are independent of X_t, X_{t-1}, X_{t-2}, ... Then for $m \geq \ell$,

$$E(X_{t+m}|\mathfrak{F}^t_{-\infty}) = E(X_{t+m}),$$

hence $\psi_m = 0$ for $m \geq \ell$. We may now choose

$$\psi_m = 1 \text{ for } m < \ell$$

$$c_t = \max_{0\leq m\leq \ell}\left(E\{[E(X_{t+m}|\mathfrak{F}^t_{-\infty}) - E(X_{t+m})]^2\right)^{1/2}$$

(3) *AR(1) processes.* Let

$$X_t = \rho X_{t-1} + U_t$$

where $|\rho| < 1$ and (U_t) is an independent process with

$$E(U_t) = 0, E(U_t^2) = \sigma^2 < \infty.$$

Then

$$X_t = \textstyle\sum_{j=0}^{\infty}\rho^j U_{t-j}.$$

Since X_t, X_{t-1}, X_{t-2}, ... can be constructed from U_t, U_{t-1}, U_{t-2}, ... and vice versa, the Borel field $\mathfrak{F}^t_{-\infty}$ is also the Borel field generated by the latter sequence. We now have

$$\begin{aligned} E(X_{t+m}|\mathfrak{F}^t_{-\infty}) &= E(\textstyle\sum_{j=0}^{\infty}\rho^j U_{t+m-j}|U_t,U_{t-1},...) \\ &= E(\textstyle\sum_{j=0}^{m-1}\rho^j U_{t+m-j} + \sum_{j=m}^{\infty}\rho^j U_{t+m-j}|U_t,U_{t-1},...) \\ &= \textstyle\sum_{j=m}^{\infty}\rho^k U_{t+m-j} \end{aligned}$$

and $E(X_{t+m}) = 0$. Thus

$$\left(E\{[E(X_{t+m}|\mathfrak{F}^t_{-\infty}) - E(X_{t+m})]^2\}\right)^{1/2} = (\textstyle\sum_{j=m}^{\infty}\rho^{2j}\sigma^2)^{1/2} = |\rho|^m\{\sum_{j=0}^{\infty}\rho^{2j}\sigma^2)^{1/2}.$$

So we may choose

$$c_t = \sigma, \psi_m = |\rho|^m/\surd(1-\rho^2)$$

(4) *ARMA(p,q) processes.* Let

$$X_t = \rho_1 X_{t-1} + \rho_2 X_{t-2} + \dots + \rho_p X_{t-p} + U_t - \tau_1 U_{t-1} - \dots \\ - \tau_q U_{t-q}, \quad (6.2.7)$$

where (U_t) is an independent sequence with

$E(U_t) = 0,\ E(U_t^2) = \sigma^2 < \infty,$

and the lag polynomials

$$\rho(L) = 1 - \rho_1 L - \rho_2 L - \dots - \rho_p L^p \quad (6.2.8)$$

$$\tau(L) = 1 - \tau_1 L - \tau_2 L - \dots - \tau_q L^p \quad (6.2.9)$$

have roots all outside the complex unit circle. Then X_t has a moving-average representation:

$$X_t = \sum_{j=0}^{\infty} \beta_j U_{t-j} \quad (6.2.10)$$

where the β_j's are exponentially decreasing:

$$|\beta_j| \le c_. \rho^j \text{ for some } c_. > 0,\ \rho \in (0,1), \quad (6.2.11)$$

and U_t has a moving average representation:

$$U_t = \sum_{j=0}^{\infty} \gamma_j X_{t-j}. \quad (6.2.12)$$

Cf. Harvey (1981). Therefore, again,

$\mathfrak{F}_{-\infty}^{t}$ is also the Borel field generated by $U_t, U_{t-1}, U_{t-2}, \dots,$

and so

$$E(X_{t+m}|\mathfrak{F}_{-\infty}^{t}) = E(\textstyle\sum_{j=0}^{\infty} \beta_j U_{t+m-j} | U_t, U_{t-1}, \dots) = \sum_{j=m}^{\infty} \beta_j U_{t+m-j},$$
$$E(X_{t+m}) = 0.$$

Consequently,

$$\sup_{t \ge 1} \left(E\{[E(X_{t+m}|\mathfrak{F}_{-\infty}^{t}) - E(X_{t+m})]^2\} \right)^{1/2} \\ = \left(\textstyle\sum_{j=m}^{\infty} \beta_j^2 \sigma^2\right)^{1/2} \to 0 \text{ as } m \to \infty$$

So we may take

$$c_t = \sigma,\ \psi_m = \left(\textstyle\sum_{j=m}^{\infty} \beta_j^2\right)^{1/2} \le c_. |\rho|^m / \sqrt{(1-\rho^2)}.$$

6.2.2 Uniform and strong mixing

A disadvantage of the mixingale concept is that it does not necessarily carry over to functions of mixingales. However, it is desirable to work with conditions that are invariant under Borel measurable transformations. We consider here two of these invariant conditions, namely the *uniform* (or φ-) *mixing* condition and the *strong* (or α-) *mixing* condition. Cf. Iosifescu and Theodorescu (1969) and Rosenblatt (1956a).

Definition 6.2.2 Let (X_t) be a sequence of random variables or vectors defined on a common probability space. Denote for $m \geq 0$,

$$\varphi(m) = \sup_t \sup_{A \in \mathfrak{F}^t_{-\infty}, B \in \mathfrak{F}^{\infty}_{t+m}, P(A)>0} |P(B|A) - P(B)|$$

$$\alpha(m) = \sup_t \sup_{A \in \mathfrak{F}^t_{-\infty}, B \in \mathfrak{F}^{\infty}_{t+m}} |P(A \cap B) - P(A)P(B)|$$

If $\lim_{m \to \infty} \varphi(m) = 0$ then (X_t) is called a uniform (or φ-) mixing process, and if $\lim_{m \to \infty} \alpha(m) = 0$ then (X_t) is called a strong (or α-) mixing process, with mixing coefficients φ and α, respectively.

The quantities $\varphi(m)$ and $\alpha(m)$ measure how much dependence exists between events separated by at least m time periods. Clearly, the φ-mixing concept implies the α-mixing concept, for $P(B|A) = P(A \cap B)/P(A)$, hence $\alpha(m) \leq \varphi(m)$. Thus the strong mixing concept is a weaker condition than the uniform mixing concept.

Examples of φ-mixing processes are independent processes ($\varphi(m) = 0$ for $m \geq 1$), finite dependent processes ($\varphi(m) = 0$ for m larger than some finite integer) and stationary Markov processes with finite state space (cf. Billingsley [1968, pp. 167–168]). An example of an α-mixing process that is not φ-mixing is a Gaussian AR(1) process (cf. Ibragimov and Linnik [1971, pp. 312–313]).

An important feature of the mixing concepts is that they are invariant under arbitrary Borel measurable transformations:

$$\text{If } (X_t) \text{ is an } \varphi-(\alpha-) \text{ mixing process, then so is } (\psi_t(X_t)), \tag{6.2.13}$$

where (ψ_t) is an arbitrary sequence of conformable Borel measurable functions. Moreover, a φ- or α-mixing process is a mixingale, provided a certain moment condition holds. The following theorem points out the relation between the mixing and the mixingale concepts.

Theorem 6.2.1. Let (X_t) be a sequence of random vectors satisfying

$$[E(|X_t|^r)]^{1/r} < \infty \text{ for some } r \geq 1, r \leq \infty.$$

Then for $1 \leq p \leq r$,

$$\{E[|E(X_{t+m}|\mathfrak{F}^t_{-\infty}) - E(X_{t+m})|^p]\}^{1/p} \leq 2\varphi(m)^{1-1/r}[E(|X_{t+m}|^r)]^{1/r},$$

$$\{E[|E(X_{t+m}|\mathfrak{F}^t_{-\infty}) - E(X_{t+m})|^p]\}^{1/p}$$
$$\leq 2(2^{1/p}+1)\alpha(m)^{1/p-1/r}[E(|X_{t+m}|^r)]^{1/r}.$$

Proof: Serfling (1968) for the φ-mixing case and McLeish (1975, lemma 2.1) for the α-mixing case.

Thus, if

$$c_t = [E(|X_t|^r)]^{1/r} < \infty \text{ for some } r > 2 \quad (6.2.14)$$

then the mixingale coefficient ψ_m equals

$$\psi_m = 2\varphi(m)^{1-1/r}, \; \psi_m = 2(1 + \sqrt{2})\alpha(m)^{1/2-1/r}, \quad (6.2.15)$$

respectively.

6.2.3 *υ-stability*

A disadvantage of the mixing conditions is that they are hard to verify. The traditional time series models, in particular ARMA(p,q) and AR(p) models, however, can be represented by moving averages of mixing variables, provided the errors are assumed to be independent. For example, a standard ARMA(p,q) model may be considered as an AR(p) model with q-dependent hence φ- and α-mixing, errors, and if the AR lag polynomial (6.2.8) has roots all outside the unit circle the process can be represented by an infinite moving average of these q-dependent errors. A natural extension of these kinds of process is therefore to consider processes of the type

$$X_t = f_t(U_t, U_{t-1}, U_{t-2}, \ldots), \quad (6.2.16)$$

where (U_t) is a mixing process and f_t is a mapping from the space of one-sided infinite sequences in the range of the U_t's such that the right-hand side of (6.2.16) is a properly defined random variable or vector.

In order to limit the memory of this process (X_t) we need a condition which ensures that the impact of remote U_{t-m}'s on X_t vanishes:

Definition 6.2.3 Let (U_t) be a sequence of random vectors in R^ℓ and let $X_t \in R^k$ be defined by (6.2.16). For some $r \geq 1$ and all $t \geq 1$, let $E(|X_t|^r) < \infty$, and denote

$$\upsilon(m) = \sup_{t\geq 1}\{E[|E(X_t|\mathfrak{G}^t_{t-m}) - X_t|^r]\}^{1/r},$$

where

$\mathfrak{G}^t_{t-m}$ is the Borel field generated by $U_t, U_{t-1}, \ldots, U_{t-m}$.

If $\lim_{m\to\infty}\upsilon(m) = 0$, then (X_t) is a *υ-stable* process in L^r with respect to the *base* (U_t).

Cf. McLeish (1975) and Bierens (1983). This concept is reminiscent of the stochastic stability concept of Bierens (1981), which is somewhat weaker a condition. See also Potscher and Prucha (1991) for a discussion of the relationship between υ-stability and Gallant and White's (1988) near epoch dependency concept.

The actual content of this definition is *not* in the first place the condition that $\upsilon(m) \to 0$, for this is always satisfied if the processes (X_t) and (U_t) are strictly stationary, as in that case we may delete "$\sup_{t\geq 1}$" and take for t some arbitrary fixed index, say $t = 1$:

$$\upsilon(m) = \{E|E(X_1|\mathfrak{G}^1_{1-m}) - X_1|^r]\}^{1/r}$$

From theorem 6.1.3 it then follows

$$\lim_{m\to\infty} E(X_1|\mathfrak{G}^1_{1-m}) = E(X_1|\mathfrak{G}^1_{-\infty}) \text{ a.s.}$$

where

$$\mathfrak{G}^1_{-\infty} = \vee_{m\geq 0}\mathfrak{G}^1_{1-m}$$

is the Borel Field generated by $U_1, U_0, U_{-1}, \ldots$ Since X_1 is a function of this one-sided infinite sequence, the Borel field generated by X_1 is contained in $\mathfrak{G}^1_{-\infty}$, by which

$$E(X_1|\mathfrak{G}^1_{-\infty}) = X_1 \text{ a.s.}$$

Cf. theorem 6.1.1(iib). Thus,

$$\lim_{m\to\infty} E(X_1|\mathfrak{G}^1_{1-m}) = X_1 \text{ a.s.}$$

and consequently by dominated convergence (theorem 2.2.2),

$$\upsilon(m) \to 0 \text{ as } m \to \infty.$$

Summarizing, we have shown:

> *Theorem 6.2.2* Let (U_t) be a strictly stationary stochastic process in R^ℓ and let for each t
>
> $$X_t = f(U_t, U_{t-1}, U_{t-2}, \ldots)$$
>
> be a well-defined random vector in R^k, where f does not depend on t. If $E(|X_t|^r) < \infty$ for some $r \geq 1$ then (X_t) is υ-stable in L^r with respect to the base (U_t).

Therefore, the actual content of definition 6.2.3 is that this result goes through if the X_t's and/or U_t's are heterogeneously distributed (that means that the distributions of U_t and/or X_t depend on t). In other words, the υ-stability condition actually imposes restrictions on the extent of heterogeneity of (X_t) and (U_t).

In checking the υ-stability condition the following result is useful.

Theorem 6.2.3 Let X_t be of the form (6.2.16). If there exist Borel measurable mappings $f_{t,m}$ such that for some $r \geq 1$,

$$E|X_t|^r < \infty, t \geq 1,$$
$$\upsilon^*(m) = \sup_{t\geq 1}[E(|f_{t,m}(U_t,U_{t-1},...,U_{t-m}) - X_t|^r\})]^{1/r} \rightarrow 0 \text{ as } m \rightarrow \infty,$$

then (X_t) is υ-stable in L^r with respect to the base (U_t), where

$$\upsilon(m) \leq 2\upsilon^*(m).$$

Proof: Observe that

$$E(X_t|\mathfrak{G}^t_{t-m}) = E(X_t|U_t,U_{t-1},...,U_{t-m})$$

is a Borel measurable function of the conditioning variables. By Jensen's inequality for conditional expectations (theorem 3.2.6) it follows that

$$|E(X_t|U_t,U_{t-1},...,U_{t-m}) - f_{t,m}(U_t,...,U_{t-m})|^r \leq E[|X_t - f_{t,m}(U_t,...,U_{t-m})|^r|U_t,...,U_{t-m}]$$

hence

$$E[|E(X_t|\mathfrak{G}^t_{t-m}) - f_{t,m}(U_t,...,U_{t-m})|]^r \leq E(|X_t - f_{t,m}(U_t,...,U_{t-m})|^r)$$

Using Minkowski's inequality (cf. section 1.4) it now follows that:

$$\{E[|E(X_t|\mathfrak{G}^t_{t-m}) - X_t|^r]\}^{1/r} \leq 2\{E[|X_t - f_{t,m}(U_t,...,U_{t-m})|]^r\}^{1/r}. \quad \text{Q.E.D.}$$

It should be noted that the υ-stability concept is only meaningful if we make further assumptions on the dependence of the base (U_t), for every sequence (X_t) is υ-stable with respect to itself. In the next section we shall impose mixing conditions on (U_t), in order to prove various laws of large numbers.

The υ-stability concept, like the mixingale concept, is not generally invariant under Borel measurable transformations. However, an invariance property holds under bounded uniformly continuous transformation, and this is just what we need to generalize the *weak* law of large numbers in sections 2.5 and 2.7 to υ-stable processes in L^2 with respect to a mixing base. Thus, let (X_t) obey the conditions in definition 6.2.3 and let ψ be a bounded uniformly continuous function on the domain of the X_t's. For notational convenience, let for $m \geq 0$

$$X_t^{(m)} = E(X_t|\mathfrak{G}^t_{t-m})$$

and let for $a \geq 0$

$$\zeta(a) = \sup_{|x_1 - x_2| \leq a}|\psi(x_1) - \psi(x_2)| \tag{6.2.17}$$

Then for arbitrary $q > 0$

$$E(|\psi(X_t^{(m)}) - \psi(X_t)|)^q \leq \zeta(a)^q + 2\sup_x|\psi(x)|^q P(|X_t^{(m)} - X_t| > a)$$
$$\leq \zeta(a)^q + 2\sup_x|\psi(x)|^q E(|X_t^{(m)} - X_t|^r)/a^r$$
$$\leq \zeta(a)^q + 2\sup_x|\psi(x)|^q \upsilon(m)^r/a^r,$$

where the second inequality follows from Chebishev's inequality. Then

$$\sup_{t\geq 1}[E(|\psi(X_t^{(m)}) - \psi(X_t)|^q)]^{1/q} \leq \tfrac{1}{2}\upsilon^*(m),$$

where

$$\upsilon^*(m) = 2\cdot\inf_{a\geq 0}(\zeta(a)^q + 2\sup_x|\psi(X_1)|^q \upsilon(m)^r/a^r)^{1/q} \tag{6.2.18}$$

Using the fact that $\zeta(a) \to 0$ for $a \downarrow 0$, it is easy to show $\upsilon^*(m) \to 0$ for $m \to \infty$. It follows now from theorem 6.2.3 that $\psi(X_t)$ is $\upsilon^*(m)$-stable in L^q with respect to the base (U_t):

> *Theorem 6.2.4* Let (X_t) be υ-stable in L^r with respect to the base (U_t). Let ψ be a bounded uniformly continuous function on the domain of the X_t's. Let $q > 0$ be arbitrary. Then $\psi(X_t)$ is υ^*-stable in L^q with respect to the base (U_t), where υ^* is defined by (6.2.17) and (6.2.18).

6.3 Weak laws of large numbers for dependent random variables

In section 6.2 we have already derived a weak law of large numbers for mixingales. We shall now generalize this result to processes that are υ-stable in L^1 with respect to a φ- or α-mixing base. Let (X_t) be a sequence of *bounded* random variables, i.e., for some $M < \infty$ and all t,

$$P(|X_t| \leq M) = 1, \tag{6.3.1}$$

with the structure (6.2.16). Define the Borel fields

$$\mathfrak{F}_{-\infty}^t, \mathfrak{F}_t^\infty, \mathfrak{G}_{-\infty}^t \text{ and } \mathfrak{G}_t^\infty$$

as in section 6.2. Moreover, let the base (U_t) be φ-mixing or α-mixing and denote

$$X_t^{(m)} = E(X_t|\mathfrak{G}_{t-m}^t) = g_{t,m}(U_t,U_{t-1},\ldots,U_{t-m}), \tag{6.3.2}$$

say. Note that $X_t^{(m)}$ is bounded too by M. We shall now derive an upper bound of $|\text{cov}(X_{t+\ell},X_t)|$ in terms of υ, φ and/or α. First observe that by (6.3.1) and the definition of υ-stability,

$$|\text{cov}(X_{t+\ell}, X_t) - \text{cov}(X_{t+\ell}^{(m)}, X_t)| \leq 2\cdot E[|X_{t+\ell} - X_{t+\ell}^{(m)}||X_t - E(X_t)|]$$
$$\leq 4M\cdot\upsilon(m), \text{ uniformly in } \ell. \tag{6.3.3}$$

Next observe that for fixed m, and α-mixing (U_t)

$$X_t^{(m)} - E(X_t^{(m)}) = g_{t,m}(U_t,U_{t-1},...,U_{t-m}) - E(X_t^{(m)}) \text{ is } \alpha^*\text{-mixing} \quad (6.3.4)$$

with

$$\alpha^*(m^*) = 1 \text{ if } m^* < m, \alpha^*(m^*) = \alpha(m^* - m) \text{ if } m^* \geq m. \quad (6.3.5)$$

Similarly, if (U_t) is φ-mixing the process (6.3.3) is φ^*-mixing, with

$$\varphi^*(m^*) = 1 \text{ if } m^* < m, \varphi^*(m^*) = \varphi(m^* - m) \text{ if } m^* \geq m \quad (6.3.6)$$

Thus by theorem 6.2.1 with $p = 1$ and $r = \infty$ it follows that

$$\begin{aligned} &E[|E(X_{t+\ell}^{(m)}|\mathfrak{G}^t_{-\infty}) - E(X_{t+\ell})|] \leq 2M\varphi^*(\ell), \\ &E[|E(X_{t+\ell}^{(m)}|\mathfrak{G}^t_{-\infty}) - E(X_{t+\ell})|] \leq 6M\alpha^*(\ell). \end{aligned} \quad (6.3.7)$$

Hence, similarly to (6.2.3), we have

$$|\text{cov}(X_{t+\ell}^{(m)},X_t)| \leq 2M^2\varphi(\ell-m), |\text{cov}(X_{t+\ell}^{(m)},X_t)| \leq 6M^2\alpha(\ell-m), \quad (6.3.8)$$

where $\varphi(m) = \alpha(m) = 1$ if $m \leq 0$. Combining (6.3.3) and (6.3.8) now yields:

> *Lemma 6.3.1* Let (X_t) be υ-stable in L^k with respect to a base (U_t) and let φ and α be the mixing coefficients corresponding to (U_t). Moreover, let for some $M < \infty$ and all t, $P(|X_t| \leq M) = 1$. Then for $\ell \geq 1$, $m \geq 0$
>
> $$|\text{cov}(X_{t+\ell},X_t)| \leq M^2\psi(\ell-m) + 4M\cdot\upsilon(m),$$
>
> where
>
> $$\psi(\ell-m) = \min(2\varphi(\ell-m),6\alpha(\ell-m)) \text{ if } \ell-m > 0,$$
> $$\psi(\ell-m) = 1 \text{ if } \ell-m \leq 0.$$

Using this result in (6.2.1) now yields:

$$|\text{var}[(1/n)\textstyle\sum_{t=1}^n X_t]| \leq M^2/n + 8\upsilon(m)M + 2n^{-1}M^2[m\psi(0) + \sum_{\ell=0}^{\infty}\psi(\ell)].$$

Letting $m \to \infty$ with n at rate o(n), we now see that the following lemma holds

> *Lemma 6.3.2* Let the bounded stochastic process (X_t) be υ-stable in L^1 with respect to the base (U_t). Assume either
>
> (a) (U_t) is φ-mixing with $\sum_{\ell=0}^{\infty}\varphi(\ell) < \infty$, or
>
> (b) (U_t) is α-mixing with $\sum_{\ell=0}^{\infty}\alpha(\ell) < \infty$.
>
> Then $\lim_{n\to\infty}\text{var}[(1/n)\sum_{t=1}^n X_t] = 0$.

We are now ready to generalize theorem 2.5.2 to υ-stable processes in L^1 with respect to a mixing base.

Theorem 6.3.1 Let (X_t) be an R^k-valued υ-stable process in L^1 with respect to a φ- or α-mixing base. Let ψ be a continuous function on R^k and let F_t be the distribution function of X_t. If

$(1/n)\sum_{t=1}^{n} F_t \to G$ properly, pointwise,
$\sup_{n\geq 1}(1/n)\sum_{t=1}^{n} E(|\psi(X_t)|^{1+\delta}) < \infty$ for some $\delta > 0$

and either

$\sum_{\ell=0}^{\infty}\varphi(\ell) < \infty$ or $\sum_{\ell=0}^{\infty}\alpha(\ell) < \infty$,
then $\text{plim}_{n\to\infty}(1/n)\sum_{t=1}^{n}\psi(X_t) = \int\psi(x)dG(x)$

Proof: We prove the theorem for the case $X_t \in R$. The proof for the case $X_t \in R^k$ is almost the same. We show that (2.5.7) in the proof of theorem 2.5.2 goes through. Thus, define similarly to (2.5.1)

$$\begin{aligned} \psi_a(x) &= \psi(x) \text{ if } |\psi(x)| \leq a, \\ \psi_a(x) &= a \quad \text{ if } \psi(x) > a, \\ \psi_a(x) &= -a \quad \text{ if } \psi(x) < -a, \end{aligned} \tag{6.3.9}$$

and let for $b > 0$,

$$\psi_{ab}(x) = \psi_a(x) \text{ if } |x| \leq b, \tag{6.3.10}$$

$$\psi_{ab}(x) = \psi_a(b\cdot x/|x|) \text{ if } |x| > b, \tag{6.3.10}$$

Then $\psi_{ab}(x)$ is bounded and uniformly continuous, for the set

$\{x \in R^k: |x| \leq b\}$

is a closed and bounded subset of R^k and hence compact, whereas continuous functions on a compact set are uniformly continuous on that set. The proof of the uniform continuity outside this set is left as an exercise (exercise 1). It follows from theorem 6.2.4 that $\psi_{ab}(X_t)$ is υ-stable in L^1 with respect to the mixing base involved. Thus it follows from lemma 6.3.1 that

$$\lim_{n\to\infty}\text{var}[(1/n)\textstyle\sum_{t=1}^{n}\psi_{ab}(X_t)] = 0,$$

hence by Chebishev's inequality,

$$\text{plim}_{n\to\infty}(1/n)\textstyle\sum_{t=1}^{n}\{\psi_{ab}(X_t) - E[\psi_{ab}(X_t)]\} = 0.$$

Since

$$\begin{aligned} \lim_{n\to\infty}E\Big(\Big|(1/n)\textstyle\sum_{t=1}^{n}\{\psi_a(X_t) - E[\psi_a(X_t)]\} \\ - (1/n)\textstyle\sum_{t=1}^{n}\{\psi_{ab}(X_t) - E[\psi_{ab}(X_t)]\}\Big|\Big) \\ \leq 2a\cdot\lim_{n\to\infty}(1/n)\textstyle\sum_{t=1}^{n}E[I(|X_t| > b)] \\ \leq 2a\cdot\lim_{n\to\infty}(1/n)\textstyle\sum_{t=1}^{n}(1 - F_t(b) + F_t(-b)) \\ = 2a(1 - G(b) + G(-b)) \to 0 \text{ as } b \to \infty, \end{aligned}$$

we now have

$$\mathrm{plim}_{n\to\infty}(1/n)\sum_{t=1}^{n}\{\psi_a(X_t)-E[\psi_a(X_t)]\}=0.$$

Thus (2.5.7) in the proof of theorem 2.5.2 goes through. Since the rest of the proof of theorem 2.5.2 does not employ the independence condition, this result is sufficient for theorem 6.3.1 to hold. Q.E.D.

Refering in the proof of theorem 2.7.2 to theorem 6.3.1 rather than to theorem 2.5.2, it immediately follows:

Theorem 6.3.2 Let (X_t) be an R^k-valued υ-stable process in L^1 with respect to a φ- or α-mixing base. Let F_t be the distribution function of X_t and let $f(x,\theta)$ be a continuous function on $R^k \times \Theta$, where Θ is a compact Borel set in R^m. If

$$(1/n)\sum_{t=1}^{n}F_t \to G, \text{ properly, pointwise,}$$
$$\sup_{n\geq 1}(1/n)\sum_{t=1}^{n}E[\sup_{\theta\in\Theta}|f(X_t,\theta)|^{1+\delta}] < \infty$$

for some $\delta > 0$, and either

$$\sum_{\ell=0}^{\infty}\varphi(\ell) < \infty \text{ or } \sum_{\ell=0}^{\infty}\alpha(\ell) < \infty,$$

then

$$\mathrm{plim}_{n\to\infty}\sup_{\theta\in\Theta}|(1/n)\sum_{t=1}^{n}f(X_t,\theta)-\int f(x,\theta)dG(x)| = 0,$$

where the limit function involved is continuous on Θ

Next we want to allow the function ψ in theorem 6.3.1 to be Borel measurable rather than continuous. There is no problem if the process (X_t) is strictly stationary and of the type $X_t = f(U_t,U_{t-1},\ldots)$ with (U_t) a strictly stationary mixing base, as we then may apply theorem 6.2.2.

Theorem 6.3.3 Let $X_t \in R^k$ be such that

$$X_t = f(U_t,U_{t-1},U_{t-2},\ldots)$$

where (U_t) is a strictly stationary φ- or α-mixing process and the time-invariant mapping f is such that (X_t) is a well-defined strictly stationary stochastic process. Let ψ be a Borel measurable real function on R^k. If $E[|\psi(X_t)|] < \infty$ and either

$$\sum_{\ell=0}^{\infty}\varphi(\ell) < \infty \text{ or } \sum_{\ell=0}^{\infty}\alpha(\ell) < \infty,$$

then $\mathrm{plim}_{n\to\infty}(1/n)\sum_{t=1}^{n}\psi(X_t) = E[\psi(X_1)]$.

Proof: Define ψ_a as in (6.3.9). Then for fixed $a > 0$, ψ_a is a bounded Borel measurable real function, and by theorem 6.2.2, $\psi_a(X_t)$ is υ-stable in L^1 with respect to (U_t). From lemma 6.3.2 and Chebishev's inequality it follows that

$\text{plim}_{n\to\infty}(1/n)\sum_{t=1}^{n}\psi_a(X_t) = E[\psi_a(X_1)]$.

Now by (6.3.9) and theorem 1.4.1

$$E[|(1/n)\sum_{t=1}^{n}\psi(X_t)-(1/n)\sum_{t=1}^{n}\psi_a(X_t)|] \leq 2\cdot E[|\psi(X_1)|I(|\psi(X_1)| > a)] \to 0 \text{ as } a \to \infty,$$

for $P(|\psi(X_1)| > a) \to 0$ as $a \to \infty$, as otherwise $E[|\psi(X_1)|] = \infty$. Similarly

$$|E[\psi(X_1)]-E[\psi_a(X_1)]| \to 0 \text{ as } a \to \infty.$$

The theorem under review now follows from the argument in the proof of theorem 2.7.2. Q.E.D.

Again, referring to theorem 6.3.3 instead of theorem 2.7.2 (with $\delta = 0$), theorem 2.7.5 carries over.

Theorem 6.3.4 Let (X_t) be as in theorem 6.3.3. Let $f(x,\theta)$ be a Borel measurable real function on $R^k \times \Theta$, where Θ is a compact Borel set in R^m, such that for each $x \in R^k$, $f(x,\theta)$ is continuous on Θ. If in addition

$$E[\sup_{\theta\in\Theta}|f(X_1,\theta)|] < \infty$$

then

$$\text{plim}_{n\to\infty}\sup_{\theta\in\Theta}|(1/n)\sum_{t=1}^{n}f(X_t,\theta)-E[f(X_1,\theta)]| = 0,$$

where $E[f(X_1,\theta)]$ is continuous on Θ.

For generalizing theorem 6.3.1 to Borel measurable functions ψ we need the following lemma.

Lemma 6.3.3 Let ψ be a Borel measurable real function on R^k and let X be a random vector in R^k such that for some $r \geq 1$, $E[|\psi(X)|^r] < \infty$. For every $\varepsilon > 0$ there exists a function ψ_ε on R^k that is bounded, continuous and zero outside a compact set (hence uniformly continuous), such that

$$E[|\psi(X)-\psi_\varepsilon(X)|^r] < \varepsilon$$

Proof: Dunford and Schwartz (1957, p. 298).

A direct corollary of this lemma is:

Lemma 6.3.4 Let (X_t) be a sequence of random vectors in R^k and let (F_t) be the sequence of corresponding distribution functions. Assume

$$(1/n)\sum_{t=1}^{n}F_t \to G \text{ properly setwise.}$$

Let ψ be a Borel measurable real function on R^k such that

$\sup_{n\geq 1}(1/n)\sum_{t=1}^{n}E[|\psi(X_t)|^{1+\delta}] < \infty$ for some $\delta > 0$.

For every $\varepsilon > 0$ there exists a uniformly continuous bounded function ψ_ε on R^k such that

$\limsup_{n\to\infty}E[|(1/n)\sum_{t=1}^{n}\psi(X_t)-(1/n)\sum_{t=1}^{n}\psi_\varepsilon(X_t)|] < \varepsilon$

Proof: Exercise 2 (Hint: Combine lemma 6.3.3 with theorem 2.5.5.)

Combining lemma 6.3.4 with theorem 6.3.2 yields:

Theorem 6.3.5 Let the conditions of theorem 6.3.1 be satisfied, except that now ψ is Borel measurable and

$(1/n)\sum_{t=1}^{n}F_t \to G$ properly, setwise.

Then the conclusion of theorem 6.3.1 carries over.

Proof: Exercise 3.

Finally, referring in the proof of theorem 2.7.4 to theorem 6.3.5 rather than to theorem 2.5.6, yields:

Theorem 6.3.6. Let the conditions of theorem 6.3.2 be satisfied, except that now

$(1/n)\sum_{t=1}^{n}F_t \to G$ properly, setwise,

$f(x,\theta)$ is Borel measurable on $R^k \times \Theta$ and for each $x \in R^k$ a continuous function on Θ. Then the conclusions of theorem 6.3.2 carry over.

Remark: It seems possible to generalize the results in this section further to strong laws, using theorem 3.1 of McLeish (1975). This, however, will require further conditions on the rate of convergence to zero of υ, φ, and α.

Exercises

1. Prove that the function (6.3.10) is uniformly continuous.
2. Prove lemma 6.3.4.
3. Prove theorem 6.3.5.

6.4 Proper heterogeneity and uniform laws for functions of infinitely many random variables

For some time series models, such as ARMA and ARMAX models least squares parameter estimation is conducted by minimizing a sum of functions of a one-sided infinite sequence of random variables. See chapter 7. In order to prove consistency of these parameter estimators under data heterogeneity we need an extension of the proper convergence concept to distributions of one-sided infinite sequences of random variables (cf. definitions 2.3.1 and 2.5.1), as well as some generalizations of the uniform laws in section 6.3.

Definition 6.4.1 Let (X_t) be a sequence of random variables in R^k, and let $F_{t,m}$ be the distribution function of $(X_t,...,X_{t-m})$. The process (X_t) is said to be pointwise (setwise) properly heterogenous if there exists a one-sided infinite sequence (X_t^*), $t \leq 0$, of R^k-valued random variables such that for m = 0,1,2,...,

$(1/n)\sum_{t=1}^{n} F_{t,m} \rightarrow H_m$ properly pointwise (setwise),

where H_m is the distribution function of $(X_0^*, X_{-1}^*, ..., X_{-m}^*)$. The sequence (X_t^*), $t \leq 0$ will be called the mean process.

The following theorem now specializes theorem 6.3.2. This theorem is the basis for the consistency results of linear ARMAX models, in chapter 8.

Theorem 6.4.1 Let (X_t) be a stochastic process in R^k which is υ-stable in L^1 with respect to an α- or φ-mixing base, where either

$\sum_{j=0}^{\infty}\varphi(j) < \infty$ or $\sum_{j=0}^{\infty}\alpha(j) < \infty$,

and pointwise properly heterogenous with mean process (X_t^*). Let $(\gamma_{j,i}(\theta))$, $j \geq 0$, $i=1,2,...,p$, be sequences of continuous mappings from a compact subset Θ of a Euclidean space into R^k, such that for $i=1,2,...,p$,

$$\sum_{j=0}^{\infty}\sup_{\theta\in\Theta}|\gamma_{j,i}(\theta)| < \infty. \tag{6.4.1}$$

Let ψ be a differentiable real function on R^p such that for $c \rightarrow \infty$,

$$\sup_{|\xi|\leq c}|(\partial/\partial\xi)\psi(\xi)| = O(c^{\mu}), \tag{6.4.2}$$

where $\mu > 0$ is such that for some $\delta > 0$,

$$\sup_t E(|X_t|^{1+\mu+\delta}) < \infty. \tag{6.4.3}$$

Denote

$$\Gamma_j(\theta) = (\gamma_{j,1}(\theta),....,\gamma_{j,p}(\theta))'.$$

Then

$$\text{plim}_{n\rightarrow\infty}\sup_{\theta\in\Theta}|(1/n)\sum_{t=1}^{n}\psi(\sum_{j=0}^{t-1}\Gamma_j(\theta)'X_{t-j}) - E[\psi(\sum_{j=0}^{\infty}\Gamma_j(\theta)'X_{-j}^*)]| = 0.$$

Moreover, the limit function $E[\psi(\sum_{j=0}^{\infty}\Gamma_j(\theta)'X_{-j}^*)]$ is a continuous real function on Θ.

Proof: Denote

$$\rho_j = \max_{i=1,\ldots,p}\sup_{\theta\in\Theta}|\gamma_{j,i}(\theta)|. \tag{6.4.4}$$

Then condition (6.4.1) implies

$$\sum_{j=0}^{\infty}\rho_j < \infty. \tag{6.4.5}$$

Moreover, denote for non-negative integers s,

$$\xi_t^{(s)}(\theta) = \sum_{j=0}^{s}\Gamma_j(\theta)'X_{t-j}. \tag{6.4.6}$$

We shall now prove theorem 6.4.1 in four steps, each stated in a lemma.

Lemma 6.4.1 There exists a constant K such that for every $n \geq 1$ and every $s \geq 0$,

$$E[\sup_{\theta\in\Theta}|(1/n)\sum_{t=1}^{n}\psi(\xi_t^{(\infty)}(\theta)) - (1/n)\sum_{t=1}^{n}\psi(\xi_t^{(s)}(\theta))|] \leq K\cdot\sum_{j=s+1}^{\infty}\rho_j.$$

Lemma 6.4.2 For every fixed $s \geq 0$,

$$\text{plim}_{n\to\infty}\sup_{\theta\in\Theta}|(1/n)\sum_{t=1}^{n}\psi(\sum_{j=0}^{s}\Gamma_j(\theta)'X_{t-j}) - E[\psi(\sum_{j=0}^{s}\Gamma_j(\theta)'X_{-j}^*)]| = 0.$$

Lemma 6.4.3 There exists a constant K such that for every s ≥ 0,

$$\sup_{\theta\in\Theta}|E[\psi(\sum_{j=0}^{s}\Gamma_j(\theta)'X_{-j}^*)] - E[\psi(\sum_{j=0}^{\infty}\Gamma_j(\theta)'X_{-j}^*)]| \leq K\cdot\sum_{j=s+1}^{\infty}\rho_j.$$

Lemma 6.4.4 The function $E[\psi(\sum_{j=0}^{\infty}\Gamma_j(\theta)'X_{-j}^*)]$ is continuous on Θ.

Realizing that (6.4.5) implies

$$\lim_{m\to\infty}\sum_{j=m+1}^{\infty}\rho_j = 0,$$

the theorem under review now easily follows from these four lemmas.

Proof of lemma 6.4.1: Observe from (6.4.4) and (6.4.6) that for $\theta \in \Theta$,

$$|\xi_t^{(\infty)}(\theta) - \xi_t^{(s)}(\theta)| \leq \sum_{j=s+1}^{\infty}|\Gamma_j(\theta)'X_{t-j}| \leq \sum_{j=s+1}^{\infty}\max_{i=1,2,\ldots,p}|\gamma_{j,i}(\theta)'X_{t-j}| \leq \sum_{j=s+1}^{\infty}\rho_j|X_{t-j}|.$$

Moreover, by the mean value theorem there exists a mean value $\lambda_{t,s}(\theta) \in [0,1]$ such that

$$|\psi(\xi_t^{(\infty)}(\theta)) - \psi(\xi_t^{(s)}(\theta))|$$
$$= |(\xi_t^{(\infty)}(\theta) - \xi_t^{(s)}(\theta))'(\partial/\partial\xi)\varphi(\lambda_{t,s}(\theta)\xi_t^{(\infty)}(\theta) + (1-\lambda_{t,s}(\theta))\xi_t^{(s)}(\theta))|$$
$$\leq |\xi_t^{(\infty)}(\theta) - \xi_t^{(s)}(\theta)|\sup_{|\xi|\leq \max(|\xi_t^{(\infty)}(\theta)|,|\xi_t^{(s)}(\theta)|)}|(\partial/\partial\xi)\psi(\xi)|$$
$$\leq \textstyle\sum_{j=s+1}^{\infty}\rho_j|X_{t-j}|\sup_{|\xi|\leq\sum_{j=0}^{\infty}\rho_j|X_{t-j}|}|(\partial/\partial\xi)\psi(\xi)|, \qquad (6.4.7)$$

where the last inequality follows from (6.4.4). According to condition (6.4.2) there exists a constant C such that

$$\sup_{|\xi|\leq a}|(\partial/\partial\xi)\psi(\xi)| = Ca^{\mu}, \qquad (6.4.8)$$

hence by (6.4.7) and Holder's and Liapounov's inequalities

$$E[\sup_{\theta\in\Theta}|\psi(\xi_t^{(\infty)}(\theta)) - \psi(\xi_t^{(s)}(\theta))|]$$
$$\leq C\cdot E[(\textstyle\sum_{j=s+1}^{\infty}\rho_j|X_{t-j}|)(\sum_{j=0}^{\infty}\rho_j|X_{t-j}|)^{\mu}]$$
$$\leq C\{E[(\textstyle\sum_{j=s+1}^{\infty}\rho_j|X_{t-j}|)^{1+\mu}]\}^{1/(1+\mu)}\{E[(\sum_{j=0}^{\infty}\rho_j|X_{t-j}|)^{1+\mu}]\}^{\mu/(1+\mu)}$$
$$\leq C\{(\textstyle\sum_{j=s+1}^{\infty}\rho_j)^{\mu}[\sum_{j=s+1}^{\infty}\rho_j E(|X_{t-j}|^{1+\mu})]\}^{1/(1+\mu)}$$
$$\times\{(\textstyle\sum_{j=0}^{\infty}\rho_j)^{\mu}[\sum_{j=0}^{\infty}\rho_j E(|X_{t-j}|^{1+\mu})]\}^{\mu/(1+\mu)}$$
$$\leq C(\textstyle\sum_{j=0}^{\infty}\rho_j)^{\mu}\sup_t E(|X_t|^{1+\mu})(\sum_{j=s+1}^{\infty}\rho_j) = K\cdot\sum_{j=s+1}^{\infty}\rho_j, \qquad (6.4.9)$$

say. This proves the lemma. Q.E.D.

Proof of lemma 6.4.2: Lemma 6.4.2 follows straightforwardly from theorem 6.3.2.

Proof of lemma 6.4.3: From lemma 6.4.1 and the conditions of theorem 6.4.1 it follows that

$$\lim_{n\to\infty}(1/n)\textstyle\sum_{t=1}^{n}E(|X_{t-s}|^{1+\mu}) = E(|X_{-s}^{*}|^{1+\mu}),$$

hence

$$\sup_{j\geq 0}E(|X_{-j}^{*}|^{1+\mu}) < \infty.$$

The lemma now follows similarly to lemma 6.4.1. Q.E.D.

Proof of lemma 6.4.4: Let $\theta_1 \in \Theta$ and $\theta_2 \in \Theta$. Similarly to (6.4.7) (with (6.4.8)) we have

$$|\psi(\textstyle\sum_{j=0}^{\infty}\Gamma_j(\theta_1)'X_{-j}^{*}) - \psi(\sum_{j=0}^{\infty}\Gamma_j(\theta_2)'X_{-j}^{*})|$$
$$\leq C|\textstyle\sum_{j=0}^{\infty}(\Gamma_j(\theta_1) - \Gamma_j(\theta_2))'X_{-j}^{*}|(\sum_{j=0}^{\infty}\rho_j|X_{-j}^{*}|)^{\mu}$$
$$\leq C[\textstyle\sum_{j=0}^{\infty}(\sum_{i=0}^{p}|\gamma_{j,i}(\theta_1) - \gamma_{j,i}(\theta_2)|)|X_{-j}^{*}|](\sum_{j=0}^{\infty}\rho_j|X_{-j}^{*}|)^{\mu}. \qquad (6.4.10)$$

Thus similarly to (6.4.9) it follows from (6.4.10) that

$$|E[\psi(\textstyle\sum_{j=0}^{\infty}\Gamma_j(\theta_1)'X_{-j}^{*})] - E[\psi(\sum_{j=0}^{\infty}\Gamma_j(\theta_2)'X_{-j}^{*})]|$$
$$\leq C.(\textstyle\sum_{j=0}^{\infty}\rho_j)^{\mu}\sup_{j\geq 0}E(|X_{-j}^{*}|^{1+\mu})\sum_{j=0}^{\infty}\sum_{i=0}^{p}|\gamma_{j,i}(\theta_1) - \gamma_{j,i}(\theta_2)|.$$

Since the $\gamma_{j,i}(\theta)$'s are continuous on Θ, this result proves the lemma. Q.E.D.

The next theorems are easy extensions of theorem 6.4.1. They will enable us to prove consistency of least squares parameter estimators of nonlinear ARMAX models. Cf. chapter 8.

Theorem 6.4.2 Let Θ, ψ, μ, (X_t), and (X_t^*) be as in theorem 6.4.1. Let the functions $\gamma_{i,j}(\theta,x)$, $j=0,1,2,\ldots$, $i=1,2,\ldots,p$, be continuous real functions on $\Theta \times R^k$, such that

$$\max_{i=1,\ldots,p}\sup_{\theta\in\Theta}|\gamma_{j,i}(\theta,x)| \leq \rho_j\bar{b}(x), \tag{6.4.11}$$

where

$$\textstyle\sum_{j=0}^{\infty}\rho_j < \infty \tag{6.4.12}$$

and $\bar{b}$ (x) is a non-negative continuous real function on R^k such that for some $\delta > 0$,

$$\sup_t E(\bar{b}\,(X_t)^{1+\mu+\delta}) < \infty. \tag{6.4.13}$$

Finally, let

$$\Gamma_j(\theta,x) = (\gamma_{j,1}(\theta,x),\ldots,\gamma_{j,p}(\theta,x))'. \tag{6.4.14}$$

Then

$$\text{plim}_{n\to\infty}\sup_{\theta\in\Theta}|(1/n)\textstyle\sum_{t=1}^{n}\psi(\sum_{j=0}^{t-1}\Gamma_j(\theta,X_{t-j})) - E[\psi(\sum_{j=0}^{\infty}\Gamma_j(\theta,X_{-j}^*))]| = 0.$$

Moreover, the limit function $E[\psi(\sum_{j=0}^{\infty}\Gamma_j(\theta,X_{-j}^*))]$ is continuous on Θ.

Proof: Replacing $|X_{t-j}|$ and $|X_{-j}^*|$ in the proofs of lemmas 6.4.1–6.4.4 by $\bar{b}\,(X_{t-j})$ and $\bar{b}\,(X_{-j}^*)$, respectively, the theorem easily follows. Q.E.D.

Theorem 6.4.3 Let the conditions of theorem 6.4.2 be satisfied, except that (X_t) is now setwise properly heterogenous and the functions $\gamma_{i,j}(\theta,x)$, $j=0,1,2,\ldots$, $i=1,2,\ldots,p$, are for each $x \in R^k$ continuous real functions on Θ and for each $\theta \in \Theta$ Borel measurable real functions on R^k. Then the conclusions of theorem 6.4.2 carry over.

Proof: Note that the function $\bar{b}$ (.) may now be merely Borel measurable. The proof of this theorem is similar to the proof of theorem 6.4.2, referring to theorem 6.3.6 instead of theorem 6.3.2. Q.E.D.

7

Functional specification of time series models

7.1 Introduction

Consider a vector time series process (Z_t) in R^k with $E(|Z_t|) < \infty$ for each t. In time series regression analysis we are interested in modeling and estimating the conditional expectation of Z_t relative to its entire past. The reason for our interest in this conditional expectation is that it represents the best forecasting scheme for Z_t; best in the sense that the mean square forecast error is minimal. To see this, compare this forecast, i.e.,

$$\hat{Z}_t = E(Z_t|Z_{t-1},Z_{t-2},\ldots), \tag{7.1.1}$$

with an alternative forecasting scheme, say

$$\tilde{Z}_t = G_t(Z_{t-1},Z_{t-2},\ldots), \tag{7.1.2}$$

where G_t is a R^k-valued (non-random) function on the space of all one-sided infinite sequences in R^k such that $\tilde{Z}_t$ is a well-defined random vector. Denote the forecast errors by

$$U_t = Z_t - \hat{Z}_t, \tag{7.1.3}$$

and

$$W_t = Z_t - \tilde{Z}_t, \tag{7.1.4}$$

respectively. Then

$$E(W_tW_t') = E(U_tU_t') + E[(\hat{Z}_t - \tilde{Z}_t)(\hat{Z}_t - \tilde{Z}_t)'], \tag{7.1.5}$$

due to the fact that by (7.1.1) and (7.1.3)

$$E(U_t|Z_{t-1},Z_{t-2},\ldots) = 0 \text{ a.s.} \tag{7.1.6}$$

Thus the mean square error matrix $E(W_tW_t')$ of the alternative forecasting scheme dominates $E(U_tU_t')$ by a positive semi-definite matrix.

7.2 Linear time series regression models

7.2.1 The Wold decomposition

The central problem in time series modeling is to find a suitable functional specification of the conditional expectation (7.1.1). Often the model is specified directly or indirectly as a linear AR(∞) model. This linear AR(∞) specification can be motivated on the basis of the famous Wold (1954) decomposition theorem, together with the assumption that the process Z_t is stationary and Gaussian, and some regularity conditions. Here we present Wold's theorem for univariate Gaussian time series processes.

> *Theorem 7.2.1 (Wold decomposition).* Let (Z_t) be a univariate stationary Gaussian time series process satisfying $\sigma^2 = \text{var}(U_t) > 0$, where U_t is defined by (7.1.3), and let for $s \geqslant 0$,
>
> $\gamma_s = E(Z_t U_{t-s}/\sigma^2)$ (note that $\gamma_0 = 1$).
>
> Then $\sum_{s=0}^{\infty}\gamma_s^2 < \infty$ and
>
> $Z_t = \sum_{s=0}^{\infty}\gamma_s U_{t-s} + W_t,$
>
> where the process (W_t) is such that
>
> $E(W_j U_t) = 0$ for all j and t and (W_t) is deterministic,
>
> i.e., W_t is a (possibly infinite) linear combination of W_{t-1}, W_{t-2}, ... without error. Moreover,
>
> (U_t) is an independent Gaussian process. (7.2.1)

Proof: Let $\{\Omega,\mathfrak{F},P\}$ be the probability space. From the definition of γ_s it easily follows that $E[(Z_t-\sum_{s=0}^{n}\gamma_s U_{t-s})^2] = E(Z_t^2-\sum_{s=0}^{n}\gamma_s^2)$, hence $\sum_{s=0}^{\infty}\gamma_s^2 < \infty$. Let $\mathfrak{G}_{t-n}^{t}$ be the Borel field generated by $U_t,...U_{t-n}$ and denote $Y_{t,n} = \sum_{s=0}^{n}\gamma_s U_{t-s}$. Then for fixed t, $Y_{t,n}$ is a martingale defined on $\{\Omega,\mathfrak{G}_{t-n}^{t},P\}$, with $\sup_n E(|Y_{t,n}|) \leq \sqrt{[\sum_{s=0}^{\infty}\gamma_s^2]} < \infty$. Therefore, it follows from theorem 6.1.2 that $\lim_{n\to\infty} Y_{t,n} = Y_{t,\infty}$ a.s., where $Y_{t,\infty} = \sum_{s=0}^{\infty}\gamma_s U_{t-s}$. Consequently,

$$\sum_{s=0}^{\infty}\gamma_s U_{t-s} \text{ exists a.s.} \tag{7.2.2}$$

Next, denote $W_t = Z_t-\sum_{s=0}^{\infty}\gamma_s U_{t-s}$. For $j > 0$ we have

$$\begin{aligned} E(W_{t-j}U_t) &= E(U_t Z_{t-j}) - \sum_{s=0}^{\infty}\gamma_s E(U_t U_{t+j-s}) \\ &= E[E(U_t|Z_{t-1},Z_{t-2},...)Z_{t-j}] \\ &\quad - \sum_{s=0}^{\infty}\gamma_s E[E(U_t|Z_{t-1},Z_{t-2},...)U_{t-j-s}] = 0, \end{aligned} \tag{7.2.3}$$

whereas for $j \geq 0$, by definition of γ_s,

$$E(W_{t+j}U_t) = E(Z_{t+j}U_t) - \sum_{s=0}^{\infty}\gamma_s E(U_{t+j-s}U_t)$$
$$= E(Z_{t+j}U_t) - \sigma^2\gamma_j = 0. \quad (7.2.4)$$

The proof that W_t is deterministic is quite difficult, and therefore we refer for it to Anderson (1971, p. 421). Since Z_t is stationary and Gaussian, $E(Z_t|Z_{t-1},...,Z_{t-m})$ is a linear function of $Z_{t-1},...,Z_{t-m}$, i.e., there exist constants $\beta_{1,m},...,\beta_{m,m}$ not depending on t, such that

$$E(Z_t|Z_{t-1},...,Z_{t-m}) = \sum_{j=1}^{m}\beta_{j,m}Z_{t-j} \quad (7.2.5)$$

(cf. exercise 1). Defining

$$U_{t,m} = Z_t - E(Z_t|Z_{t-1},...,Z_{t-m}), \quad (7.2.6)$$

it follows that $(U_{t,m},Z_{t-1},...,Z_{t-m})$ is $(m+1)$-variate normally distributed with $U_{t,m}$ independent of $Z_{t-1},...,Z_{t-m}$. Since by theorem 6.1.4,

$$\lim_{m\to\infty}U_{t,m} = U_t \text{ a.s.}, \quad (7.2.7)$$

it follows that U_t is independent of $(Z_{t-1},...,Z_{t-m})$ for every $m \geq 1$, $U_t \sim N(0,\sigma^2)$ and U_t is a linear combination of $Z_t,Z_{t-1}, Z_{t-2},...$ With these hints, (7.2.1) is not hard to prove (cf. exercise 2). Q.E.D.

Next, assume that the lag polynomial $\gamma(L) = \sum_{s=0}^{\infty}\gamma_s L^s$ is invertible:

$$\beta(L) = \gamma(L)^{-1} = \sum_{s=0}^{\infty}\beta_s L^s, \quad (7.2.8)$$

say. See Anderson (1971, pp. 423–424) for precise conditions under which (7.2.8) holds. If Z_t is stationary and Gaussian with $E(Z_t) = 0$ and the deterministic part W_t is a.s. zero then

$$\sum_{s=0}^{\infty}\beta_s Z_{t-s} = U_t, \quad (7.2.9)$$

hence, since $\beta_0 = 1$,

$$Z_t = \sum_{s=1}^{\infty}(-\beta_s)Z_{t-s} + U_t, \quad (7.2.10)$$

which is an AR(∞) model.

In practice one often assumes that the lag polynomial $\gamma(L)$ is rational, i.e.

$$\gamma(L) = \theta(L)/\alpha(L), \quad (7.2.11)$$

where

$$\theta(L) = 1 - \sum_{s=1}^{q}\theta_s L^s \quad (7.2.12)$$

$$\alpha(L) = 1 - \sum_{s=1}^{p}\alpha_s L^s \quad (7.2.13)$$

are finite-order lag polynomials with no common roots, and all roots outside the unit circle. If Z_t is a zero-mean stationary Gaussian process with $W_t = 0$ a.s. then

$$\alpha(L)Z_t = \theta(L)U_t, \tag{7.2.14}$$

which is an ARMA(p,q) model.

7.2.2 Linear vector time series models

Similar results also hold for vector time series processes. If (Z_t) is a k-variate zero mean stationary Gaussian process then under some regularity conditions we have

$$Z_t = \sum_{s=0}^{\infty} \Gamma_s U_{t-s} \tag{7.2.15}$$

where $\Gamma_s = [E(Z_t U_{t-s}')][E(U_t U_t')]^{-1}$. Again assuming that the matrix-valued lag polynomial

$$\Gamma(L) = \sum_{s=0}^{\infty} \Gamma_s L^s \qquad (\Gamma_0 = I) \tag{7.2.16}$$

is invertible with inverse

$$B(L) = \Gamma(L)^{-1} = \sum_{s=0}^{\infty} B_s L^s \qquad (B_0 = I) \tag{7.2.17}$$

the model becomes a VAR(∞) model:

$$Z_t = \sum_{s=1}^{\infty} (-B_s) Z_{t-s} + U_t. \tag{7.2.18}$$

If $\Gamma(L)$ is rational, i.e.

$$\Gamma(L) = A(L)^{-1}\Theta(L) \tag{7.2.19}$$

with

$$A(L) = I - \sum_{s=1}^{p} A_s L^s \tag{7.2.20}$$

$$\Theta(L) = I - \sum_{s=1}^{q} \Theta_s L^s, \tag{7.2.21}$$

then (under some regularity conditions), the model becomes a VARMA(p,q) model:

$$A(L)Z_t = \Theta(L)U_t \tag{7.2.22}$$

with $A(0) = \Theta(0) = I$.

VARMA models, however, may be considered as systems of ARMAX models. This is obvious if $\Theta(L)$ is diagonal, but it is also true if not each equation in (7.2.22) can be written as an ARMAX model. To see this, observe that

$$\Theta(L)^{-1} = (\det \Theta(L))^{-1} C(L),$$

where C(L) is the matrix of co-factors of $\Theta(L)$. Multiplying both sides of (7.2.22) by C(L) then yields

$$C(L)A(L)Z_t = (\det \Theta(L))U_t. \tag{7.2.23}$$

The polynomial matrix $\Psi(L) = C(L)A(L)$ consists of finite-order lag polynomials, and also $\varphi(L) = \det \Theta(L)$ is a finite-order lag polynomial. The first equation of (7.2.23) therefore takes the form

$$Z_{1,t} + \sum_{i=1}^{k}\sum_{j=1}^{p^*}\psi_{1,i,j}Z_{i,t-j} = U_{1,t} + \sum_{j=1}^{q^*}\gamma_j U_{1,t-j} \tag{7.2.24}$$

Denoting

$$Y_t = Z_{1,t},\ X_t = (Z_{2,t},\ldots,Z_{k,t}),\ V_t = U_{1,t}$$

$$\alpha_j = -\psi_{1,1,j},\ \beta_j = (-\psi_{1,2,j},\ldots,-\psi_{1,k,j})',$$

we can now write (7.2.24) in ARMAX form as

$$Y_t = \sum_{j=1}^{p^*}\alpha_j Y_{t-j} + \sum_{j=1}^{p^*}\beta_j' X_{t-j} + V_t + \sum_{j=1}^{q^*}\gamma_j V_{t-j} \tag{7.2.25}$$

Finally, for the case $q^* = 0$ we get an ARX-model.

Exercises

1. Prove (7.2.5).
2. Prove (7.2.1).

7.3 ARMA memory index models

7.3.1 Introduction

The linearity of the time series models discussed in section 7.2 is due to the assumption of normality of the time series involved. Normality, however, is by no means a necessity for time series. So the question arises what can be said about the functional form of the conditional expectation (7.1.1) if the process (Z_t) is non-Gaussian.

In this section we discuss the ARMA memory index modeling approach of Bierens (1988a,b). This approach exploits the fact that all time series are rational-valued. One could consider the rationality condition as an assumption, but in practice one cannot deal with irrational numbers, hence time series are always reported in a finite number of decimal digits and consequently time series are rational-valued by nature. Thus, the rationality condition is an indisputable fact rather than an assumption. In this section it will be shown that in conditioning a k-variate rational-valued time series process on its entire past it is possible to capture the information contained in the past of the process by a single random variable. This random variable, containing all relevant information about the past of the process involved, can be formed as an autoregressive moving average of past observations. Hence the conditional expectation involved then takes the form of a nonlinear function of an autoregressive moving average of past observations. In particular, for univariate rational-valued time series processes (Z_t) it will be shown that there exist uncountably many real numbers $\tau \in (-1,1)$ such that

$$E(Z_t|Z_{t-1},Z_{t-2},Z_{t-3},\ldots) = E(Z_t|\textstyle\sum_{j=1}^{\infty}\tau^{j-1}Z_{t-j}) \text{ a.s.} \tag{7.3.1}$$

Moreover, if Z_t is k-variate rational-valued there exist uncountably many $\tau \in (-1,1)$ and $\theta \in R^k$ such that for $i=1,\ldots,k$,

$$E(Z_{i,t}|Z_{t-1},Z_{t-2},Z_{t-3},\ldots) = E(Z_{i,t}|\textstyle\sum_{j=1}^{\infty}\tau^{j-1}\theta' Z_{t-j}) \text{ a.s.} \tag{7.3.2}$$

where $Z_{i,t}$ is the i-th component of Z_t.

This result is not specific for the geometric weighting scheme involved. More generally, it will be shown that there exist uncountably many sets of rational lag polynomials

$$\psi_{i,j}(L) = \psi_{i,j}^{(1)}(L)/\psi_i^{(2)}(L),\ i,j = 1,2,\ldots,k,$$

where $\psi_{i,j}^{(1)}(L)$ and $\psi_i^{(2)}(L)$ are finite-order lag polynomials, such that for $i=1,2,\ldots,k$,

$$E(Z_{i,t}|Z_{t-1},Z_{t-2},Z_{t-3},\ldots) = E(Z_{i,t}|\textstyle\sum_{j=1}^{k}\psi_{i,j}(L)Z_{j,t-1}) \text{ a.s.} \tag{7.3.3}$$

Since a conditional expectation can be written as a Borel measurable function of the conditioning variable, the result (7.3.3) implies that for each permissible lag polynomial $\psi_{i,j}(L)$ there exists a Borel measurable real function $f_{i,t}$ such that

$$E(Z_{i,t}|Z_{t-1},Z_{t-2},Z_{t-3},\ldots) = f_{i,t}(\textstyle\sum_{j=1}^{k}\psi_{i,j}(L)Z_{j,t-1}) \text{ a.s.} \tag{7.3.4}$$

Denoting

$$\xi_{i,t} = \textstyle\sum_{j=1}^{k}\psi_{i,j}(L)Z_{j,t-1} = \sum_{j=1}^{k}\{\psi_{i,j}^{(1)}(L)/\psi_i^{(2)}(L)\}Z_{j,t-1}, \tag{7.3.5}$$

we see that the conditioning variable in (7.3.3) can be written in ARMA form:

$$\psi_i^{(2)}(L)\xi_{i,t} = \textstyle\sum_{j=1}^{k}\psi_{i,j}^{(1)}(L)Z_{j,t-1}. \tag{7.3.6}$$

Consequently, specifying the data-generating process as an ARMA process is equivalent to specifying the response functions $f_{i,t}$, for a particular set of rational lag polynomials $\psi_{i,j}(L)$, as time-invariant linear functions. Moreover, in the multivariate case one may interpret the conditioning variable $\xi_{i,t}$ as a one-step ahead forecast with an almost arbitrary linear ARMAX model for $Z_{i,t}$. This can be seen if one replaces $\xi_{i,t}$ in (7.3.6) by $Z_{i,t}-V_{i,t}$, where $(V_{i,t})$ is the error process. The X-vector involved then consists of all components of Z_t except $Z_{i,t}$. Thus, the best one-step-ahead forecasting scheme is a Borel measurable real function of a one-step-ahead forecast with an almost arbitrary linear ARMAX model. Specifying the equations in the VARMA model (7.2.22) as ARMAX models is therefore equivalent to specifying the corresponding functions $f_{i,t}$ in (7.3.4) as linear time-invariant functions. Furthermore, all the nonlinearity of the conditional expectation function (7.3.4) is now captured by the nonlinearity of the functions $f_{i,t}$, and the impact of heterogeneity of the process (Z_t) on the conditional expectation involved is captured by the time dependence of $f_{i,t}$.

As the conditioning variable (7.3.5) carries the memory of the process, plays a similar role as the index in the index modeling approach of Sargent and Sims (1977) and Sims (1981), and can be written in ARMA(X) form, we have called our approach *autoregressive moving average (ARMA) memory index modeling* and the index (7.3.5) will be called the *ARMA memory index*.

7.3.2 Finite conditioning of univariate rational-valued time series

Let (Z_t) be a Q-valued stochastic process, where Q is the set of rational numbers. If

$$E(|Z_t|) < \infty \text{ for every t,} \tag{7.3.7}$$

then $E(Z_t|Z_{t-1},...,Z_{t-m})$ exists for any integers t and $m \geq 1$ (see chapter 3). Now our aim is to show that the conditioning variables $Z_{t-1},...,Z_{t-m}$ in this conditional expectation may be replaced by $\sum_{j=1}^{m}\tau^{j-1}Z_{t-j}$ for some real numbers τ, provided m is finite.

Suppose there exists a Borel measurable one-to-one mapping Φ_m from Q^m (the m-dimensional space of vectors with rational-valued components) to a subset of R. Then $(Z_{t-1},...,Z_{t-m})$ and $\Phi_m(Z_{t-1},...,Z_{t-m})$ generate the same Borel field, hence by the definition of conditional expectation

$$E(Z_t|Z_{t-1},...,Z_{t-m}) = E[Z_t|\Phi_m(Z_{t-1},...,Z_{t-m})] \tag{7.3.8}$$

for each t, provided (7.3.7) holds. Thus we see that by using such a one-to-one mapping Φ_m we can reduce the number of conditioning variables from m to one. This easy result is the core of our approach.

The function Φ_m may be constructed as follows. Let

$$\Phi_m(w|\tau) = \sum_{j=1}^{m}w_j\tau^{j-1}, \tag{7.3.9}$$

where

$$w = (w_1,...,w_m)' \in Q^m,\ \tau \in R. \tag{7.3.10}$$

Moreover, let for $w^{(1)} \in Q^m$, $w^{(2)} \in Q^m$,

$$R_m(w^{(1)},w^{(2)}) = \{\tau \in R\colon \Phi_m(w^{(1)}|\tau) = \Phi_m(w^{(2)}|\tau)\}. \tag{7.3.11}$$

In other words, $R_m(w^{(1)},w^{(2)})$ is the set of real roots of the $(m-1)$-order polynomial

$$\Phi_m(w^{(1)}|\tau) - \Phi_m(w^{(2)}|\tau) = \textstyle\sum_{j=1}^{m}(w_j^{(1)} - w_j^{(2)})\tau^{j-1}. \tag{7.3.12}$$

It is well known that if $w^{(1)} \neq w^{(2)}$, so that for at least one j, $w_j^{(1)} \neq w_j^{(2)}$, the number of real roots of the polynomial (7.3.12) does not exceed $m-1$. Thus if $w^{(1)} \neq w^{(2)}$ then $R_m(w^{(1)},w^{(2)})$ is a finite set of size less than or equal to $m-1$. Since Q is a countable set (see Royden [1968, proposition 6, p. 21]) and since the union of a countable collection of countable sets is countable itself (Royden [1968, proposition 7, p.21]), we now obviously have that the set

$$S_m = \cup R_m(w^{(1)},w^{(2)}) \tag{7.3.13}$$

is countable, where the union is over all Q^m-valued unequal $w^{(1)}$ and $w^{(2)}$. Thus for $\tau \in R\backslash S_m$ we have that

$$w^{(1)} \in Q^m,\ w^{(2)} \in Q^m,\ \Phi_m(w^{(1)}|\tau) = \Phi_m(w^{(2)}|\tau) \Rightarrow w^{(1)} = w^{(2)} \tag{7.3.14}$$

and vice versa. This proves that for $\tau \in R\backslash S_m$ the function $\Phi_m(w|\tau)$ is a one-to-one mapping from Q^m to a subset of R. Taking

$$S = \cup_{m=1}^{\infty} S_m, \tag{7.3.15}$$

which is a countable union of countable sets and therefore countable itself, we now see that the following theorem holds.

> *Theorem 7.3.1* Let (Z_t) be a Q-valued stochastic process satisfying $E(|Z_t|) < \infty$ for all t. Then there exists a countable subset S of R such that $\tau \in R\backslash S$ implies
>
> $$E(Z_t|Z_{t-1},\ldots,Z_{t-m}) = E(Z_t|\textstyle\sum_{j=1}^{m} Z_{t-j}\tau^{j-1}) \text{ a.s.} \tag{7.3.16}$$
>
> for $m = 1,2,3,\ldots$ and $t = \ldots,-2,-1,0,1,2,3,\ldots$

Remark: Note that this result carries over for processes (Z_t) in any countable subset of R, as we have only used the countability of Q for proving theorem 7.3.1. Thus, the theorem remains valid if the Z_t are Borel measurable transformations of Q-valued random variables, for countability is always preserved.

7.3.3 *Infinite conditioning of univariate rational-valued time series*

In this subsection we shall set forth conditions such that (7.3.1) holds for each t and each $\tau(-1,1)\backslash S$, where S is the same as in theorem 7.3.1. Intuitively we feel that (7.3.1) requires the following condition:

The process (Z_t) is such that for every t and every $\tau \in (-1,1)$, $\sum_{j=1}^{\infty} Z_{t-j}\tau^{j-1}$ converges a.s. (7.3.17)

As has been shown in Bierens (1988a), this condition is implied by the following assumption:

Assumption 7.3.1 Let $\sup_t E(|Z_t|) < \infty$.

Now if condition (7.3.17) holds then $(Z_{t-1},Z_{t-2},\ldots)$ and $(\sum_{j=1}^{\infty} Z_{t-j}\tau^{j-1},Z_{t-m-1},Z_{t-m-2},\ldots)$ generate the same Borel field, because both sequences can then be constructed from $(\sum_{j=1}^{m} Z_{t-j}\tau^{j-1},Z_{t-m-1},Z_{t-m-2},\ldots)$ and vice versa. Since this conclusion holds for every $m \geq 1$, it follows that under the conditions of theorem 7.3.1 and condition (7.3.17) or assumption 7.3.1, $\tau \in (-1,1)\backslash S$ implies

$$E(Z_t|Z_{t-1},Z_{t-2},\ldots) = E(Z_t|\textstyle\sum_{j=1}^{\infty} Z_{t-j}\tau^{j-1},Z_{t-m-1},Z_{t-m-2},\ldots) \text{ a.s.}$$

for every $m \geq 1$ and t, hence for every t,

$$E(Z_t|Z_{t-1},Z_{t-2},\ldots)$$
$$= \lim_{m\to\infty} E(Z_t|\textstyle\sum_{j=1}^{\infty} Z_{t-j}\tau^{j-1},Z_{t-m-1},Z_{t-m-2},\ldots) \text{ a.s.} \quad (7.3.18)$$

For showing (7.3.1) we now need additional conditions ensuring that the impact of $Z_{t-m-1},Z_{t-m-2},\ldots$ on the conditional expectation at the right-hand side of (7.3.18) vanishes as $m \to \infty$. In Bierens (1988a,b) we have shown that υ-stability with respect to an α-mixing base, together with some regularity conditions, will do. However, the proof involved is rather complicated. Therefore we impose here the following extension of the mixingale condition.

> *Assumption 7.3.2* Let $\mathfrak{F}^t_{-\infty}$ be the Borel field generated by
>
> $Z_t,Z_{t-1},Z_{t-2},Z_{t-3},\ldots$
>
> and let $\mathfrak{F}_t^{\infty}$ be the Borel field generated by
>
> $Z_t,Z_{t+1},Z_{t+2},Z_{t+3},\ldots$
>
> Let $\ell < \infty$ be an arbitrary integer and let W_t be an arbitrary random variable defined on $\mathfrak{F}_{t-\ell}^{\infty}$ satisfying $E(W_t^2) < \infty$. Moreover, let $\{\mathfrak{G}^t_{-\infty}\}$ and $\{\mathfrak{H}^t_{-\infty}\}$ be arbitrary sequences of Borel fields such that $\mathfrak{G}^t_{-\infty} \subset \mathfrak{F}^t_{-\infty}$ and $\mathfrak{H}^t_{-\infty} \subset \mathfrak{F}^t_{-\infty}$. For every t and every $m \geq 0$ there exist constants c_t, ψ_m, with $\psi_m \to 0$ as $m \to \infty$, such that
>
> $$\{E[E(W_t|\mathfrak{G}^{t-1}_{-\infty} \vee \mathfrak{H}^{t-m-1}_{-\infty}) - E(W_t|\mathfrak{G}^{t-1}_{-\infty})]^2\}^{1/2} \leq c_t\psi_m.$$

This assumption is stated more generally than needed here. We will need its full extent in chapter 8.

Admittedly, assumption 7.3.2 looks quite complicated. However, it simply states that the impact of the remote past of Z_t, where the remote past involved is represented by $\mathfrak{H}_{-\infty}^{t-m-1}$, vanishes as $m \to \infty$

In the case (7.3.18), $W_t = Z_t$, $\mathfrak{H}_{-\infty}^{t} = \mathfrak{F}_{-\infty}^{t}$ and $\mathfrak{G}_{-\infty}^{t-1}$ is the Borel field generated by $\sum_{j=1}^{\infty} Z_{t-j}\tau^{j-1}$, hence assumption 7.3.2 and Chebishev's inequality imply

$$\text{plim}_{m\to\infty} E(Z_t|\sum_{j=1}^{\infty} Z_{t-j}\tau^{j-1}, Z_{t-m-1}, Z_{t-m-2},\ldots)$$
$$= E(Z_t|\sum_{j=1}^{\infty} Z_{t-j}\tau^{j-1}).$$

From theorem 2.1.6 it now follows that there exists a subsequence (m_ℓ) such that

$$E(Z_t|\sum_{j=1}^{\infty} Z_{t-j}\tau^{j-1}, Z_{t-m_\ell-1}, Z_{t-m_\ell-2},\ldots)$$
$$\to E(Z_t|\sum_{j=1}^{\infty} Z_{t-j}\tau^{j-1}) \text{ a.s. as } \ell \to \infty,$$

hence the limit (7.3.18) must be equal to the latter conditional expectation as well. Thus we have:

Theorem 7.3.2 Let the conditions of theorem 7.3.1 and assumptions 7.3.1 and 7.3.2 be satisfied. There exists a countable subset S of R such that $\tau \in (-1,1)\backslash S$ implies

$$E(Z_t|Z_{t-1}, Z_{t-2},\ldots) = E(Z_t|\sum_{j=1}^{\infty} Z_{t-j}\tau^{j-1}) \text{ a.s.}$$

for $t = \ldots, -2, -1, 0, 1, 2, \ldots$

7.3.4 The multivariate case

If $Z_t \in Q^k$ we may proceed in the same way as before, hence theorems 7.3.1 and 7.3.2 carry over to rational-valued vector time series processes. However, the ARMA memory index $\sum_{j=1}^{\infty} Z_{t-j}\tau^{j-1}$ is then multivariate too.

We can get a scalar ARMA memory index by using the concept of a linear separator introduced in Bierens and Hartog (1988):

Definition 7.3.1 A vector θ is a linear separator of a countable subset Ξ of R^k if for all pairs $(x_1, x_2) \in \Xi \times \Xi$, $\theta' x_1 = \theta' x_2$ implies $x_1 = x_2$.

The existence of a linear separator of a countable set is always guaranteed. In fact the set of all linear separators is uncountable, as is illustrated by the following theorem.

Theorem 7.3.3 Let Ξ be a countable subset of R^k and let S be the set of all linear separators of Ξ. Then the set $R^k\backslash S$ has Lebesgue measure zero.

Proof: Let

$$C = \{(x_1,x_2): x_1 \in \Xi, x_2 \in \Xi, x_1 \neq x_2\}$$

and let

$$T(x_1,x_2) = \{\theta \in R^k: \theta'(x_1-x_2) = 0\}.$$

For $x_1 \neq x_2$ the set $T(x_1,x_2)$ is of lower dimension than k, hence $T(x_1,x_2)$ has Lebesgue measure zero. Now

$$R^k \backslash S = \cup_{(x_1,x_2)\in C} T(x_1,x_2)$$

is a countable union of sets with Lebesgue measure zero and therefore a set with Lebesgue measure zero itself. Q.E.D.

From definition 7.3.1 it follows that for any linear separator θ of Ξ each point in the range of $\theta'x$ ($x \in \Xi$) can uniquely be associated to a point in the domain Ξ, and vice versa. Thus $\theta'x$ is a one-to-one mapping from Ξ into R. Thus, let $\theta \in R^k$ be a linear separator of the countable set Q^k. Then it follows from theorem 3.2.1(viii):

$$E(Z_t|Z_{t-1},Z_{t-2},\ldots) = E(Z_t|\theta'Z_{t-1},\theta'Z_{t-2},\ldots) \text{ a.s.}$$

and moreover the process $(\theta'Z_t)$ is still countable-valued. Applying theorem 7.3.2 we now conclude that for each linear separator θ of Q^k there exists a countable subset S_θ of R such that for each $\tau(-1,1)\backslash S_\theta$,

$$E(Z_t|Z_{t-1},Z_{t-2},\ldots) = E(Z_t|\textstyle\sum_{j=1}^{\infty}\theta'Z_{t-j}\tau^{j-1}) \text{ a.s.} \quad (7.3.19)$$

We recall that the set Θ_0 of vectors $\theta \in R^k$ that are *not* linear separators of Q^k has Lebesgue measure zero; see theorem 7.3.3. This result, together with the countability of S_θ for each linear separator θ, imply that there exists a set $N \subset R^{k+1}$ with Lebesgue measure zero such that (7.3.19) holds for $(\theta,\tau) \in R^k \times (-1,1)\backslash N$. To see this, draw τ from the uniform $[-1,1]$ distribution, draw the components of θ independently from say the uniform [a,b] distribution and let

$$\zeta_t(\tau,\theta) = E\{I[E(Z_t|Z_{t-1},Z_{t-2},\ldots) = E(Z_t|\textstyle\sum_{j=1}^{\infty}\theta'Z_{t-j}\tau^{j-1})]|\tau,\theta\}.$$

Then

$$E[\zeta_t(\tau,\theta)] = \int_{\times_{i=1}^{k}[a,b]}\{\int_{[-1,1]}\zeta_t(\tau,\theta)d\tau\}d\theta$$
$$= \int_{\{\times_{i=1}^{k}[a,b]\}\backslash\Theta_0}\{\int_{(-1,1)\backslash S_\theta}\zeta_t(\tau,\theta)d\tau\}d\theta = 1,$$

which implies that (7.3.19) holds except for (θ,τ) in a set with Lebesgue measure zero. Thus we have:

Theorem 7.3.4 Let $(Z_t) = ((Z_{1,t},\ldots,Z_{k,t})')$ be a Q^k-valued stochastic process satisfying $E(|Z_t|) < \infty$ for every t. There exists a subset N of R^{k+1} with Lebesgue measure zero such that $(\theta,\tau) \in R^k \times (-1,1)\backslash N$ implies

$$E(Z_{i,t}|Z_{t-1},...,Z_{t-m}) = E(Z_{i,t}|\textstyle\sum_{j=1}^{m}\theta' Z_{t-j}\tau^{j-1}) \text{ a.s.} \qquad (7.3.20)$$

for $m=1,2,...,i=1,2,...,k$, and $t=...,-2,-1,0,1,2,...$ If, in addition, assumptions 7.3.1 and 7.3.2 are satisfied, then

$$E(Z_{i,t}|Z_{t-1},Z_{t-2},...) = E(Z_{i,t}|\textstyle\sum_{j=1}^{\infty}\theta' Z_{t-j}\tau^{j-1}) \text{ a.s.} \qquad (7.3.21)$$

for $i=1,2,...,k$ and $t=...,-2,-1,0,1,2,...$

For showing that (7.3.3) holds for uncountably many rational lag polynomials we need the following generalization of theorems 7.3.1 and 7.3.2.

Lemma 7.3.1 Let (Z_t) be a Q-valued stochastic process with $E(|Z_t|) < \infty$. Let q be an arbitrary positive integer. Let C_1 be the set of complex numbers with absolute value less than 1. There exists a subset S of C^q with Lebesgue measure zero such that $(\tau_1,...,\tau_q)' \in C_1^q\backslash S$ implies

$$E(Z|Z_{t-1},...,Z_{t-mq}) = E\{Z_t|\Pi_{\ell=1}^{q}[(1-(\tau_\ell L)^m)/(1-\tau_\ell L)]Z_{t-1}) \text{ a.s.} \qquad (7.3.22)$$

for $m=1,2,3,...$ and all t. If in addition assumptions 7.3.1 and 7.3.3 hold, then for each t,

$$E(Z_t|Z_{t-1},Z_{t-2},...) = E(Z_t|\Pi_{\ell=1}^{q}[1/(1-\tau_\ell L)]Z_{t-1}) \text{ a.s.} \qquad (7.3.23)$$

Proof: Let (w_t) be an arbitrary sequence of rational numbers. Denote for $q \geq 1$, $m \geq 1$,

$$x_t^{(1)}(\tau_1) = \textstyle\sum_{j=0}^{m-1}\tau_1^j w_{t-j} = \{[1-(\tau_1 L)^m]/(1-\tau_1 L)\}w_t,$$

$$x_t^{(q)}(\tau_1,\tau_2,...,\tau_q) = \textstyle\sum_{j=0}^{m-1}\tau_q^j x_{t-j}^{(q-1)}(\tau_1,\tau_2,...,\tau_{q-1})$$
$$= \Pi_{\ell=1}^{q}\{[1-(\tau_\ell L)^m]/(1-\tau_\ell L)\}w_t.$$

Suppose for the moment that $\tau_1,...,\tau_q$ are real-valued. Now draw $\tilde{\tau}_1,...,\tilde{\tau}_q$ independently from the uniform [0,1] distribution. Then

$$P(x_t^{(q)}(\tilde{\tau}_1,...,\tilde{\tau}_q) = 0|\tilde{\tau}_1,...,\tilde{\tau}_q) = 0 \text{ a.s.}$$

if at least one of the $x_{t-j}^{(q-1)}(\tilde{\tau}_1,...,\tilde{\tau}_{q-1})$, $j=0,...,m-1$, is unequal to zero, whereas

$$P(x_t^{(q)}(\tilde{\tau}_1,...,\tilde{\tau}_q) = 0|\tilde{\tau}_1,...,\tilde{\tau}_q) = 1 \text{ a.s.}$$

if all the $x_{t-j}^{(q-1)}(\tilde{\tau}_1,...,\tilde{\tau}_{q-1})$ are zero. Thus

$$P(x_t^{(q)}(\tilde{\tau}_1,...,\tilde{\tau}_q) = 0|\tilde{\tau}_1,...,\tilde{\tau}_q)$$
$$= \min_{j=0,...,m-1} I(x_{t-j}^{(q-1)}(\tilde{\tau}_1,...,\tilde{\tau}_{q-1}) = 0)$$

and consequently

$$P(x_t^{(q)}(\tilde{\tau}_1,...,\tilde{\tau}_q) = 0) = E[\min_{j=0,...,m-1} I(x_{t-j}^{(q-1)}(\tilde{\tau}_1,...,\tilde{\tau}_{q-1}) = 0)]$$
$$\leq \min_{j=0,...,m-1} P(x_{t-j}^{(q-1)}(\tilde{\tau}_1,...,\tilde{\tau}_{q-1}) = 0).$$

By recursion it therefore follows that

$$P(x_t^{(q)}(\tilde{\tau}_1,..,\tilde{\tau}_q) = 0) \leq \min_{j=0,...,q(m-1)} P(x_{t-j}^{(1)}(\tilde{\tau}_1) = 0). \tag{7.3.24}$$

But $P(x_t^{(1)}(\tilde{\tau}_1) = 0) = 0$ if at least one w_{t-j} ($j=0,...,m-1$) is unequal to zero, $P(x_t^{(1)}(\tilde{\tau}_1) = 0) = 1$ if $w_{t-j} = 0$ for $j=0,..,m-1$, hence

$$P(x_t^{(1)}(\tilde{\tau}_1) = 0) = \min_{j=0,..,m-1} I(w_{t-j} = 0). \tag{7.3.25}$$

Combining (7.3.24) and (7.3.25) now yields

$$P(x_t^{(q)}(\tilde{\tau}_1,...,\tilde{\tau}_q) = 0) \leq \min_{j=0,...,(m-1)q} I(w_{t-j} = 0).$$

This result shows that there exists a subset S_* of $\times_{j=1}^{q}(-1,1)$, depending on $w_t,w_{t-1},...,w_{t-q(m-1)}$, which has Lebesgue measure zero if one of these w_{t-j}'s is unequal to zero. The set S in lemma 7.3.1 is now the countable union of all these null sets S_*.

The case that the $\tilde{\tau}_\ell$ are complex-valued is similar. For example, let

$$\tilde{\tau}_\ell = \tilde{\rho}_\ell(\cos\tilde{\psi}_\ell + i\cdot\sin\tilde{\psi}_\ell),$$

where the $\tilde{\rho}_\ell$ are drawn independently from the uniform $[-1,1]$ distribution and the $\tilde{\psi}_\ell$ are drawn independently from say the standard normal distribution.

The rest of the proof of lemma 7.3.1 is similar to the proofs of theorems 7.3.1 and 7.3.2. Q.E.D.

Now let Γ_q be the set of vectors $\gamma = (\gamma_1,...,\gamma_q)' \in R^q$ for which the polynomial $1+\sum_{s=1}^{q}\gamma_s L^s$ has roots all outside the unit circle. Realizing that these roots are related to $\gamma_1,...,\gamma_q$ by a one-to-one mapping, the following corollary of part (7.3.23) of lemma 7.3.1 is easy to verify.

Lemma 7.3.2 Let the conditions of part (7.3.23) of lemma 7.3.1 hold. There exists a subset S of Γ_q with Lebesgue measure zero such that $\gamma = (\gamma_1,...,\gamma_q)' \in \Gamma_q \backslash S$ implies that for each t,

$$E(Z_t|Z_{t-1},Z_{t-2},...) = E\{Z_t|[1/(1+\textstyle\sum_{s=1}^{q}\gamma_s L^s)]Z_{t-1}\} \text{ a.s.}$$

Moreover, part (7.3.21) of theorem 7.3.4 can now be generalized as follows:

Lemma 7.3.3 Let the conditions of part (7.3.21) of theorem 7.3.3 hold and let q be an arbitrary positive integer. There exists a subset N of $R^k \times \Gamma_q$ with Lebesgue measure zero such that $(\theta,\gamma) \in R^k \times \Gamma_q \backslash N$ implies

$$E(Z_t|Z_{t-1},Z_{t-2},...) = E\{Z_{i,t}|[1/(1+\sum_{s=1}^{q}\gamma_s L^s)]\theta' Z_{t-1}\} \text{ a.s.}$$

for $i=1,2,...,k$ and $t=...,-2,-1,0,1,2,...$

Proof: Similarly to theorem 7.3.4.

Applying lemma 7.3.3 to the sequence:

(Z_t^*) with $Z_t^* = (Z_t', Z_{t-1}', ..., Z_{t-p}')'$,

our main theorem below now easily follows.

Theorem 7.3.5 Let p and q be arbitrary integers satisfying $p \geq 0$, $q \geq 1$. Let

$$\psi(L|\beta,\gamma) = (\sum_{s=0}^{p}\beta_s L^s)/(1+\sum_{s=1}^{q}\gamma_s L^s),$$

where $\beta = (\beta_0,\beta_1,..,\beta_p) \in R^{p+1}$, $\gamma = (\gamma_1,...,\gamma_q) \in R^q$. Moreover, let Γ_q be the set of all $\gamma \in R^q$ for which the lag polynomial $1+\sum_{s=1}^{q}\gamma_s L^s$ has roots all outside the unit circle. Under the conditions of theorem 7.3.4 (part (7.3.21)) there exists a subset N of $R^{(p+1)k} \times \Gamma_q$ with Lebesgue measure zero such that $(\beta_{i,1},...,\beta_{i,k},\gamma_i) \in R^{(p+1)k} \times \Gamma_q \backslash N$ implies

$$E(Z_{i,t}|Z_{t-1},Z_{t-2},...) = E[Z_{i,t}|\sum_{j=1}^{k}\psi(L|\beta_{i,j},\gamma_i)Z_{j,t-1}] \text{ a.s.} \quad (7.3.26)$$

for $i=1,2,...,k$ and $t=...,-2,-1,0,1,2,...$ Consequently, for each permissible rational lag polynomial $\psi(L|\beta_{i,j},\gamma_i)$ there exist Borel measurable real functions $f_{i,t}(.)$ depending on $\beta_{i,1}$, $\beta_{i,2},...,\beta_{i,k}$ and γ_i such that for $i=1,2,...,k$ and $t=...,-2,-1, 0,1,2,...,$

$$E(Z_{i,t}|Z_{t-1},Z_{t-2},...) = f_{i,t}(\sum_{j=1}^{k}\psi(L|\beta_{i,j},\gamma_i)Z_{j,t-1}) \text{ a.s.} \quad (7.3.27)$$

7.3.5 The nature of the ARMA memory index parameters and the response functions

In discussing the nature of the ARMA memory index parameters we shall first focus on the univariate case. We ask the question what the nature of a permissible τ in (7.3.1) is, i.e., is τ in general irrational or are rational τ's also permissible? We recall that a permissible τ is such that the polynomial

$$\sum_{j=1}^{m} w_j \tau^{j-1} \quad (7.3.28)$$

in nonzero for arbitrary $m \geq 1$ and arbitrary rational numbers w_j not all equal to zero. But for $m = 2$, $w_1 + w_2\tau = 0$ for $\tau = -w_1/w_2$, so that for given rational τ we can always find rational numbers w_j such that the polynomial (7.3.28) equals zero. Obviously the same applies if only integer-valued w_j's are allowed. Consequently, the permissible τ's are in general irrational. By a similar argument it can be shown that in the case of (7.3.26) at least some of the parameters in $\beta_{i,j}$ and γ_i will likely be irrational.

What is the consequence of the irrationality of the ARMA memory index parameters for the nature of the response functions? If we would pick an arbitrary permissible τ the Borel measurable real function $f_{t,\tau}$ for which

$$E(Z_t|Z_{t-1},Z_{t-2},...) = E(Z_t|\textstyle\sum_{j=1}^{\infty}\tau^{j-1}Z_{t-j}) = f_{t,\tau}(\sum_{j=1}^{\infty}\tau^{j-1}Z_{t-j}) \text{ a.s.}$$

will likely be highly discontinuous, as this function has to sort out $Z_{t-1},Z_{t-2},Z_{t-3},...$ from $\sum_{j=1}^{\infty}\tau^{j-1}Z_{t-j}$. See Sims(1988). On the other hand, if we choose τ such that Z_t and $\sum_{j=1}^{\infty}\tau^{j-1}Z_{t-j}$ are strongly correlated, and thus that $f_{t,\tau}(\sum_{j=1}^{\infty}\tau^{j-1}Z_{t-j})$ and $\sum_{j=1}^{\infty}\tau^{j-1}Z_{t-j}$ are strongly correlated, then the function $f_{t,\tau}$ will be close to a linear function. In any event, lemma 6.3.3 shows that the possible discontinuity of $f_{t,\tau}$ is not too dramatic, as $f_{t,\tau}$ can always be approximated arbitrarily close by a uniformly continuous function. Thus, given an arbitrary $\delta \in (0,1)$, a permissible $\tau \in (-1,1)$ and the condition $E(|Z_t|) < \infty$, there exists a uniformly continuous real function $g_{t,\tau}$ such that

$$E[|f_{t,\tau}(\textstyle\sum_{j=1}^{\infty}\tau^{j-1}Z_{t-j}) - g_{t,\tau}(\sum_{j=1}^{\infty}\tau^{j-1}Z_{t-j})|] < \delta^2 \qquad (7.3.29)$$

and consequently by Chebishev's inequality,

$$P[|f_{t,\tau}(\textstyle\sum_{j=1}^{\infty}\tau^{j-1}Z_{t-j}) - g_{t,\tau}(\sum_{j=1}^{\infty}\tau^{j-1}Z_{t-j})| < \delta\,] \geq 1-\delta. \qquad (7.3.30)$$

We have argued that the ARMA memory index parameters are likely irrational. Since computers deal only with rational numbers we therefore cannot calculate the ARMA memory index exactly in practice. However, it is possible to choose a rational τ_* close to τ such that "almost" all information about the past of the data-generating process is preserved. The argument goes as follows. Because of the uniform continuity of $g_{t,\tau}$, there exist real numbers $\eta > 0, \rho \in (0,1)$ and a rational number τ_* close to τ such that

$$\begin{aligned} &P[|g_{t,\tau}(\textstyle\sum_{j=1}^{\infty}\tau^{j-1}Z_{t-j}) - g_{t,\tau}(\sum_{j=1}^{\infty}\tau_*^{j-1}Z_{t-j})| < \delta\,] \\ &\quad \geq P[|\textstyle\sum_{j=1}^{\infty}\tau^{j-1}Z_{t-j} - \sum_{j=1}^{\infty}\tau_*^{j-1}Z_{t-j}| < \eta] \\ &\qquad \geq P[|\tau-\tau_*|\textstyle\sum_{j=2}^{\infty}(j-1)\rho^{j-2}|Z_{t-j}| < \eta], \end{aligned} \qquad (7.3.31)$$

where $1 > \rho > \max(|\tau|,|\tau_*|)$. The last inequality follows from the mean value theorem. Thus by Chebishev's inequality

$$\begin{aligned} &P[|g_{t,\tau}(\textstyle\sum_{j=1}^{\infty}\tau^{j-1}Z_{t-j}) - g_{t,\tau}(\sum_{j=1}^{\infty}\tau_*^{j-1}Z_{t-j})| < \delta] \\ &\quad \geq 1-|\tau-\tau_*|\textstyle\sum_{j=2}^{\infty}(j-1)\rho^{j-2}E|Z_{t-j}|/\eta \geq 1-\delta \end{aligned} \qquad (7.3.32)$$

if

$$|\tau-\tau_*| \leq \delta\eta(1-\rho)^2/\sup_t E(|Z_t|). \tag{7.3.33}$$

Combining (7.3.30) and (7.3.32) we see that for arbitrary $\delta \in (0,½)$,

$$P[|f_{t,\tau}(\sum_{j=1}^{\infty}\tau^{j-1}Z_{t-j}) - g_{t,\tau}(\sum_{j=1}^{\infty}\tau_*^{j-1}Z_{t-j})| < \delta] \geq 1-2\delta \text{ if (7.3.33) holds.} \tag{7.3.34}$$

It should be noted that the rational-valued τ_* depends in general on the time index t. However, if the process (Z_t) is strictly stationary we can pick a constant τ_*, as is not too hard to verify from (7.3.29) – (7.3.34). In that case the functions $f_{t,\tau}$ and $g_{t,\tau}$ are independent of t. Summarizing, we have shown:

> *Theorem 7.3.6* Let (Z_t) be a strictly stationary univariate rational-valued process. Let assumptions 7.3.1 and 7.3.2 hold and let $\delta \in (0,½)$ and $\tau \in (-1,1)\backslash S$ be arbitrary, where S is the same as in theorem 7.3.1. There exists a uniformly continuous real function g_τ and a rational number τ_* in a neighborhood of τ such that
>
> $$P[|E(Z_t|Z_{t-1},Z_{t-2},\ldots) - g_\tau(\sum_{j=1}^{\infty}\tau_*^{j-1}Z_{t-j})| < \delta] \geq 1-2\delta. \tag{7.3.35}$$

Finally, a similar result can be shown for the general case in theorem 7.3.5. Thus:

> *Theorem 7.3.7* Let the conditions of theorem 7.3.5 hold and assume in addition that (Z_t) is strictly stationary. For arbitrary $\delta \in (0,½)$ and $(\beta_{i,1},\ldots,\beta_{i,k},\gamma_i) \in R^{(p+1)k} \times \Gamma_q\backslash N$ there exist uniformly continuous real functions g_i and vectors $(\beta^*_{i,1},\ldots,\beta^*_{i,k},\gamma^*_i) \in Q^{(p+1)k} \times (\Gamma_q \cap Q^q)$ such that
>
> $$P[|E(Z_{i,t}|Z_{t-1},Z_{t-2},\ldots) - g_i(\sum_{j=1}^{k}\psi(L|\beta^*_{i,j},\gamma^*_i)Z_{j,t-1})| < \delta] \geq 1-2\delta \tag{7.3.36}$$
>
> for i = 1,2,...,k and each t.

7.3.6 Discussion

We have shown that in modeling rational-valued time series processes as conditional expectations relative to the entire past of the process involved, it is possible to capture the relevant information about the past of the process by a single random variable, called an ARMA memory index. Given this ARMA memory index, the specification of the model then amounts to specifying a nonlinear response function defined on the real line. Although this response function might be highly discontinuous, it can be approximated arbitrarily close by a uniformly continuous real function of an ARMA memory index with rational-valued parameters.

One might argue that our approach is merely a sophisticated variant of representing a one-sided infinite sequence of variables as a decimal expansion of a real variable. For example, let the univariate stochastic process (Z_t) be integer-valued with values 0,1,...,9, and define

$$\xi_t = \sum_{j=1}^{\infty}(0.1)^{j-1}Z_{t-j}.$$

Then ξ_t contains all the information about the past Z_{t-1}, Z_{t-2}, ... of the process under review, hence

$$E(Z_t|Z_{t-1},Z_{t-2},...) = E(Z_t|\xi_t) \text{ a.s.}$$

In particular if

$$E(Z_t|Z_{t-1},Z_{t-2},...) = \psi(Z_{t-1},Z_{t-2},...),$$

where ψ is a real function on the space of one-sided infinite sequences of integers, then

$$E(Z_t|Z_{t-1},Z_{t-2},...)$$
$$= \psi([\xi_t],[10\xi_t]-10[\xi_t],[10^2\xi_t]-10[10\xi_t],[10^3\xi_t]-10[10^2\xi_t],..) = \psi^*(\xi_t),$$

say, where [x] denotes truncation to the largest integer less than or equal to x. Even if the function ψ is wellshaped, the function ψ^* is highly discontinuous. Moreover, one might argue that knowing ψ^* is not of much help, as it is impossible to store ξ_t exactly in the memory of a computer. Admittedly, the above primitive index is in general of limited use. The main contribution of our approach, however, is that a one-period-ahead forecast on the basis of an almost arbitrary ARMAX model will work too. Modeling time series by ARMAX models can therefore be interpreted as specifying the response function $f_{i,t}$ in theorem 7.3.5 as a linear time-invariant function, and estimation of an ARMAX model can be interpreted as looking for an ARMA memory index for which the response function is linear. Fitting an ARMAX model to the data forces the nonlinear response function towards a linear function. A good forecasting performance of the estimated ARMAX model then indicates that the corresponding response function $f_{i,t}$ is close to a linear function, as the best forecasting scheme is the one which represents the expectation of the dependent variable conditional on an ARMA memory index. Thus, if one accepts ARMAX models as useful approximations of time series processes, then one accepts the existence of a tractable ARMA memory index with corresponding response function close to a linear function.

The problem of storage of the ARMA memory index is not peculiar to our approach but a universal problem. For example, transforming the data by, say, a log transformation will result in loss of information, because of the finiteness of data storage in a computer. Whether this problem is serious or not for our ARMA memory index depends on the dependence of the data. Take, for example, the above primitive index ξ_t. Storing ξ_t as a double precision variable yields 29 significant decimal digits (in CDC Fortran 5). Thus at least we can sort out $Z_{t-1},\ldots,Z_{t-29}$ from ξ_t. If Z_t is almost independent of Z_{t-j} for $j > 29$ then

$$E(Z_t|Z_{t-1},Z_{t-2},\ldots) \approx E(Z_t|Z_{t-1},\ldots,Z_{t-29}) \approx E(Z_t|\xi_t).$$

7.4 Nonlinear ARMAX models

The lesson we learn from the argument in sections 7.2 and 7.3 is that the class of linear ARMAX models forms a good starting point for modeling vector time series processes. In modeling the conditional expectation $E(Z_{i,t}|Z_{t-1},Z_{t-2},\ldots)$ one should first look for the best-fitting linear ARMAX model, as this strategy forces the nonlinear function f_i, which maps the corresponding ARMA memory index $\xi_{i,t}$ into this conditional expectation, towards a linear function. Then apply various model misspecification tests to check the validity of the linear ARMAX model. We will consider these tests in the next chapter. If these tests indicate the presence of misspecification one could then try to model the nonlinear function f_i, for which $E(Z_{i,t}|\xi_{i,t}) = f_i(\xi_{i,t})$, for example by specifying f_i as a polynomial of a bounded one-to-one transformation of $\xi_{i,t}$. Moreover, one could run a nonparametric regression of $Z_{i,t}$ on $\xi_{i,t}$ to find a suitable functional form of f_i. The latter approach is suggested in Bierens (1988a, section 6.2) and worked out further in Bierens (1990). Also, plotting $Z_{i,t}$ and $\xi_{i,t}$ may reveal the form of this function f_i. Thus, if the linear ARMAX model fails to pass model misspecification tests we may think of specifying a parametric family for the function f_i, say $f(.,\alpha)$, where α is a parameter vector. This approach gives rise to a model of the form

$$Y_t = f[(1+\textstyle\sum_{j=1}^{q}\gamma_j L^j)^{-1}(\sum_{j=1}^{p}\beta_j' Z_{t-j}),\alpha] + U_t.$$

where Y_t is one of the components of Z_t, (U_t) is the error process (which should now satisfy $E(U_t|Z_{t-1},Z_{t-2},\ldots) = 0$ a.s.) and the β_j's and $\gamma = (\gamma_1,\ldots,\gamma_q)'$ are parameter vectors. In what follows, however, we shall not deal with this class of models, for the simple reason that these models have not yet been considered in the literature, hence the sampling theory involved is still absent. The mean reason for introducing the ARMA memory index modeling theory is that it plays a key role in our consistent model misspecification testing approach, in chapter 8.

Alternatively, if a linear ARMAX model does not pass our model misspecification tests one could follow Sims' (1988) common-sense approach and add nonlinear terms to the best linear ARMAX model to capture the possible nonlinearity of the conditional expectation function. How these nonlinear terms should be specified depends on prior knowledge about the phenomena one wishes to model. This specification issue falls outside the scope of this book. Quoting Sims (1988):

> There is no more general procedure available for inference in infinite-dimensional parameter spaces than the common sense one of guessing a set of finite-dimensional models, fitting them, and weighting together the results according to how well the models fit. This describes the actual behavior of most researchers and decision makers ... Thus, if we are unsure of lag length and also believe that there may be nonlinearity in the system, a reasonable way to proceed is to introduce both a flexible distributed lag specification and some nonlinear terms that can be thought of as part of a Taylor or Fourier expansion of the nonlinear function to be estimated.

Sims' common-sense approach will lead to a nonlinear ARMAX model of the form

$$Y_t = g(Z_{t-1},...,Z_{t-p},\beta) + U_t + \textstyle\sum_{j=1}^{q}\gamma_j U_{t-j}. \qquad (7.4.1)$$

where $g(.,\beta)$ is a known parametric functional form for the AR part of the ARMAX model, with β a parameter vector. The MA part of this model may be considered as a flexible distributed lag specification, together with the AR lag structure implied by the function $g(.,\beta)$.

In chapter 8 we consider the problem of estimating the parameters of model (7.4.1), taking the function $g(.,\beta)$ as given, and we derive the asymptotic properties of these estimators under strict stationarity of the data-generating process (Z_t) as well as under data heterogeneity. Also, we consider various model misspecification tests, in particular consistent tests based on the ARMA memory index approach.

8

ARMAX models: estimation and testing

In this chapter we first consider the asymptotic properties of least squares estimators of the parameters of linear ARMAX models, and then we extend the results involved to nonlinear ARMAX models. A new feature of our approach is that we allow the *X*-variables to be stochastic time series themselves, possibly depending on lagged *Y*-values. Moreover, we allow the data-generating process to be heterogeneous. Furthermore, we propose consistent tests of the null hypothesis that the errors are martingale differences, and a less general but easier test of the null hypothesis that the errors are uncorrelated. Most of these results are obtained by further elaboration of the results in Bierens (1987a, 1991b). Moreover, we refer to Bierens and Broersma (1993) for empirical applications of the ARMAX modeling approach.

8.1 Estimation of linear ARMAX models

8.1.1 Introduction

We recall that, given a k-variate time series process $\{(Y_t,X_t)\}$, where Y_t and the $k-1$ components of X_t are real-valued random variables, the linear ARMAX model assumes the form:

$$(1-\textstyle\sum_{s=1}^{p}\alpha_s L^s)Y_t=\mu+\sum_{s=1}^{r}\beta_s{'}L^s X_t+(1+\sum_{s=1}^{q}\gamma_s L^s)U_t, \qquad (8.1.1)$$

where L is the usual lag operator, $\mu \in R$, $\alpha_s \in R$, $\beta_s \in R^{k-1}$ and $\gamma_s \in R$ are unknown parameters, the U_t's are the errors and p, q and r are natural numbers specified in advance. The exclusion of X_t in this model is no loss of generality, as we may replace X_t by $X_t^* = X_{t+1}$.

The correctness of this linear ARMAX model specification now corresponds to the null hypothesis

$$H_0\colon E[U_t|(Y_{t-1},X_{t-1}),(Y_{t-2},X_{t-2}),\ldots]=0 \text{ a.s.} \qquad (8.1.2)$$

for each t. Assuming that the lag polynomial $1+\sum_{s=1}^{r}\gamma_s L^s$ is invertible, this hypothesis implies that the ARMAX model (8.1.1) represents the mathematical expectation of Y_t conditional on the entire past of the process.

The ARMAX model specification is particularly suitable for macroeconomic vector time series modeling without imposing *a priori* restrictions prescribed by macroeconomic theory. Such macroeconomic analysis has been advocated and conducted by Sims (1980, 1981) and Doan, Litterman and Sims (1984) in the framework of unrestricted vector autoregressions and observable index models. Cf. Sargent and Sims (1977) for the latter models. The advantage of ARMAX models over the VAR models used by Sims (1980) is that ARMAX models allow an infinite lag structure with a parsimonious parameterization, by which we get a tractable model that may better reflect the strong dependence of macroeconomic time series.

Estimation of the parameters of a linear ARMAX model for the case that the X_t's are exogenous (in the sense that the X_t's are either nonstochastic or independent of the U_t's) has been considered by Hannan, Dunsmuir and Deistler (1980), among others. This estimation theory, however, is not straightforwardly applicable to the model under review. The condition that the X_t's are exogenous is too strong a condition, as then feedback from Y_t to X_t is excluded. Also, we do not assume that the errors U_t are Gaussian or independent, but merely that (U_t) is a martingale difference sequence.

We recall that the ARMAX model (8.1.1) represents the conditional expectation of Y_t given the entire past of the process $\{(Y_t,X_t)\}$, provided condition (8.1.2) holds and the MA lag polynomial $1+\sum_{s=1}^{q}\gamma_s L^s$ is invertible. We then have

$$E[Y_t|(Y_{t-1},X_{t-1}),(Y_{t-2},X_{t-2}),...] = \mu/(1+\textstyle\sum_{s=1}^{q}\gamma_s) + [(\sum_{s=1}^{p}\alpha_s L^s + \sum_{s=1}^{q}\gamma_s L^s)/(1+\sum_{s=1}^{q}\gamma_s L^s)]Y_t + [(\sum_{s=1}^{r}\beta_s' L^s)/(1+\sum_{s=1}^{q}\gamma_s L^s)]X_t \text{ a.s.} \qquad (8.1.3)$$

and

$$U_t = Y_t - E[Y_t|(Y_{t-1},X_{t-1}),(Y_{t-2},X_{t-2}),...] \text{ a.s.} \qquad (8.1.4)$$

Since the MA lag polynomial can be written as

$$1+\textstyle\sum_{s=1}^{q}\gamma_s L^s = \Pi_{s=1}^{q}(1-\lambda_s L),$$

where $\lambda_1^{-1},...,\lambda_q^{-1}$ are its possibly complex-valued roots, invertibility requires $|\lambda_s| < 1$ for $s=1,...,q$. In particular, for $0<\delta<1$ the set

$$\Gamma_\delta = \{(\gamma_1,...,\gamma_q)' \in R^q: |\lambda_s| \le 1-\delta \text{ for } s=1,...,q\} \qquad (8.1.5)$$

is a compact set of vectors $(\gamma_1,...,\gamma_q)'$ with this property. The compactness of Γ_δ follows from the fact that the γ_s's are continuous functions of

$\gamma_1,...,\gamma_q$, hence Γ_δ is the continuous image of a compact set and therefore compact itself. Cf. Royden (1968, proposition 4, p. 158).

From now on we assume that there are known compact subsets M of R, A of R^p, B of $R^{(k-1)r}$ and Γ_δ of R^q such that, if (8.1.2) is true,

$$\mu \in M,\ (\alpha_1,...,\alpha_p)' \in A,\ (\beta_1',...,\beta_r')' \in B \text{ and } (\gamma_1,...,\gamma_q)' \in \Gamma_\delta. \tag{8.1.6}$$

Stacking all these parameters in a vector θ_0:

$$\theta_0 = (\mu,\alpha_1,...,\alpha_p,\beta_1',...,\beta_r',\gamma_1,..,\gamma_q)' \tag{8.1.7}$$

and denoting the parameter space by

$$\Theta = M \times A \times B \times \Gamma_\delta \subset R^m \text{ with } m = 1 + p + (k-1)r + q, \tag{8.1.8}$$

which is a compact set, we thus have $\theta_0 \in \Theta$ if (8.1.2) is true.

Denoting $Z_t = (Y_t,X_t')'$, the conditional expectation (8.1.3) can now be written as

$$E(Y_t|Z_{t-1},Z_{t-2},...) = \varphi(\theta_0) + \textstyle\sum_{s=1}^{\infty}\eta_s(\theta_0)'Z_{t-s}, \tag{8.1.9}$$

where

$$\varphi(\theta_0) = \mu/(1 + \textstyle\sum_{s=1}^{q}\gamma_s)$$

and the $\eta_s(.)$ are continuously differentiable vector-valued functions defined by:

$$(1+\textstyle\sum_{s=1}^{q}\gamma_s L^s)(\sum_{s=1}^{\infty}\eta_s(\theta_0)L^s) = (\sum_{s=1}^{p}\alpha_s L^s + \sum_{s=1}^{q}\gamma_s L^s,\ \sum_{s=1}^{r}\beta_s' L^s)' \tag{8.1.10}$$

It is not too hard to verify that each component $\eta_{i,s}(\theta)$ of $\eta_s(\theta)$ satisfies

$$\textstyle\sum_{s=1}^{\infty}\sup_{\theta\in\Theta}|\eta_{i,s}(\theta)| < \infty, \tag{8.1.11}$$

$$\textstyle\sum_{s=1}^{\infty}\sup_{\theta\in\Theta}|(\partial/\partial\theta_j)\eta_{i,s}(\theta)| < \infty \ (j=1,2,...,m) \tag{8.1.12}$$

$$\textstyle\sum_{s=1}^{\infty}\sup_{\theta\in\Theta}|(\partial/\partial\theta_j)(\partial/\partial\theta_\ell)\eta_{i,s}(\theta)| < \infty \ (j,\ell=1,2,...,m) \tag{8.1.13}$$

etc. Cf. exercise 1. These properties will play a crucial role in our estimation theory. In particular, the model (8.1.3) can now be written as a nonlinear regression model:

$$Y_t = g_t(\theta_0) + U_t, \tag{8.1.14}$$

where the response function

$$g_t(\theta) = \varphi(\theta) + \textstyle\sum_{s=1}^{\infty}\eta_s(\theta)'Z_{t-s} \tag{8.1.15}$$

and its first and second partial derivatives are well-defined random functions.

Assuming that only $Z_1,\dots,Z_n$ have been observed, we now propose to estimate θ_0 by nonlinear least squares, as follows. Let

$$\tilde{g}_t(\theta)=\varphi(\theta)+\sum_{s=1}^{t-1}\eta_s(\theta)'Z_{t-s} \text{ if } t\geq 2,\ \tilde{g}_t(\theta)=\varphi(\theta) \text{ if } t\leq 1. \quad (8.1.16)$$

Thus (8.1.16) is $g_t(\theta)$ with Z_t set equal to the zero vector for $t < 1$. Alternatively, we may set $Z_t = Z_1$ for $t < 1$, but for convenience the analysis below will be conducted for the case (8.1.16) only. Moreover, denote

$$\hat{Q}(\theta) = (1/n)\sum_{t=1}^{n}[Y_t - \tilde{g}_t(\theta)]^2. \quad (8.1.17)$$

Then the proposed least squares estimator $\hat{\theta}$ of θ_0 is a (measurable) solution of

$$\hat{\theta}\in\Theta : \hat{Q}(\hat{\theta}) = \inf_{\theta\in\Theta}\hat{Q}(\theta). \quad (8.1.18)$$

Similar to the results in chapter 4 we can set forth conditions such that under the null hypothesis (8.1.2),

$$\surd n(\hat{\theta}-\theta_0) \to N_m(0,\Omega_1^{-1}\Omega_2\Omega_1^{-1}) \text{ in distr.,} \quad (8.1.19)$$

where Ω_1 is the probability limit of

$$\hat{\Omega}_1 = (1/n)\sum_{t=1}^{n}[(\partial/\partial\theta')\tilde{g}_t(\hat{\theta})][(\partial/\partial\theta)\tilde{g}_t(\hat{\theta})] \quad (8.1.20)$$

and Ω_2 is the probability limit of

$$\hat{\Omega}_2 = (1/n)\sum_{t=1}^{n}(Y_t-\tilde{g}_t(\hat{\theta}))^2[(\partial/\partial\theta')\tilde{g}_t(\hat{\theta})][(\partial/\partial\theta)\tilde{g}_t(\hat{\theta})]. \quad (8.1.21)$$

Moreover, when the null hypothesis (8.1.2) is false we show that there exists a $\theta_*\in\Theta$ such that

$$\text{plim}_{n\to\infty}\hat{\theta}=\theta_*. \quad (8.1.22)$$

8.1.2 Consistency and asymptotic normality

In this section we set forth conditions such that the results in section 8.1.1 hold.

> *Assumption 8.1.1* The data-generating process (Z_t) in R^k, with $Z_t = (Y_t,X_t')'$, is υ-stable in L^1 with respect to an α-mixing base, where $\sum_{j=0}^{\infty}\alpha(j) < \infty$, and is properly heterogeneous. Moreover, $\sup_t E(|Z_t|^{4+\delta}) < \infty$ for some $\delta > 0$.

(Cf. Definitions 6.2.2, 6.2.3, and 6.4.1 and theorem 6.4.1.)

In the sequel we shall denote the base involved by (v_t) where $v_t\in V$ with V a Euclidean space, and the mean process of (Z_t) (cf. definition 6.4.1) will be denoted by (Z_t^*). It should be noted that the error U_t of the ARMAX model (8.1.1) need not be a component of v_t, as it is possible that the U_t's themselves are generated by a one-sided infinite sequence of v_t's.

If we would make the strict stationarity assumption then assumption 8.1.1 simplifies to:

Assumption 8.1.1* There exists a strictly stationary α-mixing process (v_t) in a Euclidean space V, with α the same as in assumption 8.1.1, and a Borel measurable mapping G from the space of one-sided infinite sequences in V into R^k such that

$$Z_t = (Y_t,X_t')' = G(v_t,v_{t-1},v_{t-2}....) \text{ a.s.}$$

Moreover, $E(|Z_t|)^{4+\delta} < \infty$ for some $\delta > 0$.

Thus assumption 8.1.1* implies assumption 8.1.1. The proof of this proposition follows straightforwardly from theorem 6.2.2 and the fact that by the strict stationarity assumption the proper heterogeneity condition automatically holds with mean process (Z_t).

Next consider the function $\hat{Q}(\theta)$ defined by (8.1.17). Let Y_0^* be the first component of Z_0^* and let

$$\bar{Q}(\theta) = E(Y_0^* - \varphi(\theta) - \textstyle\sum_{s=1}^{\infty}\eta_s(\theta)'Z_{-s}^*)^2. \tag{8.1.23}$$

Then it follows from theorem 6.4.1:

Theorem 8.1.1 Under assumption 8.1.1,

$$\text{plim}_{n\to\infty}\sup_{\theta\in\Theta}|\hat{Q}(\theta) - \bar{Q}(\theta)| = 0.$$

Proof: Condition (6.4.1) is implied by (8.1.11). Since the function ψ in theorem 6.4.1 is now $\psi(.) = (.)^2$, condition (6.4.2) holds with $\mu = 1$. The other conditions of theorem 6.4.1 now follow from assumption 8.1.1. Q.E.D.

Next, we assume:

Assumption 8.1.2 There exists a unique $\theta_* \in \theta$ such that

$$\bar{Q}(\theta_*) = \inf_{\theta\in\Theta}\bar{Q}(\theta).$$

Since Θ is compact and $\bar{Q}(\theta)$ is continuous there is always a θ_* in Θ which minimizes $\bar{Q}(\theta)$ over Θ. Thus the actual contents of this assumption is the uniqueness of θ_*. If the null hypothesis (8.1.2) is true then $\theta_* = \theta_0$, so that assumption 8.1.2 then identifies the parameters of model (8.1.1). However, this assumption is also supposed to hold in the case that the null hypothesis (8.1.2) is false.

Applying theorem 4.2.1 it follows from theorem 8.1.1 and assumption 8.1.2:

Theorem 8.1.2 Under assumptions 8.1.1 and 8.1.2 the least squares estimator $\hat{\theta}$ defined by (8.1.18) satisfies

$$\text{plim}_{n\to\infty}\hat{\theta} = \theta_*.$$

This proves (8.1.22).

Next we show the consistency and asymptotic normality of $\hat{\theta}$ under the assumption that (8.1.2) holds for each t. Since (8.1.1) and (8.1.2) are equivalent to (8.1.9), we now assume:

Assumption 8.1.3 There exists a point θ_0 in an open convex subset Θ_0 of Θ such that (8.1.9) holds for each t.

This assumption is hardly a condition. The sets M, A, and B (cf. (8.1.6) and (8.1.8)) can be chosen to be the closures of open convex sets M_0, A_0, and B_0, respectively, whereas the set

$$\Gamma_{0,\delta} = \{(\gamma_1,...,\gamma_q)' \in R^q\colon \lambda_s < 1-\delta \text{ for } s=1,2,...,q\}$$

(cf. (8.1.5)) is for $\delta \in (0,1)$ the continuous image of an open set and therefore open itself, with closure Γ_δ. Assuming that γ_0 corresponding to θ_0 is an interior point of Γ_δ for some δ, hence $\gamma_0 \in \Gamma_{0,\delta}$, there exists an open convex neighborhood Γ_0 of γ_0 contained in Γ_δ. Thus $\Theta_0 = M_0 \times A_0 \times B_0 \times \Gamma_0$ (cf. (8.1.7)) is then an open convex subset of Θ.

In order to establish the consistency of the least squares estimator $\hat{\theta}$ it suffices to show that θ_0 minimizes $\bar{Q}(\theta)$, as then by the uniqueness condition in assumption 8.1.2, θ_* must be equal to θ_0. To show this, let

$$\tilde{Q}(\theta) = (1/n)\textstyle\sum_{t=1}^{n}(Y_t - \varphi(\theta) - \sum_{s=1}^{\infty}\eta_s(\theta)'Z_{t-s})^2. \tag{8.1.24}$$

It follows from lemmas 6.4.2 and 6.4.3 that

$$\lim_{n\to\infty}\sup_{\theta\in\Theta}|E[\tilde{Q}(\theta)] - \bar{Q}(\theta)| = 0 \tag{8.1.25}$$

and from (8.1.4) and (8.1.9) it follows that under assumption 8.1.3

$$E[\tilde{Q}(\theta)] = (1/n)\textstyle\sum_{t=1}^{n}E(U_t^2) + (1/n)\sum_{t=1}^{n}E[\varphi(\theta) - \varphi(\theta_0) + \sum_{s=1}^{\infty}(\eta_s(\theta) - \eta_s(\theta_0))'Z_{t-s}]^2. \tag{8.1.26}$$

Consequently, under assumption 8.1.3, we have:

$$\bar{Q}(\theta) = \lim_{n\to\infty}(1/n)\textstyle\sum_{t=1}^{n}E(U_t^2) + E[\varphi(\theta) - \varphi(\theta_0) + \sum_{s=1}^{\infty}(\eta_s(\theta) - \eta_s(\theta_0))'Z_{-s}^*]^2. \tag{8.1.27}$$

Clearly θ_0 minimizes $\bar{Q}(\theta)$ and hence $\theta_0 = \theta_*$. This proves:

Theorem 8.1.3 Under assumptions 8.1.1, 8.1.2, and 8.1.3,

$$\text{plim}_{n\to\infty}\hat{\theta} = \theta_0.$$

The asymptotic normality proof follows the classical lines. Cf. chapter 4. Thus we first apply the mean value theorem to $(\partial/\partial\theta_i)\hat{Q}(\hat{\theta})$, where θ_i is the i-th component of θ. This yields

$$(\partial/\partial\theta_i)\hat{Q}(\hat{\theta}) = (\partial/\partial\theta_i)\hat{Q}(\theta_0) + (\hat{\theta} - \theta_0)'(\partial/\partial\theta')(\partial/\partial\theta_i)\hat{Q}(\tilde{\theta}^{(i)}), \tag{8.1.28}$$

with $\tilde{\theta}^{(i)}$ a mean value satisfying

$$|\tilde{\theta}^{(i)} - \theta_0| \le |\hat{\theta} - \theta_0| \text{ a.s.} \tag{8.1.29}$$

Theorem 8.1.3 and assumption 8.1.3 imply that $\hat{\theta}$ is an interior point of Θ with probability converging to 1. Thus $\hat{\theta}$ and $\tilde{\theta}^{(i)}$ are with probability converging to 1 contained in the open convex subset Θ_0 of Θ. Cf. assumption 8.1.3. Consequently, we have similarly to (4.2.7),

$$\text{plim}_{n\to\infty}\sqrt{n}(\partial/\partial\theta_i)\hat{Q}(\hat{\theta}) = 0. \tag{8.1.30}$$

The next step is to establish

$$\text{plim}_{n\to\infty}[(\partial/\partial\theta')(\partial/\partial\theta_1)\hat{Q}(\tilde{\theta}^{(1)}),\ldots,(\partial/\partial\theta')(\partial/\partial\theta_m)\hat{Q}(\tilde{\theta}^{(m)})] = 2\Omega_1, \tag{8.1.31}$$

where Ω_1 is a nonsingular matrix, and the last step is to show

$$\sqrt{n}(\partial/\partial\theta')\hat{Q}(\theta_0) \to N_m(0,4\Omega_2). \tag{8.1.32}$$

Combining (8.1.28) through (8.1.32) then yields

$$\sqrt{n}(\hat{\theta} - \theta_0) \to N_m(0,\Omega_1^{-1}\Omega_2\Omega_1^{-1}) \text{ in distr.} \tag{8.1.33}$$

For proving (8.1.31) and (8.1.32) the following lemma is convenient. Let

$$g^*(\theta) = \varphi(\theta) + \textstyle\sum_{s=1}^{\infty}\eta_s(\theta)'Z^*_{-s}, \tag{8.1.34}$$

where we recall that (Z^*_t) is the mean process of (Z_t).

Lemma 8.1.1 Under assumptions 8.1.1 and 8.1.3,

$$E[(Y^*_0 - g^*(\theta_0))Z^*_{-s}] = 0 \text{ for } s = 1,2,..,$$

where Y^*_0 is the first component of Z^*_0.

Proof: Since $E[(Y_t - g_t(\theta_0))Z_{t-s}] = E(U_tZ_{t-s}) = 0$ under assumption 8.1.3 and since by theorem 6.4.1,

$$\lim_{n\to\infty}E[(Y_t - g_t(\theta_0))Z_{t-s}] = E[(Y^*_0 - g^*(\theta_0))Z^*_{-s}],$$

the lemma follows. Q.E.D.

Now consider the derivatives

$$(\partial/\partial\theta_i)\hat{Q}(\theta) = -2(1/n)\textstyle\sum_{t=1}^{n}(Y_t - \tilde{g}_t(\theta))(\partial/\partial\theta_i)\tilde{g}_t(\theta),$$

$$(\partial/\partial\theta_i)(\partial/\partial\theta_j)\hat{Q}(\theta) = 2(1/n)\textstyle\sum_{t=1}^{n}[(\partial/\partial\theta_i)\tilde{g}_t(\theta)][(\partial/\partial\theta_j)\tilde{g}_t(\theta)]$$
$$-2(1/n)\textstyle\sum_{t=1}^{n}[Y_t - \tilde{g}_t(\theta)](\partial/\partial\theta_i)(\partial/\partial\theta_j)\tilde{g}_t(\theta).$$

It follows from theorem 6.4.1 and (8.1.11), (8.1.12), and (8.1.13) that

Lemma 8.1.2 Under assumptions 8.1.1 and 8.1.2,

$$\text{plim}_{n\to\infty}\sup_{\theta\in\Theta}|(1/n)\textstyle\sum_{t=1}^{n}[(\partial/\partial\theta_i)\tilde{g}_t(\theta)][(\partial/\partial\theta_j)\tilde{g}_t(\theta)] - E[(\partial/\partial\theta_i)g^*(\theta)][(\partial/\partial\theta_j)g^*(\theta)]| = 0 \quad (8.1.35)$$

and

$$\text{plim}_{n\to\infty}\sup_{\theta\in\Theta}|(1/n)\textstyle\sum_{t=1}^{n}(Y_t - \tilde{g}_t(\theta))(\partial/\partial\theta_i)(\partial/\partial\theta_j)\tilde{g}_t(\theta) - E[(Y_0^* - g^*(\theta))(\partial/\partial\theta_i)(\partial/\partial\theta_j)g^*(\theta)]| = 0, \quad (8.1.36)$$

Proof: We only prove (8.1.35). The proof of (8.1.36) is left as exercise 2. We verify the conditions of theorem 6.4.1. For $t \geq 2$ we have

$$(\partial/\partial\theta_i)\tilde{g}_t(\theta) = (\partial/\partial\theta_i)\varphi(\theta) + \textstyle\sum_{s=1}^{t-1}(\partial/\partial\theta_i)\eta_s(\theta)'Z_{t-s},$$

hence

$$[(\partial/\partial\theta_i)\tilde{g}_t(\theta)][(\partial/\partial\theta_j)\tilde{g}_t(\theta)] = [(\partial/\partial\theta_i)\varphi(\theta)][(\partial/\partial\theta_j)\varphi(\theta)] + \psi_1(\textstyle\sum_{s=1}^{t-1}\Gamma_s^{(1)}(\theta)'Z_{t-s}) + \psi_1(\sum_{s=1}^{t-1}\Gamma_s^{(2)}(\theta)'Z_{t-s}) + \psi_2(\sum_{s=1}^{t-1}\Gamma_s^{(3)}(\theta)'Z_{t-s}),$$

where

$$\Gamma_s^{(1)}(\theta)' = [(\partial/\partial\theta_i)\varphi(\theta)][(\partial/\partial\theta_j)\eta_s(\theta)'],$$
$$\Gamma_s^{(2)}(\theta)' = [(\partial/\partial\theta_j)\varphi(\theta)][(\partial/\partial\theta_i)\eta_s(\theta)'],$$
$$\Gamma_s^{(3)}(\theta)' = \begin{pmatrix} (\partial/\partial\theta_i)\eta_s(\theta)' \\ (\partial/\partial\theta_j)\eta_s(\theta)' \end{pmatrix}$$

and for $\xi, \xi_1, \xi_2 \in R$, $\psi_1(\xi) = \xi$, $\psi_2(\xi_1,\xi_2) = \xi_1\xi_2$. Moreover, the parameter μ in (6.4.2) is

$\mu = 0$ for ψ_1, $\mu = 1$ for ψ_2.

Now part (8.1.35) of the lemma follows easily from (8.1.11), (8.1.12), assumptions 8.1.1 and 8.1.2, and theorem 6.4.1. The proof of (8.1.36) is similar. Q.E.D.

Next, observe that lemma 8.1.1 implies

$$E[(Y_0^* - g^*(\theta_0))(\partial/\partial\theta_i)(\partial/\partial\theta_j)g^*(\theta_0)] = 0. \quad (8.1.37)$$

Since

$$\text{plim}_{n\to\infty}\tilde{\theta}_i = \theta_0$$

because of (8.1.29) and theorem 8.1.3, (8.1.31) follows from (8.1.35), (8.1.36), and (8.1.37) with

$$\Omega_1 = E\{[(\partial/\partial\theta')g^*(\theta_0)][(\partial/\partial\theta)g^*(\theta_0)]\}. \tag{8.1.38}$$

The nonsingularity of Ω_1 cannot be derived, but has to be assumed as part of the identification assumption. Moreover, in order that this matrix is also defined in the case that the null hypothesis (8.1.2) fails to hold we redefine Ω_1 as

$$\Omega_1 = E\{[(\partial/\partial\theta')g^*(\theta_*)][(\partial/\partial\theta)g^*(\theta_*)]\}. \tag{8.1.39}$$

Since $\theta_* = \theta_0$ under the null hypothesis, there is no loss of generality in doing so.

Assumption 8.1.4 The matrix Ω_1 defined by (8.1.39) is non-singular.

This assumption is part of the set of maintained hypotheses which are assumed to hold regardless of whether or not the null hypothesis is true.

Using lemma 8.1.2 it easily follows that the matrix $\hat{\Omega}_1$ defined by (8.1.20) is a consistent estimator of Ω_1:

Lemma 8.1.3 Under assumptions 8.1.1 and 8.1.2,

$$\text{plim}_{n\to\infty}\hat{\Omega}_1 = \Omega_1.$$

Note that assumption 8.1.3 is not needed for this result, due to the more general definition (8.1.39) of Ω_1.

For proving (8.1.32), we observe first that

$$\begin{aligned}\sqrt{n}(\partial/\partial\theta_i)\hat{Q}(\theta_0) &= -2(1/\sqrt{n})\textstyle\sum_{t=1}^{n}(U_t + g_t(\theta_0) - \tilde{g}_t(\theta_0))(\partial/\partial\theta_i)\tilde{g}_t(\theta_0)\\ &= -2(1/\sqrt{n})\textstyle\sum_{t=1}^{n}U_t(\partial/\partial\theta_i)\tilde{g}_t(\theta_0)\\ &\quad + 2(1/\sqrt{n})\textstyle\sum_{t=1}^{n}(g_t(\theta_0) - \tilde{g}_t(\theta_0))(\partial/\partial\theta_i)\tilde{g}_t(\theta_0).\end{aligned} \tag{8.1.40}$$

Secondly, we shall prove:

$$\text{plim}_{n\to\infty}(1/\sqrt{n})\textstyle\sum_{t=1}^{n}(g_t(\theta_0) - \tilde{g}_t(\theta_0))(\partial/\partial\theta_i)\tilde{g}_t(\theta_0) = 0, \tag{8.1.41}$$

so that

$$\text{plim}_{n\to\infty}[\sqrt{n}(\partial/\partial\theta_i)\hat{Q}(\theta_0) + 2(1/\sqrt{n})\textstyle\sum_{t=1}^{n}U_t(\partial/\partial\theta_i)\tilde{g}_t(\theta_0)] = 0 \tag{8.1.42}$$

Thirdly, denoting

$$X_{n,t} = U_t(\partial/\partial\theta)\tilde{g}_t(\theta_0)\xi, \tag{8.1.43}$$

cf. theorem 6.1.7, where ξ is an arbitrary non-random vector in R^m, we show that $(X_{n,t})$ is a sequence of martingale differences for which the martingale central limit theorem 6.1.7 applies:

$$(1/\sqrt{n})\textstyle\sum_{t=1}^{n}X_{n,t} \to N(0,\sigma^2) \text{ in distr.,} \tag{8.1.44}$$

where

$$\sigma^2 = \text{plim}_{n\to\infty}(1/n)\sum_{t=1}^{n} X_{n,t}^2 = \xi'\Omega_2\xi \tag{8.1.45}$$

with

$$\Omega_2 = E\{(Y_0^* - g^*(\theta_*))^2[(\partial/\partial\theta')g^*(\theta_*)][(\partial/\partial\theta)g^*(\theta_*)]\}. \tag{8.1.46}$$

From these results it then follows

$$\sqrt{n}(\partial/\partial\theta)\hat{Q}(\theta_0)\xi \to N(0,\xi'\Omega_2\xi) \text{ in distr. for every } \xi \in R^m, \tag{8.1.47}$$

which implies (8.1.32).

For proving (8.1.41) we need the following extension of (8.1.11).

Lemma 8.1.4 For $s\to\infty$ and $i = 1,...,m$,

$$\sup_{\theta\in\Theta}|\eta_{i,s}(\theta)| = O[s^q(1-\delta)^s],$$

where δ is defined by (8.1.5).

Proof: It follows from (8.1.5) that

$$(1 + \sum_{s=1}^{q}\gamma_s L^s)^{-1} = \prod_{s=1}^{q}(1-\lambda_s L)^{-1} = \prod_{s=1}^{q}(\sum_{\ell=0}^{\infty}\lambda_s^\ell L^\ell)$$
$$= \sum_{s=0}^{\infty}(\sum_{\ell_1+\ell_2+\ldots+\ell_r = s,\ell_j=0,1,2,\ldots,s}\lambda_1^{\ell_1}\lambda_2^{\ell_2}\ldots\lambda_r^{\ell_r})L^s$$

and

$$\sum_{\ell_1+\ell_2+\ldots+\ell_r=s,\ell_j=0,1,2,\ldots,s}\lambda_1^{\ell_1}\lambda_2^{\ell_2}\ldots\lambda_r^{\ell_r}$$
$$\leq \sum_{\ell_1+\ell_2+\ldots+\ell_r=s,\ell_j=0,1,2,\ldots,s}(1-\delta)^s \leq s^q(1-\delta)^s.$$

Combining these results with (8.1.10), the lemma easily follows. Q.E.D.

Using this lemma, Cauchy–Schwarz inequality and the fact that

$$\sum_{s=t}^{\infty}s^q(1-\delta)^s = O[t^q(1-\delta)^t]$$

we see that there are constants C_* and C_{**} such that

$$E[|(1/\sqrt{n})\sum_{t=1}^{n}(g_t(\theta_0) - \tilde{g}_t(\theta_0))(\partial/\partial\theta_i)\tilde{g}_t(\theta_0)|]$$
$$\leq (1/\sqrt{n})\sum_{t=1}^{n}\sum_{s=t}^{\infty}|\eta_s(\theta_0)|E[|Z_{t-s}||(\partial/\partial\theta_i)\tilde{g}_t(\theta_0)|]$$
$$\leq (1/\sqrt{n})\sum_{t=1}^{n}\sum_{s=t}^{\infty}C_* s^q(1-\delta)^s[E(|Z_{t-s}|^2)]^{1/2}[E(|(\partial/\partial\theta_i)\tilde{g}_t(\theta_0)|^2)]^{1/2}$$
$$\leq \sup_t[E(|Z_t|^2)]^{1/2}(1/\sqrt{n})\sum_{t=1}^{n}[\sum_{s=t}^{\infty}C_* s^q(1-\delta)^s][E(|(\partial/\partial\theta_i)\tilde{g}_t(\theta_0)|^2)]^{1/2}$$
$$\leq C_{**}(1/\sqrt{n})\sum_{t=1}^{n}t^q(1-\delta)^t[E(|(\partial/\partial\theta_i)\tilde{g}_t(\theta_0)|^2)]^{1/2}. \tag{8.1.48}$$

Moreover, denoting.

$$\rho_s = \max_i|(\partial/\partial\theta_i)\eta_s(\theta_0)|,\ \rho_0 = \max_i|(\partial/\partial\theta_i)\varphi(\theta_0)|$$

we have from (8.1.12) and Liapounov's inequality,

$$E[|(\partial/\partial\theta_i)\tilde{g}_t(\theta_0)|^2] \leq E(|\rho_0 + \sum_{s=1}^{\infty}\rho_s|Z_{t-s}||^2)$$
$$\leq 2\rho_0^2 + 2(\sum_{s=1}^{\infty}\rho_s)\sum_{s=1}^{\infty}\rho_s E(|Z_{t-s}|^2) \leq 2\rho_0^2 + 2(\sum_{s=1}^{\infty}\rho_s)^2 \sup_t E(|Z_t|^2). \tag{8.1.49}$$

Thus the right-hand side of (8.1.48) is of order

$$O[(1/\sqrt{n})\sum_{t=1}^{n} t^q(1-\delta)^t] = O(1/\sqrt{n})$$

and converges therefore to zero. Now (8.1.41) follows from Chebishev's inequality.

With $X_{n,t}$ defined by (8.1.43), condition (6.1.14) and thus condition (6.1.13) of theorem 6.1.7 follow from

$$\begin{aligned} E(|X_{n,t}|^{2+\delta^*}) &\le E\{|U_t|^{2+\delta^*}\max_i|(\partial/\partial\theta_i)\tilde{g}_t(\theta_0)|^{2+\delta^*}\}|\xi|^{2+\delta^*} \\ &\le [E(|U_t|^{4+2\delta^*})]^{½}\max_i[E(|(\partial/\partial\theta_i)\tilde{g}_t(\theta_0)|^{4+2\delta^*})]^{½}|\xi|^{2+\delta^*} \\ &\le \{2^{4+2\delta^*}E(|Y_t|^{4+2\delta^*})E[|\tilde{g}_t(\theta_0)|^{4+2\delta^*}]\}^{½} \\ &\quad \times \max_i\{E[|(\partial/\partial\theta_i)\tilde{g}_t(\theta_0)|^{4+2\delta^*}]\}^{½}|\xi|^{2+\delta^*} \end{aligned}$$

and the fact that $\sup_t E(|Z_t|^{4+2\delta^*}) < \infty$ implies

$$\sup_t E(|Y_t|^{4+2\delta^*}) < \infty$$

and, similarly to (8.1.49),

$$\sup_t E(|g_t(\theta_0)|^{4+2\delta^*}) < \infty \text{ and } \sup_t E[|(\partial/\partial\theta_i)\tilde{g}_t(\theta_0)|^{4+2\delta^*} < \infty.$$

The δ^* for which this holds must therefore be smaller than $½\delta$, with δ as in assumption 8.1.1.

Condition (6.1.12) of theorem 6.1.7 follows easily from theorem 6.4.1, where σ^2 is given by (8.1.45) and (8.1.46). So (8.1.47) is proved.

Furthermore, we note that similarly to lemma 8.1.3 we have:

Lemma 8.1.5 Under assumptions 8.1.1 and 8.1.2,

$$\text{plim}_{n\to\infty}\hat{\Omega}_2 = \Omega_2.$$

Proof: Exercise 3.

Summarizing, we have:

Theorem 8.1.4 Under assumptions 8.1.1–8.1.4,

$$\sqrt{n}(\hat{\theta} - \theta_0) \to N_m(0,\Omega_1^{-1}\Omega_2\Omega_1^{-1}) \text{ in distr.} \qquad (8.1.50)$$

and under assumptions 8.1.1, 8.1.2, and 8.1.4,

$$\text{plim}_{n\to\infty}\hat{\Omega}_1^{-1}\hat{\Omega}_2\hat{\Omega}_1^{-1} = \Omega_1^{-1}\Omega_2\Omega_1^{-1}. \qquad (8.1.51)$$

Note that assumption 8.1.3 is not needed for (8.1.51). However, if assumption 8.1.3 does not hold then $\Omega_1^{-1}\Omega_2\Omega_1^{-1}$ is no longer the variance matrix of the limiting distribution of $\hat{\theta}$. Moreover, note that nonsingularity of Ω_2 is not required: if Ω_2 is singular the limiting normal distribution (8.1.50) is singular too.

Exercises

1. Prove (8.1.11), (8.1.12), and (8.1.13).
2. Prove (8.1.36).
3. Prove lemma 8.1.5.

8.2 Estimation of nonlinear ARMAX models

In this section we consider the asymptotic properties of the least squares parameter estimators of model (7.4.1):

$$Y_t = g(Z_{t-1},\ldots,Z_{t-p},\beta_0) + U_t + \sum_{j=1}^{q}\gamma_{0,j}U_{t-j},\ \beta_0 \in B, \tag{8.2.1}$$

with $B \subset R^r$ a parameter space. Let again

$$\gamma_0 = (\gamma_{0,1},\ldots,\gamma_{0,q})' \in \Gamma_\delta,$$

where Γ_δ is defined by (8.1.5) and let

$$\theta_0 = (\beta_0',\gamma_0')',\ \Theta = B \times \Gamma_\delta \subset R^m, \text{ with } m = r+q.$$

Since the lag polynomial $1 + \sum_{s=1}^{q}\gamma_s L^s$ is invertible, we can write

$$\sum_{s=0}^{\infty}\rho_s(\gamma)L^s = (1 + \sum_{s=1}^{q}\gamma_s L^s)^{-1},$$

where the $\rho_s(\gamma)$'s are continuously differentiable functions on Γ_δ such that

$$\rho_0(\gamma) = 1,\ \sum_{s=1}^{\infty}\sup_{\gamma\in\Gamma_\delta}|\rho_s(\gamma)| < \infty, \tag{8.2.2}$$

$$\sum_{s=1}^{\infty}\sup_{\gamma\in\Gamma_\delta}|(\partial/\partial\gamma_i)\rho_s(\gamma)| < \infty,\ i=1,\ldots,q, \tag{8.2.3}$$

$$\sum_{s=1}^{\infty}\sup_{\gamma\in\Gamma_\delta}|(\partial/\partial\gamma_i)(\partial/\partial\gamma_j)\rho_s(\gamma)| < \infty,\ i,j=1,..,q. \tag{8.2.4}$$

Cf. (8.1.11), (8.1.12), and (8.1.13). Similarly to (8.1.15) we can write the model in nonlinear ARX(∞) form as

$$Y_t = g_t(\theta) + U_t,$$

where now

$$g_t(\theta) = \sum_{s=0}^{\infty}\rho_s(\gamma)g(Z_{t-1},\ldots,Z_{t-p},\beta). \tag{8.2.5}$$

Moreover, similarly to (8.1.16) we truncate the response function $g_t(\theta)$ to

$$\left.\begin{aligned}\tilde{g}_t(\theta) &= \sum_{s=0}^{t-p-1}\rho_s(\gamma)g(Z_{t-1},\ldots,Z_{t-p},\beta) \text{ for } t \geq p+1,\\ \tilde{g}_t(\theta) &= 0 \text{ for } t < p+1,\end{aligned}\right\} \tag{8.2.6}$$

and we define the least squares estimator $\hat{\theta}$ of θ_0 as a (measurable) solution of

$$\hat{\theta} \in \theta : \hat{Q}(\hat{\theta}) = \inf_{\theta\in\Theta}\hat{Q}(\theta),$$

where

$\hat{Q}(\theta) = [1/(n-p)]\sum_{t=p+1}^{n}(Y_t - \tilde{g}_t(\theta))^2.$

Now assume:

Assumption 8.2.1

(a) The process (Z_t) is υ-stable in L^1 with respect to an α-mixing base, where $\sum_{j=0}^{\infty}\alpha(j) < \infty$.

(b) The function $g(w,\beta)$ is for each $w \in R^{pk}$ a continuous real function on B, and for each $\beta \in B$ a Borel measurable real function on R^{pk}, where B is a compact subset of R^r.

(c) The process (Z_t) is setwise or pointwise properly heterogeneous.

(d) If (Z_t) is pointwise properly heterogeneous, then $g(w,\beta)$ is continuous on $R^{pk} \times B$.

(e) For some $\delta > 0$,

$\sup_t E(|Z_t|^{4+\delta}) < \infty$, $\sup_t E[\sup_{\beta\in B}|g(Z_{t-1},\ldots,Z_{t-p},\beta)|^{4+\delta}] < \infty$.

Let similarly to (8.1.23)

$\bar{Q}(\theta) = E\{[Y_0^* - \sum_{s=0}^{\infty}\rho_s(\gamma)g(Z_{-1-s}^*,\ldots,Z_{-p-s}^*,\beta)]^2\}.$

where Y_0^* and Z_{-j}^* are the same as before. Then

Theorem 8.2.1 Under assumption 8.2.1,

$\text{plim}_{n\to\infty}\sup_{\theta\in\Theta}|\hat{Q}(\theta) - \bar{Q}(\theta)| = 0.$

Proof: We verify the conditions of theorems 6.4.2 and 6.4.3. Let for $w = (w_1,\ldots,w_{1+pk})' \in R^{1+pk}$,

$\gamma_s(\theta,w) = w_1 - g(w_2,\ldots,w_{1+pk},\beta)$ if $s = 0$,
$\gamma_s(\theta,w) = -\rho_s(\gamma)g(w_2,\ldots,w_{1+pk},\beta)$ if $s \geq 1$,

and let

$\rho_s = \sup_{\gamma\in\Gamma_\delta}|\rho_s(\gamma)|,$
$\bar{b}(w) = |w_1| + \sup_{\beta\in B}|g(w_2,\ldots,w_{1+pk},\beta)|.$

Note that $\bar{b}(w)$ is continuous on R^{1+pk} if $g(w_2,\ldots,w_{1+pk},\beta)$ is continuous in all its arguments. Cf. theorem 1.6.1. Then

$\sup_{\theta\in\Theta}|\gamma_s(\theta,w)| \leq \rho_s\bar{b}(w)$, $\sum_{s=0}^{\infty}\rho_s < \infty$.

The latter result follows from (8.2.2). Moreover, denoting

$W_t = (Y_t,Z_{t-1}',\ldots,Z_{t-p}')'$

it follows from assumption 8.2.1 that (W_t) is υ-stable in L^1 with respect to an α-mixing base and that

$$\sup_t E(|\bar{b}(W_t)|^{2+\delta}) < \infty.$$

The theorem under review now easily follows from theorems 6.4.2 and 6.4.3. Q.E.D.

Next, assume:

Assumption 8.2.2 There exists a unique $\theta_* \in \Theta$ such that

$$\bar{Q}(\theta_*) = \inf_{\theta\in\Theta}\bar{Q}(\theta).$$

Assumption 8.2.3 There exists a point θ_0 in an open convex subset Θ_0 of Θ, such that for each t,

$$E(Y_t|Z_{t-1},Z_{t-2},\dots) = g_t(\theta_0) \text{ a.s.}$$

Then similarly to theorems 8.1.2 and 8.1.3 we have:

Theorem 8.2.2 Under assumptions 8.2.1 and 8.2.2,

$$\text{plim}_{n\to\infty}\hat{\theta} = \theta_*.$$

Theorem 8.2.3 Under assumptions 8.2.1, 8.2.2, and 8.2.3,

$$\text{plim}_{n\to\infty}\hat{\theta} = \theta_0.$$

The proof of the asymptotic normality of $\hat{\theta}$ is left as an exercise. We only give here the additional assumptions involved.

Assumption 8.2.4 The function $g(w,\beta)$ is for each $w \in R^{pk}$ twice continuously differentiable on B. If (Z_t) is pointwise properly heterogeneous then for $i,i_1,i_2=1,\dots,r$, $(\partial/\partial\beta_i)g(w,\beta)$ and $(\partial/\partial\beta_{i_1})(\partial/\partial\beta_{i_2})g(w,\beta)$ are continuous functions on $R^{pk}\times B$. Moreover, for $i,i_1,i_2=1,\dots,r$ and some $\delta > 0$,

$$\sup_t E[|(\partial/\partial\beta_i)g(Z_{t-1},\dots,Z_{t-p},\beta)|^{4+\delta}] < \infty,$$
$$\sup_t E[|(\partial/\partial\beta_{i_1})(\partial/\partial\beta_{i_2})g(Z_{t-1},\dots,Z_{t-p},\beta)|^{2+\delta}] < \infty.$$

Let $\hat{\Omega}_1$, $\hat{\Omega}_2$, Ω_1, and Ω_2 be defined as in section 8.1.2, with n replaced by $n-p$ and $g^*(\theta)$ replaced by

$$g^*(\theta)=\textstyle\sum_{s=0}^{\infty}\rho_s(\gamma)g(Z^*_{-1-s},\dots,Z^*_{-p-s},\beta), \quad (8.2.7)$$

and assume:

Assumption 8.2.5 The matrix Ω_1 is nonsingular.

Then

Theorem 8.2.4 Under assumptions 8.2.1–8.2.5,

$$\sqrt{(n-p)}\,(\hat{\theta} - \theta_0) \to N_{r+q}(0,\Omega_1^{-1}\Omega_2\Omega_1^{-1}) \text{ in distr.}$$

and under assumptions 8.2.1, 8.2.2, 8.2.4 and 8.2.5,

$$\text{plim}_{n\to\infty}\hat{\Omega}_1^{-1}\hat{\Omega}_2\hat{\Omega}_1^{-1} = \Omega_1^{-1}\Omega_2\Omega_1^{-1}.$$

Exercise

1. Prove theorem 8.2.4 along the lines of the proof of theorem 8.1.4.

8.3 A consistent N(0,1) model specification test

In Bierens (1984) we have proposed a consistent model specification test for nonlinear time series regressions. This tests the null hypothesis that the errors of a nonlinear ARX(p) model obey a condition of the type (8.1.2). This model specification test is in principle also applicable to the ARMAX case considered in sections 8.1 and 8.2. A disadvantage of this test, however, is that the distribution of the test statistic under the null hypothesis is of an unknown type, so that the critical region of the test involved has to be derived on the basis of Chebishev's inequality for first absolute moments. This approach will lead, of course, to overestimating the effective type I error of the test, as Chebishev's inequality is not very sharp. Moreover, this test is quite laborious for relatively large data sets and models. On the other hand, the test involved is consistent in the sense that any model misspecification will be detected as the sample size grows to infinity, provided the data-generating process is strictly stationary. To the best of our knowledge no other model specification test for time series regressions has this consistency property.

We shall now propose a new test which has a known limiting distribution under the null hypothesis and is consistent in the above sense. In particular, in this section we shall construct a test statistic $\sqrt{n}\hat{T}$, say, with the property that under the null hypothesis (8.1.2), $\sqrt{n}\hat{T} \to N(0,1)$ in distribution as $n \to \infty$, whereas under the alternative hypothesis that (8.1.2) does not hold and under the stationarity hypothesis, $\text{plim}_{n\to\infty}\sqrt{n}\hat{T} = \infty$. This test is a further elaboration of the test of Bierens (1987a) and is reminiscent of the consistent conditional moment tests in chapter 5.

The consistency of our test requires that assumption 8.1.1* holds. Thus, strict stationarity of (Z_t) and thus of $\{(U_t,Z_t)\}$ is part of our maintained hypothesis. Some of our results below also hold under data heterogeneity. This will be indicated by not explicitly referring to assumption 8.1.1*. The reason for imposing the stationarity assumption is that under data heterogeneity the null hypothesis (8.1.2) may be false for only finitely many t's. Clearly, no test based on asymptotic arguments can detect this.

Let $U_t = Y_t - g_t(\theta_*)$, where g_t is defined by (8.2.5) and θ_* is defined in assumption 8.2.2. The null hypothesis of a correct model specification can now be restated as

$$H_0: P[E(U_t|Z_{t-1},Z_{t-2},Z_{t-3},\ldots)=0]=1. \tag{8.3.1}$$

The alternative hypothesis we consider is that H_0 is false. Under stationarity this general alternative hypothesis becomes

$$H_1: P[E(U_t|Z_{t-1},Z_{t-2},Z_{t-3},\ldots)=0] < 1. \tag{8.3.2}$$

Let us assume for the moment that H_1 is true. Then theorem 6.1.5 implies that there exists an integer ℓ_0 such that

$$\sup_{\ell\geq\ell_0}P[E(U_t|Z_{t-1}^{(\ell)},Z_{t-2}^{(\ell)},\ldots)=0] < 1, \tag{8.3.3}$$

where $Z_t^{(\ell)}$ is the vector of components of Z_t rounded off to ℓ decimal digits. Cf. exercise 1. Since $\{(U_t,Z_t)\}$ is strictly stationary, ℓ_0 is independent of t. Because the process $(Z_t^{(\ell)})$ is rational-valued, we may now apply theorem 7.3.4:

> *Lemma 8.3.1* Let assumptions 7.3.2, 8.1.1*, and 8.2.1 hold. There exists a subset N of R^{k+1} with Lebesgue measure zero such that (8.3.3) implies
>
> $$\sup_{\ell\geq\ell_0}P\{E(U_t|\textstyle\sum_{s=1}^{\infty}\tau^{s-1}\xi' Z_{t-s}^{(\ell)}) = 0\} < 1$$
>
> for all $(\xi,\tau) \in R^k \times (-1,1)\backslash N$.

Proof: Let $\theta_* = (\beta_*',\gamma_*')'$ and

$$U_t^{(j)} = Y_t - \textstyle\sum_{s=0}^{j-p}\rho_s(\gamma_*)g(Z_{t-1-s},\ldots,Z_{t-p-s},\beta_*)$$

Cf. (8.2.5). Then $U_t^{(j)} \in \mathfrak{F}_{t-j}^{\infty}$ (cf. assumption 7.3.2) and

$$E(|U_t - U_t^{(j)}|) \leq \textstyle\sum_{s=j+p+1}^{\infty}|\rho_s(\gamma_*)|E[|g(Z_{t-1-s},\ldots,Z_{t-p-s},\beta_*)|] \to 0 \text{ as } j \to \infty.$$

Consequently,

$$E[|E(U_t|\textstyle\sum_{s=1}^{\infty}\tau^{s-1}\xi' Z_{t-s}^{(\ell)}) - E(U_t^{(j)}|\sum_{s=1}^{\infty}\tau^{s-1}\xi' Z_{t-s}^{(\ell)})|] \leq E(|U_t - U_t^{(j)}|) \to 0 \text{ as } j \to \infty \tag{8.3.4}$$

and

$$E[|E(U_t|Z_{t-1}^{(\ell)},Z_{t-2}^{(\ell)},\ldots) - E(U_t^{(j)}|Z_{t-1}^{(\ell)},Z_{t-2}^{(\ell)},\ldots)|] \leq E(|U_t - U_t^{(j)}|) \to 0 \text{ as } j \to \infty. \tag{8.3.5}$$

Moreover, from theorem 7.3.4 and assumption 7.3.2 it follows that there exists a subset $N_{j,\ell}$ of R^{k+1} with Lebesgue measure zero such that for all $(\xi,\tau) \in R^k \times (-1,1)\backslash N_{j,\ell}$,

$$E(U_t^{(j)}|Z_{t-1}^{(\ell)},Z_{t-2}^{(\ell)},\ldots) = E(U_t^{(j)}|\textstyle\sum_{s=1}^{\infty}\tau^{s-1}\xi' Z_{t-s}^{(\ell)}). \tag{8.3.6}$$

Combining (8.3.4), (8.3.5), and (8.3.6) and taking for N the union of all the sets $N_{j,\ell}$, the lemma follows. Q.E.D.

Next, we combine lemma 8.3.1 with lemma 3.3.1:

Lemma 8.3.2 Let ψ be an arbitrary bounded Borel measurable one-to-one mapping from R into R. Let the conditions of lemma 8.3.1 hold. There exists a subset S of R^{k+2} with Lebesgue measure zero such that (8.3.3) implies

$$E\{U_t \cdot \exp[\rho \cdot \psi(\textstyle\sum_{s=1}^{\infty}\tau^{s-1}\xi' Z_{t-s}^{(\ell)})]\} \neq 0 \tag{8.3.7}$$

for all $\ell \geq \ell_0$ and all $(\rho,\xi,\tau) \in R \times R^k \times (-1,1)\backslash S$.

Proof: Lemmas 3.3.1 and 8.3.1 imply that for each $(\xi,\tau) \in R^k \times (-1,1)\backslash N$ there exists a countable subset $C_\ell(\xi,\tau)$ of R such that (8.3.7) holds for $\rho \notin C_\ell(\xi,\tau)$. The proof can now easily be completed along the lines of the proof of theorem 3.3.5. Cf. exercise 2. Q.E.D.

Let

$$\hat{U}_t = Y_t - \tilde{g}_t(\hat{\theta}),$$

where $\tilde{g}_t$ is defined by (8.2.6). Denoting

$$w_{t,\ell}(\rho,\xi,\tau) = \exp[\rho \cdot \varphi(\textstyle\sum_{j=1}^{\infty}\tau^{j-1}\xi' Z_{t-j}^{(\ell)})]; \tag{8.3.8}$$

$$\left.\begin{aligned} &\hat{w}_{t,\ell}(\rho,\xi,\tau) = \exp[\rho \cdot \varphi(\textstyle\sum_{j=1}^{t-1}\tau^{j-1}\xi' Z_{t-j}^{(\ell)})] \text{ if } t \geq 2,\\ &\hat{w}_{t,\ell}(\rho,\xi,\tau) = 1 \text{ if } t \leq 1; \end{aligned}\right\} \tag{8.3.9}$$

$$c_{n,\ell}(\rho,\xi,\tau) = [1/(n-p)]\textstyle\sum_{t=p+1}^{n} U_t w_{t,\ell}(\rho,\xi,\tau); \tag{8.3.10}$$

$$\hat{c}_{n,\ell}(\rho,\xi,\tau) = [1/(n-p)]\textstyle\sum_{t=p+1}^{n} \hat{U}_t \hat{w}_{t,\ell}(\rho,\xi,\tau), \tag{8.3.11}$$

$$\bar{c}_\ell(\rho,\xi,\tau) = \lim_{n\to\infty} E[c_{n,\ell}(\rho,\xi,\tau)], \tag{8.3.12}$$

where ψ is now a bounded *uniformly continuous* one-to-one mapping from R into R, it follows:

Theorem 8.3.1 Let the conditions of theorem 8.2.2 be satisfied. Then

$$\text{plim}_{n\to\infty}\hat{c}_{n,\ell}(\rho,\xi,\tau) = \bar{c}_\ell(\rho,\xi,\tau).$$

Under H_1 and assumptions 7.3.2 and 8.1.1* there exists an integer ℓ_0 and a subset S of R^{k+2} with Lebesgue measure zero such that for all $\ell \geq \ell_0$ and all $(\rho,\xi,\tau) \in R \times R^k \times (-1,1)\backslash S$,

$\bar{c}_\ell(\rho,\xi,\tau) \neq 0,$

whereas under H_0,

$\bar{c}_\ell(\rho,\xi,\tau) = 0$

for all ℓ and all $(\rho,\xi,\tau) \in R \times R^k \times (-1,1)$.

Proof: This theorem follows easily from lemma 8.3.2 and theorems 6.4.3 and 8.2.2. Cf. exercise 3. Q.E.D.

Theorem 8.3.1 suggests using $\hat{c}_{n,\ell}(\rho,\xi,\tau)$ as a basis for a consistent test of the null hypothesis (8.3.1) versus the alternative hypothesis (8.3.2). The next two lemmas establish the asymptotic normality of $\hat{c}_{n,\ell}(\rho,\xi,\tau)$ under H_0.

Lemma 8.3.3 Under the null hypothesis (8.3.1) and the conditions of theorem 8.2.4,

$$\text{plim}_{n\to\infty}\{\surd(n\text{-}p)\hat{c}_{n,\ell}(\rho,\xi,\tau) - [1/\surd(n-p)]\textstyle\sum_{t=1}^{n} U_t[w_{t,\ell}(\rho,\xi,\tau) - \bar{b}_\ell(\rho,\xi,\tau)'\Omega_1^{-1}(\partial/\partial\theta')g_t(\theta_*)]\} = 0, \quad (8.3.13)$$

where Ω_1 is defined by (8.1.38) with g^* defined by (8.2.7), and

$$\bar{b}_\ell(\rho,\xi,\tau) = \lim_{n\to\infty}(1/n)\textstyle\sum_{t=1}^{n} E[w_{t,\ell}(\rho,\xi,\tau)(\partial/\partial\theta')g_t(\theta_*)]. \quad (8.3.14)$$

Proof: Exercise 4.

Denoting

$$\bar{s}_\ell^2(\rho,\xi,\tau) = \lim_{n\to\infty}(1/n)\textstyle\sum_{t=1}^{n} E\{U_t^2[w_{t,\ell}(\rho,\xi,\tau) - \bar{b}_\ell(\rho,\xi,\tau)'\Omega_1^{-1}(\partial/\partial\theta')g_t(\theta_*)]^2\}, \quad (8.3.15)$$

it follows now from lemma 8.3.3 and the martingale central limit theorem 6.1.7 that

Lemma 8.3.4 Under the null hypothesis (8.3.1) and the conditions of theorem 8.2.4,

$$\surd(n\text{-}p)\ \hat{c}_{n,\ell}(\rho,\xi,\tau) \to N(0,\bar{s}_\ell^2(\rho,\xi,\tau)) \text{ in distr.} \quad (8.3.16)$$

for each $(\rho,\xi,\tau) \in R \times R^k \times (-1,1)$ and each ℓ.

Proof: Exercise 5.

Moreover, denoting

$$\hat{s}_{n,\ell}^2(\rho,\xi,\tau) = [1/(n-p)]\textstyle\sum_{t=p+1}^{n} \hat{U}_t^2[\hat{w}_{t,\ell}(\rho,\xi,\tau) - b_{n,\ell}(\rho,\xi,\tau)'\hat{\Omega}_1^{-1}(\partial/\partial\theta')\tilde{g}_t(\hat{\theta})]^2 \quad (8.3.17)$$

with

$$\hat{b}_{n,\ell}(\rho,\xi,\tau)=[1/(n-p)]\sum_{t=p+1}^{n}\hat{w}_{t,\ell}(\rho,\xi,\tau)(\partial/\partial\theta')\tilde{g}_t(\hat{\theta}) \tag{8.3.18}$$

we have:

> *Lemma 8.3.5* Under assumptions 8.2.1, 8.2.2, 8.2.4, and 8.2.5,
>
> $\text{plim}_{n\to\infty}\hat{s}^2_{n,\ell}(\rho,\xi,\tau) = \bar{s}^2_\ell((\rho,\xi,\tau),$
>
> regardless whether or not the null is true.

Proof: Exercise 6.

Our test statistic is now

$$\hat{T}_\ell(\rho,\xi,\tau)=\hat{c}_{n,\ell}(\rho,\xi,\tau)/\sqrt{(\hat{s}^2_{n,\ell}(\rho,\xi,\tau))}. \tag{8.3.19}$$

However, before we can draw conclusions about the limiting behavior of $\hat{T}_\ell(\rho,\xi,\tau)$ under H_0 and H_1 we have to address the question whether $\bar{s}^2_\ell(\rho,\xi,\tau) > 0$ for all (ρ,ξ,τ). The answer is no, i.e., if the model contains a constant term then at least

$\bar{s}^2_\ell(0,\xi,\tau) = 0$ and $\bar{s}^2_\ell(\rho,0,\tau) = 0,$

where in the latter case 0 is the zero vector. If $\xi = 0$ then clearly

$\hat{w}_{t,\ell}(\rho,\xi,\tau) = w_{t,\ell}(\rho,\xi,\tau) = \exp(\rho\cdot\psi(0))$

and consequently

$\hat{c}_{n,\ell}(\rho,\xi,\tau) = \exp(\rho\cdot\psi(0))[1/(n-p)]\sum_{t=p+1}^{n}\hat{U}_t.$

Similarly, if $\rho = 0$ then

$\hat{c}_{n,\ell}(\rho,\xi,\tau) = [1/(n-p)]\sum_{t=p+1}^{n}\hat{U}_t.$

But if model (8.2.1) contains a constant term then

$\sum_{t=p+1}^{n}\hat{U}_t = 0$ a.s.,

hence

$\bar{s}^2_\ell(\rho,\xi,\tau) = 0.$

We may exclude this case by including $\rho = 0$ and/or $\xi = 0$ in the set S. Because the new set S is then the union of the original set S with another set with Lebesgue measure zero, it still has Lebesgue measure zero. The following assumption guarantees that the points $(\rho,\xi,\tau) \in R\times R^k\times(-1,1)$ for which $\bar{s}^2_\ell(\rho,\xi,\tau) = 0$ are indeed contained in a set with Lebesgue measure zero.

> *Assumption 8.3.1* The process (Z_t) is strictly stationary. There exists a stationary process (f_t), where f_t is defined on the Borel field generated by $Z_{t-1},Z_{t-2},\ldots$, such that the random vector κ_t

$= (f_t,(\partial/\partial\theta)g_t(\theta_*))'$ has positive definite second moment matrix $E(\kappa_t\kappa_t')$.

Lemma 8.3.6 Under assumption 8.3.1 and the conditions of lemma 8.3.5 there exists a natural number ℓ_1 such that for all $\ell > \ell_1$ the set

$$S^*_\ell = \{(\rho,\xi,\tau) \in R \times R^k \times (-1,1): \bar{s}^2_\ell(\rho,\xi,\tau) = 0\}$$

has Lebesgue measure zero.

Proof: Without loss of generality we may assume $P(U_t = 0) < 1$. Let $(\rho,\xi,\tau) \in S^*_\ell$. Then

$$w_{t,\ell}(\rho,\xi,\tau) = \bar{b}_\ell(\rho,\xi,\tau)'\Omega_1^{-1}(\partial/\partial\theta')g_t(\theta_*) \text{ a.s.}$$

Hence

$$E[f_t \cdot w_{t,\ell}(\rho,\xi,\tau)] = \bar{b}_\ell(\rho,\xi,\tau)'\Omega_1^{-1}E[(\partial/\partial\theta')g_t(\theta_*)f_t]$$
$$= E[(\partial/\partial\theta')g_t(\theta_*)\lambda\, w_{t,\ell}(\rho,\xi,\tau)],$$

where

$$\lambda = \Omega_1^{-1}E[(\partial/\partial\theta')g_t(\theta_*)f_t].$$

Since $P[f_t = (\partial/\partial\theta')g_t(\theta_*)\lambda] = 1$ would imply that $E(\kappa_t\kappa_t')$ is singular, it follows from assumption 8.3.1 that

$$P[f_t = (\partial/\partial\theta')g_t(\theta_*)\lambda] < 1.$$

Similarly to lemma 8.3.2 it follows now that for sufficiently large ℓ, S^*_ℓ has Lebesgue measure zero. Q.E.D.

Taking the union of the former set S with the union of the S^*_ℓ over $\ell \geq \ell_1$ and denoting the new set again by S we now have:

Theorem 8.3.2 There exists a natural number ℓ_0 and a subset S of R^{k+2} with Lebesgue measure zero such that for all $(\rho,\xi,\tau) \in R \times R^k \times (-1,1)\backslash S$ and all $\ell \geq \ell_0$ the following hold.

(i) Under the null hypothesis, the conditions of theorem 8.2.4 and assumption 8.3.1, we have

$$\sqrt{(n-p)}\hat{T}_\ell(\rho,\xi,\tau) \to N(0,1) \text{ in distr.} \tag{8.3.20}$$

(ii) If the null is false then under assumptions 7.3.2, 8.1.1*, 8.3.1, 8.2.1, 8.2.2, 8.2.4, and 8.2.5,

$$\text{plim}_{n\to\infty}\sqrt{(n-p)}\hat{T}_\ell(\rho,\xi,\tau) = \infty. \tag{8.3.21}$$

In practice the exceptional set S is unknown. However, similarly to theorem 5.3.1 we have:

Theorem 8.3.3 Draw ρ and the components of ξ randomly from continuous distributions and draw τ randomly from the uniform $(-1,1)$ distribution. Let $\ell \geq \ell_0$. Then the conclusions of theorem 8.3.2 carry over.

Proof: Exercise 7.

Next we propose a slightly modified version of the test under review, for the very same reason as in section 5.3. Suppose we have chosen

$$\psi(.) = \mathrm{tg}^{-1}(\delta(.)), \text{ where } \delta > 0 \text{ is some constant.} \tag{8.3.22}$$

Moreover, suppose that

$$\hat{x}_{t,\ell}(\tau,\xi) = \sum_{j=1}^{t-1} \tau^{j-1} \xi' Z_{t-j}^{(\ell)} \tag{8.3.23}$$

takes with high probability only large positive values. Then $\psi(\hat{x}_{t,\ell}(\tau,\xi))$ takes with high probability only values close to $\frac{1}{2}\pi$, which is the upper bound of the function ψ. Hence the function

$$\hat{w}_{t,\ell}(\rho,\xi,\tau) = \exp[\rho \cdot \psi(\hat{x}_{t,\ell}(\tau,\xi))] \tag{8.3.24}$$

takes values close to $\exp(\rho\,\frac{1}{2}\pi)$ and consequently

$$\hat{c}_{n,\ell}(\rho,\xi,\tau) \approx [(1/n)\textstyle\sum_{t=1}^{n} \hat{U}_t]\exp(\rho\,\frac{1}{2}\pi).$$

But if the $\hat{U}_t$ are least squares residuals of a model with a constant term they sum up to zero and hence $\hat{c}_{n,\ell}(\rho,\xi,\tau)$ will then be close to zero. Clearly this will destroy the power of the test. Therefore we propose to standardize the argument of ψ, i.e., we propose to replace $\hat{x}_{t,\ell}(\tau,\xi)$ in (8.3.24) by $\hat{\hat{x}}_{t,\ell}(\tau,\xi)$ defined as follows:

$$\left.\begin{aligned} \hat{\hat{x}}_{t,\ell}(\tau,\xi) &= [\hat{x}_{t,\ell}(\tau,\xi) - (1/t)\textstyle\sum_{s=1}^{t}\hat{x}_{s,\ell}(\tau,\xi)]/ \\ &\quad \{(1/t)\textstyle\sum_{s=1}^{t}\hat{x}_{s,\ell}(\tau,\xi)^2 - [(1/t)\sum_{s=1}^{t}\hat{x}_{s,\ell}(\tau,\xi)]^2\}^{1/2} \text{ if } t \geq 3, \\ \hat{\hat{x}}_{t,\ell}(\tau,\xi) &= 0 \text{ if } t \leq 2, \end{aligned}\right\} \tag{8.3.25}$$

where $\hat{x}_{t,\ell}(\tau,\xi) = 0$ if $t \leq 1$ and defined by (8.3.24) if $t \geq 2$. The function $\hat{w}_{t,\ell}(\rho,\xi,\tau)$ is thus redefined as

$$\left.\begin{aligned} \hat{w}_{t,\ell}(\rho,\xi,\tau) &= \exp[\rho\cdot\varphi(\hat{\hat{x}}_{t,\ell}(\tau,\xi))] \text{ if } t \geq 3, \\ \hat{w}_{t,\ell}(\rho,\xi,\tau) &= 1 \text{ if } t \leq 2. \end{aligned}\right\} \tag{8.3.26}$$

Redefine the function $w_{t,\ell}(\rho,\xi,\tau)$ accordingly as

$$w_{t,\ell}(\rho,\xi,\tau) = \exp[\rho\cdot\varphi(\bar{x}_{t,\ell}(\tau,\xi))], \tag{8.3.27}$$

where

$$\bar{x}_{t,\ell}(\tau,\xi) = \{x_{t,\ell}(\tau,\xi) - E[x_{t,\ell}(\tau,\xi)]\}/\{var[x_{t,\ell}(\tau,\xi)]\}^{1/2} \quad (8.3.28)$$

with

$$x_{t,\ell}(\tau,\xi) = \sum_{j=1}^{\infty}\tau^{j-1}\xi' Z_{t-j}^{(\ell)}. \quad (8.3.29)$$

Then

Theorem 8.3.4 With (8.3.26) instead of (8.3.9) and (8.3.27) instead of (8.3.8), all the previous results in this section go through.

Proof: Exercise 8.

Remark 1: It is easy to verify that the results in this section also go through if we use more general ARMA memory indices than (8.3.29). In particular, we may replace (8.3.29) by, say,

$$x_{t,\ell}(\tau,\xi) = (1+\tau_1 L^1+\ldots+\tau_{q_1}L^{q_1})^{-1}(\xi_1 L+\ldots+\xi_{p_1}L^{p_1})' Z_t^{(\ell)})$$

and replace (8.3.23) by

$$\hat{x}_{t,\ell}(\tau,\xi) = (1+\tau_1 L^1+\ldots+\tau_{q_1}L^{q_1})^{-1}(\xi_1 L+\ldots+\xi_{p_1}L^{p_1})'\hat{Z}_t^{(\ell)}),$$

where now

$$\tau = (\tau_1,\ldots,\tau_{q_1})' \in \Delta,\ \xi = (\xi_1',\ldots,\xi_{p_1}')' \in R^{k+p_1}$$

with Δ such that the lag polynomial $1+\tau_1 L^1+\ldots+\tau_{q_1}L^{q_1}$ has roots all outside the complex unit circle, and

$$\hat{Z}_t^{(\ell)} = Z_t^{(\ell)} \text{ for } t \geq 1, \qquad \hat{Z}_t^{(\ell)} = 0 \text{ for } t < 1.$$

Remark 2: In chapter 7 we argued that the parameters τ and ξ for which

$$E(U_t|Z_{t-1}^{(\ell)},Z_{t-2}^{(\ell)},\ldots) = E(U_t|\sum_{j=1}^{\infty}\tau^{j-1}\xi' Z_{t-j}^{(\ell)}) \text{ a.s.}$$

are likely to be irrational. Since this result plays a key role in the proof of theorem 8.3.1, one might therefore think that the consistency of our test cannot hold as consistency requires irrational τ and ξ, whereas in practice it is impossible to deal with irrational numbers. However, the functions $\bar{c}_\ell(\rho,\xi,\tau)$ and $\bar{s}_\ell^2(\rho,\xi,\tau)$ are continuous, and so is

$$\bar{T}_\ell(\rho,\xi,\tau) = \text{plim}_{n\to\infty}\hat{T}_\ell(\rho,\xi,\tau) = \bar{c}_\ell(\rho,\xi,\tau)/\sqrt{(\bar{s}_\ell^2(\rho,\xi,\tau))},$$

provided $\bar{s}_\ell^2(\rho,\xi,\tau) > 0$, hence if

$$\bar{T}_\ell(\rho,\xi,\tau) \neq 0$$

holds then it holds too on an open neighborhood of (ρ,ξ,τ) and thus also for all rational (ρ^*,ξ^*,τ^*) in this neighborhood.

Exercises

1. Prove (8.3.3).
2. Complete the proof of lemma 8.3.2.
3. Complete the proof of theorem 8.3.1.
4. Prove lemma 8.3.3.
5. Prove lemma 8.3.4.
6. Prove lemma 8.3.5.
7. Prove theorem 8.3.3.
8. Prove theorem 8.3.4.

8.4 An autocorrelation test

In this section we briefly discuss a test for first- or higher-order autocorrelation of the errors U_t of model (8.2.1). The null hypothesis is still H_0 defined by (8.3.1), but instead of (8.3.2) we consider the less general alternative

$$H_1^{(r)}: \mathrm{cov}(U_t,U_{t-j}) \neq 0 \text{ for some } j \in \{1,2,...,r\}.$$

The reason for considering the problem of testing H_0 against $H_1^{(r)}$ is threefold. First, in traditional times analysis most tests for model specification test the null hypothesis of white-noise errors against an alternative of the type $H_1^{(r)}$. Second, such a test is rather easy to construct, and its construction is a very useful exercise that highlights the essence of the approach in the previous sections. Third, severe model misspecification will likely be covered by $H_1^{(r)}$ for r sufficiently large. Therefore we advocate conducting the test below first, as a pretest of model misspecification. If H_0 is rejected in favor of $H_1^{(r)}$ there is no need to conduct a consistent test. However, since $H_1^{(r)}$ may be false while H_0 is false, not rejecting H_0 in favor of $H_1^{(r)}$ does not provide sufficient evidence that H_0 is true. In that case the consistent tests in section 8.3 should be used in order to verify whether H_0 is true or not.

The test involved can simply be based on the statistic

$$\hat{c} = [1/(n\text{-}r\text{-}p)]\textstyle\sum_{t=r+p+1}^{n}\hat{U}_t\hat{V}_t.$$

where

$$\hat{U}_t = Y_t - \tilde{g}_t(\hat{\theta}),$$

with $\tilde{g}_t$ defined by (8.2.6), and

$$\hat{V}_t = (\hat{U}_{t-1},...,\hat{U}_{t-r})'.$$

Let

$$U_t = Y_t - g_t(\theta^*),$$

where g_t is defined by (8.2.5) and θ_* is defined in assumption 8.2.2, and let

$V_t = (U_{t-1},...,U_{t-r})'$.

We recall that under H_0, $\theta_* = \theta_0$. Denoting

$$\Delta = A - B_1\Omega_1^{-1}B_2' - B_2\Omega_1^{-1}B_1' + B_1\Omega_1^{-1}\Omega_2\Omega_1^{-1}B_1',$$
$$\hat{\Delta} = \hat{A} - \hat{B}_1\hat{\Omega}_1^{-1}\hat{B}_2' - \hat{B}_2\hat{\Omega}_1^{-1}\hat{B}_1' + \hat{B}_1\hat{\Omega}_1^{-1}\hat{\Omega}_2\hat{\Omega}_1^{-1}\hat{B}_1',$$

with

$$B_1 = \lim_{n\to\infty}[1/(n-r-p)]\textstyle\sum_{t=r+p+1}^{n} E[V_t(\partial/\partial\theta)g_t(\theta_*)],$$
$$B_2 = \lim_{n\to\infty}[1/(n-r-p)]\textstyle\sum_{t=r+p+1}^{n} E[U_t^2 V_t(\partial/\partial\theta)g_t(\theta_*)],$$
$$A = \lim_{n\to\infty}[1/(n-r-p)]\textstyle\sum_{t=r+p+1}^{n} E(U_t^2 V_t V_t')$$
$$\hat{B}_1 = [1/(n-r-p)]\textstyle\sum_{t=r+p+1}^{n} E[\hat{V}_t(\partial/\partial\theta)\tilde{g}_t(\hat{\theta})],$$
$$\hat{B}_2 = [1/(n-r-p)]\textstyle\sum_{t=r+p+1}^{n} E[\hat{U}_t^2\hat{V}_t(\partial/\partial\theta)\tilde{g}_t(\hat{\theta})],$$
$$\hat{A} = [1/(n-r-p)]\textstyle\sum_{t=r+p+1}^{n} E(\hat{U}_t^2\hat{V}_t\hat{V}_t'),$$

the test statistic involved is now

$$\hat{a}_r = (n-r-p)\hat{c}'\hat{\Delta}^{-1}\hat{c}.$$

Theorem 8.4.1 Let $\det(\Delta) \neq 0$.

(i) Under the null hypothesis (8.3.1) and assumptions 8.2.1–8.2.5 we have

$$\hat{a}_r \to \chi_r^2 \text{ in distr.}$$

(ii) Under $H_1^{(r)}$ and the assumptions 8.1.1*, 8.2.1, 8.2.2, 8.2.4 and 8.2.5 we have

$$\text{plim}_{n\to\infty}\hat{a}_r = \infty.$$

Proof: The details of the proof are left as exercises. Below we only give the main steps of the argument. First, under the conditions of part (ii) of the theorem we have

$$\text{plim}_{n\to\infty}\hat{c} \neq 0. \tag{8.4.1}$$

Next, let the conditions of part (i) hold. Let $\hat{c}_i$ be the i-th component of $\hat{c}$. By the mean value theorem there exists a mean value $\hat{\theta}^{(i)}$ satisfying $|\hat{\theta}^{(i)} - \theta_0| \leq |\hat{\theta} - \theta_0|$ such that

$$\begin{aligned}\hat{c}_i = {} & [1/(n-r-p)]\textstyle\sum_{t=r+p+1}^{n}(Y_t - \tilde{g}_t(\theta_0))(Y_{t-i} - \tilde{g}_{t-i}(\theta_0)) \\ & -\{[1/(n-r-p)]\textstyle\sum_{t=r+p+1}^{n}(Y_t - \tilde{g}_t(\hat{\theta}^{(i)}))((\partial/\partial\theta)\tilde{g}_{t-i}(\hat{\theta}^{(i)})) \\ & + [1/(n-r-p)]\textstyle\sum_{t=r+p+1}^{n}((\partial/\partial\theta)\tilde{g}_t(\hat{\theta}^{(i)}))(Y_{t-i} - \tilde{g}_{t-i}(\hat{\theta}^{(i)}))\} \\ & \times(\hat{\theta} - \theta_0)\end{aligned}$$

Since

$$\text{plim}_{n\to\infty}\{[1/\surd(n-r-p)]\textstyle\sum_{t=r+p+1}^{n}(Y_t-\tilde{g}_t(\theta_0))(Y_{t-i}-\tilde{g}_{t-i}(\theta_0)] \\ -[1/\surd(n-r-p)]\textstyle\sum_{t=r+p+1}^{n}U_tU_{t-i}\} = 0,$$

$$\text{plim}_{n\to\infty}[1/(n-r-p)]\textstyle\sum_{t=r+p+1}^{n}(Y_t-\tilde{g}_t(\hat{\theta}^{(i)}))((\partial/\partial\theta)\tilde{g}_{-i}(\hat{\theta}^{(i)}))$$

$$= \text{plim}_{n\to\infty}[1/(n-r-p)]\textstyle\sum_{t=r+p+1}^{n}U_t(\partial/\partial\theta)g_{t-i}(\theta_0) = 0,$$

$$\text{plim}_{n\to\infty}[1/(n-r-p)]\textstyle\sum_{t=r+p+1}^{n}((\partial/\partial\theta)\tilde{g}_t(\hat{\theta}^{(i)}))(Y_{t-i}-\tilde{g}_{t-i}(\hat{\theta}^{(i)}))$$

$$= \text{plim}_{n\to\infty}[1/(n-r-p)]\textstyle\sum_{t=r+p+1}^{n}U_{t-i}(\partial/\partial\theta)g_t(\theta_0)$$

and

$$\text{plim}_{n\to\infty}\{\surd(n-r-p)(\hat{\theta}-\theta_0) \\ -[1/\surd(n-r-p)]\textstyle\sum_{t=r+p+1}^{n}U_t\Omega_1^{-1}(\partial/\partial\theta')g_t(\theta_0)\} = 0$$

it follows now that

$$\text{plim}_{n\to\infty}\{\surd(n-r-p)\hat{c} \\ -[1/\surd(n-r-p)]\textstyle\sum_{t=r+p+1}^{n}U_t(V_t-B_1\Omega_1^{-1}(\partial/\partial\theta')g_t(\theta_0))\} = 0,$$

hence by theorem 6.1.7,

$$\surd(n-r-p)\hat{c} \to N_r(0,\Delta) \text{ in distr.} \qquad (8.4.2)$$

Finally, we have

$$\text{plim}_{n\to\infty}\hat{\Delta} = \Delta. \qquad (8.4.3)$$

Combining (8.4.1), (8.4.2), and (8.4.3), the theorem follows. Q.E.D.

9

Unit roots and cointegration

If a time series is modeled as an ARMA(p,q) process while the true data-generating process is an ARIMA(p−1,1,q) process, strange things may happen with the asymptotic distributions of parameter estimators. For example, if a time series process Y_t is modeled as $Y_t = \alpha Y_{t-1} + U_t$, with U_t Gaussian white noise and α assumed to be in the stable region (-1,1), while in reality the process is a random walk, i.e., $\Delta Y_t = U_t$, then the OLS estimator α_n of α (on the basis of a sample of size n) is n-consistent rather than $\sqrt{}$n-consistent, and the asymptotic distribution of $n(\alpha_n\text{-}\alpha)$ is non-normal. Therefore, in testing the hypothesis $\alpha = 1$ standard asymptotic theory is no longer valid. See Fuller (1976), Dickey and Fuller (1979, 1981), Evans and Savin (1981, 1984), Said and Dickey (1984), Dickey, Hasza, and Fuller (1984), Phillips (1987), Phillips and Perron (1988), Hylleberg and Mizon (1989), and Haldrup and Hylleberg (1989), among others, for various unit root tests (all based on testing $\alpha = 1$ in an AR model) and Schwert (1989) for a Monte Carlo analysis of the power of some of these tests. Moreover, see Diebold and Nerlove (1990) for a review of the unit root literature, and see Bierens (1993) and Bierens and Guo (1993) for alternative tests of the unit root hypothesis.

In this chapter we shall review and explain the most common unit root tests. However, since understanding the asymptotic theory involved requires some knowledge of the theory of convergence of probability measures on metric spaces, we shall start with reviewing the latter first.

The concept of cointegration was first introduced by Granger (1981) and elaborated further by Engle and Granger (1987), Engle and Yoo (1987), Stock and Watson (1988) and Johansen (1988, 1991), to mention a few. Recently it has become an increasingly popular topic in the econometrics literature. The basic idea is that if all the components X_{it} of a *vector* time series process X_t have a unit root there may exist linear combinations $\alpha' X_t$ without a unit root. These linear combinations may then be interpreted as long-term relations between the components of X_t. Since the theory of cointegration is rapidly developing, any attempt to cover the whole literature will soon be outdated. In this chapter we shall therefore outline the basic principles only, on the basis of Engle and

Granger (1987), Engle (1987), Engle and Yoo (1989) and Johansen (1988).

9.1 Weak convergence of random functions

9.1.1 Introduction

In order to derive tests for a unit root in time series processes we need to generalize the concept of convergence in distribution of random variables or vectors to weak convergence of random functions on the unit interval [0,1]. Therefore we briefly review some terminology and results related to convergence of probability measures on metric spaces. The emphasis is on intuition rather than on mathematical rigor. For a full account, see Royden (1968) for a general treatment of the theory of metric spaces, and, in particular, Billingsley (1968) for a rigorous treatment of convergence of probability measures on metric spaces.

Let $\{\Omega,\mathfrak{F},P\}$ be a probability space and let f(t) be a random function on [0,1] defined on $\{\Omega,\mathfrak{F},P\}$. We recall that by definition f is a mapping from $\Omega \times [0,1]$ onto R such that for each $r \in R$, $t \in [0,1]$, $\{\omega\in\Omega: f(\omega,t) \leq r\} \in \mathfrak{F}$. Cf. definition 1.6.1. Now assume that f belongs to a class S of real function on [0,1], in the sense that the set

$$N = \{\omega\in\Omega: f(\omega,.) \notin S\}$$

is a null set in $\mathfrak{F}$: $N \in \mathfrak{F}$, $P(N) = 0$. Then we may interpret f as a mapping from Ω onto S. In order to make probability statements about f we need to define a Borel field $\mathfrak{B}$ of subsets of S such that for each set $B \in \mathfrak{B}$, $f^{-1}(B) \in \mathfrak{F}$. These sets B play a similar role to the Borel sets in a Euclidean space. Thus, we need to define Borel sets of *functions* in S.

We recall that the Euclidean Borel field of subsets of R (that is, the collection of Borel sets in R) is defined as the minimal Borel field containing the collection of all half-open intervals $(-\infty,b]$, $b \in R$. It is quite easy to verify that the same Euclidean Borel field can be defined as the minimal Borel field containing the collection of all open intervals (a,b), $a,b \in R$, $a < b$. This suggests to define the collection of Borel sets in S as the minimal Borel field containing the collection of all open sets in S. However, since we have not yet defined a distance measure for functions in S, topological terms like "open", "closed", "closure", "dense", "boundary", etc., have no meaning yet for subsets of S. Therefore we shall endow the set S with a metric ρ, i.e., let ρ be a mapping from $S \times S$ into R with the following properties: for all functions f, g, and h in S,

$$\rho(f,f) = 0;\ 0 < \rho(f,g) < \infty \text{ iff } f \neq g;\ \rho(f,g) = \rho(g,f);$$
$$\rho(f,h) \leq \rho(f,g) + \rho(g,h) \text{ (triangular inequality).} \qquad (9.1.1)$$

An example of such a metric is the "sup" norm:

$$\rho(f,g) = \sup_{0 \leqslant t \leqslant 1}|f(t)-g(t)|. \tag{9.1.2}$$

The pair (S,ρ) is called a *metric space*. The metric ρ allows us to define the following attributes of subsets of S. A set A is *open* if for every $f \in A$ there exists an $\varepsilon > 0$ such that the open ε-sphere $\{g\in S: \rho(f,g) < \varepsilon\}$ about f is contained in A. An element f of S is called a *point of closure* of a set A if for every $\varepsilon > 0$ there is an element $g \in A$ such that $\rho(f,g) < \varepsilon$. The set of points of closure of A is called the *closure* of A and is denoted by A^-. A set A is *closed* if $A^- = A$. An element f of A is called an *interior point* if there exists an $\varepsilon > 0$ such that $\{g\in S: \rho(f,g) < \varepsilon\} \subset A$. The set of interior points of A is called the *interior* of A, and is denoted by A^0. Clearly, A^0 is an open set. The *boundary* of a set A, denoted by ∂A, is defined by $\partial A = A^-\backslash A^0$. A set A is *dense* in B if $A \subset B \subset A^-$. Finally, a set A is *compact* if every open cover of A (that is a union of open sets in S containing A) contains a finite subcover.

We now define the Borel sets of S as the members of the minimal Borel field $\mathfrak{B}$ containing the collection of open sets in S. It is not too hard to prove that open sets, closed sets, boundaries and closures of Borel sets, and compact sets are all Borel sets. Note that this notion of a Borel set of functions is relative to the metric ρ: if we choose another metric ρ then $\mathfrak{B}$ may change.

In chapter 1 we defined a random variable X as a real function $x(\omega)$ on Ω such that for each $b \in R$, $\{\omega\in\Omega: x(\omega)\leq b\} \in \mathfrak{F}$, and we have seen that this property implies that for all Borel sets B in R, $\{\omega\in\Omega: x(\omega)\in B\} \in \mathfrak{F}$, and vice versa. Thus an equivalent condition for X being a random variable is that for each Borel set B in R, $\{\omega\in\Omega: x(\omega)\in B\} \in \mathfrak{F}$. This suggests to define a *random element* X of S as a mapping $x: \Omega \rightarrow S$ such that for each Borel set B in S, $\{\omega\in\Omega: x(\omega,.) \in B\} \in \mathfrak{F}$. Similarly to random variables, a random element X of S induces a probability measure μ on $\{S,\mathfrak{B}\}$ by the correspondence

$$\mu(B) = P[\{\omega\in\Omega: x(\omega,.) \in B\}], B \in \mathfrak{B}. \tag{9.1.3}$$

This probability measure μ describes the distribution of X.

Let φ be a real function on S. In order that $\varphi(X)$, with X a random element of S, is a well-defined random variable the sets $\{f\in S: \varphi(f) \leq b\}$, $b \in R$, should be Borel sets in S. If so, we will also in this case call the function φ Borel measurable. Actually, the notion of Borel measurability of real functions on metric spaces does not differ from the notion of Borel measurability of real functions on Euclidean spaces. Thus the definitions (in particular the definition of simple function) and results in section 1.3 carry over to real functions on metric spaces, provided of course that the Euclidean metric $\rho(x,y) = |x-y|$ is replaced by the metric of the metric space under review. Consequently, the expectation $E[\varphi(X)]$, with X a random element of a metric space and φ a Borel measurable function on S, can also be defined along the lines of section 1.4.

Next, let (S_1,ρ_1) and (S_2,ρ_2) be two metric spaces, and let $\mathfrak{B}_1$ and $\mathfrak{B}_2$ be the corresponding collections of Borel sets. A mapping Φ: $S_1 \rightarrow S_2$ is called Borel measurable if for all $B_2 \in \mathfrak{B}_2$, $\{f \in S_1: \Phi(f) \in B_2\} \in \mathfrak{B}_1$. Thus, if X is a random element of S_1 and Φ is Borel measurable then $\Phi(X)$ is a random element of S_2. A mapping Φ: $S_1 \rightarrow S_2$ is continuous if for each $f \in S_1$ and arbitrary $\varepsilon > 0$ there exists a $\delta > 0$ such that $\rho_2(\Phi(f),\Phi(g)) < \varepsilon$ if $g \in S_1$ and $\rho_1(f,g) < \delta$. Continuous mappings are Borel measurable.

Now consider a sequence (X_n) of random elements of S, defined on a common probability space $\{\Omega,\mathfrak{F},P\}$. Each X_n induces a probability measure μ_n on $\{S,\mathfrak{B}\}$ by the correspondence

$$\mu_n(B) = P[\{\omega \in \Omega: x_n(\omega,.) \in B\}],\ B \in \mathfrak{B}. \tag{9.1.4}$$

Analogously to proper convergence of distribution functions we can now define the *weak* convergence of μ_n to a probability measure μ on {S,B} as follows:

Definition 9.1.1 A sequence (μ_n) of probability measures on $\{S,\mathfrak{B}\}$ converges weakly to μ, denoted by $\mu_n \Rightarrow \mu$, if μ is a probability measure on $\{S,\mathfrak{B}\}$ such that for all Borel sets $B \in \mathfrak{B}$ with $\mu(\partial B) = 0$, $\lim_{n\rightarrow\infty}\mu_n(B) = \mu(B)$.

The condition $\mu(\partial B) = 0$ corresponds to the exclusion of discontinuity points of the limiting distribution F in the case of proper convergence of F_n to F. Cf. definition 2.3.1.

Similarly to convergence in distribution of random variables we can now define:

Definition 9.1.2 Let X_n, $n=1,2,\ldots$, and X be random elements of a metric space $\{S,\rho\}$ defined on a common probability space. Then X_n converges weakly to X, denoted by $X_n \Rightarrow X$, if $\mu_n \Rightarrow \mu$, where μ_n and μ are the induced probability measures of X_n and X, respectively.

We recall that for random variables X_n and X, $X_n \rightarrow X$ in distribution if and only if for all bounded continuous real functions φ on R, $E[\varphi(X_n)] \rightarrow E[\varphi(X)]$. Cf. theorem 2.3.1. A similar result also holds in the case of weak convergence:

Theorem 9.1.1 Let X_n, $n=1,2,\ldots$, and X be random elements of a metric space $\{S,\rho\}$ defined on a common probability space. Then $X_n \Rightarrow X$ if and only if for all bounded continuous real functions φ on S, $E[\varphi(X_n)] \rightarrow E[\varphi(X)]$.

Proof: Billingsley (1968, theorem 2.1, pp. 11–12).

From theorems 2.3.1 and 9.1.1 it now follows easily that in the case S = R and of $\mathfrak{B}$ the Euclidean Borel field, definition 9.1.1 is equivalent to the definition of proper convergence of distribution functions.

We have seen in theorem 2.3.4 that convergence in distribution of random variables is invariant under continuous transformations. Also this property carries over to weak convergence:

> *Theorem 9.1.2 (Continuous mapping theorem)* Let $X_n \Rightarrow X$, where X_n and X are random elements of a metric space (S,ρ), and let μ be the probability measure induced by X. Let Φ be a Borel measurable mapping from (S,ρ) into a metric space (S^*,ρ^*) such that Φ is continuous on a Borel set $S_0 \subset S$ with $\mu(S_0) = 1$. Then $\Phi(X_n) \Rightarrow \Phi(X)$.

Proof: Billingsley (1968, theorem 5.1, p.30).

For random variables and random vectors, convergence in distribution implies stochastic boundedness. Cf. theorem 2.5.9. Thus, stochastic boundedness is a necessary condition for convergence in distribution. The same applies to weak convergence. The counterpart of stochastic boundedness in the case of random elements of S is called *tightness*:

> *Definition 9.1.3* A sequence of probability measures μ_n on a metric space $\{S,\rho\}$ is tight if for every $\varepsilon \in (0,1)$ there exists a compact set $K \subset S$ such that for all $n \geq 1$, $\mu_n(K) > 1-\varepsilon$. If μ_n is induced by a random element X_n of S, then the sequence (X_n) is called tight.

9.1.2 Weak convergence in C; Wiener process

We now consider a special but important case of a metric space of real functions, namely the metric space C of *continuous* real functions on [0,1], endowed with the "sup" norm ρ defined in (9.1.2).

The concept of tightness, together with the concept of finite dimensional distribution below, plays a crucial role in determining weak convergence in C:

> *Definition 9.1.4* Let X be a random element of C. A finite distribution of X is the distribution of a finite dimensional random vector of the form $(X(t_1),X(t_2),...,X(t_m))'$, where $t_i \in [0,1]$, $i=1,..,m < \infty$.

We now have:

> *Theorem 9.1.3*. Let X_n and X be random elements of C. Then $X_n \Rightarrow X$ if and only if
> (i) all finite distributions of X_n converge properly pointwise to the corresponding finite distributions of X, and
> (ii) X_n is tight.

Proof: Billingsley (1968, p.35)

Next, we consider the concept of Wiener process (also called Brownian motion). Let (U_n) be a sequence of independent standard normal random variables, and define the random function $Y_n(t)$ on [0,1] by

$$\left.\begin{aligned} Y_n(t) &= (1/\sqrt{n})\textstyle\sum_{j=1}^{[nt]} U_j \text{ if } t \in [n^{-1},1]; \\ &= 0 \text{ if } t \in [0,n^{-1}), \end{aligned}\right\} \quad (9.1.5)$$

where [x] stands for the largest integer $\leq$ x. This is not a continuous random function and hence not a random element in C, but we can smooth out the jumps in $Y_n(t)$ by adding the term

$$Z_n(t) = (nt-[nt])(1/\sqrt{n})U_{[nt]+1}. \quad (9.1.6)$$

Thus, let

$$X_n(t) = Y_n(t) + Z_n(t). \quad (9.1.7)$$

Then $X_n(t)$ is a.s. continuous and therefore a random element of C. Note that for fixed t, $Y_n(t)$ and $Z_n(t)$ are independent normal random variables with zero means and variances:

$$\text{var}(Y_n(t)) = [nt]/n, \ \text{var}(Z_n(t)) = (nt-[nt])^2/n,$$

hence

$$\text{var}(X_n(t)) = [nt]/n + (nt-[nt])^2/n \rightarrow t \text{ as } n \rightarrow \infty. \quad (9.1.8)$$

Moreover for $0 \leq t < s \leq 1$ we have

$$\begin{pmatrix} X_n(s) - X_n(t) \\ X_n(t) \end{pmatrix} \rightarrow N_2\left(\begin{pmatrix} 0 \\ 0 \end{pmatrix}, \begin{pmatrix} s-t & 0 \\ 0 & t \end{pmatrix}\right), \quad (9.1.9)$$

as is not hard to verify. Thus $X_n(s)-X_n(t)$ and $X_n(t)$ are asymptotically independent. This result suggests the existence of a random element W in C with the following properties: For $0 \leq t < s \leq 1$,

$$\begin{pmatrix} W(s) - W(t) \\ W(t) \end{pmatrix} \sim N_2\left(\begin{pmatrix} 0 \\ 0 \end{pmatrix}, \begin{pmatrix} s-t & 0 \\ 0 & t \end{pmatrix}\right). \quad (9.1.10a)$$

or equivalently, for s, t $\in$ [0,1],

$$\begin{pmatrix} W(s) \\ W(t) \end{pmatrix} \sim N_2\left(\begin{pmatrix} 0 \\ 0 \end{pmatrix}, \begin{pmatrix} s & \min(s,t) \\ \min(s,t) & t \end{pmatrix}\right). \quad (9.1.10b)$$

Such a random element is called a *Wiener process* or *Brownian motion*. However, does a Wiener process exist in C ? According to theorem 9.1.3, we have to verify that all finite distributions of X_n converge properly pointwise to the corresponding finite distributions of W, and that X_n is tight. The proof of the latter is rather complicated; we refer for it to Billingsley (1968, pp. 61–64). On the other hand, it is easy to verify that for arbitrary unequal $t_1,...,t_m$ in [0,1],

$$(X_n(t_1),...,X_n(t_m))' \to (W(t_1),...,W(t_m))',$$

where the random variables $W(t_j)$ are such that for $s=t_i$, $t=t_j$, (9.1.10b) holds. Thus a Wiener process exists.

Summarizing, we have shown $X_n \Rightarrow W$, where X_n is defined by (9.1.5)–(9.1.7) with the U_j's independent standard normally distributed, and W a Wiener process. More generally, we have the following functional central limit theorem:

> *Theorem 9.1.4* Let X_n be defined by (9.1.5)–(9.1.7), where the U_j's are independent random variables with zero mean and finite variance $\sigma^2 > 0$. Then $X_n/\sigma \Rightarrow W$, where W is a Wiener process.

Proof: Billingsley (1968, theorem 10.1, p. 68)

Note that this theorem generalizes the central limit theorem 2.4.1, i.e., theorem 2.4.1 follows from theorem 9.1.4 by confining attention to $t = 1$.

A Wiener process is an (important) example of a Gaussian process. A Gaussian process Z in C is a random element of C such that all finite distributions of Z are multivariate normal. They are uniquely determined by their expectation function E[Z(t)] and covariance function cov[Z(s),Z(t)], $s,t \in [0,1]$. Consequently, a Wiener process is uniquely determined by (9.1.10b). Another example of a Gaussian process in C is the so-called *Brownian bridge*: $W^0(t) = W(t) - tW(1)$, where W is a Wiener process. Note that $W^0(0) = W^0(1) = 0$ a.s.

Exercises

1. Let W be a Wiener process.
   (a) What is the distribution of $\int_0^1 tW(t)dt$?
   (b) Calculate $E[W(1)\int_0^1 W(t)dt]$.
   (c) Calculate $E[W(½)\int_0^1 W(t)dt]$
2. Calculate $E[W^0(t)^2]$, where W^0 is a Brownian bridge.

9.1.3 Weak convergence in D

The random function $Y_n(t)$ defined by (9.1.5) is a right-continuous real random function: $\lim_{s\downarrow t} Y_n(s) = Y_n(t)$ a.s, has finite left-hand limits: $\lim_{s\uparrow t} Y_n(s) = Y_n(t-)$ exists a.s., and has finitely many discontinuities. In order to consider weak convergence properties of such random functions we have to extend the set C to the set D of all right-continuous real functions on [0,1] with left-hand limits. As is shown in Billingsley (1968, p.110), these two conditions ensure that all functions in D have countably many discontinuities. However, endowing the space D with the "sup" norm (9.1.2) would lead to too conservative a distance measure. For example, let

$$f(t) = I(t \geq \tfrac{1}{2}),\ f_n(t) = f(t - \tfrac{1}{2}n^{-1}), \tag{9.1.11}$$

where I(.) is the indicator function. Then for all n, $\sup_{0 \leqslant t \leqslant 1} |f_n(t) - f(t)| = 1$, although $f_n \to f$ for all continuity points of f. Therefore we endow the space D with the so-called Skorohod metric:

> *Definition 9.1.5* Let Λ be the space of strictly increasing continuous real functions on [0,1] satisfying $\lambda(0) = 0$, $\lambda(1) = 1$. The Skorohod metric $\rho^0(f,g)$ is the infimum of those positive ε for which Λ contains some λ with
>
> $$\sup_{s \neq t, 0 \leqslant s \leqslant 1, 0 \leqslant t \leqslant 1} |\ln[(\lambda(t) - \lambda(s))/(t-s)]| \leq \varepsilon \tag{9.1.12a}$$
>
> and
>
> $$\sup_{0 \leqslant t \leqslant 1} |f(t) - g(\lambda(t))| \leq \varepsilon \tag{9.1.12b}$$

It is shown in Billingsley (1968, p.113) that ρ^0 is indeed a metric. Note that condition (9.1.12a) says that a suitable function λ should be close to unity: $\lambda(t) \approx t$. Furthermore, taking $\lambda(t) = t$ we see that ρ^0 is dominated by the "sup" norm:

$$\rho^0(f,g) \leq \sup_{0 \leqslant t \leqslant 1} |f(t) - g(t)|. \tag{9.1.13}$$

This easy inequality is quite convenient, as it will often enable us to verify continuity properties by working with the "sup" metric rather than with the more complicated Skorohod metric.

The idea behind this definition is that in comparing the distance between two functions f and g in D one should allow for a small deformation $\lambda(t)$ of the time index t in order to bring the discontinuity points of f and g closer together. As an illustration of this point, consider again example (9.1.11). Let for $n \geq 2$,

$$\lambda_n(t) = (1 - \alpha_n)t + \alpha_n t^2, \text{ where } \alpha_n = 1/[n - n^{-1}].$$

Then λ_n is a strictly increasing continuous function on [0,1] such that $\lambda_n(0) = 0$, $\lambda_n(\frac{1}{2} + \frac{1}{2}n^{-1}) = \frac{1}{2}$, $\lambda_n(1) = 1$, $f(\lambda_n(t)) = f_n(t)$, hence

$\sup_{0 \leqslant t \leqslant 1}|f_n(t) - f(\lambda_n(t))| = 0$, and

$\sup_{s \neq t, 0 \leqslant s \leqslant 1, 0 \leqslant t \leqslant 1}|\ln[(\lambda_n(t) - \lambda_n(s))/(t-s)]| = \ln(1+\alpha_n)$.

Thus, for the case (9.1.11) we have $\rho^0(f_n,f) = O(n^{-1})$, so that $f_n \to f$ in the Skorohod topology.

Having endowed D with the Skorohod metric ρ^0, we can now state the following version of theorem 9.1.4:

> *Theorem 9.1.5* Let Y_n be defined by (9.1.5), where the U_j's are independent random variables with zero mean and finite variance $\sigma^2 > 0$. Then $Y_n/\sigma \Rightarrow W$, where W is a Wiener process.

Proof: Billingsley (1968, theorem 16.1, p. 137)

9.2 Estimating an AR(1) model without intercept when the true data-generating process is a white-noise random walk

As a first application of the material in section 9.1 we consider the limiting distribution of the OLS estimator of the parameter α in the AR(1) model

$$Y_t = \alpha Y_{t-1} + U_t, \tag{9.2.1}$$

where

> *Assumption 9.2.1* The U_t's are i.i.d. and satisfy
>
> $E(U_t) = 0$, $E(U_t^2) = \sigma^2$, $E(|U_t|^{2+\delta}) < \infty$ for some $\delta > 0$.

If $|\alpha| < 1$ it is well known that under assumption 9.2.1 the OLS estimator

$$\alpha_n = \sum_{t=2}^{n} Y_t Y_{t-1} \Big/ \sum_{t=2}^{n} Y_{t-1}^2 \tag{9.2.2}$$

of α is asymptotically normally distributed:

$$\sqrt{n}(\alpha_n - \alpha) \to N(0, 1-\alpha^2). \tag{9.2.3}$$

If the true value of α equals one, then (9.2.3) is still valid, in the sense that then indeed $\sqrt{n}(\alpha_n - 1) \to 0$ in probability, hence $\sqrt{n}(\alpha_n - 1) \to N(0,0)$ in distr., but this result is of no help in making inference about α. As is shown by Fuller (1976) and Dickey and Fuller (1979), in the case $\alpha = 1$ we have that $n(\alpha_n\text{-}1)$ converges weakly (and in distribution) to a function of a Wiener process, namely:

Theorem 9.2.1 Let $\Delta Y_t = U_t$ and let assumption 9.2.1 hold. Then

$$n(\alpha - 1) \Rightarrow Z_1 = \frac{\frac{1}{2}(W(1)^2 - 1)}{\int_0^1 W(r)^2 dr}. \tag{9.2.4}$$

The limiting distribution Z_1 is tabulated in Fuller (1976, table 8.5.1, p.371). In particular,

$P(Z_1 < -8) \approx 0.05, P(Z_1 < -5.7) \approx 0.1.$

Fuller (1976) and Dickey and Fuller (1979) derive the result (9.2.4) in a rather complicated way. Here we shall follow the more transparant approach of Phillips (1987), using the results in section 9.1.

Proof of Theorem 9.2.1:
First, observe from (9.2.1) and (9.2.2) that

$$\alpha_n - 1 = \sum_{t=2}^n U_t Y_{t-1} / \sum_{t=2}^n Y_{t-1}^2. \tag{9.2.5}$$

Now consider the denominator in (9.2.5). For the case $\alpha = 1$ we have

$$\begin{aligned}\sum_{t=2}^n Y_{t-1}^2 &= \sum_{t=1}^n Y_t^2 - Y_n^2 = \sum_{t=1}^n (\sum_{j=1}^t U_j + Y_0)^2 - (\sum_{t=1}^n U_t + Y_0)^2 = \\ &\sum_{t=1}^n (\sum_{j=1}^t U_j)^2 + 2Y_0 \sum_{t=1}^n (\sum_{j=1}^t U_j) + nY_0^2 \\ &\qquad - (\sum_{t=1}^n U_t)^2 - 2Y_0 \sum_{t=1}^n U_t - Y_0^2 \\ &= n\sigma^2[\sum_{t=1}^n W_n(t/n)^2 - W_n(1)^2] \\ &\qquad + 2Y_0\sigma\sqrt{n}[\sum_{t=1}^n W_n(t/n) - W_n(1)] + (n-1)Y_0^2,\end{aligned} \tag{9.2.6}$$

where

$$\left.\begin{aligned} W_n(r) &= [1/(\sigma\sqrt{n})]\sum_{t=1}^{[rn]} U_t \text{ if } r \in [n^{-1},1], \\ W_n(r) &= 0 \text{ if } r \in [0,n^{-1}). \end{aligned}\right\} \tag{9.2.7}$$

Note that by theorem 9.1.5,

$$W_n \Rightarrow W, \tag{9.2.8}$$

with W a Wiener process. Moreover, for any Borel measurable real function f on R we have

$$\begin{aligned}\int_0^1 f(W_n(r))dr &= \sum_{t=0}^{n-1} \int_{t/n}^{(t+1)/n} f(W_n(r))dr = (1/n)\sum_{t=0}^{n-1} f[W_n(t/n))] \\ &= (1/n)\sum_{t=1}^n f[W_n(t/n)] + f(0)/n - f(W_n(1))/n.\end{aligned} \tag{9.2.9}$$

Since for continuous real functions f on R and functions g in D

$\Phi_f(g) = f(g(1))$ and $\Psi_f(g) = \int_0^1 f(g(r))dr$

are continuous real functions on D, it follows now from (9.2.8), (9.2.9), and the continuous mapping theorem 9.1.2 that

Lemma 9.2.1 Under assumption 9.2.1,

$$(1/n)\sum_{t=1}^{n} f[W_n(t/n)] = \int_0^1 f(W_n(r))dr + O_p(n^{-1}) \Rightarrow \int_0^1 f(W(r))dr$$

for any continuous real function f on R.

Application of this lemma (for $f(x) = x^2$ and $f(x) = x$, respectively) to the right-hand side of (9.2.6) yields:

Lemma 9.2.2 Let $\Delta Y_t = U_t$ and let assumption 9.2.1 hold. Then

$$(1/n^2)\sum_{t=2}^{n} Y_{t-1}^2 = \sigma^2 \int_0^1 W_n(r)^2 dr + O_p(1/\sqrt{n}) \Rightarrow \sigma^2 \int_0^1 W(r)^2 dr.$$

Note that the results in lemmas 9.2.1 and 9.2.2 involve random variables rather than random functions, so that in this case weak convergence is equivalent to convergence in distribution.

Next we consider the limiting distribution of the numerator on the right-hand side of (9.2.5). If $\alpha = 1$ we can write

$$\begin{aligned}
(1/n)\sum_{t=2}^{n} U_t Y_{t-1} &= (1/n)\sum_{t=2}^{n} U_t (Y_0 + \textstyle\sum_{j=1}^{t-1} U_j) \\
&= (1/n)\sum_{t=2}^{n} U_t \textstyle\sum_{j=1}^{t-1} U_j + Y_0 (1/n)\sum_{t=1}^{n} U_t - Y_0 U_1/n \\
&= (1/n)\sum_{t=2}^{n} U_t \textstyle\sum_{j=1}^{t-1} U_j + o_p(1) \\
&= \tfrac{1}{2}(1/n)\sum_{t=2}^{n} [(\textstyle\sum_{j=1}^{t} U_j)^2 - (\sum_{j=1}^{t-1} U_j)^2 - U_t^2] + o_p(1) \\
&= \tfrac{1}{2}(1/n)[\textstyle\sum_{j=1}^{n} U_j]^2 - \tfrac{1}{2}(1/n)\sum_{t=1}^{n} U_t^2 + o_p(1) \\
&= \tfrac{1}{2}\sigma^2 [W_n(1)^2 - (1/n)\textstyle\sum_{t=1}^{n} (U_t^2/\sigma^2)] + o_p(1) \\
&= \tfrac{1}{2}\sigma^2 [W_n(1)^2 - 1] + o_p(1),
\end{aligned} \qquad (9.2.10)$$

where the third and last equalities follow from the fact that by the weak law of large numbers,

$$(1/n)\sum_{t=1}^{n} U_t = o_p(1); \; (1/n)\sum_{t=1}^{n} (U_t^2/\sigma^2) = 1 + o_p(1).$$

Combining (9.2.8) and (9.2.10) now yields:

Lemma 9.2.3 Let $\Delta Y_t = U_t$ and let assumption 9.2.1 hold. Then

$$(1/n)\sum_{t=2}^{n} U_t Y_{t-1} = \tfrac{1}{2}\sigma^2 (W_n(1)^2 - 1) + o_p(1) \Rightarrow \tfrac{1}{2}\sigma^2 (W(1)^2 - 1).$$

Finally, denoting

$$X_n = [(1/n)\sum_{t=2}^{n} U_t Y_{t-1}, (1/n^2)\sum_{t=2}^{n} Y_{t-1}^2]',$$
$$X_n^* = \sigma^2 [\tfrac{1}{2}(W_n(1)^2 - 1), \int_0^1 W_n(r)^2 dr]',$$
$$X = \sigma^2 [\tfrac{1}{2}(W(1)^2 - 1), \int_0^1 W(r)^2 dr]',$$

lemmas 9.2.2 and 9.2.3 imply that

$X_n = X_n^* + o_p(1) \to X$ in distr.

In other words, the results of lemmas 9.2.2 and 9.2.3 hold jointly. Referring to one of the continuous mapping theorems 2.3.4 or 9.1.2, this result now proves theorem 9.2.1. Q.E.D.

Exercises:

1. Prove (9.2.3).
2. Calculate $P(Z_1 < 0)$, where Z_1 is defined in (9.2.4).
3. Suppose $U_t = V_t + \frac{1}{2}V_{t-1}$, where the V_t's are i.i.d. $N(0,\sigma^2)$ random variables. How will (9.2.4) change?

9.3 Estimating an AR(1) model with intercept when the true data-generating process is a white noise random walk

The test suggested by theorem 9.2.1 tests the null hypothesis H_0: $Y_t - Y_{t-1} = U_t$, with (U_t) a white-noise process, against the alternative that Y_t is a *zero mean* AR(1) process. However, if the true data-generating process is AR(1) with *nonzero mean* , i.e., $Y_t = c + \alpha Y_{t-1} + U_t$, $c \neq 0$, $|\alpha| < 1$, then the probability limit of the OLS estimate α_n defined by (9.2.2) is

$$\text{plim}_{n\to\infty}\alpha_n = E(Y_1Y_o)/E(Y_0^2) = \alpha + \frac{1+\alpha}{[(1+\alpha)/(1-\alpha)] + [\sigma^2/c^2]}. \qquad (9.3.1)$$

It is easy to see that the right-hand side of (9.3.1) approaches 1 if σ^2/c^2 approaches zero. Thus if c^2 is large, relative to σ^2, then α_n will be close to 1, even if α itself is not. Take for example the case $\alpha = 0.5$, $\sigma^2 = 1$, $c = 10$. Then $\text{plim}_{n\to\infty}\alpha_n \approx 0.998$, hence for large n, $n(\alpha_n - 1) \approx$ -0.002n. In order that this value is less than the 5 percent critical value -8, n should be at least 4000! This example therefore suggests including an intercept in the AR(1) model to be estimated, so that the OLS estimator of α now becomes:

$$\alpha_n = \textstyle\sum_{t=2}^n(Y_t - \bar{Y}_1)(Y_{t-1} - \bar{Y}_0) / \sum_{t=2}^n(Y_{t-1} - \bar{Y}_0)^2,$$
$$\text{with } \bar{Y}_0 = [1/(n-1)]\textstyle\sum_{t=2}^n Y_{t-1};\ \bar{Y}_1 = [1/(n-1)]\sum_{t=2}^n Y_t. \qquad (9.3.2)$$

Now let us assume again that the data-generating process is the random walk $\Delta Y_t = U_t$, where U_t satisfies assumption 9.2.1. Then similarly to (9.2.5) we can write

$$\alpha_n - 1 = \textstyle\sum_{t=2}^n U_t(Y_{t-1} - \bar{Y}_0) / \sum_{t=2}^n(Y_{t-1} - \bar{Y}_0)^2$$
$$= (\textstyle\sum_{t=2}^n U_tY_{t-1} - \bar{Y}_0\sum_{t=2}^n U_t)/[(\sum_{t=2}^n Y_{t-1}^2) - (n-1)\bar{Y}_0^2]. \qquad (9.3.3)$$

Now observe that

$$\begin{aligned}(n-1)\bar{Y}_0 &= \textstyle\sum_{t=2}^{n} Y_{t-1} = \sum_{t=2}^{n} Y_t - Y_n \\ &= \textstyle\sum_{t=1}^{n}(\sum_{j=1}^{t} U_j + Y_0) - (\sum_{j=1}^{n} U_j + Y_0) \\ &= \sigma n\sqrt{n}(1/n)\textstyle\sum_{t=2}^{n} W_n(t/n) - \sigma\sqrt{n}W_n(1) + (n-1)Y_0,\end{aligned}$$

hence by (9.2.8) and lemma 9.2.1 we have:

Lemma 9.3.1 Let $\Delta Y_t = U_t$ and let assumption 9.2.1 hold. Then

$$\bar{Y}_0/\sqrt{n} = \sigma\int_0^1 W_n(r)dr + O_p(1/\sqrt{n}) \Rightarrow \sigma\int_0^1 W(r)dr.$$

From this lemma it easily follows:

Lemma 9.3.2 Let $\Delta Y_t = U_t$ and let assumption 9.2.1 hold. Then

$$\bar{Y}_0\textstyle\sum_{t=2}^{n} U_t/n = \sigma^2 W_n(1)\int_0^1 W_n(r)dr + O_p(1/\sqrt{n}) \Rightarrow \sigma^2 W(1)\int_0^1 W(r)dr$$

and

$$(n-1)\bar{Y}_0^2/n^2 = \sigma^2\left(\int_0^1 W_n(r)dr\right)^2 + O_p(1/\sqrt{n}) \Rightarrow \sigma^2\left(\int_0^1 W(r)dr\right)^2.$$

Combining the results of lemmas 9.2.2 and 9.2.3 with the results in lemma 9.3.2 now yields:

Theorem 9.3.1 Let $\Delta Y_t = U_t$, let assumption 9.2.1 hold and let α_n now be defined by (9.3.2). Then

$$n(\alpha_n - 1) \Rightarrow Z_2 = \frac{\frac{1}{2}(W(1)^2 - 1) - W(1)\int_0^1 W(r)dr}{\int_0^1 W(r)^2 dr - \left(\int_0^1 W(r)dr\right)^2}. \tag{9.3.4}$$

Also the limiting distribution Z_2 is tabulated in Fuller (1976, table 8.5.1, p. 371). In particular,

$P(Z_2 < -14) \approx 0.05$, $P(Z_2 < -11.3) \approx 0.1$.

Exercises

1. Prove (9.3.1).
2. Suppose $U_t = V_t - \frac{1}{2}V_{t-1}$, where the V_t's are i.i.d. $N(0,\sigma^2)$ random variables. How will (9.3.4) change?

9.4 Relaxing the white-noise assumption

9.4.1 The augmented Dickey–Fuller test

The condition that the errors of the AR(1) model (9.2.1) are white noise (assumption 9.2.1) is, of course, too restrictive for econometric applications. In practice we much more often encounter time series that are better approximated by an ARIMA(p,1,q) model than by the ARIMA(0,1,0) model considered in the previous two sections. Since under fairly general conditions an ARIMA (p,1,q) model can be written as an ARIMA(∞,1,0) model, and the latter can be approximated by an ARIMA(k,1,0) model, with k possibly increasing with the sample size, Said and Dickey (1984) proposed basing a test on the OLS estimate α_n of the parameter α in the model:

$$Y_t = c + \alpha Y_{t-1} + \beta_1 \Delta Y_{t-1} + \ldots + \beta_k \Delta Y_{t-k} + U_t,$$

with $(1 - \beta_1 L - \ldots - \beta_k L^k)$ a lag polynomial with roots all outside the unit circle. They showed that if $k \to \infty$ at rate $o(n^{1/3})$ then the *t*-test statistic of the hypothesis $\alpha = 1$ has the same limiting distribution as in the case $\beta_i = 0$, U_t is white noise. The latter distribution is tabulated in Fuller (1976). However, we shall not discuss this result further, but focus on the Phillips (1987) and Phillips–Perron (1988) tests, because the latter tests require less distributional assumptions.

9.4.2 The Phillips and Phillips–Perron tests

Phillips (1987) and Phillips and Perron (1988) propose to test the null hypothesis

$$H_0: \Delta Y_t = U_t,$$

where (U_t) is a zero mean mixing process rather than white noise (cf. assumption 9.2.1):

Assumption 9.4.1.

(a) $E(U_t) = 0$ for all t;

(b) $\sup_t E(|U_t|^\beta) < \infty$ for some $\beta > 2$;

(c) $\sigma^2 = \lim_{n\to\infty} E\{[(1/\sqrt{n})\sum_{t=1}^n U_t]^2\}$ exists and $\sigma^2 > 0$;

(d) $\sigma_u^2 = \lim_{n\to\infty}(1/n)\sum_{t=1}^n E[(U_t)^2]$ exists and $\sigma_u^2 > 0$;

(e) $\{U_t\}$ is α-mixing with mixing coefficients $\alpha(s)$ satisfying $\sum_{s=1}^\infty \alpha(s)^{1-2/\beta} < \infty$.

Note that in general $\sigma^2 \neq \sigma_u^2$, i.e.,

$$\sigma^2 = \sigma_u^2 + 2.\lim_{n\to\infty}(1/n)\sum_{t=2}^n \sum_{j=1}^{t-1} E(U_t U_j).$$

Moreover, note that assumption 9.4.1 allows for a fair amount of heterogeneity.

The main difference between the Phillips and the Phillips–Perron test is that Phillips (1987) considers the alternative

$$H_1\colon Y_t = \alpha_1 Y_{t-1} + U_t,\ |\alpha_1| < 1, \tag{9.4.1}$$

whereas Phillips and Perron (1988) consider the alternative

$$H_1\colon Y_t = c + \alpha_2 Y_{t-1} + U_t,\ |\alpha_2| < 1. \tag{9.4.2}$$

where in both cases the U_t satisfy assumption 9.4.1.

Phillips (1987) and Phillips–Perron (1988) now use Herrndorf's (1984) functional central limit theorem for mixing processes:

> *Lemma 9.4.1* Let W_n be defined by (9.2.7), with U_t satisfying assumption 9.4.1. Then $W_n \Rightarrow W$, with W a Wiener process.

Moreover, we have

> *Lemma 9.4.2* Under Assumption 9.4.1, $\text{plim}_{n\to\infty}(1/n)\sum_{t=1}^{n} U_t^2 = \sigma_u^2$.

Proof: Exercise for the reader.

Now replacing in section 9.2 the references to assumption 9.2.1 by references to assumption 9.4.1, the only change we have to make is in (9.2.10) and consequently in lemma 9.2.3. Due to lemma 9.4.1 the last equality in (9.2.10) now becomes:

$$\begin{aligned} &\tfrac{1}{2}\sigma^2[W_n(1)^2 - (1/n)\textstyle\sum_{t=1}^{n}(U_t^2/\sigma^2)] + o_p(1) \\ &\qquad = \tfrac{1}{2}\sigma^2[W_n(1)^2 - \sigma_u^2/\sigma^2] + o_p(1), \end{aligned}$$

hence lemma 9.2.3 becomes:

> *Lemma 9.4.3* Let $\Delta Y_t = U_t$ and let assumption 9.4.1 hold. Then
>
> $$\begin{aligned} (1/n)\textstyle\sum_{t=2}^{n} U_t Y_{t-1} &= \tfrac{1}{2}\sigma^2[W_n(1)^2 - \sigma_u^2/\sigma^2] + o_p(1) \\ &\Rightarrow \tfrac{1}{2}\sigma^2[W(1)^2 - \sigma_u^2/\sigma^2]. \end{aligned}$$

Also the lemmas in section 9.3 carry over. In view of the result in lemma 9.4.3 we can now restate theorems 9.2.1 and 9.3.1 as follows:

> *Theorem 9.4.1* Let α_{1n} and α_{2n} be the OLS estimators of the parameters α_1 and α_2 in the auxiliary regressions (9.4.1) and (9.4.2), respectively. Moreover, let $\Delta Y_t = U_t$ with U_t obeying assumption 9.4.1. Then
>
> $$n(\alpha_{1n} - 1) \Rightarrow Z_1^* = \frac{\frac{1}{2}[W(1)^2 - \sigma_u^2/\sigma^2]}{\int_0^1 W(r)^2 dr}. \tag{9.4.3}$$

and

$$n(\alpha_{2n} - 1) \Rightarrow Z_2^* = \frac{\frac{1}{2}[W(1)^2 - \sigma_u^2/\sigma^2] - W(1)\int_0^1 W(r)dr}{\int_0^1 W(r)^2 dr - (\int_0^1 W(r)dr)^2}. \quad (9.4.4)$$

The problem now arises that the distributions of Z_1^* and Z_2^* depend on the unknown variance ratio σ_u^2/σ^2. In order to solve this problem, let us *assume* for the moment that we have a consistent estimator $\hat{\sigma}^2$ of σ^2, and choose

$$\hat{\sigma}_u^2 = (1/(n-1))\sum_{t=2}^n e_t^2 \quad (9.4.5)$$

as a consistent estimator of σ_u^2, where the e_t's are the OLS residuals of the auxiliary regression (9.4.1) in the case of the Phillips test and auxiliary regression (9.4.2) in the case of the Phillips–Perron test. The consistency of $\hat{\sigma}_u^2$ under H_0 follows straightforwardly from lemma 9.4.2 and theorem 9.4.1. It now follows easily from lemmas 9.2.2 and 9.3.1 (with assumption 9.2.1 replaced by assumption 9.4.1) that under H_0 and assumption 9.4.1,

$$\frac{\frac{1}{2}(\hat{\sigma}^2 - \hat{\sigma}_u^2)}{(1/n^2)\sum_{t=1}^n Y_t^2} \Rightarrow \frac{\frac{1}{2}(1 - \sigma_u^2/\sigma^2)}{\int_0^1 W(r)^2 dr} \quad (9.4.6)$$

and

$$\frac{\frac{1}{2}(\hat{\sigma}^2 - \hat{\sigma}_u^2)}{(1/n^2)\sum_{t=1}^n (Y_t - \bar{Y})^2} \Rightarrow \frac{\frac{1}{2}(1 - \sigma_u^2/\sigma^2)}{\int_0^1 W(r)^2 dr - (\int_0^1 W(r)dr)^2} \quad (9.4.7)$$

where $\bar{Y} = (1/n)\sum_{t=1}^n Y_t$. Hence, denoting

$$Z_{1n} = n(\alpha_{1n} - 1) - \frac{\frac{1}{2}(\hat{\sigma}^2 - \hat{\sigma}_u^2)}{(1/n^2)\sum_{t=1}^n Y_t^2} \quad (9.4.8)$$

$$Z_{2n} = n(\alpha_{2n} - 1) - \frac{\frac{1}{2}(\hat{\sigma}^2 - \hat{\sigma}_u^2)}{(1/n^2)\sum_{t=1}^n (Y_t - \bar{Y})^2} \quad (9.4.9)$$

we then have:

Theorem 9.4.2 Let $\hat{\sigma}^2$ be a consistent estimator of σ^2. Under the null hypothesis $\Delta Y_t = U_t$ with U_t obeying assumption 9.4.1, we have $Z_{in} \Rightarrow Z_i$, $i=1,2$, where Z_{1n} and Z_{2n} are defined in (9.4.8) and (9.4.9), and Z_1 and Z_2 are defined in theorems 9.2.1 and 9.3.1.

The statistics Z_{1n} and Z_{2n} are now the test statistics of the Phillips and Phillips–Perron unit root tests, respectively. Next, consider the case that Y_t is stationary. Since

$$\text{plim}_{n\to\infty} \frac{\hat{\sigma}_u^2}{(1/n)\sum_{t=1}^n Y_t^2} \leq 1 \text{ in the case (9.4.1)}, \tag{9.4.10}$$

$$\text{plim}_{n\to\infty} \frac{\hat{\sigma}_u^2}{(1/n)\sum_{t=1}^n (Y_t - \bar{Y})^2} \leq 1 \text{ in the case (9.4.2)}, \tag{9.4.11}$$

it follows easily

Theorem 9.4.3 Let $\hat{\sigma}^2$ be a consistent estimator of σ^2. Under the alternative hypotheses (9.4.1) and (9.4.2) respectively, with U_t obeying assumption 9.4.1, we have: $\text{plim}_{n\to\infty} Z_{in}/n < 0$, hence $\text{plim}_{n\to\infty} Z_{in} = -\infty$ $(i=1,2)$.

In other words, the tests involved are consistent. Note that the inequalities (9.4.10) and (9.4.11) and theorem 9.4.3 do not necessarily hold if $\hat{\sigma}_u^2$ would have been based on $Y_t - Y_{t-1}$ rather than on the OLS residuals of the auxiliary regressions (9.4.1) and (9.4.2).

Exercises
1. Prove (9.4.10) and (9.4.11).
2. Prove theorem 9.4.3.

9.5 The Newey–West estimator of σ^2

Phillips (1987) and Phillips–Perron (1988) propose to estimate σ^2 by the following Newey–West (1987) type estimator:

$$\hat{\sigma}^2 = \hat{\sigma}_u^2 + 2[1/(n-1)]\sum_{j=1}^{m_n} w_j(m_n)\sum_{t=j+2}^{n} e_t e_{t-j}, \tag{9.5.1}$$

where

$$w_j(m) = 1 - j/(m+1) \tag{9.5.2}$$

and m_n is chosen such that $m_n = o(n^{1/4})$. This estimator has the advantage over the White–Domowitz (1984) estimator (which is equal to (9.5.1) with $w_j(m) = 1$) that it is a.s. non-negative.

In the discussion of the Newey–West estimator it is convenient to drop the subscript of m_n and to assume that Y_0 is observable, so that (9.5.1) then becomes:

$$\hat{\sigma}^2 = \hat{\gamma}(0) + 2\sum_{i=1}^{m} w_i(m)\hat{\gamma}(i), \tag{9.5.3}$$

where for $i=0,1,2,\ldots$,

$$\hat{\gamma}(i) = (1/n)\sum_{t=1+i}^{n} e_{t-i}e_t. \tag{9.5.4}$$

Similarly, denote

$$\tilde{\sigma}^2 = \tilde{\gamma}(0) + 2\sum_{i=1}^{m} w_i(m)\gamma(i), \tag{9.5.5}$$

with

$$\tilde{\gamma}(i) = (1/n)\sum_{t=1+1}^{n} U_{t-i}U_t. \tag{9.5.6}$$

> *Theorem 9.5.1* Let $\Delta Y_t = U_t$ and let assumption 9.4.1 hold. Then $\hat{\sigma}^2 - \tilde{\sigma}^2 = O_p(m\sqrt{m/n})$.

Proof: We prove the theorem only for the case that U_t is strictly stationary and e_t is the residual of the auxiliary regression (9.4.1). Substituting $e_t = U_t - (\alpha_{1n} - 1)Y_{t-1}$ yields

$$\begin{aligned}(\hat{\gamma}(i) - \tilde{\gamma}(i))/(\alpha_{1n} - 1) &= -(1/n)\sum_{t=1+i}^{n} U_{t-i}Y_{t-1} \\ &\quad -(1/n)\sum_{t=1+i}^{n} Y_{t-i-1}U_t + (\alpha_{1n} - 1)(1/n)\sum_{t=1+i}^{n} Y_{t-i-1}Y_{t-1} \\ &= -(1/n)\sum_{t=1+i}^{n} U_{t-i}(Y_{t-1} - Y_{t-i-1}) \\ &\quad -(1/n)\sum_{t=1+i}^{n} U_{t-i}Y_{t-i-1} - (1/n)\sum_{t=1+i}^{n} (Y_{t-i-1} - Y_{t-1})U_t \\ &\quad -(1/n)\sum_{t=1+i}^{n} Y_{t-1}U_t + (\alpha_{1n} - 1)(1/n)\sum_{t=1+i}^{n} Y_{t-i-1}Y_{t-1}.\end{aligned} \tag{9.5.7}$$

It follows easily from (9.2.10) that for $i \leq m$ and $m = o(n)$,

$$(1/n)\sum_{t=1+i}^{n} U_{t-i}Y_{t-i-1} = (1/n)\sum_{t=1}^{n-i} U_tY_{t-1} = O_p(1) \tag{9.5.8}$$

and similarly,

$$(1/n)\sum_{t=1+i}^{n} U_tY_{t-1} = O_p(1). \tag{9.5.9}$$

Moreover, it is easy to verify that for some constant M, not depending on t and i, $E[|U_{t-i}(Y_{t-1} - Y_{t-i-1})|] \leq Mi^{1/2}$, hence for $i \leq m$,

$$(1/n)\sum_{t=1+i}^{n} U_{t-i}(Y_{t-1} - Y_{t-i-1}) = O_p(\sqrt{m}), \tag{9.5.10}$$

and similarly

$$(1/n)\sum_{t=1+i}^{n} (Y_{t-i-1} - Y_{t-1})U_t = O_p(\sqrt{m}). \tag{9.5.11}$$

Furthermore, using the Cauchy–Schwarz inequality and lemma 9.2.2 it follows easily that

$$(1/n)\sum_{t=1+i}^{n} Y_{t-i-1}Y_{t-1} \leq (1/n)\sum_{t=1}^{n} Y_t^2 = O_p(n). \tag{9.5.12}$$

Finally, under H_0 we have:

$$\alpha_{1n} - 1 = O_p(1/n). \tag{9.5.13}$$

Combining (9.5.7)–(9.5.13) now yields:

$$\max_{0\leq i\leq m}|\hat{\gamma}(i) - \tilde{\gamma}(i)| = O_p(n^{-1}\surd m), \tag{9.5.14}$$

from which the theorem easily follows. Q.E.D.

Theorem 9.5.2 Under assumption 9.4.1, $\tilde{\sigma}^2 = \tilde{\tilde{\sigma}}^2 + O_p(m^2/n)$, where $\tilde{\tilde{\sigma}}^2 = (1/n)\sum_{t=1}^{n-m+1}[(1/\surd m)\sum_{j=0}^{m-1} U_{t+j}]^2$.

Proof: Exercise 2.

Theorem 9.5.3 Under assumption 9.4.1, strict stationarity and the condition $m \to \infty$ at rate $o(\surd n)$, $\text{plim}_{n\to\infty}\tilde{\tilde{\sigma}}^2 = \sigma^2$.

Proof: We can write $\tilde{\tilde{\sigma}}^2 = (1/n)\sum_{t=1}^{n} V_t(m)$, where

$$V_t(m) = [(1/\surd m)\sum_{j=0}^{m-1} U_{t-j}]^2 \text{ if } t \geq m;\ V_t(m) = 0 \text{ if } t < m. \tag{9.5.15}$$

Now for fixed m, $V_t(m)$ is an α-mixing process with mixing coefficient $\alpha_m(j) = \alpha(j-m)$ if $j \geq m$, $\alpha_m(j) = 1$ if $j < m$, and so is $V_t(m)I[V_t(m)\leq K]$ for $K > 0$, where I(.) is the indicator function. It follows now from (6.2.3), Holder's inequality and theorem 6.2.1 (with $r = \infty$) that for some constant c,

$$\text{cov}\{V_{t+j}(m)I[V_{t+j}(m)\leq K],\ V_t(m)I[V_t(m)\leq K]\} \leq cK\alpha_m(j)^{1/2}. \tag{9.5.16}$$

hence

$$\text{var}\{(1/n)\sum_{t=1}^{n} V_t(m)I[V_t(m)\leq K]\} \leq (1/n)K^2 + cKm/n$$
$$+ cK(1/n)\sum_{j=m}^{n}\alpha(j-m)^{1/2} = O(K^2/n + mK/n). \tag{9.5.17}$$

Thus if $K = o(\surd n)$ and $m = o(\surd n)$, then

$$\text{plim}_{n\to\infty}(1/n)\sum_{t=1}^{n}\left(V_t(m)I[V_t(m)\leq K] - E\{V_t(m)I[V_t(m)\leq K]\}\right) = 0. \tag{9.5.18}$$

Next, define for fixed K,

$$f_K(x) = x \text{ if } 0 \leq x \leq K,\ f_K(x) = 0 \text{ if } x < 0,\ f_K(x) = K \text{ if } x > K. \tag{9.5.19}$$

Since $V_1(m) \Rightarrow \sigma^2 W(1)^2$ if $m \to \infty$, it follows from the continuous mapping theorem (theorem 9.1.2) that $f_K(V_1(m)) \Rightarrow f_K(\sigma^2 W(1)^2)$, hence by the dominated convergence theorem and strict stationarity,

$$E[f_K(V_t(m))] \to E[f_K(\sigma^2 W(1)^2)] \text{ if } m \to \infty, \tag{9.5.20}$$

uniformly in t. Moreover, by assumption we have

$$E[V_t(m)] \to \sigma^2 \text{ if } m \to \infty, \tag{9.5.21}$$

uniformly in t. Combining (9.5.19)-(9.5.21) yields

$$E\{V_t(m)I[V_t(m) > K]\} \to E\{\sigma^2 W(1)^2 I[\sigma^2 W(1)^2 > K]\} \text{ if } m \to \infty, \tag{9.5.22}$$

for fixed K, uniformly in t, hence

$$E\{V_t(m)I[V_t(m) > K]\} \to 0 \text{ if } m \to \infty \text{ and } K \to \infty. \tag{9.5.23}$$

Combining (9.5.18) and (9.5.23), the theorem follows. Q.E.D.

Combining theorems 9.5.1–9.5.3 now yields:

> *Theorem 9.5.4* Under assumption 9.4.1, strict stationarity and the condition $m \to \infty$ at rate $o(\sqrt{n})$, the Newey–West estimator (9.5.3) is consistent: $\text{plim}_{n\to\infty}\hat{\sigma}^2 = \sigma^2$.

Note that this result (and its proof) differs from the original result of Newey and West in that here $m = o(\sqrt{n})$ rather than $m = o(n^{1/4})$. However, Andrews (1991) following different lines arrives at the same conclusion as theorem 9.5.4.

Finally, one may wonder why we have not based the Newey–West estimator involved on $\Delta Y_t = U_t$ directly rather than on the OLS residuals e_t. The reason is that if we replace e_t by ΔY_t then under the stationarity hypothesis, $\text{plim}_{n\to\infty}\hat{\sigma}^2 = 0$. Consequently, $\text{plim}_{n\to\infty}Z_{in}/n$ would then be less negative than in the case of a residual-based Newey–West estimator, and therefore the tests would have less power.

Exercises

1. Prove theorem 9.5.1 for the case that the e_t's are the residuals of the auxiliary regression (9.4.2).
2. Prove theorem 9.5.2.
3. Suppose that the Y_t's are i.i.d. $N(0,\sigma^2)$. Let Z_{1n}^* be the test statistic Z_{1n} with $\hat{\sigma}^2$ and $\hat{\sigma}_u^2$ based on $Y_t - Y_{t-1}$ rather than on the OLS residuals, e_t, of auxiliary regression (9.4.1). Show that $\text{plim}_{n\to\infty}Z_{1n}/n < \text{plim}_{n\to\infty}Z_{1n}^*/n < 0$.

9.6 Unit root versus deterministic trend

We have seen that the Phillips test has low power against the alternative $Y_t = \alpha Y_{t-1} + c + U_t$, $|\alpha| < 1$, (cf. (9.4.2)) if c^2/σ^2 is large. However, the

Phillips–Perron test will suffer from a similar problem, namely in the case that the true data-generating process is of the type

$$H_1: Y_t = \alpha Y_{t-1} + \beta t + \gamma + U_t \tag{9.6.1}$$

with $|\alpha| < 1, \beta \neq 0$ and U_t satisfying assumption 9.4.1. Take for example the case $Y_t = \beta t + \gamma + \varepsilon_t$; $\varepsilon_t \sim$ NID(0,1), with $\beta \neq 0$. Then it is easy to verify that the OLS estimator α_{2n} of the parameter α_2 in model (9.4.2) satisfies $n(\alpha_{2n} - 1) = o_p(1)$, hence the Dickey–Fuller test in section 9.3 and the Phillips–Perron test in section 9.4 will have no power against this alternative. In order to cover this case as well, Dickey and Fuller (1979, 1981) also propose a test of the null hypothesis $\alpha = 1, \beta = \gamma = 0$ in model (9.6.1) with (U_t) white noise. Phillips and Perron (1988) modified this test for the case of mixing (U_t).

In deriving this test it is convenient to rewrite model (9.6.1) as

$$Y_t = \theta' X_t + U_t, \text{ where } X_t = (Y_{t-1},t,1)'; \ \theta = (\alpha,\beta,\gamma)'. \tag{9.6.2}$$

Again the null hypothesis to be tested is that $\Delta Y_t = U_t$, where (U_t) satisfies assumption 9.4.1. Clearly, under H_0 we have $\theta = (1,0,0)'$. The OLS estimator $\theta_n = (\alpha_n,\beta_n,\gamma_n)'$ of θ satisfies

$$\theta_n - \theta = (\alpha_n - 1,\beta_n,\gamma_n)' = [\textstyle\sum_{t=2}^n X_t X_t']^{-1}\sum_{t=2}^n X_t U_t$$

$$= \begin{pmatrix} \sum_{t=2}^n Y_{t-1}^2 & \sum_{t=2}^n tY_{t-1} & \sum_{t=2}^n Y_{t-1} \\ \sum_{t=2}^n tY_{t-1} & \sum_{t=2}^n t^2 & \sum_{t=2}^n t \\ \sum_{t=2}^n Y_{t-1} & \sum_{t=2}^n t & n-1 \end{pmatrix}^{-1} \begin{pmatrix} \sum_{t=2}^n Y_{t-1}U_t \\ \sum_{t=2}^n tU_t \\ \sum_{t=2}^n U_t \end{pmatrix}. \tag{9.6.3}$$

Most of the partial sums in (9.6.3) involving Y_t and U_t have been encountered before, except $\sum_{t=2}^n tY_{t-1}$ and $\sum_{t=2}^n tU_t$. Their limiting behavior under H_0 is derived in the following two lemmas.

Lemma 9.6.1 Let $\Delta Y_t = U_t$ and let assumption 9.4.1 hold. Then

$$[1/(n^2\sqrt{n})]\textstyle\sum_{t=2}^n tY_{t-1} = \sigma\int_0^1 rW_n(r)dr + O_p(1/\sqrt{n}) \Rightarrow \sigma\int_0^1 rW(r)dr.$$

Proof: The lemma follows from the following equalities:

$$\begin{aligned}
[1/(n^2\sqrt{n})]\textstyle\sum_{t=2}^n tY_{t-1} &= [1/(n^2\sqrt{n})]\textstyle\sum_{t=1}^{n-1}(t+1)Y_t \\
&= [1/(n^2\sqrt{n})]\textstyle\sum_{t=1}^{n-1}tY_t + [1/(n^2\sqrt{n})]\sum_{t=1}^{n-1}Y_t \\
&= [1/(n^2\sqrt{n})]\textstyle\sum_{t=1}^{n-1}t(Y_0 + \sum_{j=1}^t U_j) \\
&\quad + [1/(n^2\sqrt{n})]\textstyle\sum_{t=1}^{n-1}(Y_0 + \sum_{j=1}^t U_j) \\
&= [1/(n^2\sqrt{n})]\textstyle\sum_{t=1}^{n-1}t[Y_0 + \sigma\sqrt{n}W_n(t/n)] \\
&\quad + [1/(n^2\sqrt{n})]\textstyle\sum_{t=1}^{n-1}[Y_0 + \sigma\sqrt{n}W_n(t/n)] \\
&= [1/(n^2\sqrt{n})]\textstyle\sum_{t=1}^{n-1}tY_0 + \sigma(1/n^2)\sum_{t=1}^{n-1}tW_n(t/n)
\end{aligned}$$

$$+ [1/(n^2\sqrt{n})]\textstyle\sum_{t=1}^{n-1} Y_0 + \sigma(1/n^2)\sum_{t=1}^{n-1} W_n(t/n)$$
$$= \sigma(1/n^2)\textstyle\sum_{t=1}^{n-1} tW_n(t/n) + O_p(1/\sqrt{n}),$$

and

$$\int_0^1 rW_n(r)dr = \textstyle\sum_{t=0}^{n-1}\int_{t/n}^{(t+1)/n} rW_n(r)dr = (1/n)\sum_{t=0}^{n-1} W_n(t/n)\int_{t/n}^{(t+1)/n} rdr$$
$$= (1/n)\textstyle\sum_{t=0}^{n-1} W_n(t/n)[(t/n) + \tfrac{1}{2}n^{-2}]$$
$$= (1/n^2)\textstyle\sum_{t=0}^{n-1} tW_n(t/n)) + \tfrac{1}{2}n^{-2}\int_0^1 W_n(r)dr. \qquad \text{Q.E.D.}$$

Lemma 9.6.2 Let assumption 9.4.1 hold. Then

$$[1/(n\sqrt{n})]\textstyle\sum_{t=2}^{n} tU_t = \sigma W_n(1) - \sigma\int_0^1 W_n(r)dr + O_p[1/(n\sqrt{n})]$$
$$\Rightarrow \sigma W(1) - \sigma\textstyle\int_0^1 W(r)dr.$$

Proof: This lemma is a straightforward corollary of the following more general lemma:

Lemma 9.6.3 Let F be a differentiable real function on [0,1] with derivative f, let (x_t) be an arbitrary sequence in R and let $S_n(r) = \sum_{t=1}^{[rn]} x_t$ if $r \in [n^{-1},1]$; $S_n(r) = 0$ if $r \in [0,n^{-1})$. Then $\sum_{t=1}^{n} F(t/n)x_t = F(1)S_n(1) - \int_0^1 f(r)S_n(r)dr$.

Proof: Without loss of generality we may assume that F is constant on $(1,\infty)$, so that $F(x) = F(1)$ for $x > 1$. Now observe that

$$\textstyle\sum_{t=1}^{n}\{F[(t+1)/n]-F[t/n]\}S_n(t/n) = \sum_{t=0}^{n-1}\{F[(t+1)/n]-F[t/n]\}S_n(t/n)$$
$$= \textstyle\sum_{t=0}^{n-1}\int_{t/n}^{(t+1)/n} f(x)S_n(x)dx = \int_0^1 f(x)S_n(x)dx.$$

Moreover, by rearranging terms it easily follows that:

$$\textstyle\sum_{t=1}^{n}\{F[(t+1)/n]-F[t/n]\}S_n(t/n) = \sum_{t=1}^{n}\{F[(t+1)/n]-F[t/n]\}\sum_{j=1}^{t} x_j$$
$$= \textstyle\sum_{t=1}^{n}\sum_{j=t}^{n}\{F[(j+1)/n]-F[j/n]\}x_t = \sum_{t=1}^{n}[F(1+n^{-1})-F(t/n)]x_t$$
$$= F(1+n^{-1})\textstyle\sum_{j=1}^{n} x_j - \sum_{t=1}^{n} F(t/n)x_t = F(1)S_n(1) - \sum_{t=1}^{n} F(t/n)x_t.$$

Combining these results, the lemma follows. Q.E.D.

Denoting

$$\Gamma_n = \begin{pmatrix} n & 0 & 0 \\ 0 & n\sqrt{n} & 0 \\ 0 & 0 & \sqrt{n} \end{pmatrix},$$

it is now easy to verify that

$$\Gamma_n^{-1}(\textstyle\sum_{t=2}^{n} X_t X_t')\Gamma_n^{-1}$$

$$= \begin{pmatrix} (1/n^2)\sum_{t=2}^n Y_{t-1}^2 & [1/(n^2\sqrt{n})]\sum_{t=2}^n tY_{t-1} & [1/(n\sqrt{n})]\sum_{t=2}^n Y_{t-1} \\ [1/(n^2\sqrt{n})]\sum_{t=2}^n tY_{t-1} & (1/n^3)\sum_{t=2}^n t^2 & (1/n^2)\sum_{t=2}^n t \\ [1/(n\sqrt{n})]\sum_{t=2}^n Y_{t-1} & (1/n^2)\sum_{t=2}^n t & (n-1)/n \end{pmatrix}$$

$$= \begin{pmatrix} \sigma & 0 & 0 \\ 0 & 1 & 0 \\ 0 & 0 & 1 \end{pmatrix} \begin{pmatrix} \int_0^1 W_n(r)^2 dr & \int_0^1 rW_n(r)dr & \int_0^1 W_n(r)dr \\ \int_0^1 rW_n(r)dr & 1/3 & 1/2 \\ \int_0^1 W_n(r)dr & 1/2 & 1 \end{pmatrix} \begin{pmatrix} \sigma & 0 & 0 \\ 0 & 1 & 0 \\ 0 & 0 & 1 \end{pmatrix} + o_p(1).$$

$$\Gamma_n^{-1}\sum_{t=2}^n X_t U_t = \begin{pmatrix} (1/n)\sum_{t=2}^n Y_{t-1}U_t \\ [1/(n\sqrt{n})]\sum_{t=2}^n tU_t \\ (1/\sqrt{n})\sum_{t=2}^n U_t \end{pmatrix}$$

$$= \sigma \begin{pmatrix} \sigma & 0 & 0 \\ 0 & 1 & 0 \\ 0 & 0 & 1 \end{pmatrix} \begin{pmatrix} \frac{1}{2}(W_n(1)^2 - \sigma_u^2/\sigma^2) \\ W_n(1) - \int_0^1 W_n(r)dr \\ W_n(1) \end{pmatrix} + o_p(1).$$

Thus we have:

Theorem 9.6.1 Let $\Delta Y_t = U_t$ and let assumption 9.4.1 hold. Then the OLS estimators α_n, β_n, and γ_n of the parameters α, β, and γ of model (9.6.1) satisfy $[n(\alpha_n - 1), n\sqrt{n}\beta_n/\sigma, \sqrt{n}\gamma_n/\sigma]' \Rightarrow M^{-1}V$, where

$$M = \begin{pmatrix} \int_0^1 W(r)^2 dr & \int_0^1 rW(r)^2 dr & \int_0^1 W(r)dr \\ \int_0^1 rW(r)dr & 1/3 & 1/2 \\ \int_0^1 W(r)dr & 1/2 & 1 \end{pmatrix};$$

$$V = \begin{pmatrix} \frac{1}{2}(W(1)^2 - \sigma_u^2/\sigma^2) \\ W(1) - \int_0^1 W(r)dr \\ W(1) \end{pmatrix}.$$

Next we derive a more explicit expression for the limiting distribution of $n(\alpha_n - 1)$. Denote

$$X_1 = \int_0^1 W(r)^2 dr - (\int_0^1 W(r)dr)^2,$$

$$X_2 = \int_0^1 (r - ½)W(r)dr,$$

$$X_3 = \int_0^1 W(r)dr,$$

$$X_4 = X_1 - 12X_2^2 \ (= 12\det(M)).$$

Then

$$M^{-1} = X_4^{-1}\begin{pmatrix} 1 & -12X_2 & 6X_2 - X_3 \\ -12X_2 & 12X_1 & -6X_1 + 12X_2X_3 \\ 6X_2 - X_3 & -6X_1 - 12X_2X_3 & X_4 + 3X_1 - 12X_2X_3 + X_3^2 \end{pmatrix}$$

and

$$V = \begin{pmatrix} \frac{1}{2}(W(1)^2 - 1) \\ W(1) - X_3 \\ W(1) \end{pmatrix} + \begin{pmatrix} \frac{1}{2}(1 - \sigma_u^2) \\ 0 \\ 0 \end{pmatrix}.$$

Hence we have:

$$n(\alpha_n - 1) \Rightarrow \frac{\frac{1}{2}(W(1)^2 - 1) - W(1)(6X_2 + X_3) + 12X_2X_3}{X_4} + \frac{\frac{1}{2}(1 - \sigma_u^2/\sigma^2)}{X_4}$$

This result can be restated as:

Theorem 9.6.2 Let $\Delta Y_t = U_t$ and let assumption 9.4.1 hold. Then the OLS estimator α_n of the parameter α in model (9.6.1) satisfies

$$n(\alpha_n - 1) \Rightarrow Z_3 + \frac{\sigma^2 - \sigma_u^2}{24\sigma^2 \det(M)}$$

where

$$Z_3 = \frac{\frac{1}{2}(W(1)^2 - 1) - 2W(1)\int_0^1 (3r - 1)W(r)dr + 6\int_0^1 (2r - 1)W(r)dr \int_0^1 W(r)dr}{12\det(M)}.$$

Note that the distribution of Z_3 is tabulated in Fuller (1976, table 8.5.1). In particular,

$P(Z_3 < -21.5) \approx 0.05$, $P(Z_3 < -18.1) \approx 0.1$.

Finally, observe that under H_0,

$\det[\Gamma_n{}^{-1}[\sum_{t=2}^n X_t X_t']\Gamma_n{}^{-1}] \Rightarrow \sigma^2 \det(M)$,

hence:

Theorem 9.6.3 Let $\Delta Y_t = U_t$ with U_t obeying assumption 9.4.1. Denote

$$Z_{3n} = n(\alpha_n - 1) - \frac{\hat{\sigma}^2 - \hat{\sigma}_u^2}{(24/n^6)\det(\sum_{t=2}^{n} X_t X_t')}$$

where α_n is the OLS estimator of the parameter α in model (9.6.1), and $\hat{\sigma}^2$ and $\hat{\sigma}_u^2$ are defined in (9.4.5) and (9.5.1), where the e_t's are the OLS residuals of the auxiliary regression (9.6.1). Then $Z_{3n} \Rightarrow Z_3$.

Along similar lines we can construct test statistics for the hypotheses $\beta = 0$ and $\gamma = 0$, and the joint hypothesis $\alpha = 1, \beta = \gamma = 0$.

Exercise

1. An alternative to the above test is to apply the Phillips test to the OLS residuals $\hat{e}_t$ of the auxiliary regression

   $Y_t = \beta t + \gamma + V_t$.

   Derive the asymptotic distribution of this alternative test statistic under the unit root hypothesis, and compare it with Z_3. (Hint: Denote

   $W_n^D(r) = \hat{e}_{[rn]}/(\sigma\sqrt{n})$ if $r \in [n^{-1},1]$; $W_n^D(r) = 0$ if $r \in [0,n^{-1}]$

   and show that $W_n^D \Rightarrow W^D$, with W^D a function of a Wiener process W [W^D is called the detrended Wiener process]. Then replace W in (9.4.3) by W^D.)

9.7 Introduction to cointegration

Consider a vector time series process $X_t \in R^k$ such that each component X_{it} is integrated of order one, i.e., each of the series X_{it} contains a unit root, but ΔX_{it} is a zero mean stationary process. Referring to the Wold decomposition theorem (cf. theorem 7.2.1), we may therefore write:

$$\Delta X_t = C(L)U_t = (\textstyle\sum_{j=0}^{\infty} C_j L^j)U_t = \sum_{j=0}^{\infty} C_j U_{t-j}, \quad (9.7.1)$$

where L is the lag operator, U_t is a k-variate white-noise process:

$$E(U_t) = 0,\ E(U_t U_t') = I,\ E(U_t U_{t-j}') = O \text{ for } j = 1,2,..., \quad (9.7.2)$$

and the coefficients matrices C_j are such that

$$\textstyle\sum_{j=0}^{\infty} C_j C_j' \text{ exists.} \quad (9.7.3)$$

Note that there is no loss of generality in assuming $E(U_t U_t') = I$. If $E(U_t U_t') = \Omega$, then one may replace U_t by $U_t^* = \Omega^{-1/2} U_t$ and the C_j's by $C_j \Omega^{-1/2}$. Moreover, note that (9.7.3) implies that

$$C(1) = \sum_{j=0}^{\infty} C_j \text{ exists.} \tag{9.7.4}$$

Denote $B(L) = C(L) - C(1)$. Then $B(1) = O$, hence all the elements of $B(L)$ have a unit root, and consequently we can write

$$C(L) = C(1) + (1-L)C^*(L). \tag{9.7.5}$$

Thus,

$$(1-L)X_t = C(1)U_t + (1-L)C^*(L)U_t.$$

Now assume that the matrix $C(1)$ is singular. Then there exists a nonzero vector α such that $\alpha' C(1) = 0'$. Denoting

$$Z_t = \alpha' X_t,$$

we then have

$$\begin{aligned}(1-L)Z_t = (1-L)\alpha' X_t &= \alpha' C(1)U_t + (1-L)\alpha' C^*(L)U_t \\ &= (1-L)\alpha' C^*(L)U_t,\end{aligned}$$

hence,

$$Z_t = \alpha' C^*(L)U_t.$$

Thus Z_t is stationary if $C^*(L)U_t$ is. A sufficient condition for the latter is that the elements of $C^*(L)$ are rational lag polynomials,

$$C^*(L) = [c^*_{ij}(L)], \text{ with } c^*_{ij}(L) = a^*_{ij}(L)/b^*_{ij}(L),$$

where $a^*_{ij}(L)$ and $b^*_{ij}(L)$ are finite lag polynomials with roots all outside the unit circle. In its turn a sufficient condition for this is that the elements of $C(L)$ are rational lag polynomials:

$C(L) = (c_{ij}(L))$, with $c_{ij}(L) = a_{ij}(L)/b_{ij}(L)$, where $a_{ij}(L)$ and $b_{ij}(L)$ are finite lag polynomials with roots all outside the unit circle. (9.7.6)

Then

$$c_{ij}(L) - c_{ij}(1) = [a_{ij}(L) - a_{ij}(1)b_{ij}(L)/b_{ij}(1)]/b_{ij}(L) = d_{ij}(L)/b_{ij}(L),$$

say, where $d_{ij}(L)$ is a finite lag polynomial. Denoting the order of d_{ij} by m_{ij}, we can write

$$d_{ij}(L) = \Pi_{s=1}^{m_{ij}}(\delta_{ijs} - L),$$

where the δ_{ijs} are the roots of $d_{ij}(L)$. However, since by construction $d_{ij}(L)$ contains a unit root, one of the δ_{ijs} equals one, say $\delta_{ij1} = 1$. Then

$$C^*(L) = (c^*_{ij}(L)), \text{ with } c^*_{ij}(L) = \Pi_{s=2}^{m_{ij}}(\delta_{ijs} - L)/b_{ij}(L).$$

We may take α equal to an eigenvector of $C(1)'$ corresponding to a zero eigenvalue. Thus let A be the matrix of eigenvectors of C(1)' corresponding to the zero eigenvalues. Then $A'X_t$ is stationary.

Summarizing, we have shown:

> *Theorem 9.7.1* Let the k-variate time series process (X_t) be defined by (9.7.1)–(9.7.3) and (9.7.6). If $m = \text{rank}(C(1)) < k$ then there exists a $k \times (k-m)$ matrix A with rank $k-m$ such that $Z_t = A'X_t$ is stationary.

If C(1) is indeed singular then X_t is called a *cointegrated system*, and the columns of A are called the *cointegrated vectors.*

9.8 Error correction form of cointegrated systems

Following Engle (1987) and Engle and Yoo (1989), we show now how to write the model in autoregressive error correction form. Assume for simplicity that $\text{rank}(C(1)) = k-1$, so that there is only one cointegrated vector α. Without loss of generality we may normalize α as follows:

$$\alpha = (1,\alpha_2,\ldots,\alpha_k). \tag{9.8.1}$$

Now consider the matrix

$$\Phi = \begin{pmatrix} 1 & | & \alpha_2\ldots\alpha_k \\ \cdots & \text{ı} & \cdots\cdots\cdots \\ 0 & | & \\ \vdots & | & I_{k-1} \\ 0 & | & \end{pmatrix} = \begin{pmatrix} \alpha \\ \cdots \\ \Phi_* \end{pmatrix}, \text{ where } \Phi_* = [0, I_{k-1}]. \tag{9.8.2}$$

Denoting

$$V^{-1}(L) = \begin{pmatrix} \alpha' C^*(L) \\ \phi_* C(L) \end{pmatrix}, M(L) = \begin{pmatrix} 1-L & | & O' \\ \cdots\cdots & \text{ı} & \cdots \\ O & | & I_{k-1} \end{pmatrix}, \tag{9.8.3}$$

we can write

$$\Phi\Delta X_t = \begin{pmatrix} \alpha'\Delta X_t \\ \Phi_*\Delta X_t \end{pmatrix} = \begin{pmatrix} (1-L)\alpha' C^*(L) \\ \Phi_* C(L) \end{pmatrix} U_t =$$

$$= \begin{pmatrix} 1-L & | & 0' \\ \cdots\cdots & \text{ı} & \cdots \\ 0 & | & I_{k-1} \end{pmatrix} \begin{pmatrix} \alpha' C^*(L) \\ \Phi_* C(L) \end{pmatrix} U_t$$

$$= M(L)V^{-1}(L)U_t. \tag{9.8.4}$$

Next, denote

$$M^*(L) = \begin{pmatrix} 1 & | & O' \\ \cdots & | & \cdots\cdots\cdots\cdots \\ 0 & | & (1-L)I_{k-1} \end{pmatrix}, \tag{9.8.5}$$

so that $M^*(L)M(L) = (1-L)I_k$, and assume that $V^{-1}(L)$ is invertible, with inverse V(L). Then

$$(1-L)M^*(L)\Phi X_t = M^*(L)\Phi\Delta X_t = (1-L)V^{-1}(L)U_t, \tag{9.8.6}$$

hence

$$M^*(L)\Phi X_t = V^{-1}(L)U_t. \tag{9.8.7}$$

Denoting

$$A(L) = V(L)M^*(L)\Phi, \tag{9.8.8}$$

we now get the AR form of the model:

$$A(L)X_t = U_t. \tag{9.8.9}$$

Next, observe that

$$A(1) = V(1)M^*(1)\Phi$$

$$= V(1)\begin{pmatrix} 1 & | & 0' \\ \cdots & | & \cdots \\ 0 & | & O \end{pmatrix}\begin{pmatrix} 1 & | & \alpha_2..\alpha_k \\ \cdots & | & \cdots\cdots \\ 0 & | & \\ \cdot & | & I_{k-1} \\ \cdot & | & \\ 0 & | & \end{pmatrix} = V(1)\begin{pmatrix} 1 & | & \alpha_2..\alpha_k \\ \cdots & | & \cdots\cdots \\ 0 & | & \\ \cdot & | & O_{k-1} \\ \cdot & | & \\ 0 & | & \end{pmatrix} = \gamma\alpha', \tag{9.8.10}$$

where O_{k-1} is the $(k-1)\times(k-1)$ zero matrix and γ is the first column of V(1). Moreover, similarly to (9.7.5) we can write

$$A(L) = A(1)L + (1-L)A^*(L). \tag{9.8.11}$$

Combining (9.8.9), (9.8.10), and (9.8.11) now yields the error correction form of the model:

$$A^*(L)\Delta X_t + \gamma\alpha' X_{t-1} = U_t. \tag{9.8.12}$$

Note that the lag of X_t does not matter: replacing $A^*(L)$ by, say,

$$A^{**}(L) = A^*(L) + \textstyle\sum_{j=1}^{p-1}\gamma\alpha' L^j, \tag{9.8.13}$$

model (9.8.12) becomes

$$A^{**}(L)\Delta X_t + \gamma\alpha' X_{t-p} = U_t. \qquad (9.8.14)$$

The latter form is the one used by Johansen (1988), with $A^{**}(L)$ a $(p-1)$-order lag polynomial:

$$\Delta X_t = B_1\Delta X_{t-1} + \ldots + B_{p-1}\Delta X_{t-p+1} - \gamma\alpha' X_{t-p} + U_t. \qquad (9.8.15)$$

9.9 Estimation and testing of cointegrated systems

9.9.1 The Engle–Granger approach

Working in the context of a bivariate system with at most one cointegrated vector, Engle and Granger (1987) propose estimating the cointegrated vector $\alpha = (1, \alpha_2)'$ by regressing the first component X_{1t} of X_t on the second component X_{2t}, using OLS, and then testing whether the OLS residuals $\hat{Z}_t$ have a unit root, using the augmented Dickey–Fuller test of Said and Dickey (1984). However, since the latter test is conducted on estimated residuals, the tables of the critical values of this test in Fuller (1976) no longer apply. The correct critical values involved can be found in Engle and Yoo (1987).

If the test rejects the unit root hypothesis, and thus accepts the cointegration hypothesis, one may substitute for $\alpha' X_{t-1}$ in (9.8.12) the OLS residual $\hat{Z}_{t-1}$ and estimate the parameter matrices in $A^*(L)$ by OLS, assuming that $A^*(L)$ is a finite-order lag polynomial. Replacing α by its OLS estimate $\hat{\alpha} = (1, \hat{\alpha}_2)$ does not affect the asymptotic properties of the OLS estimators of the coefficients of $A^*(L)$, because $\hat{\alpha}_2$ is super consistent: $n(\hat{\alpha}_2 - \alpha_2) = O_p(1)$.

The above approach is only applicable if there is at most one cointegrated vector. Systems with dimension greater than two, however, may have multiple cointegrated vectors. In that case one may use the approach of Stock and Watson (1988), which is (more or less) a multivariate extension of the Engle–Granger approach and is related to Johansen's approach below. See Johansen (1991, sect.6).

9.9.2 Johansen's maximum likelihood approach

In a recent series of influential papers, Johansen (1988, 1991) and Johansen and Juselius (1990) propose an ingenious and practical full maximum likelihood (ML) estimation and testing approach. The basic idea is quite simple: assume that the process X_t is Gaussian, integrated of order 1, and observable for $t = 1,\ldots,n$. Moreover, assume that model (9.8.15), with α' and γ $r \times k$ matrices of rank $r \leq k$, represents the conditional expectation of ΔX_t relative to $X_{t-1}, X_{t-2}, \ldots$ Then the conditional distribution of ΔX_t, relative to $X_{t-1}, X_{t-2}, \ldots$, is k-variate normal:

$$\Delta X_t | X_{t-1}, X_{t-2}, \ldots \sim N_k(B_1 \Delta X_{t-1} + \ldots + B_{p-1} \Delta X_{t-p+1} - \gamma\alpha' X_{t-p}, \Lambda) \tag{9.9.1}$$

Consequently, the log-likelihood function takes the form

$$\begin{aligned} \ell(B_1,\ldots,B_{p-1},\alpha,\gamma,\Lambda) = & -\tfrac{1}{2} n \cdot \ln(\det \Lambda) \\ & -\tfrac{1}{2}\textstyle\sum_{t=p+1}^{n}(\Delta X_t + \gamma\alpha' X_{t-p} - \sum_{i=1}^{p-1} B_i \Delta X_{t-i})' \Lambda^{-1} \\ & \times(\Delta X_t + \gamma\alpha' X_{t-p} - \textstyle\sum_{i=1}^{p-1} B_i \Delta X_{t-i} + \text{rest}, \end{aligned} \tag{9.9.2}$$

where the rest term depends on the initial values $X_0, \ldots, X_{1-p}$ only. The actual parameter matrix of interest is α, so let us concentrate out the other parameter matrices. First, if α, γ, and Λ are assumed to be known the ML estimators of the matrices $B_1, \ldots, B_{p-1}$ can be obtained simply by regressing $\Delta X_t + \gamma\alpha' X_{t-p}$ on $\Delta X_{t-1}, \ldots, \Delta X_{t-p+1}$, using OLS. The residuals of this regression are $R_{0t} + \gamma\alpha' R_{pt}$, where

R_{0t} is the residual vector of the regression of ΔX_t on $\Delta X_{t-1}, \ldots, \Delta X_{t-p+1}$, and R_{tp} is the residual vector of the regression of X_{t-p} on $\Delta X_{t-1}, \ldots, \Delta X_{t-p+1}$. (9.9.3)

Thus the partially concentrated log-likelihood function, with only $B_1, \ldots, B_{p-1}$ concentrated out, is

$$\begin{aligned} \ell(\alpha,\gamma,\Lambda) = & -\tfrac{1}{2} n \cdot \ln(\det \Lambda) \\ & -\tfrac{1}{2}\textstyle\sum_{t=p+1}^{n}(R_{0t} + \gamma\alpha' R_{pt})' \Lambda^{-1}(R_{0t} + \gamma\alpha' R_{pt}) + \text{rest}. \end{aligned} \tag{9.9.4}$$

Similarly, we can concentrate γ out, given α and Λ, by regressing R_{0t} on $\alpha' R_{pt}$, which yields the estimate

$$\hat{\gamma}(\alpha) = -S_{0p}\alpha(\alpha' S_{pp}\alpha)^{-1}, \tag{9.9.5}$$

with

$$S_{ij} = (1/n)\textstyle\sum_{t=2}^{n} R_{it} R_{jt}', \quad i,j = 0,p. \tag{9.9.6}$$

Finally, we concentrate Λ out, given α, by substituting the well-known ML estimator of the variance matrix of a normal distribution with zero mean vector:

$$\begin{aligned} \hat{\Lambda}(\alpha) &= (1/n)\textstyle\sum_{t=1}^{n}(R_{0t} + \hat{\gamma}(\alpha)\alpha' R_{pt})(R_{0t} + \hat{\gamma}(\alpha)\alpha' R_{pt})' \\ &= S_{00} - S_{0p}\alpha(\alpha' S_{pp}\alpha)^{-1}\alpha' S_{p0}. \end{aligned} \tag{9.9.7}$$

Thus, the concentrated log-likelihood function now becomes:

$$\ell(\alpha) = -\tfrac{1}{2} n \cdot \ln(\det \hat{\Lambda}(\alpha)) + \text{rest}, \tag{9.9.8}$$

hence the ML estimator of α is found by solving the minimization problem

$$\min \det[S_{00} - S_{0p}\alpha(\alpha' S_{pp}\alpha)^{-1}\alpha' S_{p0}], \tag{9.9.9}$$

where the minimization is over all $k \times r$ matrices α.

Now consider the well-known matrix relation

$$\begin{pmatrix} A & B \\ B' & C \end{pmatrix} = \begin{pmatrix} A & O \\ B' & I \end{pmatrix}\begin{pmatrix} I & A^{-1}B \\ O & C - B'A^{-1}B \end{pmatrix} = \begin{pmatrix} I & B' \\ O & C \end{pmatrix}\begin{pmatrix} A - B'C^{-1}B & 0 \\ C^{-1}B' & I \end{pmatrix},$$

where A and C are nonsingular matrices. Then

$$\det(A)\cdot\det(C - B'A^{-1}B) = \det(C)\cdot\det(A - B'C^{-1}B).$$

Substituting $A = S_{00}$, $B = S_{0p}\alpha$ and $C = \alpha' S_{pp}\alpha$, it follows that the ML estimator of α is obtained by solving the minimization problem

$$\min \det(\alpha' S_{pp}\alpha - \alpha' S_{p0}S_{00}^{-1}S_{0p}\alpha) \,/\, \det(\alpha' S_{pp}\alpha). \tag{9.9.10}$$

Note, however, that the solution of (9.9.10) is not unique, as we may freely premultiply α' by a conformable nonsingular matrix.

Next, let D be the diagonal matrix with diagonal elements $\hat{\lambda}_1, \hat{\lambda}_2, \ldots, \hat{\lambda}_p$, where

$\hat{\lambda}_1 \geq \hat{\lambda}_2 \geq \ldots \geq \hat{\lambda}_k$ are the ordered roots of the polynomial $\det(\lambda S_{pp} - S_{p0}S_{00}^{-1}S_{0p})$, with $\hat{Q} = (\hat{q}_1, \ldots, \hat{q}_k)$ the corresponding matrix of eigenvectors. (9.9.11)

Then

$$S_{pp}\hat{Q}D = S_{p0}S_{00}^{-1}S_{0p}\hat{Q}. \tag{9.9.12}$$

Moreover, since the roots (9.9.11) are the eigenvalues of the positive semi-definite matrix $S_{pp}^{-\frac{1}{2}}S_{p0}S_{00}^{-1}S_{0p}S_{pp}^{-\frac{1}{2}}$, and $\hat{Q} = S_{pp}^{-\frac{1}{2}}\hat{Q}^*$, with $\hat{Q}^*$ the matrix of eigenvectors of $S_{pp}^{-\frac{1}{2}}S_{p0}S_{00}^{-1}S_{0p}S_{pp}^{-\frac{1}{2}}$, we can normalize $\hat{Q}$ such that

$$\hat{Q}' S_{pp}\hat{Q} = I_k. \tag{9.9.13}$$

Now choose

$$\alpha = \hat{Q}\xi, \text{ where } \xi \text{ is a } k \times r \text{ matrix.} \tag{9.9.14}$$

Then it follows from (9.9.13) and (9.9.14) that the minimization problem (9.9.10) becomes

$$\min \det(\xi'\xi - \xi' D\xi)/\det(\xi'\xi), \tag{9.9.15}$$

where without loss of generality we may normalize ξ such that $\xi'\xi = I_r$

(because we may replace ξ by $\xi(\xi'\xi)^{-1/2}$). It is now easy to verify that the solution of (9.9.15) is:

$$\xi = \begin{pmatrix} I_r \\ 0 \end{pmatrix}, \tag{9.9.16}$$

hence the ML estimator of α is equal to the first r columns of $\hat{Q}$, i.e.,

$$\hat{\alpha} = (\hat{q}_1,\ldots,\hat{q}_r), \tag{9.9.17}$$

and the corresponding maximum value of the likelihood function, given the restriction that α has rank r, is

$$L_{\max}^{-\frac{1}{2}}(r) = \text{const} \times \Pi_{i=1}^{r}(1-\hat{\lambda}_i). \tag{9.9.18}$$

Consequently, the likelihood ratio test LR(k − r) for the hypothesis that there are *at most* r cointegrated vectors is:

$$-2{\cdot}\ln(LR(k-r)) = -n\textstyle\sum_{i=r+1}^{k}\ln(1-\hat{\lambda}_i). \tag{9.9.19}$$

It is well known that under standard conditions, −2 times the log of the LR test statistic converges in distribution to a χ^2 distribution with degrees of freedom equal to the number of constraints (in the present case, k − r). The present situation however, is far from standard, and therefore the usual conclusions from maximum likelihood theory (cf. section 4.5) no longer automatically apply. In particular, the limiting distribution of the test statistic (9.9.19) is now a function of a (k − r)-variate standard Wiener process. Johansen (1988, table 1, p. 239) has calculated critical values on the basis of Monte Carlo simulations (Table 9.9.1). Moreover, Johansen (1988) shows that the ML estimators are consistent. Since the proofs are tedious, we shall not give them here.

Since cointegrated vectors represent long-run relations between integrated variables, it is important to test whether certain components of cointegrated vectors are zero. Also, in economics, for example, one may ask the question whether the log of real GNP is stationary, while the log of nominal GNP and the log of the GNP deflator are integrated. This hypothesis corresponds to a cointegrated vector proportional to (1, − 1)'. These types of hypotheses can be formulated as linear restrictions:

$$H_1\text{: } \alpha = H\varphi, \tag{9.9.20}$$

where H is a known k × s matrix of full rank and φ is an s × r matrix of parameters, with s < r. The likelihood ratio test statistic $-2{\cdot}\ln(LR^*)$ involved, which is easy to derive along the above lines, has a limiting χ^2 distribution with r(k − s) degrees of freedom. See Johansen (1988, theorem 4).

Table 9.9.1 *Asymptotic critical values of the LR test* $-2 \cdot \ln(LR(m))$

	Significance level (percent)		
m	10	5	2.5
1	2.9	4.2	5.3
2	10.3	12.0	13.9
3	21.2	23.8	26.1
4	35.6	38.6	41.2
5	53.6	57.2	60.3

Finally, in Johansen (1991) the model (9.8.15) is augmented with a vector of intercepts μ and a vector of seasonal dummies D_t orthogonal to μ:

$$\Delta X_t = B_1 \Delta X_{t-1} + \ldots + B_{p-1} \Delta X_{t-p+1} - \gamma\alpha' X_{t-p} + \Phi D_t + \mu + U_t \tag{9.9.21}$$

The derivation of the concentrated likelihood function and the LR test for the number of cointegrated vectors is similar to above. However, the presence of an intercept has a considerable impact on the asymptotic distribution of the LR test. In particular, it matters whether the vector μ of intercepts can be written as

$$\mu = \gamma\alpha_0, \text{ with } \alpha_0 \text{ an } r \times 1 \text{ vector,} \tag{9.9.22}$$

or not. If so, then

$$\gamma\alpha' X_{t-p} + \mu = \gamma\alpha^{*\prime} X^*_{t-p}, \text{ with } \alpha^* = (\alpha', \alpha_0)' \text{ and } X^*_t = (X'_t, 1)', \tag{9.9.23}$$

so that then the cointegrated relations have intercepts rather than the model for ΔX_t itself. See further, Johansen (1991).

10

The Nadaraya–Watson kernel regression function estimator

This chapter reviews the asymptotic properties of the Nadaraya-Watson type kernel estimator of an unknown (multivariate) regression function. Conditions are set forth for pointwise weak and strong consistency, asymptotic normality, and uniform consistency. These conditions cover the standard i.i.d. case with continuously distributed regressors, as well as the cases where the distribution of all, or some, regressors is discrete. Moreover, attention is paid to the problem of how the kernel and the window width should be specified. This chapter is a modified and extended version of Bierens (1987b). For further reading and references, see the monographs by Eubank (1988), Hardle (1990), and Rosenblatt (1991), and for an empirical application, see Bierens and Pott-Buter (1990).

10.1 Introduction

The usual practice in constructing regression models is to specify a parametric family for the response function. Obviously the most popular parametric family is the linear model. However, one could consider this as choosing a parametric functional form from a continuum of possible functional forms, analogously to sampling from a continuous distribution, for often the set of theoretically admissible functional forms is uncountably large. Therefore the probability that we pick the true functional form in this way is zero, or at least very close to zero.

The only way to avoid model misspecification is to specify no functional form at all. But then the problem arises how information about the functional form of the model can be derived from the data. A possible solution to this problem is to use so-called kernel estimators of regression functions.

Since the pioneering papers of Nadaraya (1964) and Watson (1964) on kernel regression function estimators, there is now a growing extent of literature on the problem of nonparametric estimation of unknown regression functions. See Collomb (1981, 1985a) and Bierens (1987b) for a bibliography. Most of the literature on nonparametric regression function estimation deals with the kernel method and its variants.

In this section we shall now introduce the kernel regression function estimator for the case where we have an i.i.d. sample $\{(Y_1,X_1),...,(Y_n,X_n)\}$ from an absolutely continuous (k+1)-variate distribution with density f(y,x), where $y \in R$ and $x \in R^k$. In this data set the Y_j's are the dependent variables and the X_j's are k-component vectors of regressors. If $E(|Y_j|) < \infty$, then by definition (cf. chapter 3) the conditional expectation of Y_j relative to X_j exists and takes the form

$$E(Y_j|X_j) = g(X_j), \tag{10.1.1}$$

with g(.) a Borel measurable real function on R^k. Denoting

$$U_j = Y_j - g(X_j), \tag{10.1.2}$$

we then get the regression model

$$Y_j = g(X_j) + U_j, \tag{10.1.3}$$

where by construction the error term U_j satisfies the usual condition that its conditional expectation relative to the vector of regressors equals zero with probability 1, i.e.,

$$E(U_j|X_j) = 0 \text{ a.s.} \tag{10.1.4}$$

The model (10.1.3) is therefore purely tautological, that is, its set up is merely a matter of definition. Now our aim is to estimate the regression function g(.) without making explicit assumptions about its functional form.

For the data-generating process under review the regression function g(.) takes the well-known form

$$g(x) = \int yf(y,x)dy/h(x), \text{ if } h(x) > 0, \tag{10.1.5}$$

where h(x) is the marginal density of f(y,x) ,i.e.,

$$h(x) = \int f(y,x)dy. \tag{10.1.6}$$

This suggests estimation of the function g(x) via estimating the densities f and h.

A convenient method for estimating unknown multivariate density functions is the kernel density estimation method proposed by Rosenblatt (1956b). Important contributions to the asymptotic theory of this class of estimators have been made by Parzen (1962) for the univariate case and Cacoullos (1966) for the multivariate case. See Fryer (1977) and Tapia and Thompson (1978) for reviews.

A kernel estimator of the density h(x) is a random function of the form

$$\hat{h}(x) = (1/n)\sum_{j=1}^{n} K[(x-X_j)/\gamma_n]/\gamma_n^k, \tag{10.1.7}$$

where K[.] is an *a priori* chosen real function on R^k, called the *kernel*, satisfying

$$\int|K(x)|dx < \infty, \int K(x)dx = 1, \tag{10.1.8}$$

and (γ_n) is an *a priori* chosen sequence of positive numbers, called *window width* parameters, satisfying

$$\lim_{n\to\infty}\gamma_n = 0, \lim_{n\to\infty}n\gamma_n^k = \infty. \tag{10.1.9}$$

Under conditions (10.1.8) and (10.1.9) the estimator $\hat{h}(x)$ is pointwise weakly consistent in every continuity point of h(x), provided

$$\sup_x h(x) < \infty. \tag{10.1.10}$$

The proof of this proposition is simple but instructive. First, the asymptotic unbiasedness follows from

$$E[\hat{h}(x)] = \int\gamma_n^{-k}K[(x-z)/\gamma_n]h(z)dz = \int h(x-\gamma_n z)K(z)dz$$
$$\to h(x)\int K(z)dz = h(x) \tag{10.1.11}$$

by bounded convergence. Second, the variance vanishes at order $O[1/(n\gamma_n^k)]$, as

$$n\gamma_n^k\text{var}(\hat{h}(x)) = n\gamma_n^k(1/n^2)\sum_{j=1}^n\text{var}\{K[(x-X_j)/\gamma_n]/\gamma_n^k)\}$$
$$= E\{\gamma_n^{-k}K[(x-X_j)/\gamma_n]^2 - \gamma_n^k(E\{\gamma_n^{-k}K[(x-X_j)/\gamma_n]\})^2$$
$$= \int h(x-\gamma_n z)K(z)^2dz - \gamma_n^k[\int h(x-\gamma_n z)K(z)dz]^2$$
$$\to h(x)\int K(z)^2dz \tag{10.1.12}$$

by bounded convergence. This completes the pointwise weak consistency proof.

We shall now construct a kernel density estimator $\hat{f}(y,x)$ of the joint density f(y,x) such that $\hat{h}(x)$ is the marginal density of $\hat{f}(y,x)$ and the integral $\int y\hat{f}(y,x)dy$ yields an expression involving the same kernel K as in (10.1.7). This kernel estimator of f(y,x) is of the form

$$\hat{f}(y,x) = (1/n)\sum_{j=1}^n K_*[(y-Y_j)/\gamma_n,(x-X_j)/\gamma_n]\gamma_n^{-k-1}, \tag{10.1.13}$$

where the kernel K_* satisfies

$$\int yK_*(y,x)dy = 0, \int K_*(y,x)dy = K(x). \tag{10.1.14}$$

Then $\hat{h}(x)$ is the marginal density of $\hat{f}(y,x)$ and moreover,

$$\int y\hat{f}(y,x)dy = (1/n)\sum_{j=1}^n Y_jK[(x-X_j)/\gamma_n]\gamma_n^{-k}, \tag{10.1.15}$$

hence the corresponding regression function estimator of (10.1.5) is

$$\hat{g}(x) = \{\sum_{j=1}^n Y_jK[(x-X_j)/\gamma_n]\}/\{\sum_{j=1}^n K[(x-X_j)/\gamma_n]\}. \tag{10.1.16}$$

This is the so-called Nadaraya-Watson kernel regression function estimator, named after Nadaraya (1964) and Watson (1964). Note that this kernel regression function estimator is a weighted mean of the dependent variables Y_j, where the weights sum up to 1. In particular, if the kernel is chosen to be a unimodal density function with zero mode, for instance let the kernel be the density of the k-variate standard normal distribution, then the closer x is to X_j, the more weight is put on Y_j.

Similarly to (10.1.11) and (10.1.12) it follows now that

$$\begin{aligned}E[\hat{g}(x)\hat{h}(x)] &= E\{Y_jK[(x-X_j)/\gamma_n]\gamma_n^{-k}\} = E\{g(X_j)K[(x-X_j)/\gamma_n]\gamma_n^{-k}\}\\ &= \int g(z)h(z)K[(x-z)/\gamma_n]\gamma_n^{-k}dz = \int g(x-\gamma_n z)h(x-\gamma_n z)K(z)dz\\ &\to g(x)h(x) \qquad (10.1.17)\end{aligned}$$

by bounded convergence, and

$$\begin{aligned}n\gamma_n^k\,\mathrm{var}[\hat{g}(x)\hat{h}(x)] &= \gamma_n^{-k}(1/n)\textstyle\sum_{j=1}^n \mathrm{var}\{Y_jK[(x-X_j)/\gamma_n]\}\\ &= E\{Y_1^2K[(x-X_1)/\gamma_n)]^2\gamma_n^{-k}\} - \gamma_n^k\left(E\{Y_1K[(x-X_1)/\gamma_n]^2\gamma_n^{-k}\}\right)^2\\ &= \int\sigma_y^2(z)h(z)K[(x-z)/\gamma_n]\gamma_n^{-k}dz - \gamma_n^k\{E[\hat{g}(x)\hat{h}(x)]\}^2\\ &= \int\sigma_y^2(x-\gamma_n z)h(x-\gamma_n z)K(z)^2dz - \gamma_n^k\{E[\hat{g}(x)h(x)]\}^2\\ &\to \sigma_y^2(x)h(x)\int K(z)^2dz \qquad (10.1.18)\end{aligned}$$

by bounded convergence, where

$$\sigma_y^2(x) = E(Y_j^2|X_j = x) \text{ for } h(x) > 0, \qquad (10.1.19)$$

provided x is a continuity point of g(x), h(x), and $\sigma_y^2(x)$ and

$$\sup_x|g(x)|h(x) < \infty,\ \sup_x\sigma_y^2(x)h(x) < \infty. \qquad (10.1.20)$$

Now it is easy to verify from (10.1.11), (10.1.12), (10.1.17), and (10.1.18) that

$$\mathrm{plim}_{n\to\infty}\hat{h}(x) = h(x),\ \mathrm{plim}_{n\to\infty}\hat{g}(x)\hat{h}(x) = g(x)h(x) \qquad (10.1.21)$$

and hence

$$\mathrm{plim}_{n\to\infty}\hat{g}(x) = g(x) \qquad (10.1.22)$$

in every continuity point x of h(x) and g(x)h(x) for which $h(x) > 0$.

The weak consistency of the kernel regression function estimator is not limited to the case that X_j is continuously distributed, as is shown by Devroye (1978) and Bierens (1983). We shall consider the (partly) discrete case later on, in section 10.4. Uniform consistency will also be considered later in this chapter. Moreover, strong consistency results have been derived by Nadaraya (1965, 1970) and Noda (1976). Here we shall give a different proof of the strong consistency of the kernel estimator.

First, consider the following special case of Whittle's (1960) lemma.

Lemma 10.1.1 Let $Z_1,..,Z_n$ be independent random variables with

$E(Z_j^4) \leq M < \infty, j = 1,...,n.$

Then $E(\{\sum_{j=1}^n [Z_j - E(Z_j)]\}^4) \leq 3n^2 M$

Proof: Exercise 1. (Hint: Relate $a_n = E\left(\{\sum_{j=1}^n [Z_j - E(Z_j)]\}^4\right)$ to a_{n-1}.

From this lemma and (10.1.10) it follows that

$$E\left(\{\hat{h}(x) - E[\hat{h}(X)]\}^4\right) \leq [3n^2/(n^4\gamma_n^{4k})]E\{K[(x - X_1)/\gamma_n]^4\}$$
$$= [3/(n^2\gamma_n^{3k})]E\{K[(x - X_1)/\gamma_n]^4\gamma_n^{-k}\} = [3/(n^2\gamma_n^{3k})]\int K[(x - z)/\gamma_n]^4\gamma_n^{-k}h(z)dz$$
$$= [3/(n^2\gamma_n^{3k})]\int h(x - \gamma_n z)K(z)^4 dz = O[1/(n^2\gamma_n^{3k})] \qquad (10.1.23)$$

hence from Chebishev's inequality

$$P\{|\hat{h}(x) - E[\hat{h}(x)]| > \varepsilon\} = O[1/(n^2\gamma_n^{3k})] \qquad (10.1.24)$$

for every $\varepsilon > 0$. Thus if γ_n is chosen such that

$$\sum_{n=1}^{\infty}(n^2\gamma_n^{3k})^{-1} < \infty \qquad (10.1.25)$$

then it follows from theorem 2.1.2 that

$$\hat{h}(x) - E[\hat{h}(x)] \to 0 \text{ a.s.} \qquad (10.1.26)$$

Now assume

$$E(Y_j^4) < \infty \qquad (10.1.27)$$

and let

$$\sigma_y^4(x) = E(Y_j^4 | X_j = x),\ h(x) > 0, \qquad (10.1.28)$$

be such that

$$\sup_x \sigma_y^4(x)h(x) < \infty. \qquad (10.1.29)$$

Then, similarly to (10.1.23),

$$E\left(\{\hat{g}(x)\hat{h}(x) - E[\hat{g}(x)\hat{h}(x)]\}^4\right)$$
$$\leq [3/(n^2\gamma_n^{3k})]\int \sigma_y^4(x - \gamma_n z)h(x - \gamma_n z)K(z)^4 dz = O[1/(n^2\gamma_n^{3k})] \qquad (10.1.30)$$

hence condition (10.1.25) implies

$$\hat{g}(x)\hat{h}(x) - E[\hat{g}(x)\hat{h}(x)] \to 0 \text{ a.s.} \qquad (10.1.31)$$

Together with (10.1.11) and (10.1.17), the results (10.1.26) and (10.1.31) imply

$\hat{g}(x) \to g(x)$ a.s., provided $h(x) > 0$.

Summarizing, we have shown:

Theorem 10.1.1 Let $x \in R^k$ be such that $h(x) > 0$.

(i) If

$\gamma_n \to 0$, $n\gamma_n^k \to \infty$, $\sup_x h(x) < \infty$, $\sup_x|g(x)|h(x) < \infty$ and $\sup\sigma_y^2(x)h(x) < \infty$,

then $\hat{g}(x) \to g(x)$ in pr.

(ii) If in addition

$E(Y_j^4) < \infty$, $\sup_x\sigma_y^4(x)h(x) < \infty$ and $\sum_{n=1}^{\infty} n^{-2}\gamma_n^{-3} < \infty$,

then $\hat{g}(x) \to g(x)$ a.s.

Exercises

1. Prove lemma 10.1.1.
2. Are the conditions on the window width for strong consistency stronger than those for weak consistency?
3. Do we need the condition that Y_j is continuously distributed?

10.2 Asymptotic normality in the continuous case

The kernel regression estimation approach distinguishes itself from other nonparametric regression methods in that asymptotic distribution theory is fairly well established. In particular, the asymptotic normality of the kernel regression function estimator under the conditions under review has been proved by Schuster (1972) for the univariate case (k = 1). Here we shall derive asymptotic normality, in a somewhat different but much easier way, for the general case k > 1.

Observe from (10.1.3), (10.1.7), and (10.1.16) that

$$
\begin{aligned}
[\hat{g}(x) - g(x)]\hat{h}(x) &= (1/n)\textstyle\sum_{j=1}^n U_j K[(x - X_j]/\gamma_n)\gamma_n^{-k} \\
&\quad + (1/n)\textstyle\sum_{j=1}^n \left([g(X_j) - g(x)]K[(x - X_j)/\gamma_n)]\gamma_n^{-k}\right. \\
&\qquad \left. - E\{[g(X_j) - g(x)]K[(x - X_j)/\gamma_n]\gamma_n^{-k}\}\right) \\
&\quad + (1/n)\textstyle\sum_{j=1}^n E\{[g(X_j) - g(x)]K[(x - X_j)/\gamma_n]\gamma_n^{-k}\} \\
&= \hat{q}_1(x) + \hat{q}_2(x) + \hat{q}_3(x), \qquad (10.2.1)
\end{aligned}
$$

say. We shall now set forth conditions such that firstly

$$\surd(n\gamma_n^k)\hat{q}_1(x) \to N(0, \sigma_u^2(x)h(x)\textstyle\int K(z)^2 dz) \text{ in distr.,} \qquad (10.2.2)$$

where, for $h(x) > 0$,

$$\sigma_u^2(x) = E(U_j^2 | X_j = x) \qquad (10.2.3)$$

is the conditional variance of U_j. Secondly, we show that

$$\lim_{n\to\infty}E\{[\surd(n\gamma_n^k)\hat{q}_2(x)]^2\}=0 \tag{10.2.4}$$

and finally we set forth condition such that

$$\lim_{n\to\infty}\gamma_n^{-2}\hat{q}_3(x) \text{ exists.} \tag{10.2.5}$$

The conditions we need are the following. Let for $p > 0$

$$\sigma_u^p(x)=E(|U_j|^p|X_j=x), \tag{10.2.6}$$

provided $E(|U_j|^p) < \infty$ and $h(x) > 0$.

> *Assumption 10.2.1* There exists a $\delta > 0$ such that $\sigma_u^{2+\delta}(x)h(x)$ is uniformly bounded. The functions $g(x)^2h(x)$ and $\sigma_u^2(x)h(x)$ are continuous and uniformly bounded. The functions $h(x)$ and $g(x)h(x)$ and their first and second partial derivatives are continuous and uniformly bounded.

First we prove (10.2.2). Denote

$$v_{n,j}(x)=U_jK[(x-X_j)/\gamma_n]/\surd(\gamma_n^k). \tag{10.2.7}$$

Since

$$\surd(n\gamma_n^k)\hat{q}_1(x) = (1/\surd n)\textstyle\sum_{j=1}^n v_{n,j}(x),$$

it suffices to show that the double array $(v_{n,j}(x))$ satisfies the conditions of Liapounov's central limit theorem (cf. theorem 2.4.3). Thus the results

$$E[v_{n,j}(x)]=0, \tag{10.2.8}$$

$$\begin{aligned}E[v_{n,j}(x)^2]&=E\{U_j^2K[(x-X_j)/\gamma_n]^2\gamma_n^{-k}\}=\textstyle\int\sigma_u^2(x-\gamma_n z)h(x-\gamma_n z)K(z)^2dz\\ &\to\sigma_u^2(x)h(x)\textstyle\int K(z)^2dz,\end{aligned} \tag{10.2.9}$$

and

$$\begin{aligned}\textstyle\sum_{j=1}^n E[|v_{n,j}(x)/\surd n|^{2+\delta}]&=[1/\surd(n\gamma_n^k)]^\delta E\{|U_j|^{2+\delta}|K[(x-X_j)/\gamma_n]|^{2+\delta}\gamma_n^{-k}\}\\ &=[1/\surd(n\gamma_n^k)]^\delta\textstyle\int\sigma_u^{2+\delta}(x-\gamma_n z)h(x-\gamma_n z)|K(z)|^{2+\delta}dz\\ &=O[1/\surd(n\gamma_n^k)^\delta]\to 0, \text{ for some } \delta > 0\end{aligned} \tag{10.2.10}$$

imply

$$(1/\surd n)\textstyle\sum_{j=1}^n v_{n,j}(x)\to N(0,\sigma_u^2(x)h(x)\int K(z)^2dz) \text{ in distr.} \tag{10.2.11}$$

This proves (10.2.2). Next, observe that similarly to (10.1.12),

$$\begin{aligned}E\{[\surd(n\gamma_n^k)\hat{q}_2(x)]^2\}&=\textstyle\int[g(x-\gamma_n z)-g(x)]^2h(x-\gamma_n z)K(z)^2dz\\ &\quad-\gamma_n^k\{\textstyle\int[g(x-\gamma_n z)-g(x)]h(x-\gamma_n z)K(z)dz\}^2\to 0\end{aligned} \tag{10.2.12}$$

by bounded convergence. This proves (10.2.4). Finally, observe that similarly to (10.1.11),

$$\begin{aligned}\hat{q}_3(x) &= \int[g(x-\gamma_n z) - g(x)]h(x-\gamma_n z)K(z)dz \\ &= \int[g(x-\gamma_n z)h(x-\gamma_n z) - g(x)h(x)]K(z)dz \\ &\quad - g(x)\int[h(x-\gamma_n z) - h(x)]K(z)dz \\ &= -\gamma_n\int z'(\partial/\partial x')[g(x)h(x)]K(z)dz \\ &\quad + \tfrac{1}{2}\gamma_n^2\int z'(\partial/\partial x)(\partial/\partial x')[g(x-\gamma_n\xi_n(x,z)z)h(x-\gamma_n\xi_n(x,z)z)]zK(z)dz \\ &\quad + \gamma_n g(x)\int z'(\partial/\partial x')h(x)K(z)dz \\ &\quad - \tfrac{1}{2}\gamma_n^2 g(x)\int z'(\partial/\partial x)(\partial/\partial x')h(x-\gamma_n\xi_n(x,z)z)zK(z)dz, \qquad (10.2.13)\end{aligned}$$

where $0 \le \xi_n(x,z) \le 1$. The last equality in (10.2.13) follows from Taylor's theorem. Thus if we choose K such that

$$\int xK(x)dx = 0, \ \int xx'K(x)dx = \Omega \text{ is finite,} \qquad (10.2.14)$$

then the first and third terms at the right-hand side of (10.2.13) vanish, while by bounded convergence the second and fourth terms, divided by γ_n^2, converge. Thus,

$$\lim_{n\to\infty}\gamma_n^{-2}\hat{q}_3(x) = b(x), \qquad (10.2.15)$$

where

$$b(x) = \tfrac{1}{2}\mathrm{tr}\{\Omega(\partial/\partial x)(\partial/\partial x')[g(x)h(x)]\} - \tfrac{1}{2}g(x)\mathrm{tr}\{\Omega(\partial/\partial x)(\partial/\partial x')h(x)\}. \qquad (10.2.16)$$

This proves (10.2.5).

From (10.2.1), (10.2.2), (10.2.4), and (10.2.5) the following theorem easily follows (exercise 1).

> *Theorem 10.2.1* Let assumption 10.2.1 and condition (10.2.14) hold and let $h(x) > 0$. If
>
> $$\lim_{n\to\infty}\gamma_n^2\sqrt{(n\gamma_n^k)} = \mu \text{ with } 0 \le \mu < \infty \qquad (10.2.17)$$
>
> then
>
> $$\sqrt{(n\gamma_n^k)}[\hat{g}(x) - g(x)] \to N\{\mu b(x)/h(x), [\sigma_u^2(x)/h(x)]\int K(z)^2dz\} \qquad (10.2.18)$$
>
> in distribution. If
>
> $$\lim_{n\to\infty}\gamma_n^2\sqrt{(n\gamma_n^k)} = \infty, \qquad (10.2.19)$$
>
> then
>
> $$\mathrm{plim}_{n\to\infty}\gamma_n^{-2}[\hat{g}(x) - g(x)] = b(x)/h(x). \qquad (10.2.20)$$

Note that the latter result may be considered as convergence in distribution to a degenerated limiting distribution.

At first sight it looks attractive to choose the window width γ_n such that $\mu=0$, as then the asymptotic bias vanishes. However, in that case the asymptotic rate of convergence in distribution is lower than in the case $\mu>0$, as (10.2.17) implies

$$\sqrt{(n\gamma_n^k)}/n^{2/(k+4)} \to \mu^{k/(k+4)} \text{ as } n\to\infty. \tag{10.2.21}$$

This corresponds to the fact that minimizing the integrated mean square error

$$E\{\int[\hat{g}(x)\hat{h}(x)-g(x)h(x)]^2dx\}$$

yields an optimal window width of the form (10.2.17) with $\mu>0$. Thus the window width γ_n which gives the maximum rate of convergence in distribution is

$$\gamma_n = cn^{-1/(k+4)}, \tag{10.2.22}$$

where $c>0$ is a constant. Since $\mu=c^{(k+4)/2}$, we have the following corollary.

> *Theorem 10.2.2* Let the conditions of theorem 10.2.1 hold. With the window width (10.2.22) we have
>
> $$n^{2/(k+4)}[\hat{g}(x)-g(x)] \to N\{c^2b(x)/h(x), c^{-k}[\sigma_u^2(x)/h(x)]\int K(z)^2dz\}. \tag{10.2.23}$$

Notice that the asymptotic rate of convergence in distribution is negatively related to the number of regressors. This is typical for nonparametric regression, for the more regressors we have, the more information we ask from the data and thus the more observations we need to get a useful answer.

The result (10.2.23) only has practical significance if it is possible to estimate the mean and the variance of the limiting normal distribution involved. As far as the variance is concerned, consistent estimation will appear to be feasible. Regarding the mean, however, the estimation problem is too hard. Inspecting the function b(x) (cf. (10.2.16)) reveals that estimating this function is awkward, as b(x) is a function of the second derivatives of the unknown functions h(x) and g(x)h(x). It would therefore be preferable to eliminate the mean of the limiting normal distribution. We have already mentioned a way of doing that, namely to choose the window width such that the limit μ in (10.2.17) is zero, but then we also sacrifice some of the speed of convergence. There is, however, another way to remove the asymptotic bias while maintaining the maximal rate of convergence in distribution of order $n^{2/(k+4)}$, namely by combining the results (10.2.18) and (10.2.20). The idea is to use (10.2.20) for estimating the mean of the limiting normal distribution in (10.2.18) by subtracting the random function at the left-hand side of (10.2.20) times μ from the left-hand side of (10.2.18).

Theorem 10.2.3 Let the conditions of theorem 10.2.1 hold. Let $\hat{g}_1(x)$ be the kernel regression estimator with window width

$$\gamma_n = cn^{-1/(k+4)}$$

and let $\hat{g}_2(x)$ be the kernel regression estimator with window width

$$\gamma_n = cn^{-\delta/(k+4)}, \text{ with } \delta \in (0,1).$$

Denote

$$\hat{g}_{\cdot}(x) = [\hat{g}_1(x) - n^{-2(1-\delta)/(k+4)}\hat{g}_2(x)]/[1 - n^{-2(1-\delta)/(k+4)}]. \quad (10.2.24)$$

Then

$$n^{2/(k+4)}[\hat{g}_{\cdot}(x) - g(x)] \to N(0, c^{-k}[\sigma_u^2(x)/h(x)]\int K(z)^2 dz) \text{ in distr.} \quad (10.2.25)$$

Note that for the estimator $\hat{g}_1(x)$ the result (10.2.18) holds with $\mu > 0$, whereas for $\hat{g}_2(x)$ the result (10.2.20) holds. The proof of this theorem therefore follows straightforwardly from the fact that by (10.2.20),

$$n^{2/(k+4)}[\hat{g}_1(x) - g(x)] - c^2(cn^{-\delta/(k+4)})^{-2}[\hat{g}_2(x) - g(x)]$$

is asymptotically distributed as

$$n^{2/(k+4)}[\hat{g}_1(x) - g(x)] - c^2 b(x)/h(x)$$

(cf. exercise 2). This easy result is related to the generalized jack-knife method of Schucany and Sommers (1977) for bias reduction of kernel density estimators.

The rate of convergence in distribution is determined by the rate of convergence of the expectation of $\hat{q}_3(x)$. If we choose the kernel K such that $\int xK(x)dx = 0$ and $\int xx'K(x)dx = O$, then it can be shown that instead of (10.2.15), $\lim_{n\to\infty}\gamma_n^{-3}\hat{q}_3(x)$ exists and is finite. The asymptotic rate of convergence in distribution then becomes $n^{3/(k+6)}$ instead of $n^{2/(k+4)}$. Thus a way to improve the convergence in distribution is to choose a kernel with zero moments up to a particular order m. More precisely, following Singh (1981) we define the class $\mathfrak{K}_{k,m}$ of these kernels as follows.

Definition 10.2.1 Let $\mathfrak{K}_{k,m}$ be the class of all bounded Borel measurable real valued functions K(.) on R^k such that, with $z=(z_1,...,z_k)'$, $z_i \in R$,

$$\int z_1^{i_1} z_2^{i_2} \ldots z_k^{i_k} K(z_1,z_2,\ldots,z_k)dz_1\ldots dz_k$$
$$= 1 \text{ if } i_1 = i_2 = \ldots = i_k = 0,$$
$$= 0 \text{ if } 0 < i_1 + \ldots + i_k < m, \tag{10.2.26}$$
$$\int |z|^i |K(z)|dz < \infty \text{ for } i=0 \text{ and } i=m, \int K(z)dz = 1.$$

With $K \in \mathfrak{K}_{k,m}$ there exists a function $b^*(x)$ such that

$$\lim_{n\to\infty} \gamma_n^{-m} \hat{q}_3(x) = b^*(x), \tag{10.2.27}$$

provided h(x) and g(x)h(x) belong to the class $\mathfrak{D}_{k,m}$:

Definition 10.2.2 Let $\mathfrak{D}_{k,m}$ be the class of all continuous real functions f on R^k such that the derivatives

$$(\partial/\partial z_1)^{i_1}(\partial/\partial z_2)^{i_2}\ldots(\partial/\partial z_k)^{i_k} f(z_1,\ldots,z_k),\ i_j \geq 0,\ j=1,\ldots,k,$$

are continuous and uniformly bounded for $0 \leq i_1 + i_2 + \ldots + i_k \leq m$.

Thus similarly to theorem 10.2.1 we have:

Theorem 10.2.4 Let assumption 10.2.1 and the additional conditions $h(x) \in \mathfrak{D}_{k,m}$, $g(x)h(x) \in \mathfrak{D}_{k,m}$, $K \in \mathfrak{K}_{k,m}$ hold, where m is an integer > 2. Let h(x) > 0. There exists a real function $b^*(x)$ on R^k such that

$$\lim_{n\to\infty} \gamma_n^m \sqrt{(n\gamma_n^k)} = \mu \text{ with } 0 \leq \mu < \infty \tag{10.2.28}$$

implies

$$\sqrt{(n\gamma_n^k)}[\hat{g}(x) - g(x)] \to N\{\mu b^*(x)/h(x), [\sigma_u^2(x)/h(x)]\int K(z)^2 dz\} \tag{10.2.29}$$

in distr., and

$$\lim_{n\to\infty} \gamma_n^m \sqrt{(n\gamma_n^k)} = \infty \tag{10.2.30}$$

implies

$$\text{plim}_{n\to\infty} \gamma_n^{-m}[\hat{g}(x) - g(x)] = b^*(x)/h(x). \tag{10.2.31}$$

The optimal rate of convergence in distribution is now $n^{m/(2m+k)}$, and the corresponding window width is

$$\gamma_n = cn^{-1/(2m+k)} \tag{10.2.32}$$

with c > 0 a constant. Moreover, similarly to theorems 10.2.2 and 10.2.3 we now have:

Theorem 10.2.5 Let the conditions of theorem 10.2.2 hold. With window width (10.2.32) we have:

$$n^{m/(2m+k)}[\hat{g}(x)-g(x)]$$
$$\to N\{c^m b^*(x)/h(x), c^{-k}[\sigma_u^2(x)/h(x)]\int K(z)^2 dz\} \text{ in distr.} \qquad (10.2.33)$$

Theorem 10.2.6 Let the conditions of theorem 10.2.4 hold. Let $\hat{g}_1(x)$ be the kernel regression estimator with window width

$$\gamma_n = cn^{-1/(2m+k)}$$

and let $\hat{g}_2(x)$ be the kernel regression estimator with window width

$$\gamma_n = cn^{-\delta/(2m+k)} \text{ with } \delta \in (0,1).$$

Denote

$$\hat{g}_*(x)=[\hat{g}_1(x)-n^{-(1-\delta)m/(2m+k)}\hat{g}_2(x)]/[1-n^{-(1-\delta)m/(2m+k)}]. \qquad (10.2.34)$$

Then

$$n^{m/(2m+k)}[\hat{g}_*(x)-g(x)]\to N\{0,c^{-k}[\sigma_u^2(x)/h(x)]\int K(z)^2 dz\}. \qquad (10.2.35)$$

As we have seen in chapter 4, the usual asymptotic normality results in parametric regression analysis hold with a rate of convergence in distribution equal to the square root of the number of observations. Now we see that in the nonparametric regression case this rate can be approached arbitrarily close by increasing m

In Singh (1981) examples are given of members of the class $\mathfrak{K}_{1,m}$ for $m=3,4,5,6$. However, a simple way to construct kernels in $\mathfrak{K}_{k,m}$ for arbitrary $k \geq 1$ and even $m \geq 2$ is the following. Let for $x \in R^k$ and $N > 1$

$$K(x)=\sum_{j=1}^N \theta_j \exp(-\tfrac{1}{2}x'\Omega^{-1}x/\sigma_j^2)/[(\surd(2\pi))^k|\sigma_j|^k\surd\det(\Omega)], \qquad (10.2.36)$$

where Ω is a positive definite matrix and the θ_j and σ_j are such that

$$\sum_{j=1}^N \theta_j = 1, \qquad (10.2.37)$$

$$\sum_{j=1}^N \theta_j \sigma_j^{2\ell} = 0 \text{ for } \ell=1,2,\ldots,N-1. \qquad (10.2.38)$$

Then it is not hard to verify that $K \in \mathfrak{K}_{k,m}$ with $m = 2N$ (exercise 3).

The choice of the θ_j and σ_j affects the asymptotic variance of the estimator $\hat{g}_*$ via the quantity

$$\int K(x)^2 dx = \sum_{i=1}^N \sum_{j=1}^N \theta_i \theta_j \surd(\sigma_i^2+\sigma_j^2)(\surd(2\pi))^k \surd\det(\Omega). \qquad (10.2.39)$$

Thus at first sight one might think of choosing the θ_j and σ_j so as to minimize (10.2.39), given Ω. However, (10.2.39) can be made arbitrarily small, for if $\theta_1,\ldots,\theta_N,\sigma_1,\ldots,\sigma_N$ is a solution of (10.2.37) and (10.2.38) then so is $\theta_1,...,\theta_N$, $\mu\sigma_1,...,\mu\sigma_N$ for any $\mu>0$. Then (10.2.39) is proportional to μ^{-1}. This indicates that the choice of the θ_j and the σ_j is not crucial, as the constant of the window width (10.2.32) may take over the role of this μ.

Finally, we consider the multivariate limiting distribution of the kernel regression estimator in distinct points. Thus let $x^{(1)}$ and $x^{(2)}$ be distinct points in R^k such that $h(x^{(1)})>0$, $h(x^{(2)})>0$. Then, similarly to (10.2.9),

$$\begin{aligned}&\mathrm{cov}[\surd(n\gamma_n^k)\hat{q}_1(x^{(1)}),\surd(n\gamma_n^k)\hat{q}_1(x^{(2)})]\\&\qquad=E\{U_j^2K[(x^{(1)}-X_j)/\gamma_n]K[(x^{(2)}-X_j]/\gamma_n\}\gamma_n^{-k}\\&=\int\sigma_u^2(x^{(1)}-\gamma_n z)h(x^{(1)}-\gamma_n z)K(z)K\{[(x^{(2)}-x^{(1)})/\gamma_n]+z\}dz\to 0,\qquad(10.2.40)\end{aligned}$$

by bounded convergence, for $K\{[(x^{(1)}-x^{(2)})/\gamma]+z\}\to 0$ as $\gamma\downarrow 0$. Using this result it is easy to show (exercise 4) that

$[\surd(n\gamma_n^k)\hat{q}_1(x^{(1)}),\ \surd(n\gamma_n^k)\hat{q}_1(x^{(2)})]' \to N_2(0,D)$ in distr., with D is a *diagonal* variance matrix. (10.2.41)

Thus $\surd(n\gamma_n^k)\hat{q}_1(x^{(1)})$ and $\surd(n\gamma_n^k)\hat{q}_1(x^{(2)})$ are asymptotically independent, and so are $\surd(n\gamma_n^k)[\hat{g}(x^{(1)})-g(x^{(1)})]$ and $\surd(n\gamma_n^k)[\hat{g}(x^{(2)})-g(x^{(2)})]$. More generally we have:

> *Theorem 10.2.7* Let the conditions of theorem 10.2.1 or theorem 10.2.4 be satisfied and let $x^{(1)},...,x^{(M)}$ be distinct points in R^k with $h(x^{(\ell)}) > 0$ for $\ell=1,2,...,M$. Then the sequence
>
> $\{\surd(n\gamma_n^k)(\hat{g}(x^{(\ell)})-g(x^{(\ell)})]\},\ \ell=1,...,M$
>
> is asymptotically independent, and so is
>
> $\{\surd(n\gamma_n^k)[\hat{g}_.(x^{(\ell)})-g(x^{(\ell)})]\},\ \ell=1,...,M.$

Finally we consider estimation of the asymptotic variance in (10.2.35). Let

$$\hat{\sigma}2(x)=\frac{c^{-k}(1/n)\sum_{j=1}^n[Y_j-\hat{g}_*(x)]^2K[(x-X_j)/\gamma_n(c)]^2/\gamma_n(c)^k}{\{(1/n)\sum_{j=1}^n K[(x-X_j)/\gamma_n(c)]/\gamma_n(c)^k\}^2}\qquad(10.2.42)$$

with

$$\gamma_n(c)=cn^{-1/(2m+k)}.\qquad(10.2.43)$$

It is not too hard to show:

> *Theorem 10.2.8* Under the conditions of theorem 10.2.6,
>
> $\mathrm{plim}_{n\to\infty}\sigma^2(x|c) = c^{-k}[\sigma_u^2(x)/h(x)]\int K(z)^2dz,$
>
> hence
>
> $\hat{\eta}(x|c) = n^{m/(2m+k)}[\hat{g}_.(x|c)-g(x)]/\hat{\sigma}(x|c) \to N(0,1)$ in distr.

Moreover, if $x^{(1)},...,x^{(M)}$ are distinct points in R^k with $h(x^{(\ell)}) > 0$, $\ell = 1,2,...,M$, then

$$(\hat{\eta}(x^{(1)}|c),...,\hat{\eta}(x^{(M)}|c))' \rightarrow N_M(O,I) \text{ in distr.}$$

Proof: Exercise 5.

On the basis of this result it is now easy to construct confidence bands for g(x). In particular, the 95 per cent asymptotic confidence interval for g(x) is:

$$\hat{g}_{\bullet}(x|c) + 1.96\,\hat{\sigma}(x|c)/n^{m/(2m+k)}.$$

Exercises

1. Complete the proof of theorem 10.2.1.
2. Complete the proof of theorem 10.2.3.
3. Verify that the kernel (10.2.36) belongs to the class $\mathfrak{K}_{k,m}$ with $m = 2N$.
4. Prove (10.2.41).
5. Prove theorem 10.2.8.

10.3 Uniform consistency in the continuous case

The uniform consistency of the kernel regression estimator is proved by Nadaraya (1965, 1970), Devroye (1978), Schuster and Yakowitz (1979) and Bierens (1983), among others. The approach in the latter two papers is based on an idea of Parzen (1962), namely to use the Fourier transform of the kernel. Suppose that the kernel has an absolutely integrable Fourier transform, i.e.,

$$\psi(t) = \int \exp(it'x)K(x)dx, \qquad \int|\psi(t)|dt < \infty. \tag{10.3.1}$$

If K is a density then $\psi(t)$ is its characteristric function. Then by the inversion formula for characteristic functions (cf. theorem 1.5.1) we have

$$K(x) = (1/(2\pi))^k \int \exp(-it'x)\psi(t)dt. \tag{10.3.2}$$

This result, however, carries over to more general Fourier transforms. In particular, for the kernel (10.2.36) we have

$$\psi(t) = \sum_{j=1}^{N}\theta_j \int \exp(it'x)\{\exp(-\tfrac{1}{2}x'\Omega^{-1}x/\sigma_j^2)/[(\sqrt{2\pi})^k|\sigma_j|^k\sqrt{\det(\Omega)}]\}dx$$
$$= \sum_{j=1}^{N}\theta_j \exp[-\tfrac{1}{2}\sigma_j^2 t'\Omega t] \tag{10.3.3}$$

and applying the inversion formula in theorem 1.5.1 to each of the terms involved we see that (10.3.2) holds. Thus $\hat{g}(x)\hat{h}(x)$ can be written as

$$\hat{g}(x)\hat{h}(x) = (1/n)\sum_{j=1}^{n}\gamma_n^{-k}[1/(2\pi)]^k Y_j \int \exp[-it'(x-X_j)/\gamma_n]\psi(t)dt$$
$$= [1/(2\pi)]^k \int [(1/n)\sum_{j=1}^{n} Y_j \exp(it'X_j)]\exp(-it'x)\psi(\gamma_n t)dt, \tag{10.3.4}$$

hence

$$E[\sup_x|\hat{g}(x)\hat{h}(x) - E(\hat{g}(x)\hat{h}(x))|] \\ \leq [1/(2\pi)]^k \int E\left(|(1/n)\sum_{j=1}^n \{Y_j\exp(it'X_j) \\ - E[Y_j\exp(it'X_j)]\}|\right)|\psi(\gamma_n t)|dt. \quad (10.3.5)$$

Moreover, using the well-known equality

$$\exp(ia) = \cos(a) + i.\sin(a)$$

and Liapounov's inequality we see that, uniformly in t,

$$E\left(|(1/n)\sum_{j=1}^n \{Y_j\exp(it'X_j) \ - E[Y_j\exp(it'X_j)]\}|\right) \\ \leq \{\text{var}[(1/n)\sum_{j=1}^n Y_j\cos(t'X_j)] + \text{var}[(1/n)\sum_{j=1}^n Y_j\sin(t'X_j)]\}^{½} \\ \leq \surd[E(Y_j^2)]/\surd n. \quad (10.3.6)$$

Combining (10.3.5) and (10.3.6) yields

$$E[\sup_x|\hat{g}(x)\hat{h}(x) - E(\hat{g}(x)\hat{h}(x))|] \leq \surd[E(Y_j^2)](1/\surd n)[1/(2\pi)]^k \int|\psi(\gamma_n t)|dt \\ = O[1/(\gamma_n^k \surd n)]. \quad (10.3.7)$$

Furthermore, if $f(x) = g(x)h(x)$ belongs to the class $\mathfrak{D}_{k,2}$ and K belongs to the class $\mathfrak{K}_{k,2}$ then it follows, similarly to (10.2.13), that

$$\gamma_n^{-2}\sup_x|E[\hat{g}(x)\hat{h}(x)] \ - g(x)h(x)| \\ = \gamma_n^{-2}\sup_x|\int[g(x-\gamma_n z)h(x-\gamma_n z) \ - g(x)h(x)]K(z)dz| \\ = \gamma_n^{-2}\sup_x|\int[f(x-\gamma_n z) \ - f(x)]K(z)dz| \\ \leq \sup_x|½\int z'(\partial/\partial x)(\partial/\partial x')f(x)zK(z)dz| \ < \ \infty. \quad (10.3.8)$$

More generally, if $g(x)h(x)$ belongs to $\mathfrak{D}_{k,m}$ and K belongs to $\mathfrak{K}_{k,m}$ then

$$\gamma_n^{-m}\sup_x|E[\hat{g}(x)\hat{h}(x)] - g(x)h(x)| \ < \ \infty, \quad (10.3.9)$$

uniformly in n. Combining (10.3.7) and (10.3.9) now yields

$$E[\sup_x|\hat{g}(x)\hat{h}(x) - g(x)h(x)|] = O\{[\min(\gamma_n^k\surd n, \gamma_n^{-m})]^{-1}\}. \quad (10.3.10)$$

Clearly, this rate of convergence is optimal for

$$\gamma_n = c.n^{-1/(2m+2k)}, \ c \ > \ 0, \quad (10.3.11)$$

and then

$$E[\sup_x|\hat{g}(x)\hat{h}(x) \ - g(x)h(x)|] = O(n^{-m/(2m+2k)}). \quad (10.3.12)$$

Changing Y_j to 1 we see that a similar results hold for $\hat{h}(x)$. It is now easy to verify:

Theorem 10.3.1 Let assumption 10.2.1 and the additional

conditions (10.3.1), $h(x)\in\mathfrak{D}_{k,m}$, $g(x)h(x)\in\mathfrak{D}_{k,m}$, and $K\in\mathfrak{K}_{k,m}$ hold, where $m \geq 2$. Let $\delta \in (0,\sup_x h(x)]$ be arbitrary. For the window width (10.3.11) we have

$$n^{m/(2m+2k)}\sup_{x\in\{x\in R^k:h(x)\geq\delta\}}|\hat{g}(x)-g(x)|=O_p(1).$$

The proof is left as an exercise.

It should be noted that the rate of uniform convergence, $n^{m/(2m+2k)}$, is not the maximum obtainable rate, as is shown by Silverman (1978) for the density case and Révész (1979), Schuster and Yakowitz (1979), Liero (1982), and Cheng (1983) for the regression case. The present conservative approach has been chosen for the simplicity with which it can easily be extended to the case with partly discrete regressors and/or time series.

10.4 Discrete and mixed continuous-discrete regressors

10.4.1 The discrete case

Economic and other social data quite often contain qualitative variables. A typical feature of such variables is that they take a countable number of values and can usually be rescaled to integer valued variables. We consider first the case where all the components of X_j are of a qualitative nature. In the next subsection we show what happens in the mixed continuous-discrete case. The following assumption formalizes the discrete nature of X_j.

Assumption 10.4.1 There exists a countable subset Δ of R^k such that

(i) $x \in \Delta$ implies $p(x) = P(X_j = x) > 0$;

(ii) $\sum_{x\in\Delta}p(x) = 1$;

(iii) every bounded subset of Δ is finite.

Part (iii) of this assumption excludes limit points in Δ. It ensures that for every $x \in \Delta$,

$$\inf_{z\in\Delta\backslash\{x\}}|z-x|=\mu(x) > 0. \qquad (10.4.1)$$

Now let the kernel and the window width be such that

$$K(0)=1,\ \gamma_n\downarrow 0,\ \sqrt{n}\ \sup_{|z|>\mu/\gamma_n}|K(z)|\rightarrow 0 \text{ for every } \mu > 0. \qquad (10.4.2)$$

This condition holds for kernels of the type (10.2.36) and window widths of the type $\gamma_n = c.n^{-\tau}$ with $\tau > 0$, $c > 0$.

Since now

$$|(1/\sqrt{n})\sum_{j=1}^{n} Y_j K[(x-X_j)/\gamma_n] \ -(1/\sqrt{n})\sum_{j=1}^{n} Y_j I(X_j=x)|$$
$$\leq (1/\sqrt{n})\sum_{j=1}^{n}|Y_j K[(x-X_j)/\gamma_n]| I(X_j \neq x)$$
$$\leq (1/n)\sum_{j=1}^{n}|Y_j|\sqrt{n}\ \sup_{|z|>\mu(x)/\gamma_n}|K(z)|\to 0 \text{ in prob.,} \tag{10.4.3}$$

where I(.) is the indicator function, and similarly

$$|(1/\sqrt{n})\sum_{j=1}^{n} K[(x-X_j)/\gamma_n]-(1/\sqrt{n})\sum_{j=1}^{n} I(X_j=x)|\to 0 \text{ in pr.,} \tag{10.4.4}$$

it is easy to verify that for every $x \in \Delta$

$$\text{plim}_{n\to\infty}\sqrt{n}[\hat{g}(x)-\hat{g}^*(x)]=0, \tag{10.4.5}$$

where

$$\hat{g}^*(x)=[\sum_{j=1}^{n} Y_j I(X_j=x)]/[\sum_{j=1}^{n} I(X_j=x)]$$
$$=[\sum_{j=1}^{n} U_j I(X_j=x)]/[\sum_{j=1}^{n} I(X_j=x)]+g(x). \tag{10.4.6}$$

It now follows straightforwardly from the law of large numbers that

$$\hat{p}^*(x)=(1/n)\sum_{j=1}^{n} I(X_j=x)\to p(x) \text{ in pr.,} \tag{10.4.7}$$

whereas by the central limit theorem

$$\sqrt{n}[\hat{g}^*(x)\hat{p}^*(x)-g(x)\hat{p}^*(x)]=(1/\sqrt{n})\sum_{j=1}^{n} U_j I(X_j=x)$$
$$\to N(0,\sigma_u^2(x)p(x)) \text{ in distr.} \tag{10.4.8}$$

Combining (10.4.5), (10.4.7) and (10.4.8) yields:

> *Theorem 10.4.1* Under assumption 10.4.1 and condition (10.4.2) we have
>
> $$\sqrt{n}[\hat{g}(x)-g(x)]\to N(0,\sigma_u^2(x)/p(x)) \text{ in distr.} \tag{10.4.9}$$

Also, similarly to theorem 10.2.7 we have:

> *Theorem 10.4.2* Let $x^{(1)},\dots,x^{(M)}$ be distinct points in Δ. Under the conditions of theorem 10.4.1 the sequence
>
> $$\{\sqrt{n}(\hat{g}(x^{(\ell)}) \ -g(x^{(\ell)})\},\ \ell=1,\dots,M$$
>
> is asymptotically independent.

Proof: Exercise 1.

Note that the discrete case differs from the continuous case in that hardly any restrictions are placed on the window width while, nevertheless, the assymptotic normal distribution has zero mean. Moreover, the aymptotic rate of convergence in distribution is now the same as for the usual parametric models. Furthermore, since every bounded subset Δ_* of Δ is finite, theorem 10.4.1 implies that

$$\max_{x\in\Delta_*}|\sqrt{n}[\hat{g}(x)-g(x)]| = O_p(1). \qquad (10.4.10)$$

10.4.2 The mixed continuous–discrete case

We now consider the case where the first k_1 components of X_j are continuous and the remaining k_2 components are discrete. Of course, this case is only relevant for $k = k_1+k_2 \geq 2$.

Assumption 10.4.2 Let $x_j = (X_j^{(1)},X_j^{(2)})' \in \Delta_1 \times \Delta_2$, where Δ_1 is a k_1-dimensional real space and Δ_2 is a subset of a k_2-dimensional real space. The set Δ_2 is such that

(i) $x^{(2)} \in \Delta_2$ implies $p(x^{(2)}) = P(X_j^{(2)} = x^{(2)}) > 0$;

(ii) $\sum_{x^{(2)}\in\Delta_2} p(x^{(2)}) = 1$;

(iii) every bounded subset of Δ_2 is finite.

Let $x = (x^{(1)},x^{(2)})' \in \Delta_1 \times \Delta_2$ and let $h(x^{(1)}|x^{(2)})$ be the density of the conditional distribution of $X_j^{(1)}$ relative to the event $X_j^{(2)} = x^{(2)}$. For every fixed $x^{(2)} \in \Delta_2$ the following holds:

(iv) $h(x^{(1)}|x^{(2)})$ and $g(x^{(1)},x^{(2)})h(x^{(1)}|x^{(2)})$ belong to the class $\mathfrak{D}_{k_1,m}$ with $m \geq 2$;

(v) there exists a $\delta > 0$ such that $\sigma_u^{2+\delta}(x^{(1)},x^{(2)})h(x^{(1)}|x^{(2)})$ is uniformly bounded on Δ_1;

(vi) the functions $g(x^{(1)},x^{(2)})^2h(x^{(1)}|x^{(2)})$ and $\sigma_u^2(x^{(1)},x^{(2)})h(x^{(1)}|x^{(2)})$ are continuous and uniformly bounded on Δ_1.

Moreover, we now choose the kernel $K(x^{(1)},x^{(2)})$ and the window width γ_n such that with $(z_1,z_2)' \in \Delta_1 \times \Delta_2$ and for $n \to \infty$,

$$\left.\begin{array}{l} \gamma_n\downarrow 0;\ \sqrt{n}\,\sup_{|z_2|>\mu/\gamma_n}\int|K(z_1,z_2)|dz_1 \to 0 \text{ for every } \mu > 0; \\ n\gamma_n^{k_1}\to\infty;\ K(z_1,0) \in \mathfrak{K}_{k_1,m} \text{ with } m \geq 2; \\ \int|K(z_1,0)|dz_1 < \infty,\ \int K(z_1,0)dz_1 = 1. \end{array}\right\} \qquad (10.4.11)$$

A suitable kernel satisfying (10.4.11) can be constructed similarly to (10.2.36), i.e., let

$$K(x) = \sum_{j=1}^N \theta_j \exp(-\tfrac{1}{2}x'\Omega^{-1}x/\sigma_j^2)/(\sqrt{(2\pi)})^{k_1}|\sigma_j|^{k_1}\sqrt{\det(\Omega_1)}, \qquad (10.4.12)$$

where Ω_1 is the inverse of the upper-left $(k_1 \times k_1)$ submatrix of Ω^{-1} and the σ_j's and θ_j's are the same as in (10.2.38). Denoting

$$h(x)=h(x^{(1)},x^{(2)})=h(x^{(1)}|x^{(2)})p(x^{(2)}), \tag{10.4.13}$$

we now have:

> *Theorem 10.4.3* Under assumption 10.4.2 and condition (10.4.11) the conclusions of theorems 10.2.1–10.2.8 and theorem 10.3.1 carry over with k replaced by k_1 and $\int K(z)^2dz$ replaced by $\int K(z_1,0)^2dz_1$.

This theorem can be proved by combining the arguments in sections 10.2 and 10.4.1. The proof is somewhat cumbersome but does not involve insurmountable difficulties. It is therefore left to the reader.

Exercises

1. Prove theorem 10.4.2.
2. Prove theorem 10.4.3.

10.5 The choice of the kernel

In the literature on kernel density and regression function estimation the problem of how the kernel should be specified has mainly been considered from an asymptotic point of view. In the case of density estimation Epanechnikov (1969) has shown that the kernel which minimizes the integrated mean squared error

$$\int[\hat{h}(x)-h(x)]^2dx \tag{10.5.1}$$

over the class of product kernels

$$K(x)=K(x^{(1)},x^{(2)},\ldots,x^{(k)})=\prod_{i=1}^{k}K_0(x^{(i)}),\ x^{(i)}\in R, \tag{10.5.2}$$

with

$$K_0(v)=K_0(-v)\geq 0,\ \ \int K_0(v)dv=\int v^2K_0(v)dv=1,\ \int vK_0(v)dv=0, \tag{10.5.3}$$

is a product kernel with

$$\begin{aligned}&K_0(v)=3/(4\surd 5)\ -3v^2/(20\surd 5)\ \text{if}\ |v|\leq\surd 5,\\&K_0(v)=0\ \text{if}\ |v|>\surd 5.\end{aligned} \tag{10.5.4}$$

Note that Epanechnikov's kernel K_0 is the solution of the problem:

$$\text{minimize}\ \int K_0(v)^2dv,\ \text{subject to (10.5.3).} \tag{10.5.5}$$

Greblicki and Krzyzak (1980) have confirmed this result for the regression case. Epanechnikov also shows that there are various kernels which are nearly optimal. For example, the standard normal density satisfies the condition (10.5.3) and is almost optimal, as

$$\int[\exp(-\tfrac{1}{2}v^2)/\sqrt{(2\pi)}]^2dv = 1.051\int K_0(v)^2dv. \tag{10.5.6}$$

A disadvantage of Epanechnikov's kernel is that its Fourier transform is not absolutely integrable, a condition employed in section 10.3. Also, the non-negativity of K_0 implies that the kernel (10.5.2) with (10.5.4) merely satisfies $K \in \mathfrak{K}_{k,2}$, whereas higher rates of convergence in distribution than $n^{2/(k+4)}$ require $K \in \mathfrak{K}_{k,m}$ with $m > 2$. Cf. theorem 10.2.4.

Since kernels of the type (10.2.36) have all the required properties, are almost arbitrarily flexible and can easily be constructed, we advocate the use of that type of kernel. However, the question now arises how the matrix Ω should be specified. A heuristic approach to solve this problem is to specify Ω such that certain properties of the true regression function carry over to the estimate $\hat{g}$. The property we shall consider is the *linear translation invariance principle*. Suppose we apply a linear translation to x and the x_j's:

$$x^* = Px + q,\ X_j^* = PX_j + q, \tag{10.5.7}$$

where P is a nonsingular $k \times k$ matrix and q is a k-component vector. Then

$$g(x) = E(Y_j|X_j = x) = E(Y_j|X_j^* = x^*) = g^*(x^*), \tag{10.5.8}$$

say. However, if we replace the X_j and x in (10.2.16) by X_j^* and x^*, respectively, and if we leave the kernel K unchanged, then the resulting kernel regression estimator $\hat{g}^*(x^*)$, say, will in general be unequal to $\hat{g}(x)$, for

$$\hat{g}^*(x^*) = \{\textstyle\sum_{j=1}^n Y_jK[P(x-X_j)/\gamma_n)]\}/\{\textstyle\sum_{j=1}^n K[P(x-X_j)/\gamma_n]\} \neq \hat{g}(x) \text{ if } P \neq I \tag{10.5.9}$$

The only way to accomplish $\hat{g}^*(x^*) = \hat{g}(x)$ in all cases (10.5.7) is to let the kernel be of the form

$$\hat{K(x)} = \eta(x'\hat{V}^{-1}x), \tag{10.5.10}$$

where η is a real function on R and $\hat{V}$ is the sample variance matrix, i.e.,

$$\hat{V} = (1/n)\textstyle\sum_{j=1}^n(X_j - \bar{X})(X_j - \bar{X})' \text{ with } \bar{X} = (1/n)\textstyle\sum_{j=1}^n X_j. \tag{10.5.11}$$

In particular, if we use kernels of the form (10.2.36) then we should specify $\Omega = \hat{V}$. Thus for $m = 2,4,6,\ldots$ we let

$$\hat{K}_m(x) = \textstyle\sum_{j=1}^{m/2}\theta_j\exp(-\tfrac{1}{2}x'\hat{V}^{-1}x/\sigma_j^2)/[(\sqrt{(2\pi)})^k|\sigma_j|^k\sqrt{\det(\hat{V})}] \tag{10.5.12a}$$

in the continuous case,

$$\hat{K}_m(x) = \textstyle\sum_{j=1}^{m/2}\theta_j\exp(-\tfrac{1}{2}x'\hat{V}^{-1}x/\sigma_j^2)/[(\sqrt{(2\pi)})^{k_1}|\sigma_j|^{k_1}\sqrt{\det((\hat{V}^{(1)})^{-1})}] \tag{10.5.12b}$$

in the mixed continuous–discrete case (with the first k_1 components of X_j continuously distributed) and

$$\hat{K}_m(x) = \hat{K}_2(x) = \exp(-\tfrac{1}{2}x'\hat{V}^{-1}x) \qquad (10.5.12c)$$

in the discrete case, where $\hat{V}^{(1)}$ is the upper-left $k_1 \times k_1$ submatrix of $\hat{V}^{-1}$ and

$$\textstyle\sum_{j=1}^{m/2} \theta_j\sigma_j^{2\ell} = 1 \text{ if } \ell = 0,\ \sum_{j=1}^{m/2} \theta_j\sigma_j^{2\ell} = 0 \text{ if } \ell = 1,2,\ldots,(m/2)-1. \qquad (10.5.13)$$

The question now arises whether the previous asymptotic results go through for kernel regression estimators with this kernel. The answer is yes, provided the following additional conditions hold.

> *Assumption 10.5.1* Let $E(|X_j|^4) < \infty$ and let the matrix
>
> $$V = E(X_jX_j') - [E(X_j)][E(X_j)]' \qquad (10.5.14)$$
>
> be nonsingular.

Denoting

$$K_m(x) = \textstyle\sum_{j=1}^{m/2}\theta_j\exp(-\tfrac{1}{2}x'V^{-1}x/\sigma_j^2)/[(\sqrt{(2\pi)})^k|\sigma_j|^k\sqrt{\det(V)}], \qquad (10.5.15a)$$

in the continuous case,

$$K_m(x) = \textstyle\sum_{j=1}^{m/2}\theta_j\exp(-\tfrac{1}{2}x'V^{-1}x/\sigma_j^2)/[(\sqrt{(2\pi)})^{k_1}|\sigma_j|^{k_1}\det((V^{(1)})^{-1})] \qquad (10.5.15b)$$

in the mixed continuous–discrete case, where $V^{(1)}$ is the upper-left $k_1 \times k_1$ submatrix of V^{-1} and the θ_j and the σ_j are the same as before, and

$$K_m(x) = K_2(x) = \exp(-\tfrac{1}{2}x'V^{-1}x) \qquad (10.5.15c)$$

in the discrete case, we can now state:

> *Theorem 10.5.1* With assumption 10.5.1 the kernel regression estimator with kernel (10.5.12) has the same asymptotic properties (as previously considered) as the kernel regression estimator with kernel (10.5.15).

Proof: We shall prove this theorem only for the continuous case with kernel $\hat{K}_2(x)$. The proof for the other cases is similar and therefore left to the reader. Let

$$\hat{s}(x) = (1/n)\textstyle\sum_{j=1}^{n} Y_j\exp[-\tfrac{1}{2}(x-X_j)'\hat{V}^{-1}(x-X_j)/\gamma_n^2] \;/[(\sqrt{(2\pi)})^k\gamma_n^k\sqrt{\det(\hat{V})}], \qquad (10.5.16)$$

$$\tilde{s}(x) = (1/n)\textstyle\sum_{j=1}^{n} Y_j\exp[-\tfrac{1}{2}(x-X_j)'V^{-1}(x-X_j)/\gamma_n^2] \;/[(\sqrt{(2\pi)})^k\gamma_n^k\sqrt{\det(\hat{V})}], \qquad (10.5.17)$$

$$\bar{s}(x) = (1/n)\sum_{j=1}^{n} Y_j \exp[-\tfrac{1}{2}(x-X_j)'V^{-1}(x-X_j)/\gamma_n^2] \\ /[(\sqrt{(2\pi)})^k \gamma_n^k \sqrt{\det(V)}]. \tag{10.5.18}$$

Moreover, let

$$\hat{M} = \max_{i,j}|\hat{v}^{(i,j)} - v^{(i,j)}|, \tag{10.5.19}$$

where $\hat{v}^{(i,j)}$ is the typical element of $\hat{V}^{-1}$ and $v^{(i,j)}$ is the typical element of V^{-1}. For every $t=(t_1,...,t_k)'R^k$ we have

$$|t'\hat{V}^{-1}t - t'V^{-1}t| \leq \hat{M}\sum_{i,j}|t_i t_j| \leq k\,\hat{M}t't \leq \rho\hat{M}t'V^{-1}t, \tag{10.5.20}$$

where ρ is the maximum eigenvalue of V times k. Using inequality (10.5.20) and the mean value theorem it is not too hard to verify that

$$|\hat{s}(x) - \tilde{s}(x)| \leq [\rho\hat{M}/(n\gamma_n^k)]\sum_{j=1}^{n}|Y_j|[(x-X_j)'V^{-1}(x-X_j)/\gamma_n^2] \\ \times \exp[\tfrac{1}{2}\rho\hat{M}(x-X_j)'V^{-1}(x-X_j)/\gamma_n^2]\exp[-\tfrac{1}{2}(x-X_j)'V^{-1}(x-X_j)/\gamma_n^2] \\ /[(\sqrt{(2\pi)})^k\sqrt{\det(\hat{V})}]. \tag{10.5.21}$$

Since the X_j's are independent and have bounded fourth moments we have for every $\varepsilon > 0$,

$$n^{\frac{1}{2}-\varepsilon}(\hat{V} - V) \to 0 \text{ in pr.}, \tag{10.5.22}$$

as is easy to verify by using Chebishev's inequality. Since the elements of an inverse matrix are continuously differentiable functions of the elements of the inverted matrix, provided the inverted matrix is nonsingular, it follows that (10.5.22) implies

$$n^{\frac{1}{2}-\varepsilon}(\hat{V}^{-1} - V^{-1}) \to 0 \text{ in pr.} \tag{10.5.23}$$

and consequently

$$\text{plim}_{n\to\infty} n^{\frac{1}{2}-\varepsilon}\,\hat{M} = 0 \text{ for every } \varepsilon > 0. \tag{10.5.24}$$

Thus also

$$\lim_{n\to\infty} P(\rho\hat{M} < 1/4) = 1. \tag{10.5.25}$$

Now (10.5.21) and (10.5.25) imply that the inequality

$$|\hat{s}(x) - \tilde{s}(x)| \leq (2\rho k\hat{M}/\gamma_n^k)(\sqrt{\det(V)}/\sqrt{\det(\hat{V})})(\sqrt{2})^k \\ \times (1/n)\sum_{j=1}^{n}|Y_j|K_*[(x-X_j)/\gamma_n] \tag{10.5.26}$$

with

$$K_*(x) = [x'V^{-1}x/(2k)]\exp[-(1/4)x'V^{-1}x]/[(\sqrt{(2\pi)})^k(\sqrt{2})^k\sqrt{\det(V)}] \tag{10.5.27}$$

holds with probability converging to 1. Since

$$E\{(1/n)\sum_{j=1}^{n}|Y_j|K_*[(x-X_j)/\gamma_n]\gamma_n^{-k}\} \leq E\{(1+Y_0^2)K_*[(x-X_0)/\gamma]\gamma_n^{-k}\}$$
$$= \int[1+\sigma_u^2(x-\gamma_n z)+g(x-\gamma_n z)^2]h(x-\gamma_n z)K_*(z)dz$$
$$\rightarrow[1+\sigma_u^2(x)+g(x)^2]h(x) \text{ as } n\rightarrow\infty \qquad (10.5.28)$$

and since (10.5.24) implies

$$\text{plim}_{n\rightarrow\infty}\surd(n\gamma_n^k)\hat{M}=0, \qquad (10.5.29)$$

it now follows that, pointwise in x,

$$\text{plim}_{n\rightarrow\infty}\surd(n\gamma_n^k)|\hat{s}(x)-\tilde{s}(x)|=0 \qquad (10.5.30)$$

Next, observe that

$$\text{plim}_{n\rightarrow\infty}\surd(n\gamma_n^k)|\tilde{s}(x)-\bar{s}(x)|=0, \qquad (10.5.31)$$

for (10.5.22) implies that

$$\text{plim}_{n\rightarrow\infty}\surd(n\gamma_n^k)(\det(\hat{V})-\det(V))=0. \qquad (10.5.32)$$

Thus,

$$\text{plim}_{n\rightarrow\infty}\surd(n\gamma_n^k)(\hat{s}(x)-\bar{s}(x))=0. \qquad (10.5.33)$$

From this result it follows straightforwardly that the asymptotic normality results go through. The proof that the uniform consistency results go through is left as an exercise.

10.6 The choice of the window width

From the preceding results it is clear that the asymptotic performance of the kernel regression function estimator heavily depends on the choice of the window width γ_n. In particular, the asymptotic normality results in theorems 10.2.3 and 10.2.6 show that the variance of the limiting normal distribution of $\hat{g}_.$ shrinks down to zero if we let the constant c of the window-width parameters approach infinity. But that will destroy the small sample performance of the kernel regression estimator. If we choose too large a γ_n the Nadaraya–Watson regression function estimate will become too flat, for

$$\hat{g}(x)\rightarrow\bar{Y}=(1/n)\sum_{j=1}^{n}Y_j \text{ if we let } \gamma_n\rightarrow\infty. \qquad (10.6.1)$$

Similarly, $\hat{g}_.(x) \rightarrow \bar{Y}$ if $c \rightarrow \infty$. On the other hand, if we choose too small a γ_n the estimate $\hat{g}$ will go wild. For example, if we employ in (10.1.16) the kernel $\hat{K}_2$ and if we let $\gamma_n\downarrow 0$, then

$$\hat{g}(x)\rightarrow\sum_{j=1}^{n}Y_jI[(x-X_j)'\hat{V}^{-1}(x-X_j)=\min_\ell(x-X_\ell)'\hat{V}^{-1}(x-X_\ell)]$$
$$/\sum_{j=1}^{n}I[(x-X_j)\hat{V}^{-1}(x-X_j)=\min_\ell(x-X_\ell)'\hat{V}^{-1}(x-X_\ell)] \qquad (10.6.2)$$

($\ell = 1,\ldots,n$), where I(.) is the indicator function. Thus $\hat{g}(x)$ converges to the Y_j for which $(x - X_j)'\hat{V}^{-1}(x - X_j)$ is minimal, so that then the estimate $\hat{g}$ degenerates to an inconsistent nearest neighbor estimate. Cf. Stone (1977). Again, a similar result holds for $\hat{g}_*$ if we let $c \to 0$.

A somewhat heuristic but effective trick to optimize the window width is the cross-validation approach introduced by Stone (1974), Geisser (1975), and Wahba and Wold (1975). See also Wong (1983). The basic idea is to split the data set in two parts. Then the first part is used for calculating the estimate and the second part is used for optimizing the fit of the estimate by minimizing the mean squared error. A variant used by Bierens (1983) is to consider various partitions and to minimize the mean of the mean squared errors. In particular, let

$$\hat{g}^{(\ell)}(x|\gamma) = \sum_{j=1}^{n} Y_j I(j \neq \ell)\hat{K}_m((x - X_j)/\gamma)/\sum_{j=1}^{n} I(j \neq \ell)\hat{K}_m[(x - X_j)/\gamma] \tag{10.6.3}$$

and denote similarly to (10.2.34),

$$\hat{g}_1^{(\ell)}(x|c) = \hat{g}^{(\ell)}(x|cn^{-1/(2m+k)}), \tag{10.6.4}$$

$$\hat{g}_2^{(\ell)}(x|c) = \hat{g}^{(\ell)}(x|cn^{-\delta/(2m+k)}), \tag{10.6.5}$$

$$\hat{g}_*^{(\ell)}(x|c) = (\hat{g}_1^{(\ell)}(x|c) \; - n^{-(1-\delta)m/(2m+k)}\hat{g}_2^{(\ell)}(x|c))/(1 - n^{-(1-\delta)m/(2m+k)}) \tag{10.6.6}$$

Then $\hat{g}_*^{(\ell)}(x|c)$ is the regression function estimator of the type (10.2.34) with kernel $\hat{K}_m$, based on the data set leaving the observation with index ℓ out. We now propose to optimize c by minimizing

$$\hat{Q}(c) = \sum_{j=1}^{n}(Y_j - \hat{g}_*^{(j)}(X_j|c))^2 \tag{10.6.7}$$

to c in an interval $[c_1,c_2]$ with $0 < c_1 < c_2 < \infty$. Denoting the resulting optimal c by $\hat{c}$, i.e.,

$$\hat{Q}(\hat{c}) = \inf(\hat{Q}(c)|c \in [c_1,c_2]), \tag{10.6.8}$$

we then propose to use

$$\hat{g}_*(x|\hat{c}) = \hat{g}_*^{(0)}(x|\hat{c}) \tag{10.6.9}$$

as the cross-validated kernel regression function estimator.

Although this approach works well in practice, it has the disadvantage that we lose control over some of the asymptotic properties of kernel estimators. From Bierens (1983) it follows that the cross-validated kernel regression estimator remains (uniformly) consistent, but it is not clear whether asymptotic normality goes through. We can regain some control over the asymptotic behaviour of $\hat{g}_*(x|\hat{c})$ if instead of (10.6.8) we use

$$\hat{Q}(\hat{c}) = \min(\hat{Q}(c^{(\ell)}|\ell = 1,2,\ldots,M), \tag{10.6.10}$$

where $c_1 = c^{(1)} < \ldots < c^{(M)} = c_2$ are grid points. It is not hard to show that in the continuous case the M-variate limiting distribution of

$$n^{m/(2m+k)}(\hat{g}_*(x|c^{(1)}) - g(x), \ldots, \hat{g}_*(x|c^{(M)}) - g(x)) \tag{10.6.11}$$

is M-variate normal with zero mean vector. Hence for x with $h(x) > 0$ we have at least

$$n^{m/(2m+k)}(\hat{g}_*(x|\hat{c}) - g(x)) = O_p(1). \tag{10.6.12}$$

A similar result holds for the mixed continuous–discrete case. However, if for this $\hat{c}$, $\text{plim}_{n\to\infty}\hat{c} = c$, then asymptotic normality goes through as if $\hat{c} = c$. Moreover, in the discrete case the cross-validated regression estimator has the same properties as before, without additional conditions.

If our sample is large, we may proceed as follows. Split the sample into two subsamples of sizes n_1 and n_2, respectively. Now apply the cross-validation procedure as described above to one of the subsamples, say subsample 2, or alternatively, determine an appropriate c by visual inspection of the nonparametric regression results based on this subsample. Then use the resulting $\hat{c}$ as constant in the regression function estimator $\hat{g}_*(x|c)$ based on subsample 1. Since now $\hat{c}$ and $\hat{g}_*(x|c)$ are independent, the asymptotic distribution results go through for $\hat{g}_*(x|\hat{c})$, conditional on $\hat{c}$.

10.7 Nonparametric time series regression

Recently the kernel regression approach has been extended to time series. Robinson (1983) shows strong consistency and asymptotic normality, using the α-mixing concept. In Bierens (1983) we proved uniform consistency under υ-stability in L^2 with respect to a φ-mixing base, and in Bierens (1987b) we generalized this result to pointwise consistency and asymptotic normality. Collomb (1985b) proves uniform strong consistency under the φ-mixing condition and Georgiev (1984) proves consistency in the case of a Markov data-generating process. In this section we shall extend the results in the previous sections to time series, employing the υ-stablity and φ-mixing concepts, on the basis of the results in Bierens (1987b).

10.7.1 Assumptions and preliminary lemmas

We first state the assumptions we need to prove pointwise and uniform consistency and asymptotic normality of kernel time series regression estimators, and we prove three basic lemmas.

Assumption 10.7.1 The data-generating process $\{(Y_t,X_t)\}$ is a strictly stationary υ-stable process in L^2 with respect to a strictly stationary φ-mixing base (W_t), where

$$\upsilon(m) = O(\exp(-c{\cdot}m)) \text{ for some } c > 0; \tag{10.7.1}$$

$$\textstyle\sum_{m=0}^{\infty}\varphi(m)^{1/2} < \infty. \tag{10.7.2}$$

Also, we assume that $g(X_t)$ represents the conditional expectation of Y_t given the entire past of the data-generating process:

Assumption 10.7.2 Let

$$g(X_t) = E(Y_t|X_t,X_{t-1},X_{t-2},\ldots,Y_{t-1},Y_{t-2},\ldots) \text{ a.s.} \tag{10.7.3}$$

The vector X_t may contain lagged Y_t's. Thus $g(X_t)$ is in fact a (non)linear ARX model with unknown functional form g(.). We note that Robinson (1983) only assumes $E(Y_t|X_t) = g(X_t)$, which is weaker than (10.7.3). However, as has been argued in chapter 7, proper time series models should satisfy condition (10.7.3). The errors U_t are then martingale differences, so that the martingale difference central limit theorem 6.1.7 is applicable.

Next, we assume:

Assumption 10.7.3.

(i) If assumption 10.2.1 holds then in addition:
  (a) $\sigma_u^4(x)h(x)$ is uniformly bounded;
  (b) $g(x)^2h(x)$ has countinuous and bounded second derivatives.

(ii) If assumption 10.4.2 holds then for every fixed $x^{(2)} \in \Delta_2$,
  (a) $\sigma_u^4(x^{(1)},x^{(2)})h(x^{(1)}|x^{(2)})$ is uniformly bounded on Δ_1;
  (b) $g(x^{(1)},x^{(2)})^2h(x^{(1)}|x^{(2)})$ has continuous and bounded second derivatives with respect to the components of $x^{(1)}$.

Finally, in order to prove theorem 10.5.1 for time series we need the following addition to assumption 10.7.1:

Assumption 10.7.4 The process $\{(Y_j,X_j)\}$ is υ-stable in L^4 with respect to the φ-mixing base considered in assumption 10.7.1.

The following lemma will be used to prove pointwise consistency and asymptotic normality of the kernel regression estimators considered in sections 10.1 through 10.4.

Lemma 10.7.1 Let $\{(Z_j,X_j)\}$ be a strictly stationary stochastic process in $R \times R^k$, with $E(Z_j^4) < \infty$ and $E(|X_j|^2) < \infty$. Let this process be υ-stable in L^2 with respect to a strictly stationary φ-mixing base, where υ satisfies condition (10.7.1) and φ satisfies condition (10.7.2). Let K be a Borel measurable real function on R^k such that

$$\int|K(x)|dx < \infty; \int|t\psi(t)|dt < \infty,$$

where

$$\psi(t) = \int \exp(i\cdot t'x)K(x)dx.$$

Denote for $x \in R^k$,

$$d_n(x) = \mathrm{var}\{(1/n)\textstyle\sum_{j=1}^{n} Z_j K[(x-X_j)/\gamma_n]\} \\ -(1/n^2)\textstyle\sum_{j=1}^{n} \mathrm{var}\{Z_j K[(x-X_j)/\gamma_n]\}, \qquad (10.7.4)$$

where $\gamma_n > 0$, $\gamma_n \downarrow 0$ as $n \to \infty$. Then

$$d_n(x) = O\big(\{\ln(n/\gamma_n) + \ln\big[1/\big(E\{Z_0^2 K[(x-X_0)/\gamma_n]^2\}\big)\big]\} \\ \times E\{Z_0^2 K[(x-X_0)/\gamma_n]^2/n\}\big)$$

Proof: We can write

$$d_n(x) = 2(1/n^2)\textstyle\sum_{\ell=1}^{n-1}\sum_{j=1}^{n-\ell} \mathrm{cov}\{Z_0 K[(x-X_0)/\gamma_n], Z_j K[(x-X_j)/\gamma_n]\} \\ = 2(1/n^2)\textstyle\sum_{\ell=1}^{n-1}\sum_{j=1}^{n-\ell} E\{Z_0 Z_j K[(x-X_0)/\gamma_n] K[(x-X_j)/\gamma_n]\} \\ -2(1/n^2)\textstyle\sum_{\ell=1}^{n-1}\sum_{j=1}^{n-\ell} E\big(\{Z_0 K[(x-X_0)/\gamma_n]\}^2.\big) \qquad (10.7.5)$$

Similarly, let

$$d_n^{(m)}(x) \\ = 2(1/n^2)\textstyle\sum_{\ell=1}^{n-1}\sum_{j=1}^{n-\ell} \mathrm{cov}\{Z_0^{(m)} K[(x-X_0^{(m)}]/\gamma_n), Z_j^{(m)} K[(x-X_j^{(m)})/\gamma_n]\} \\ = 2(1/n^2)\textstyle\sum_{\ell=1}^{n-1}\sum_{j=1}^{n-\ell} E\{Z_0^{(m)} Z_j^{(m)} K[(x-X_0^{(m)})/\gamma_n] K[(x-X_j^{(m)})/\gamma_n]\} \\ -2(1/n^2)\textstyle\sum_{\ell=1}^{n-1}\sum_{j=1}^{n-\ell} E\big(\{Z_0^{(m)} K((x-X_0^{(m)})/\gamma_n)\}^2\big), \qquad (10.7.6)$$

where

$$Z_j^{(m)} = E(Z_j|W_j, W_{j-1}, W_{j-2}, \ldots, W_{j-m}); \\ X_j^{(m)} = E(X_j|W_j, W_{j-1}, W_{j-2}, \ldots, W_{j-m}).$$

We shall prove the lemma in three steps:

Step 1:

$$|d_n^{(m)}(x)| \le 4n^{-1}\big(m + \textstyle\sum_{\ell=0}^{\infty}\varphi(\ell)^{1/2}\big)E\big(\{Z_0^{(m)} K[(x-X_0^{(m)})/\gamma_n]\}^2\big);$$

Step 2: For sufficiently large n and some constant $c_1 > 0$, independent of j and m, we have

$$E\big(\sup_x|\{Z_0 K[(x-X_0)/\gamma_n]\}\{Z_j K[(x-X_j)/\gamma_n]\} \\ -\{Z_0^{(m)} K[(x-X_0^{(m)}]/\gamma_n)\}\{Z_j^{(m)} K[(x-X_j^{(m)}]/\gamma_n)\}|\big) \le c_1\gamma_n^{-1}\upsilon(m);$$

Step 3: For sufficiently large n and some constants $c_2 > 0$, $c_3 > 0$, independent of x, j and m, we have

$$\begin{aligned}&|E\{Z_0K[(x-X_0)/\gamma_n]\}E\{Z_jK[(x-X_j)/\gamma_n]\}\\&\quad -E\{Z_0^{(m)}K[(x-X_0^{(m)})/\gamma_n]\}E\{Z_j^{(m)}K[(x-X_j^{(m)})/\gamma_n]\}|\\&\quad\quad \leq c_2(\gamma_n^{-1}\upsilon(m))^2 + c_3\gamma_n^{-1}\upsilon(m).\end{aligned}$$

We first show that the results of these three steps imply the lemma. Let (m_n) be a sequence of positive integers such that $m_n \to \infty$ and $m_n/n \to 0$, and let n be so large that

$$m_n \geq \sum_{\ell=0}^{\infty}\varphi(\ell)^{1/2}.$$

It follows from step 1 and step 2 with $j=0$ that for sufficiently large n,

$$|d_n^{(m)}(x)| \leq 8(m_n/n)E\big(\{Z_0K[(x-X_0)/\gamma_n]\}^2\big) + 8(m_n/n)c_1\gamma_n^{-1}\upsilon(m_n).$$

Moreover, it follows from steps 2 and 3 that

$$|d_n(x)-d_n^{(m)}(x)| \leq 2(c_1+c_3)\gamma_n^{-1}\upsilon(m_n) + 2c_2(\gamma_n^{-1}\upsilon(m_n))^2.$$

Without loss of generality we may assume that for sufficiently large n,

$$m_n/n \leq (c_1+c_2+c_3)/4 \text{ and } \gamma_n^{-1}\upsilon(m_n) \leq 1 \tag{10.7.7}$$

(as will appear). Then

$$\begin{aligned}|d_n(x)|&\leq 8(m_n/n)E\big(\{Z_0K[(x-X_0)/\gamma_n]\}^2\big)+4(c_1+c_2+c_3)\gamma_n^{-1}\upsilon(m_n)\\&= O(\rho_n(x)),\end{aligned}$$

where

$$\rho_n(x)=(m_n/n)E\big(\{Z_0K[(x-X_0)/\gamma_n]\}^2\big)+\gamma_n^{-1}\exp(-c\cdot m_n). \tag{10.7.8}$$

Minimizing the right-hand side of (10.7.8) to m_n yields

$$\upsilon(m_n)=\exp(-c\cdot m_n)=(1/c)(\gamma_n/n)\big(E\{Z_0K[(x-X_0)/\gamma_n]\}\big)^{-2},$$

with

$$m_n=(1/c)\big[\log(c)+\log(n/\gamma_n)-2\cdot\log\big(E\{Z_0K[(x-X_0)/\gamma_n]\}\big)\big],$$

(thus observe that indeed (10.7.7) holds). Hence

$$\begin{aligned}\rho_n(x) &\leq (1/c)|1+\log(c)+\log(n/\gamma_n)\\&\quad +\log\big[\big(E\{Z_0^2K[(x-X_0)/\gamma_n]^2\}\big)^{-1}\big]|\big(E\{Z_0^2K[(x-X_0)/\gamma_n]^2/n\}\big)\\&=O\big\{\big[\ln(n/\gamma_n)+\ln\big(E\{Z_0^2K[(x-X_0)/\gamma_n]^2\}\big)^{-1}\big]E\{Z_0^2K[(x-X_0)/\gamma_n]^2/n\}\big\},\end{aligned}$$

as was to be shown.

Proof of step 1:

Since $\{Z_j^{(m)}K[(x-X_j^{(m)})/\gamma_n]\}$ is a φ^*-mixing sequence, where

$\varphi^*(\ell)=1$ if $\ell<m$, $\varphi^*(\ell)=\varphi(\ell\text{-}m)$ if $\ell\geq m$,

it follows from (6.2.3) and theorem 6.2.1 that

$$\text{cov}\{Z_0^{(m)}K[(x-X_0^{(m)})/\gamma_n],Z_j^{(m)}K[(x-X_j^{(m)})/\gamma_n]\} \leq 2\varphi^*(j)^{1/2}E\left(\{Z_0^{(m)}K[(x-X_0^{(m)})/\gamma_n]\}^2\right).$$

Step 1 follows now from the fact that

$\sum_{j=0}^{\infty}\varphi^*(j)^{1/2}\leq m+\sum_{j=0}^{\infty}\varphi(j)^{1/2}$.

Proof of step 2:

From the inversion formula for Fourier transforms we have

$$K(x)=[1/(2\pi)]^k\int\exp(-i\cdot t'x)\psi(t)dt \tag{10.7.9}$$

From (10.7.9) it follows that for all $x\in R^k$

$$\begin{aligned}
&|Z_0Z_jK[(x-X_0)/\gamma_n]K[(x-X_j)/\gamma_n] \\
&\qquad -Z_0^{(m)}Z_j^{(m)}K[(x-X_0^{(m)})/\gamma_n]K[(x-X_j^{(m)})/\gamma_n]| \\
&\leq [1/(2\pi)]^{2k}\gamma_n^{2k}\int\int|Z_0Z_j\exp(i\cdot t_1'X_0+i\cdot t_2'X_j) \\
&-Z_0^{(m)}Z_j^{(m)}\exp(i\cdot t_1'X_0^{(m)}+i\cdot t_2'X_j^{(m)})||\psi(\gamma_nt_1)\psi(\gamma_nt_2)|dt_1dt_2. \\
&\leq [1/(2\pi)]^{2k}\gamma_n^{2k}\int\int|Z_0Z_j\exp(i\cdot t_1'X_0+i\cdot t_2'X_j) \\
&\quad -Z_0Z_j\exp(i\cdot t_1'X_0^{(m)}+i\cdot t_2'X_j^{(m)})||\psi(\gamma_nt_1)\psi(\gamma_nt_2)|dt_1dt_2 \\
&\quad +[1/(2\pi)]^{2k}\gamma_n^{2k}\int\int|Z_0Z_j\exp(i\cdot t_1'X_0^{(m)}+i\cdot t_2'X_j^{(m)}) \\
&-Z_0^{(m)}Z_j^{(m)}\exp(i\cdot t_1'X_0^{(m)}+i\cdot t_2'X_j^{(m)})||\psi(\gamma_nt_1)\psi(\gamma_nt_2)|dt_1dt_2. \\
&\leq [1/(2\pi)]^{2k}\gamma_n^{2k}|Z_0Z_j||(X_0,X_j)-(X_0^{(m)},X_j^{(m)})| \\
&\qquad\times\int\int|(t_1,t_2)||\psi(\gamma_nt_1)\psi(\gamma_nt_2)|dt_1dt_2 \\
&+[1/(2\pi)]^{2k}\gamma_n^{2k}|Z_0Z_j-Z_0^{(m)}Z_j^{(m)}|\int\int|\psi(\gamma_nt_1)\psi(\gamma_nt_2)|dt_1dt_2. \\
&\leq [1/(2\pi)]^{2k}\gamma_n^{-1}|Z_0Z_j||(X_0,X_j)-(X_0^{(m)},X_j^{(m)})| \\
&\qquad\times\int\int|(t_1,t_2)||\psi(t_1)\psi(t_2)|dt_1dt_2 \\
&+[1/(2\pi)]^{2k}|Z_0Z_j\text{-}Z_0^{(m)}Z_j^{(m)}|\int\int|\psi(t_1)\psi(t_2)|dt_1dt_2. \\
&\leq [1/(2\pi)]^{2k}\gamma_n^{-1}|Z_0Z_j|(|X_0-X_0^{(m)}|^2+|X_j-X_j^{(m)}|^2)^{1/2} \\
&\qquad\qquad\times\int|t||\psi(t)|dt\int|\psi(t)|dt \\
&\quad +[1/(2\pi)]^{2k}(|Z_0||Z_j-Z_j^{(m)}|+|Z_0-Z_0^{(m)}||Z_j^{(m)}|)(\textstyle\int|\psi(t)|dt)^2.
\end{aligned} \tag{10.7.10}$$

Applying the Cauchy–Schwarz and Liapounov inequalities and using the inequality $E[(Z_j^{(m)})^2]\leq E(Z_j^2)$ (cf. exercise 1) it follows from (10.7.10) that there exist constants $c_*^{(1)}>0$, $c_*^{(2)}>0$, independent of j and m, such that

$$E\{\sup_x|Z_0Z_jK[(x-X_0)/\gamma_n]K((x-X_j)/\gamma_n] \\ -Z_0^{(m)}Z_j^{(m)}K[(x-X_0^{(m)})/\gamma_n]K[(x-X_j^{(m)}]/\gamma_n)|\} \\ \leq [1/(2\pi)]^{2k}\gamma_n^{-1}\{E[(Z_0Z_j)^2]\}^{½}\{E[|X_0-X_0^{(m)}|^2]+E[|X_j\text{-}X_j^{(m)}|^2]\}^{½} \\ \times \int|t||\psi(t)|dt\int|\psi(t)|dt \\ +[1/(2\pi)]^{2k}[E(Z_0^2)]^{½}\{E[(Z_j-Z_j^{(m)})^2]\}^{½}(\int|\psi(t)|dt)^2 \\ +[1/(2\pi)]^{2k}\{E[(Z_0-Z_0^{(m)})^2]\}^{½}[E(Z_j^2)]^{½}(\int|\psi(t)|dt)^2 \\ \leq c_*^{(1)}\gamma_n^{-1}\upsilon(m)+c_*^{(2)}\upsilon(m) \qquad (10.7.11)$$

For n so large that $c_*^{(1)}\gamma_n^{-1} \geq c_*^{(2)}$ we may take c_1 in step 2 equal to $2\cdot c_*^{(1)}$.

Proof of step 3:

By stationarity and the trivial inequality

$$|a^2-b^2| \leq (a-b)^2+|a||a-b|$$

we have

$$|E\{Z_0K[(x-X_0)/\gamma_n]\}E\{Z_jK[(x-X_j)/\gamma_n]\} \\ -E\{Z_0^{(m)}K[(x-X_0^{(m)})/\gamma_n]\}E\{Z_j^{(m)}K[(x-X_j^{(m)})/\gamma_n]\}| \\ =|(E\{Z_0K[(x-X_0)/\gamma_n]\})^2 - (E\{Z_0^{(m)}K[(x-X_0^{(m)})/\gamma_n]\})^2| \\ \leq \{E|Z_0K[(x-X_0)/\gamma_n] - Z_0^{(m)}K[(x-X_0^{(m)})/\gamma_n]|\}^2 \\ +|E\{Z_0K[(x-X_0)/\gamma_n]\}|E|Z_0K[(x-X_0)/\gamma_n]-Z_0^{(m)}K[(x-X_0^{(m)})/\gamma_n]| \qquad (10.7.12)$$

From (10.7.9) it follows, similarly to (10.7.11), that there exist constants $c_*^{(1)} > 0$, $c_*^{(2)} > 0$, independent of x and m, such that

$$E|Z_0K[(x-X_0)/\gamma_n)]-Z_0^{(m)}K[(x-X_0^{(m)})/\gamma_n]| \\ \leq [1/(2\pi)]^k\gamma_n^k\int E|Z_0\exp(i\cdot t'X_0) - Z_0^{(m)}\exp(i\cdot t'X_0^{(m)})||\psi(\gamma_n t)|dt \\ \leq [1/(2\pi)]^k\gamma_n^kE|Z_0 - Z_0^{(m)}|\int|\psi(\gamma_n t)|dt \\ +[1/(2\pi)]^k\gamma_n^kE|X_0 - X_0^{(m)}||Z_0^{(m)}|\int|t\psi(\gamma_n t)|dt \\ \leq [1/(2\pi)]^k\{E|Z_0 - Z_0^{(m)}|\}^{½}\int|\psi(t)|dt \\ +[1/(2\pi)]^k\gamma_n^k[E(|X_0 - X_0^{(m)}|^2)]^{½}\{E[(Z_0^{(m)})]^2]\}^{½}\int|t\psi(t)|dt \\ \leq c_*^{(1)}\gamma_n^{-1}\upsilon(m)+c_*^{(2)}\upsilon(m). \qquad (10.7.13)$$

Realizing that by (10.7.9)

$$|E\{Z_0K[(x-X_0)/\gamma_n]\}| \leq [1/(2\pi)]^kE|Z_0|\int|\varphi(t)|dt < \infty,$$

step 3 now easily follows from (10.7.12) and (10.7.13). This completes the proof. Q.E.D.

The following lemma enables us to prove uniform consistency

Lemma 10.7.2 Let the conditions of lemma 10.7.1 hold, except that now $E(Z_j^2) < \infty$ suffices, and let

$$a_n(x) = (1/n)\sum_{j=1}^n Z_j K[(x - X_j)/\gamma_n]$$

Then

$$E\{\sup_x |a_n(x) - E[a_n(x)]|\} = O\{[\log(n/\gamma_n^2)]^{1/2}/\sqrt{n}\}$$

Proof: Let

$$a_n^{(m)}(x) = (1/n)\sum_{j=1}^n Z_j^{(m)} K[(x - X_j^{(m)})/\gamma_n].$$

It follows from (10.7.9), similarly to (10.7.18), that there exist constants $c_*^{(1)} > 0$, $c_*^{(2)} > 0$, independent of x and m, such that

$$E[\sup_x |a_n(x) - a_n^{(m)}(x)|] \leq c_*^{(1)}\gamma_n^{-1}\upsilon(m) + c_*^{(2)}\upsilon(m). \tag{10.7.14}$$

Moreover, it follows from (10.7.9), the well-known formula

$$\exp(i\cdot u) = \cos(u) + i\sin(u),$$

Liapounov's inequality and inequality (1.4.4) that

$$\begin{aligned} &E\{\sup_x |a_n^{(m)}(x) - E[a_n^{(m)}(x)]|\} \\ &\leq [1/(2\pi)]^k \gamma_n^k \int E|(1/n)\sum_{j=1}^n \{Z_j^{(m)}\exp(i\cdot t'X_j^{(m)}) \\ &\qquad - E[Z_j^{(m)}\exp(i\cdot t'X_j^{(m)})]\}|\,|\psi(\gamma_n t)|dt \\ &\leq (\sqrt{2})[1/(2\pi)]^k\gamma_n^k \int \{E[(1/n)\sum_{j=1}^n \{Z_j^{(m)}\cos(t'X_j^{(m)}) \\ &\qquad - E[Z_j^{(m)}\cos(t'X_j^{(m)})]\})^2]\}^{1/2}|\psi(\gamma_n t)|dt \\ &+ (\sqrt{2})[1/(2\pi)]^k\gamma_n^k \int \{E[((1/n)\sum_{j=1}^n \{Z_j^{(m)}\cos(t'X_j^{(m)}) \\ &\qquad - E[Z_j^{(m)}\cos(t'X_j^{(m)})]\})]]^2\}^{1/2}|\psi(\gamma_n t)|dt. \end{aligned} \tag{10.7.15}$$

Similarly to step 1 in the proof of lemma 10.7.1 we have, uniformly in t,

$$\begin{aligned} &E[((/n)\sum_{j=1}^n \{Z_j^{(m)}\cos(t'X_j^{(m)}) - E[Z_j^{(m)}\cos(t'X_j^{(m)})]\})^2] \\ &\leq [(1/n) + 4n^{-1}(m + \sum_{\ell=0}^\infty \varphi(\ell)^{1/2})]E[(Z_0^{(m)})^2] \\ &\leq [(1/n) + 4n^{-1}(m + \sum_{\ell=0}^\infty \varphi(\ell)^{1/2})]E[(Z_0)^2] \leq c_*(m/n), \end{aligned} \tag{10.7.16}$$

say, for sufficiently large m, and similarly,

$$E[((1/n)\sum_{j=1}^n \{Z_j^{(m)}\sin(t'X_j^{(m)}) - E[Z_j^{(m)}\sin(t'X_j^{(m)})]\})^2] \leq c_*(m/n), \tag{10.7.17}$$

Combining (10.7.15), (10.7.16) and (10.7.17) it follows that

$$\begin{aligned} &E\{\sup_x |a_n^{(m)}(x) - E[a_n^{(m)}(x)]|\} \\ &\qquad \leq \{(2\sqrt{2})[1/(2\pi)]^k \int |\psi(t)|dt\sqrt{c_*}\}(m/n)^{1/2} = c_1(m/n)^{1/2}, \end{aligned} \tag{10.7.18}$$

say. Combining (10.7.14) and (10.7.18) it follows that for sufficiently large n

$$E\{\sup_x|a_n(x) - E[a_n(x)]|\} \le 2\, E\{\sup_x|a_n(x) - a_n^{(m_n)}(x)|\}$$
$$+ E\{\sup_x|a_n^{(m_n)}(x) - E[a_n^{(m_n)}(x)]|\}$$
$$\le 2c_*^{(1)}\gamma_n^{-1}\upsilon(m_n) + 2c_*^{(2)}\upsilon(m_n) + c_1(m_n/n)^{1/2}$$
$$= O\{[(m_n/n) + \gamma_n^{-2}\exp(-2c\cdot m_n)]^{1/2}\}, \quad (10.7.19)$$

say. Minimizing the right hand side of (10.7.19) to m_n, the lemma follows. Q.E.D.

Finally, the following lemma will enable us to extend the results in section 10.5 to time series.

Lemma 10.7.3 Let (Z_j) be a strictly stationary stochastic process in R satisfying $E(Z_j^4) < \infty$. Let (Z_j) be υ-stable in L^4 with respect to a strictly stationary φ-mixing base, where

$$\upsilon(m) = O[\exp(-c\cdot m)] \text{ for some } c > 0,\ \sum_{\ell=0}^{\infty}\varphi(\ell)^{1/2} < \infty. \quad (10.7.20)$$

Then for every $\varepsilon > 0$,

$$\text{plim}_{n\to\infty} n^{1/2-\varepsilon}(1/n)\sum_{j=1}^{n}[Z_j - E(Z_j^2)] = 0 \quad (10.7.21)$$

and

$$\text{plim}_{n\to\infty} n^{1/2-\varepsilon}(1/n)\sum_{j=1}^{n}[Z_j^2 - E(Z_j^2)] = 0. \quad (10.7.22)$$

Proof: Let (W_j) be the base and let

$$Z_j^{(m)} = E(Z_j|W_j, W_{j-1}, W_{j-2}, \ldots, W_{j-m}).$$

Denote similarly to (10.7.4), (10.7.5), and (10.7.6)

$$d_n = \text{var}[(1/n)\sum_{j=1}^{n}Z_j^2] - (1/n^2)\sum_{j=1}^{n}\text{var}(Z_j^2),$$
$$d_n^{(m)} = \text{var}[(1/n)\sum_{j=1}^{n}(Z_j^{(m)})^2] - (1/n^2)\sum_{j=1}^{n}\text{var}[(Z_j^{(m)})^2].$$

Then it follows similarly to the proof of lemma 10.7.1 that for sufficiently large n

$$|d_n^{(m)}| \le 4[(m + \sum_{\ell=0}^{\infty}\varphi(\ell)^{1/2})/n]E(Z_j^4) \le c_1 m/n,$$

and

$$|d_n - d_n^{(m)}| \le c_2\upsilon(m),$$

for some $c_1 > 0, c_2 > 0$. Thus

$$d_n = O[(m_n/n) + \exp(-c\cdot m_n)]$$

Now choose $m = n^{\varepsilon}$. Then

$$n^{1-2\varepsilon}\text{var}[(1/n)\sum_{j=1}^{n}Z_j^2]$$
$$\le n^{1-2\varepsilon}\{c_1 n^{\varepsilon-1} + c_2\exp[-(1/4)cn^{\varepsilon}]\} + n^{-2\varepsilon}E(Z_0^4) \to 0$$

as $n \to \infty$. This proves (10.7.22). The proof of (10.7.21) is nearly the same.
Q.E.D.

10.7.2 Consistency and asymptotic normality of time series kernel regression function estimators

In this subsection we now generalize the approach in sections 10.1–10.6 to time series.

Theorem 10.7.1 Let

$$E(U_j^8) < \infty \text{ and } E[g(X_j)^4] < \infty \tag{10.7.23}$$

and let the kernel K be such that for $\ell = 1,2$,

$$\int |t\psi_\ell(t)|dt < \infty, \text{ where } \psi_\ell(t) = \int \exp(i \cdot t'x)K(x)^\ell dx. \tag{10.7.24}$$

Moreover,

let $\int zz'K(z)^2dz$ be finite in the continuous case, and let $\int z_1z_1'K(z_1,0)^2dz_1$ be finite in the mixed continuous–discrete case, respectively. (10.7.25)

(Note that the conditions (10.7.24) and (10.7.25) hold for kernels of the type (10.2.36).)

With assumptions 10.7.1, 10.7.2, and 10.7.3 and the conditions (10.7.23), (10.7.24), and (10.7.25) the asymptotic normality results in sections 10.2 and 10.4 go through.

Proof: We only prove the theorem for the continuous case, leaving the proofs for the discrete and mixed continuous–discrete cases as exercises. We now have to show that (10.2.2) and (10.2.4) go through and that

$$\mathrm{var}(\hat{h}(x)) \to 0 \tag{10.7.26}$$

in the time series case under review, as only in these steps has the independence assumption been employed.

Step 1: proof of (10.2.2). Since now the $v_{n,j}(x)$ defined by (10.2.7) are martingale differences, it suffices to show

$$\mathrm{plim}_{n\to\infty}(1/n)\sum_{j=1}^n [v_{n,j}(x)^2 - E(v_{n,j}(x)^2)] = 0, \tag{10.7.27}$$

as then (10.2.2) follows from theorem 6.1.7. Thus consider lemma 10.7.1 with $Z_j = U_j^2$ and K(x) replaced by $K(x)^2$. Since

$$E\{U_j^4K[(x-X_j)/\gamma_n]^4\} = \gamma_n^k\int\sigma_u^4(x-\gamma_nz)h(x-\gamma_nz)K(z)^4dz = O(\gamma_n^k),$$

it follows from lemma 10.7.1 that

$$\mathrm{var}\{(1/n)\textstyle\sum_{j=1}^{n} U_j^2 K[(x-X_j)/\gamma_n]^2/\gamma_n^k\}$$
$$= (1/n^2)\textstyle\sum_{j=1}^{n}\mathrm{var}\{U_j^2 K[(x-X_j)/\gamma_n]^2/\gamma_n^k\} + \gamma_n^{-2k} d_n(x)$$
$$= O[1/(n\gamma_n^k)] + O[(1/(n\gamma_n^k))\ln(n/\gamma_n^{k+1})] \to 0 \qquad (10.7.28)$$

as $n \to \infty$, provided γ_n is proportional to $n^{-\tau}$ with $\tau < 1/k$. Therefore, (10.7.26) follows from (10.7.28) and Chebishev's inequality.

Step 2: proof of (10.2.4). Let Z_j in lemma 10.7.1 be

$$Z_j = Y_j - U_j - g(x) = g(X_j) - g(x).$$

Then

$$\mathrm{var}\{\surd(n\gamma_n^k)(1/n)\textstyle\sum_{j=1}^{n}[g(X_j)-g(x)]K[(x-X_j)/\gamma_n]/\gamma_n^k\}$$
$$-(1/n^2)\textstyle\sum_{j=1}^{n}\mathrm{var}\{\surd(n\gamma_n^k)[g(X_j)-g(x)]K[(x-X_j)/\gamma_n]/\gamma_n^k\}$$
$$= (n/\gamma_n^k)d_n(x) = O[\gamma_n^2\ln(n/\gamma_n^{k+3})] + o(1),$$

where the last conclusion follows from the fact that by assumption 10.7.3 and Taylor's theorem

$$E\{[g(X_j)-g(x)]^2\}K[(x-X_j)/\gamma_n]^2$$
$$= \gamma_n^k\textstyle\int[g(x-\gamma_n z)-g(x)]^2 h(x-\gamma_n z)K(z)^2dz$$
$$\approx \gamma_n^{k+2}\textstyle\int\{z'(\partial/\partial x')[g(x)^2h(x)]\}^2K(z)^2dz = O(\gamma_n^{k+2}).$$

Since $\gamma_n^2\ln(n/\gamma_n^{k+3}) \to 0$ as $n \to \infty$ if γ_n is proportional to $n^{-\tau}$ with $\tau > 0$, (10.2.4) follows.

Step 3: proof of (10.7.26). Let

$$\sigma_n^2(x) = E\{K[(x-X_0)/\gamma_n]^2\}\gamma_n^{-k}.$$

Observe that similarly to (10.1.17),

$$\sigma_n^2(x) \to h(x)\textstyle\int K(z)^2dz.$$

Now let $Z_j = 1$ in lemma 10.7.1 and let x be such that $h(x) > 0$. Then

$$\mathrm{var}(\hat{h}(x)) \le \gamma_n^{-2k}d_n(x) + \sigma_n^2(x)/(n\gamma_n^k)$$
$$= O[(\log(n/\gamma_n) + \log(\gamma_n^{-k}) + 1)/(n\gamma_n^k)]$$
$$= O[(\log(n\gamma_n^{-k-1}))/(n\gamma_n^k)] \to 0$$

if γ_n is proportional to $n^{-\tau}$ with $\tau < 1/k$. Since the latter condition is satisfied throughout section 10.2, the proof of theorem 10.7.1 for the continuous case is completed. Q.E.D.

Theorem 10.7.2 Let assumption 10.7.1 hold. Then:

(i) the conclusion of theorem 10.3.1 becomes:

$$[n/\log(n)]^{m/(2m+2k)}\sup_{x\in\{x\in R^k:h(x)\geq\delta\}}|\hat{g}(x) - g(x)| = O_p(1),$$

with corresponding optimal window width of the form

$$\gamma_n = c\cdot[\log(n)/n]^{1/(2m+2k)};$$

(ii) the conclusion of theorem 10.4.1 regarding uniform consistency becomes:

$$[n/\log(n)]^{m/(2m+2k_1)}\sup_{x\in\{x\in R^k:h(x)\geq\delta\}}|\hat{g}(x) - g(x)| = O_p(1),$$

with corresponding optimal window width

$$\gamma_n = c\cdot[\log(n)/n]^{1/(2m+2k_1)},$$

where h(x) is defined by (10.4.13).

Proof: Again we confine our attention to the continuous case, i.e. part (i). The only places in section 10.3 where the independence assumption has been employed are (10.3.6) and, subsequently, (10.3.7) and (10.3.10). From lemma 10.7.2 with $Z_j = Y_j$ it follows that in the present case (10.3.7) becomes:

$$E\{\sup_x|\hat{g}(x)\hat{h}(x) - E[\hat{g}(x)\hat{h}(x)]|\}$$
$$= \gamma_n^{-k}E\{\sup_x|a_n(x) - E[a_n(x)]|\} = O\{[\log(n/\gamma_n^2)]^{1/2}/(\gamma_n^k\sqrt{n})\}. \quad (10.7.29)$$

Combining (10.7.29) with (10.3.9), there exist constants $c_1 > 0$, $c_2 > 0$ such that (10.3.10) becomes:

$$E[\sup_x|\hat{g}(x)\hat{h}(x) - g(x)h(x)|] = O\{c_1[\log(n/\gamma_n^2)]^{1/2}/(\gamma_n^k\sqrt{n}) + c_2\gamma_n^m\}$$
$$= O\{c_1[\log(n)]^{1/2}/(\gamma_n^k\sqrt{n}) + c_2\gamma_n^m\} \quad (10.7.30)$$

provided

$$\log(1/\gamma_n^2)/\log(n)\to 0. \quad (10.7.31)$$

Minimizing (10.7.30) to γ_n yields an optimal window width of the form $\gamma_n = c\cdot[\log(n)/n]^{1/(2m+2k)}$ for which indeed (10.7.31) holds. With this window width, (10.7.30) becomes

$$E[\sup_x|\hat{g}(x)\hat{h}(x) - g(x)h(x)|] = O\{[\log(n)/n]^{m/(2m+2k)}\}.$$

This proves part (a) of the theorem. Q.E.D.

Finally, we have

Theorem 10.7.3 Under the conditions of theorems 10.7.1 and 10.7.2 and the additional assumption 10.7.4 the conclusions of theorem 10.5.1 carry over.

Proof: It follows straightforwardly from lemma 10.7.3 that (10.5.22) goes through, which proves the theorem. Q.E.D.

Remark: We note that the φ-mixing condition on the base can be relaxed to the weaker α-mixing condition, but at the expense of stronger conditions on the moments of Y_j and X_j. This follows from theorem 6.2.1. This extension is left as an exercise.

Exercises

1. Prove $E[(Z_j^{(m)})^2] \leq E(Z_j^2)$. (cf. lemma 10.7.1).
2. Prove theorem 10.7.1 for the discrete and mixed continuous–discrete case.
3. Prove part (ii) of theorem 10.7.2.

References

Anderson,T.W. (1958), *An Introduction to Multivariate Statistical Analysis*, New York: John Wiley.

(1971), *The Statistical Analysis of Time Series*, New York: John Wiley.

Andrews,D.W.K. (1991), "Heteroskedasticity and Autocorrelation Consistent Covariance Matrix Estimation," *Econometrica*, 59: 817–858.

Arrow,K.J., H.B.Chenery, B.S.Minhas, and R.M.Solow (1961), "Capital–Labor Substitution and Economic Efficiency," *Review of Economics and Statistics*, 43: 225–250.

Atkinson,A.C. (1969), "A Test for Discriminating Between Models," *Biometrika*, 56: 337–347.

(1970), "A Method for Discriminating Between Models," *Journal of the Royal Statistical Society, Series B*, 32: 323–353.

Bierens,H.J. (1981), *Robust Methods and Asymptotic Theory in Nonlinear Econometrics*, Lecture Notes in Economics and Mathematical Systems, vol. 192, Berlin: Springer Verlag.

(1982), "Consistent Model Specification Tests," *Journal of Econometrics*, 20: 105–134.

(1983), "Uniform Consistency of Kernel Estimators of a Regression Function under Generalized Conditions," *Journal of the American Statistical Association*, 77: 699–707.

(1984), "Model Specification Testing of Time Series Regressions," *Journal of Econometrics*, 26: 323–353.

(1987a), "ARMAX Model Specification Testing, With an Application to Unemployment in the Netherlands," *Journal of Econometrics*, 35: 161–190.

(1987b), "Kernel Estimators of Regression Functions," in Truman F.Bewley (ed.), *Advances in Econometrics 1985*, New York: Cambridge University Press, 99–144.

(1988a), "ARMA Memory Index Modeling of Economic Time Series [with discussion]," *Econometric Theory*, 4: 35–59.

(1988b), "Reply," *Econometric Theory*, 4: 70–76.

(1990), "Model–Free Asymptotically Best Forecasting of Stationary Economic Time Series," *Econometric Theory*, 6: 348–383.

(1991a), "A Consistent Conditional Moment Test of Functional Form," *Econometrica*, 58: 1443–1458.

(1991b), "Least Squares Estimation of Linear and Nonlinear ARMAX models under Data Heterogeneity," *Annales d'Economie et de Statistique* 20/21: 143–169.

(1993), "Higher Order Sample Autocorrelations and the Unit Root Hypothesis," *Journal of Econometrics*, 57: 137—160.

Bierens,H.J. and L.Broersma (1993), "The Relation Between Unemployment and Interest Rate: Some International Evidence," *Econometric Reviews*, 12: 217–256.

Bierens,H.J. and S.Guo (1993), "Testing Stationarity and Trend Stationarity Against the Unit Root Hypothesis," *Econometric Reviews*, 12: 1–32.

Bierens,H.J. and J.Hartog (1988), "Non–Linear Regression with Discrete Explanatory Variables, with an Application to the Earnings Function," *Journal of Econometrics*, 38: 269–299.

Bierens,H.J. and H.Pott–Buter (1990), "Specification of Household Engel Curves by Nonparametric Regression [with discussion]," *Econometric Reviews*, 9: 123–184.

Billingsley,P. (1968), *Convergence of Probability Measures*, New York: John Wiley.

(1979), *Probability and Measure*, New York: John Wiley.

Box,G.E.P. and D.R.Cox (1964), "An Analysis of Transformations," *Journal of the Royal Statistical Society, Series B*, 26: 211–243.

Burguete, W.J., A.R.Gallant, and G.Souza (1982), "On Unification of the Asymptotic Theory on Nonlinear Models [with discussion]," *Econometric Reviews*, 1: 151–211.

Cacoullos,T. (1966), "Estimation of a Multivariate Density," *Annals of the Institute of Statistics and Mathematics*, 18: 179–189.

Cheng,K.F. (1983), "Strong Convergence in Nonparametric Estimation of Regression Functions," *Periodica Mathematica Hungarica*, 14: 177–187.

Chung,K.L. (1974), *A Course in Probability Theory*, New York: Academic Press.

Collomb,G. (1981), "Estimation non–paramétrique de la régression: revue bibliographique," *International Statistical Review*, 49: 75–93.

(1985a), "Nonparametric Regression: An Up–to-Date Bibliography," *Statistics*, 16: 309–324.

(1985b), "Non–parametric Time Series Analysis and Prediction: Uniform Almost Sure Convergence of the Window and K–NN Autoregression Estimates," *Statistics*, 16: 297–307.

Cox,D.R. (1961), "Tests for Separate Families of Hypotheses," *Proceedings of the 4th Berkeley Symposium*, 1: 105–123.

(1962), "Further Results on Tests of Separate Families of Hypotheses," *Journal of the Royal Statistical Society, Series B*, 24: 406–424.

Cramer,J.S. (1969), *Empirical Econometrics*, Amsterdam: North-Holland.

Dagenais, M.G and J.M. Dufour (1991), "Invariance, Nonlinear Models, and Asymptotic Tests," *Econometrica*, 59: 1601–1615.

Davidson,R. and J.G.MacKinnon (1981), "Several Tests for Model Specification in the Presence of Alternative Hypotheses," *Econometrica*, 49, 781–793.

Devroye,L.P. (1978), "The Uniform Convergence of the Nadaraya–Watson Regression Function Estimate," *Canadian Journal of Statistics*, 6: 179–191.

Dickey,D.A. and W.A.Fuller (1979), "Distribution of the Estimators for Autoregressive Time Series with a Unit Root," *Journal of the American Statistical Association*, 74: 427–431.

(1981), "Likelihood Ratio Statistics for Autoregressive Time Series with a Unit Root," *Econometrica*, 49: 1057–1072.

Dickey,D.A., D.P.Hasza, and W.A.Fuller (1984) "Testing for Unit Roots in Seasonal Time Series," *Journal of the American Statistical Association*, 79: 355–367.

Diebold,F. and M.Nerlove (1990), "Unit Roots in Economic Time Series: A Selective Survey," in T.B.Fomby and G.F.Rodes (eds.), *Co-Integration, Spurious Regressions, and Unit Roots*, London: JAI Press.

Doan,T., P.Litterman, and C.Sims (1984), "Forecasting and Conditional Projection Using Realistic Prior Distributions," *Econometric Reviews*, 3: 1–100.

Don,F.J.H. (1986), "Constrained Non–Linear Least Squares," *Statistica Neerlandica*, 40: 109–115.

Dunford,N. and J.T.Schwartz (1957), *Linear Operators*, Part I: *General Theory*, New York: Wiley Interscience.

Engle,R.F. (1987), "On the Theory of Cointegrated Economic Time Series," Invited paper presented at the Econometric Society European Meeting, Copenhagen.

Engle,R.F. and C.W.J.Granger (1987), "Cointegration and Error Correction: Representation, Estimation, and Testing," *Econometrica*, 55: 251–276.

Engle,R.F. and S.B.Yoo (1987), "Forecasting and Testing in Cointegrated Systems," *Journal of Econometrics*, 35: 143–159

(1989), "Cointegrated Economic Time Series: A Survey with New Results," mimeo, Department of Economics, University of California, San Diego.

Epanechnikov,V.A. (1969), "Non–parametric Estimation of a Multivariate Probability Density," *Theory of Probability and its Applications*, 14: 153–158.

Eubank,R. (1988), *Spline Smoothing and Nonparametric Regression*, New York: Marcel Dekker.

Evans,G.B.A. and N.E.Savin (1981), "Testing for Unit Roots: 1," *Econometrica*, 49: 753–779.

(1984), "Testing for Unit Roots: 2," *Econometrica*, 52, 1241–1269.

Feller,W. (1966), *An Introduction to Probability Theory and Its Applications*, vol. II, New York: John Wiley.

Fryer,M.J. (1977), "A Review of Some Non–parametric Methods of Density Estimation," *Journal of the Institute of Mathematics and its Applications*, 20: 335–354.

Fuller,W.A. (1976), *Introduction to Statistical Time Series*, New York: John Wiley.

Gallant,A.R. (1987), *Nonlinear Statistical Models*, New York: John Wiley.

Gallant,A.R. and H.White (1987), *A Unified Theory of the Estimation and Inference for Nonlinear Dynamic Models*, New York: Basil Blackwell.

Geisser,S. (1975), "The Predictive Sample Reuse Method with Applications," *Journal of the American Statistical Association*, 70: 320–328.

Georgiev,A.A. (1984), "Nonparametric System Identification by Kernel Methods," *IEEE Transact. Aut.Cont.*, 29: 356–358.

Gihman,I.I. and A.V.Skorohod (1974), *The Theory of Stochastic Processes*, vol. I, Berlin: Springer Verlag.

Granger,C.W.J. (1981), "Some Properties of Time Series and Their Use in Econometric Model Specification," *Journal of Econometrics*, 16: 121–130.

Greblicki,W., and A.Krzyzak (1980), "Asymptotic Properties of Kernel Estimates of a Regression Function," *Journal of Statistical Planning and Inference*, 4: 81–90.

Gregory,A.W. and M.R.Veall (1985), "Formulating Wald Tests of Non–linear Restrictions," *Econometrica*, 53: 1465–1468.

Haldrup,N. and S.Hylleberg (1989), "Unit Roots and Deterministic Trends, with Yet Another Comment on the Existence and Interpretation of a Unit Root in U.S. GNP," mimeo, Institute of Economics, University of Aarhus.

Hannan,E.J., W.T.M.Dunsmuir, and M.Deistler (1980), "Estimation of Vector ARMAX Models," *Journal of Multivariate Analysis*, 10: 275–295.

Hansen,L.P. (1982), "Large Sample Properties of Generalized Method of Moment Estimators," *Econometrica*, 50: 1029–1054.

Hardle,W. (1990), *Applied Nonparametric Regression*, Cambridge: Cambridge University Press.

Harvey,A.C. (1981), *Time Series Models*, Oxford: Philip Allen.

Hausman,J.A. (1978), "Specification Tests in Econometrics," *Econometrica*, 46: 1251–1271.

Herrndorf,N. (1984), "A Functional Central Limit Theorem for Weakly Dependent Sequences of Random Variables," *Annals of Probability*, 12: 141–153.

Hogg,R.V. and A.T.Craig (1978), *Introduction to Mathematical Statistics*, London: Macmillan.

Holly,A. (1982), "A Remark on Hausman's Specification Test," *Econometrica*, 50: 749–760.

Hylleberg,S. and G.E.Mizon (1989), "A Note on the Distribution of the Least Squares Estimator of a Random Walk with Drift," *Economics Letters*, 29: 225–230.

Ibragimov,I.A. and Y.V.Linnik (1971), *Independent and Stationary Sequences of Random Variables*, Groningen: Wolters–Noordhoff.

Iosifescu,M. and R.Theodorescu (1969), *Random Processes and Learning*, New York: Springer Verlag.

Jennrich,R.I. (1969), "Asymptotic Properties of Nonlinear Least Squares Estimators," *Annals of Mathematical Statistics*, 40: 633–643.

Johansen,S. (1988), "Statistical Analysis of Cointegrated Vectors," *Journal of Economic Dynamics and Control*, 12: 231–254.

(1991), "Estimation and Hypothesis Testing of Cointegrated Vectors in Gaussian Vector Autoregressive Models," *Econometrica*, 59: 1551–1580.

Johansen,S. and K.Juselius (1990), "Maximum Likelihood Estimation and Inference on Cointegration: With Applications to the Demand for Money," *Oxford Bulletin of Economics and Statistics*, 52: 169–210

Kolmogorov,A.N. and S.V.Fomin (1961), *Elements of the Theory of Functions and Functional Analysis*, vol. II: *Measure. The Lebesque Integral. Hilbert Space*, Rochester N.Y.: Graylock Press.

Liero,H. (1982), "On the Maximal Deviation of the Kernel Regression Function Estimate," *Mathematik, Operationsforschung und Statistik, Ser.Statist.*, 13: 171–182.

McLeish,D.L. (1974), "Dependent Central Limit Theorems and Invariance Principles," *Annals of Probability*, 2: 620–628.

(1975), "A Maximal Inequality and Dependent Strong Laws," *Annals of Probability*, 3: 829–839.

Malinvaud,E. (1970a), *Statistical Methods of Econometrics*, Amsterdam: North Holland.

(1970b), "The Consistency of Nonlinear Regression," *Annals of Mathematical Statistics*, 41: 956–969.

Nadaraya,E.A. (1964), "On Estimating Regression," *Theory of Probability and its Applications*, 9: 141–142.

(1965), "On Non–parametric Estimation of Density Functions and Regression Curves," *Theory of Probability and its Applications*, 10: 186–190.

(1970), "Remarks on Non–parametric Estimates for Density Functions and Regression Curves," *Theory of Probability and its Applications*, 15: 134–137.

Newey,W.K. (1985), "Maximum Likelihood Specification Testing and Conditional Moment Tests," *Econometrica*, 53: 1047–1070.

Newey,W.K. and K.D.West (1987), "A Simple Positive Definite Heteroskedasticity and Autocorrelation Consistent Covariance Matrix," *Econometrica*, 55: 703–708.

Neyman,J (1959), "Optimal Asymptotic Tests of Composite Statistical Hypotheses," in U.Grenander (ed.), *Probability and Statistics, the Harold Cramer Volume*, Uppsala: Almqvist and Wiksell, 213–234.

Noda,K. (1976), "Estimation of a Regression Function by the Parzen Kernel–type Density Estimators," *Annals of the Institute of Statistics and Mathematics*, 28: 221–234.

Pagan,A. and F.Vella (1989), "Diagnostic Tests for Models Based on Individual Data: A Survey," *Journal of Applied Econometrics*, 4: S29–S59.

Parthasarathy,K.R. (1977), *Introduction to Probability and Measure*, New York: Springer Verlag.

Parzen,E. (1962), "On Estimation of a Probability Density Function and Mode," *Annals of Mathematical Statistics*, 33: 1065–1076.

Pereira,B.de B. (1977), "A Note on the Consistency and on the Finite Sample Comparisons of Some Tests of Separate Families of Hypotheses," *Biometrika*, 64: 109–113.

(1978), "Tests and Efficiencies of Separate Regression Models," *Biometrika*, 65: 319–327.

Pesaran,M.H. and A.S.Deaton (1978), "Testing Non–nested Non-linear Regression Models," *Econometrica*, 46: 677–694.

Phillips,P.C.B. (1987), "Time Series Regression with a Unit Root," *Econometrica*, 55: 277–301.

Phillips,P.C.B. and J.Y.Park (1988), "On the Formulation of Wald Tests of Nonlinear Restrictions," *Econometrica*, 56 1065–1083.

Phillips,P.C.B. and P.Perron (1988), "Testing for a Unit Root in Time Series Regression," *Biometrika*, 75: 335–346.

Potscher,B.M. and I.R.Prucha (1986), "A Class of Partially Adaptive One–Step M–Estimators for the Nonlinear Regression Model with Dependent Observations," *Journal of Econometrics*, 32: 219–251.

(1991a), "Basic Structure of the Asymptotic Theory in Dynamic Nonlinear Econometric Models, Part I: Consistency and Approximation Concepts," *Econometric Reviews*, 10: 125–216.

(1991b), "Basic Structure of the Asymptotic Theory in Dynamic Nonlinear Econometric Models, Part II: Asymptotic Normality," *Econometric Reviews*, 10: 253–325.

Quandt,R.E. (1974), "A Comparison of Methods for Testing Non-nested Hypotheses," *Review of Economics and Statistics*, 56: 92–99.

Ramsey,J.B. (1969), "Tests for Specification Errors in Classical Linear Least–squares Regression Analysis," *Journal of the Royal Statistical Society, Series B*, 31: 350–371.

(1970), "Models, Specification Error, and Inference: A Discussion of Some Problems in Econometric Methodology," *Bulletin of the Oxford Institute of Economics and Statistics*, 32: 301–318.

Révész,P. (1968), *The Laws of Large Numbers*, New York: Academic Press.

(1979), "On the Nonparametric Estimation of the Regression Function," *Probl. Contr. Inf. Theory*, 8: 297–302.

Robinson,P.M. (1983), "Nonparametric Estimators for Time Series," *Journal of Time Series Analysis*, 4: 185–207.

Rosenblatt,M. (1956a), "A Central Limit Theorem and a Strong Mixing Condition," *Proceedings of the National Academy of Science* [USA], 42: 43–47.

(1956b), "Remarks on Some Non–parametric Estimates of a Density Function," *Annals of Mathematical Statistics*, 27: 832–837.

(1991), *Stochastic Curve Estimation*, Hayward, Calif.: Institute of Mathematical Statistics.

Royden,H.L. (1968), *Real Analysis*, London: Macmillan.

Rudin,W. (1976), *Principles of Mathematical Analysis*, Tokyo: McGraw-Hill Kogakusha.

Said,S.E. and D.A.Dickey (1984), "Testing for Unit Roots in Autoregressive–Moving Average of Unknown Order," *Biometrika*, 71: 599–607.

Sargent,T.J. and C.A.Sims (1977), "Business Cycle Modeling Without Pretending to Have Too Much A Priori Economic Theory," in C.A.Sims (ed.), *New Methods in Business Cycle Research: Proceedings from a Conference*, Minneapolis: Federal Reserve Bank of Minneapolis.

Schucany,W.R. and J.P.Sommers (1977), "Improvement of Kernel Type Density Estimators," *Journal of the American Statistical Association* 72: 420–423.

Schuster,E.F. (1972), "Joint Asymptotic Distribution of the Estimated Regression Function at a Finite Number of Distinct Points," *Annals of Mathematical Statistics*, 43: 84–88.

Schuster,E.F. and S.Yakowitz (1979), "Contributions to the Theory of Nonparametric Regression, with Application to System Identification," *Annals of Statistics*, 7: 139–149.

Schwert,G.W. (1989), "Tests for Unit Roots: A Monte Carlo Investigation," *Journal of Business and Economic Statistics*, 7: 147–159.

Serfling,R.J. (1968), "Contributions to Central Limit Theory for Dependent Variables," *Annals of Mathematical Statistics*, 39: 1158–1175.

Silverman,B.W. (1978), "Weak and Strong Uniform Consistency of the Kernel Estimate of a Density and its Derivates," *Annals of Statistics*, 6: 177–184.

Sims,C.A. (1980), "Macroeconomics and Reality," *Econometrica*, 48: 1–48.

(1981), "An Autogressive Index Model for the U.S., 1948–1975," in J.Kmenta and J.B.Ramsey (eds.), *Large–Scale Macro–Econometric Models*, Amsterdam: North–Holland.

(1988), "Comment on 'ARMA Memory Index Modeling of Economic Time Series'," *Econometric Theory*, 4: 64–69.

Singh,R.S. (1981), "Speed of Convergence in Non–parametric Estimation of a Multivariate M–Density and its Mixed Partial Derivatives," *Journal of Statistical Planning and Inference*, 5: 287–298.

Stock,J.H. and M.W.Watson (1988), "Testing for Common Trends," *Journal of the American Statistical Association*, 83: 1097–1107.

Stone,C. (1977), "Consistent Nonparametric Regression [with discussion]," *Annals of Statistics*, 5: 595–645.

Stone,M. (1974), "Cross–validatory Choice and Assessment of Statistical Predictions [with discussion]," *Journal of the Royal Statistical Society, Series B*, 36: 111–147.

Stout,W.F. (1974), *Almost Sure Convergence*, New York: Academic Press.

Tapia,R.A. and J.R.Thompson (1978), *Nonparametric Probability Density Estimation*, Baltimore: Johns Hopkins University Press.

Tauchen,G. (1985), "Diagnostic Testing and Evaluation of Maximum Likelihood Models," *Journal of Econometrics*, 30: 415–443.

Wahba,G. and S.Wold (1975), "A Completely Automatic French Curve: Fitting Spline Functions by Cross–validation," *Communications in Statistics*, 4: 1–17.

Watson,G.S. (1964), "Smooth Regression Analysis," *Sankhya, Series A*, 26: 359–372.

White,H. (1980a), "Using Least Squares to Approximate Unknown Regression Functions," *International Economic Review*, 21: 149–170.

(1980b), "Nonlinear Regression on Cross–Section Data," *Econometrica*, 48: 721–746.

(1981), "Consequences and Detection of Misspecified Nonlinear Regression Models," *Journal of the American Statistical Association*, 76: 419–433.

(1982), "Maximum Likelihood Estimation of Misspecified Models," *Econometrica*, 50,:1–25.

(1984), *Asymptotic Theory for Econometricians*. New York: Academic Press.

White,H and I.Domowitz (1984), "Nonlinear Regression with Dependent Observations," *Econometrica*, 52: 143–151.

Whittle,P. (1960), "Bounds on the Moments of Linear and Quadratic Forms in Independent Random Variables," *Theory of Probability and Its Applications*, 5: 302.

Wilks,S.S. (1963), *Mathematical Statistics*, Princeton: Princeton University Press.

Wold,H. (1954), *A Study in the Analysis of Stationary Time Series*, Uppsala: Almqvist and Wiksell.

Wong,W.H. (1983), "On the Consistency of Cross–validation in Kernel Nonparametric Regression," *Annals of Statistics*, 11: 1136–1141.

Index